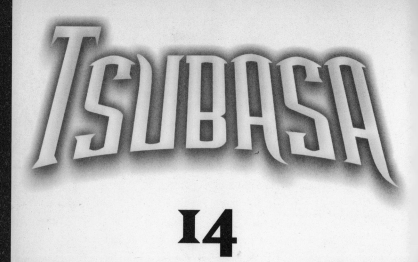

14

CLAMP

TRANSLATED AND ADAPTED BY
William Flanagan

LETTERED BY
Dana Hayward

BALLANTINE BOOKS · NEW YORK

Tsubasa, vol. 14 is a work of fiction. Names, characters, places, and incidents are the products of the author's imagination or are used fictitiously. Any resemblance to actual events, locales, or persons, living or dead, is entirely coincidental.

A Del Rey Trade Paperback Original

Published in the United States by Del Rey Books, an imprint of The Random House Publishing Group, a division of Random House, Inc., New York.

Publication rights arranged through Kodansha, Ltd.

First published in Japan in 2005 by Kodansha, Ltd., Tokyo.

ISBN 978-0-345-48534-2

Printed in the United States of America

www.delreymanga.com

9 8 7 6 5 4 3 2

Translation and adaptation—William Flanagan
Lettering—Dana Hayward

Contents

Tsubasa crosses over with *xxxHOLiC*. Although it isn't necessary
to read *xxxHOLiC* to understand the events in *Tsubasa*, you'll get to see
the same events from different perspectives if you read both series!

Honorifics Explained

Throughout the Del Rey Manga books, you will find Japanese honorifics left intact in the translations. For those not familiar with how the Japanese use honorifics and, more important, how they differ from American honorifics, we present this brief overview.

Politeness has always been a critical facet of Japanese culture. Ever since the feudal era, when Japan was a highly stratified society, use of honorifics—which can be defined as polite speech that indicates relationship or status—has played an essential role in the Japanese language. When addressing someone in Japanese, an honorific usually takes the form of a suffix attached to one's name (example: "Asuna-san"), is used as a title at the end of one's name, or appears in place of the name itself (example: "Negi-sensei," or simply "Sensei!").

Honorifics can be expressions of respect or endearment. In the context of manga and anime, honorifics give insight into the nature of the relationship between characters. Many English translations leave out these important honorifics, and therefore distort the feel of the original Japanese. Because Japanese honorifics contain nuances that English honorifics lack, it is our policy at Del Rey not to translate them. Here, instead, is a guide to some of the honorifics you may encounter in Del Rey Manga.

-san: This is the most common honorific, and is equivalent to Mr., Miss, Ms., or Mrs. It is the all-purpose honorific and can be used in any situation where politeness is required.

-sama: This is one level higher than "-san." It is used to confer great respect.

-dono: This comes from the word "tono," which means "lord." It is an even higher level than "-sama" and confers utmost respect.

-kun: This suffix is used at the end of boys' names to express familiarity or endearment. It is also sometimes used by men among friends, or when addressing someone younger or of a lower station.

-chan: This is used to express endearment, mostly toward girls. It is also used for little boys, pets, and even among lovers. It gives a sense of childish cuteness.

Bozu: This is an informal way to refer to a boy, similar to the English terms "kid" and "squirt."

Sempai/Senpai: This title suggests that the addressee is one's senior in a group or organization. It is most often used in a school setting, where underclassmen refer to their upperclassmen as "sempai." It can also be used in the workplace, such as when a newer employee addresses an employee who has seniority in the company.

Kohai: This is the opposite of "sempai," and is used toward underclassmen in school or newcomers in the workplace. It connotes that the addressee is of a lower station.

Sensei: Literally meaning "one who has come before," this title is used for teachers, doctors, or masters of any profession or art.

-[blank]: This is usually forgotten in these lists, but it is perhaps the most significant difference between Japanese and English. The lack of honorific means that the speaker has permission to address the person in a very intimate way. Usually, only family, spouses, or very close friends have this kind of permission. Known as *yobisute*, it can be gratifying when someone who has earned the intimacy starts to call one by one's name without an honorific. But when that intimacy hasn't been earned, it can be very insulting.

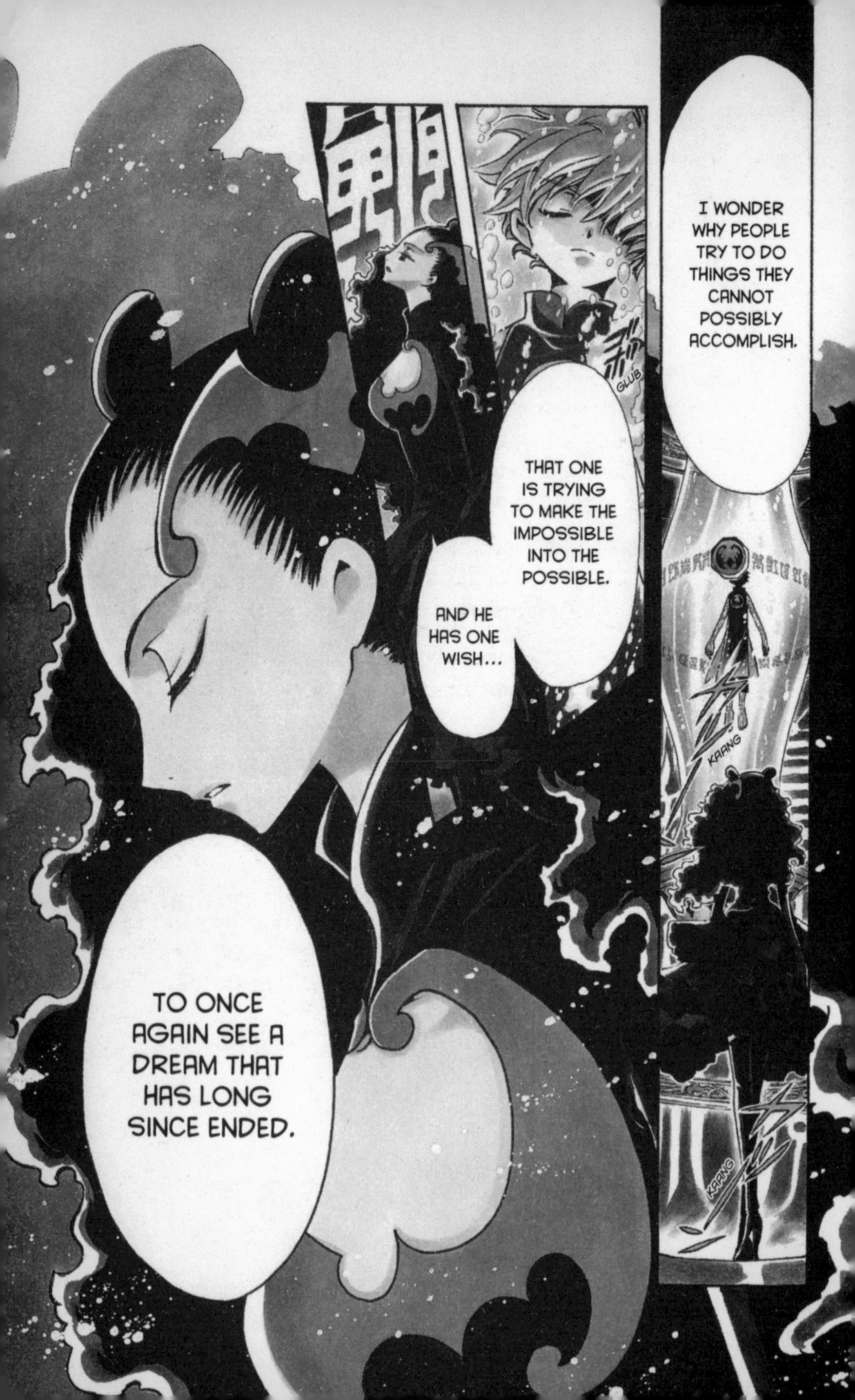
I WONDER WHY PEOPLE TRY TO DO THINGS THEY CANNOT POSSIBLY ACCOMPLISH.
KRANG
KRANG
GLUB
THAT ONE IS TRYING TO MAKE THE IMPOSSIBLE INTO THE POSSIBLE.
AND HE HAS ONE WISH...
TO ONCE AGAIN SEE A DREAM THAT HAS LONG SINCE ENDED.

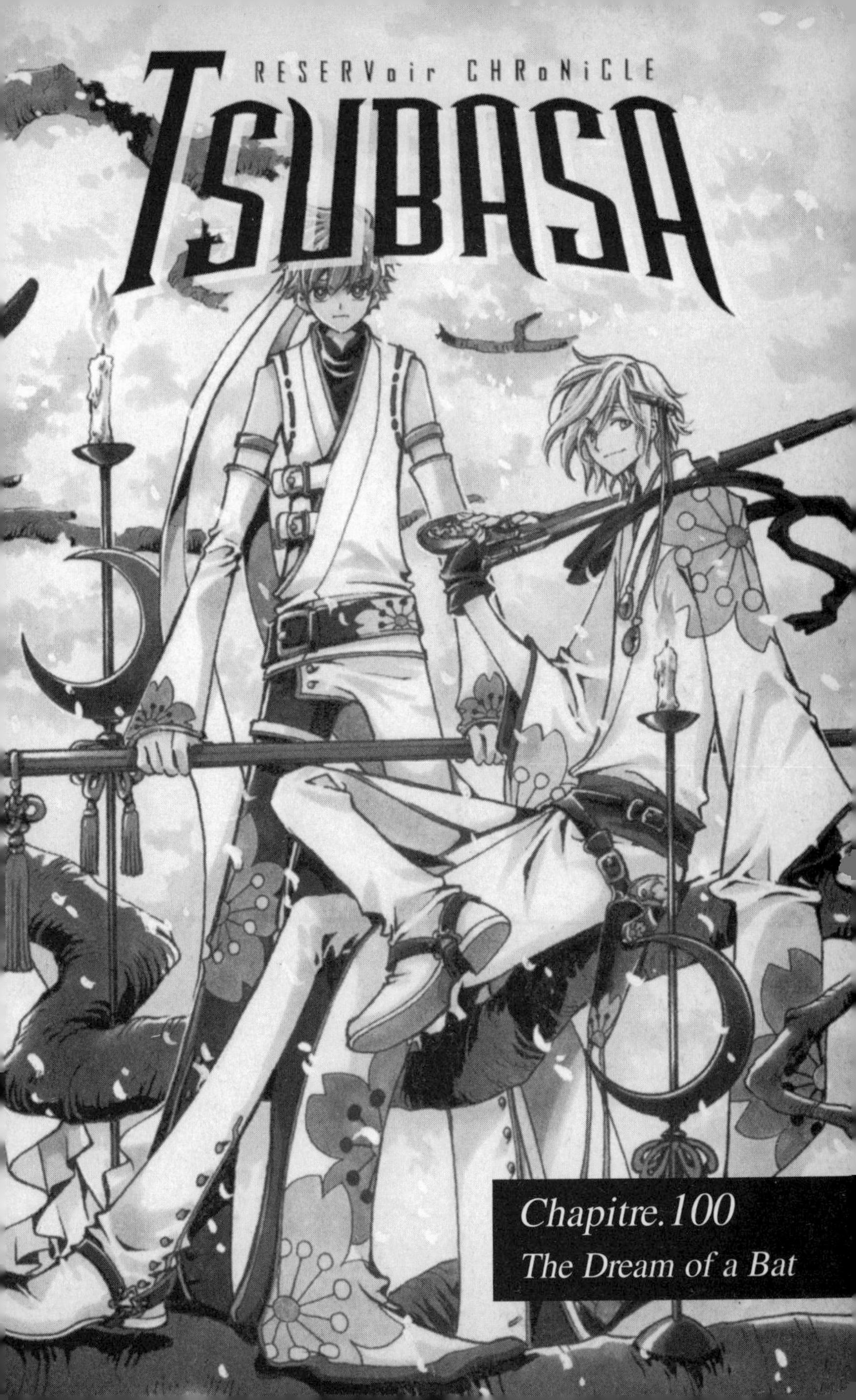
RESERVoir CHRoNiCLE
TSUBASA
Chapitre.100
The Dream of a Bat

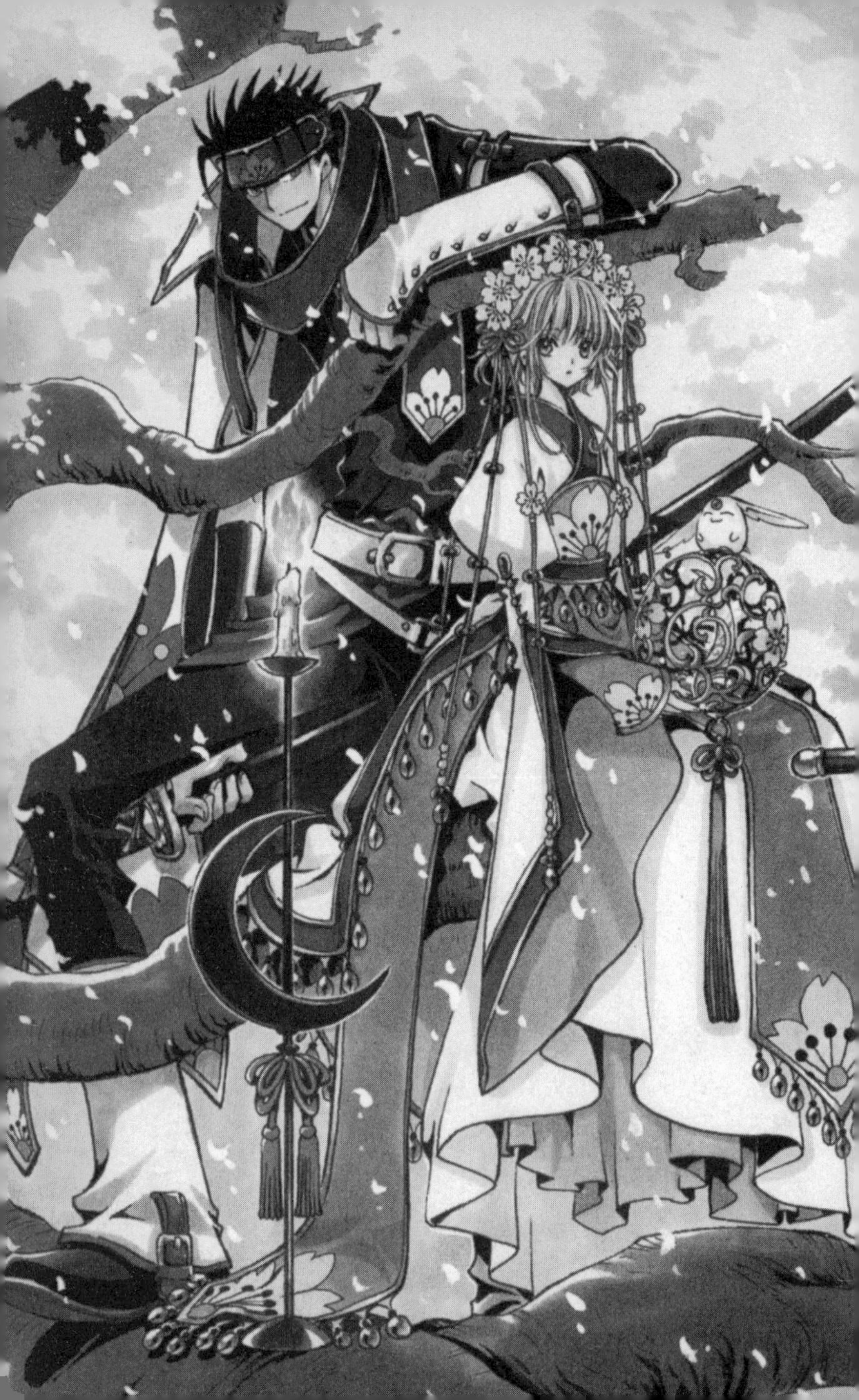

ツバサ

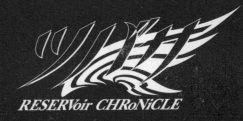

RESERVoir CHRoNiCLE

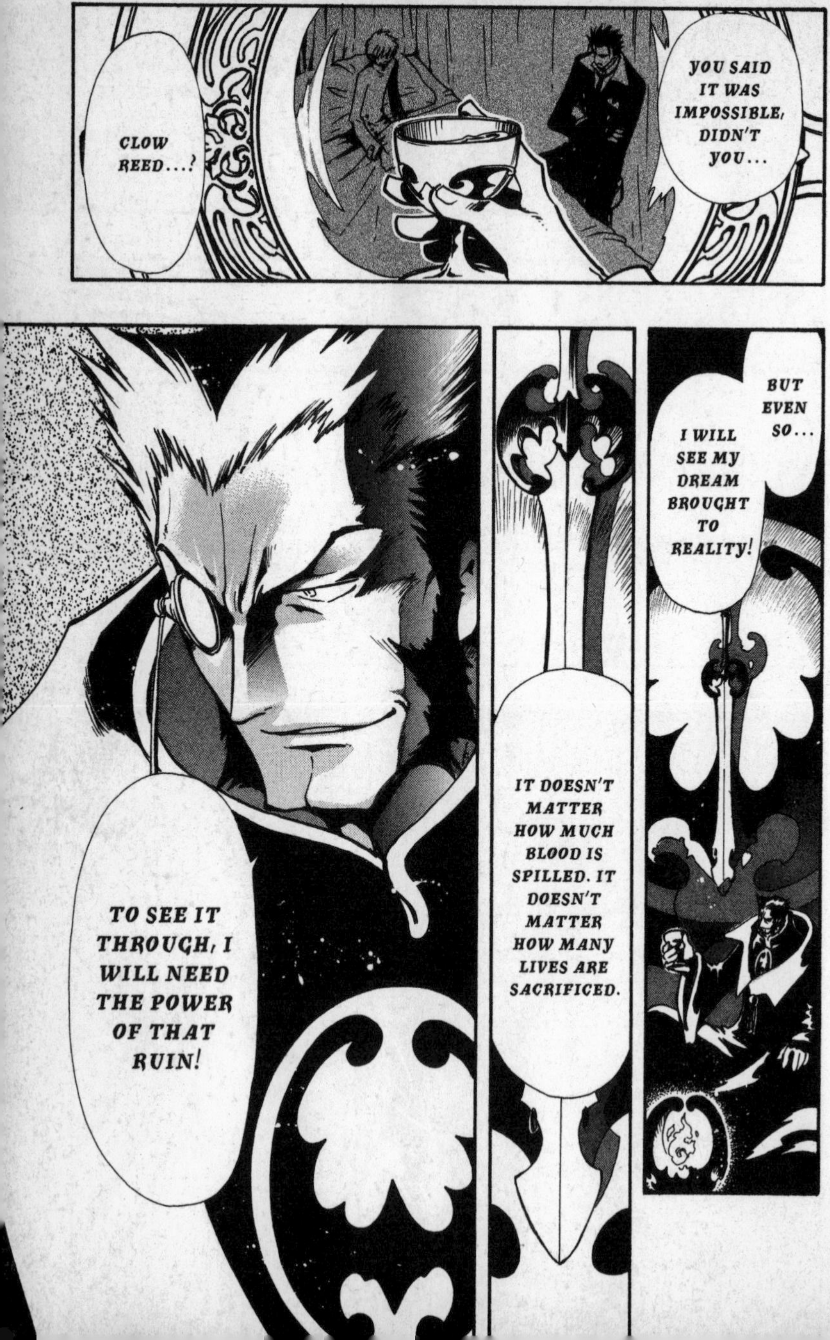
YOU SAID IT WAS IMPOSSIBLE, DIDN'T YOU...
CLOW REED...?
BUT EVEN SO...
I WILL SEE MY DREAM BROUGHT TO REALITY!
IT DOESN'T MATTER HOW MUCH BLOOD IS SPILLED. IT DOESN'T MATTER HOW MANY LIVES ARE SACRIFICED.
TO SEE IT THROUGH, I WILL NEED THE POWER OF THAT RUIN!

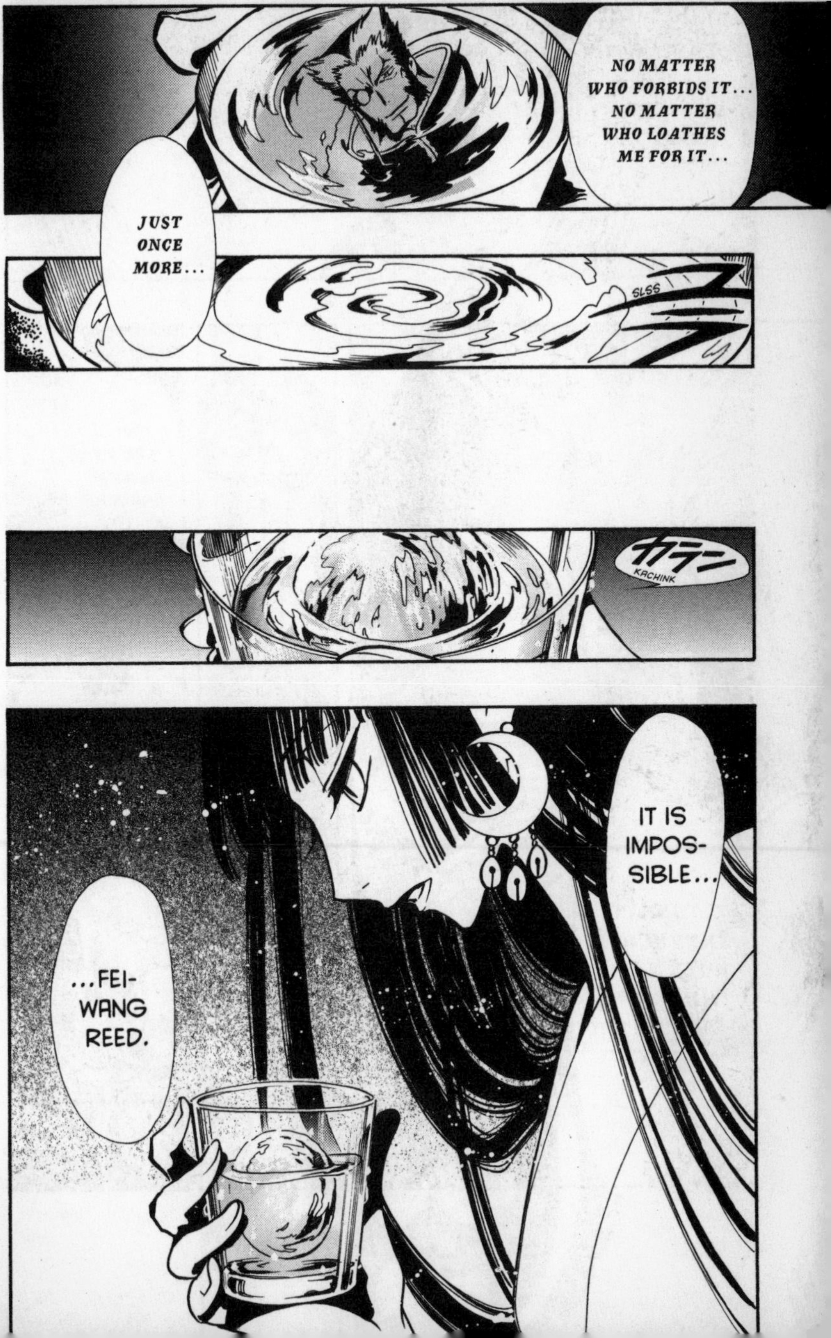
NO MATTER WHO FORBIDS IT... NO MATTER WHO LOATHES ME FOR IT...
JUST ONCE MORE...
SLSS
カラン
KACHINK
IT IS IMPOS-SIBLE...
...FEI-WANG REED.

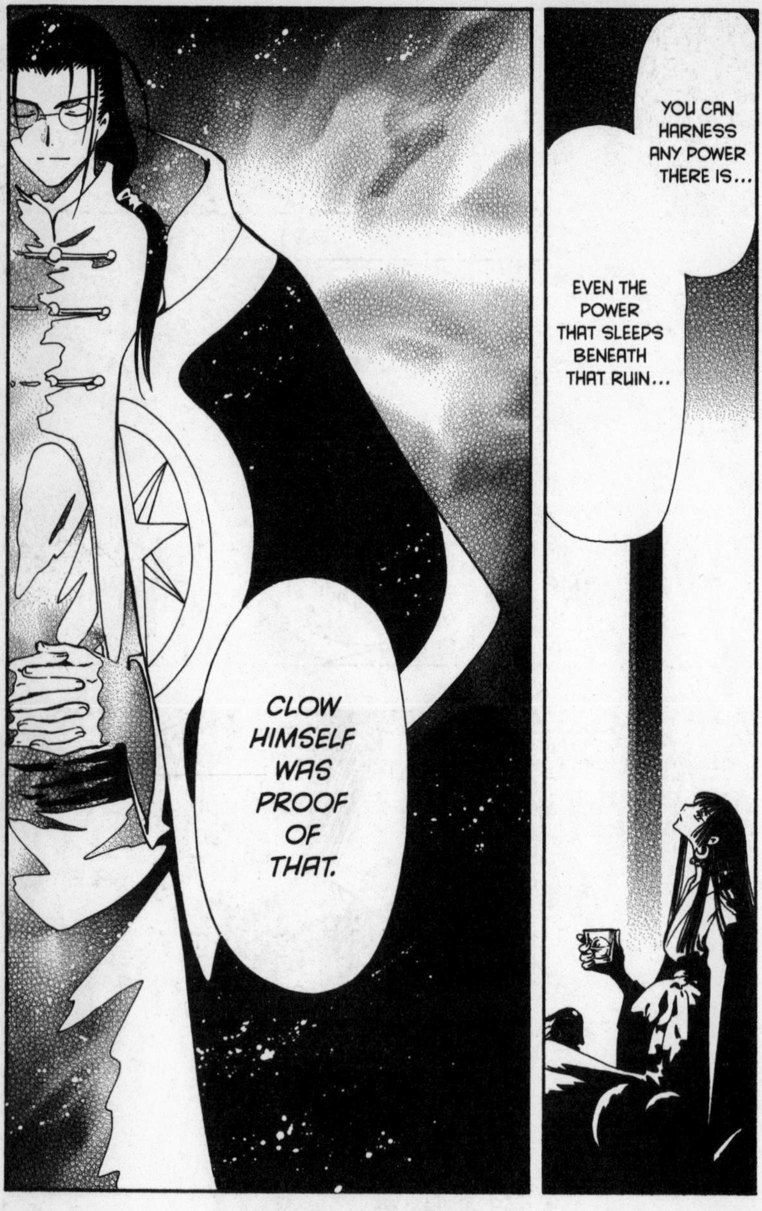
YOU CAN HARNESS ANY POWER THERE IS...
EVEN THE POWER THAT SLEEPS BENEATH THAT RUIN...
CLOW HIMSELF WAS PROOF OF THAT.

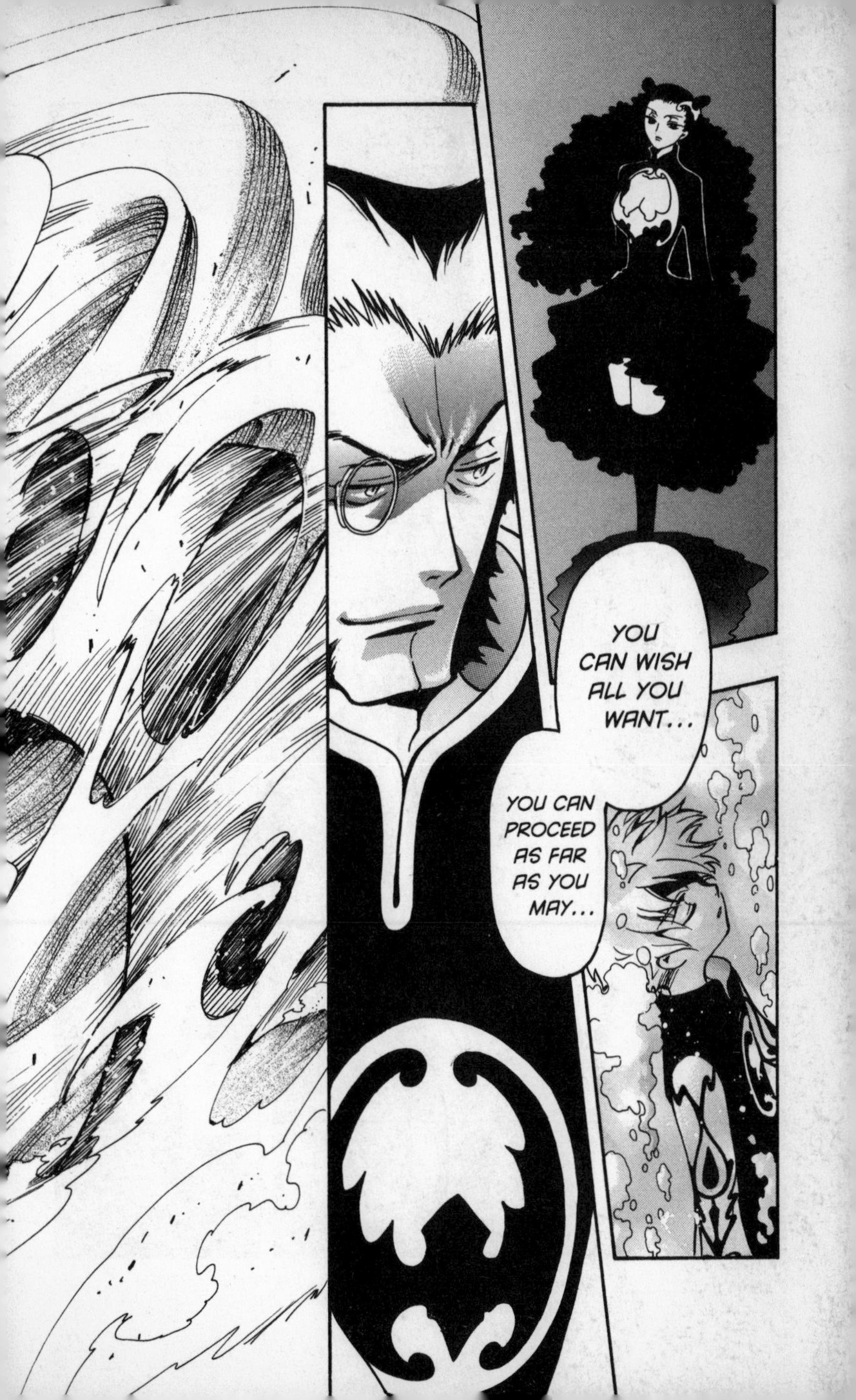
YOU CAN WISH ALL YOU WANT...
YOU CAN PROCEED AS FAR AS YOU MAY...

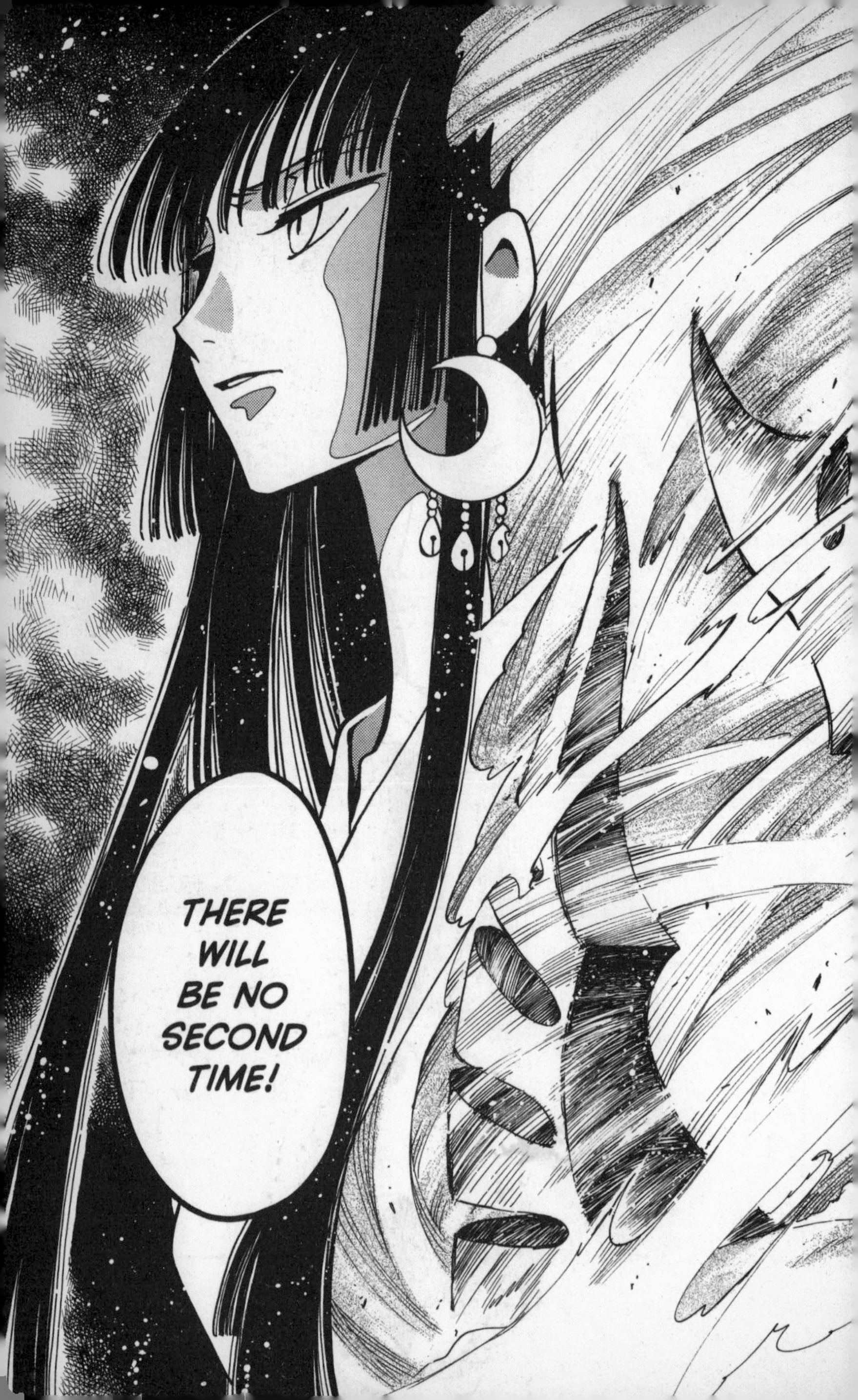
THERE WILL BE NO SECOND TIME!

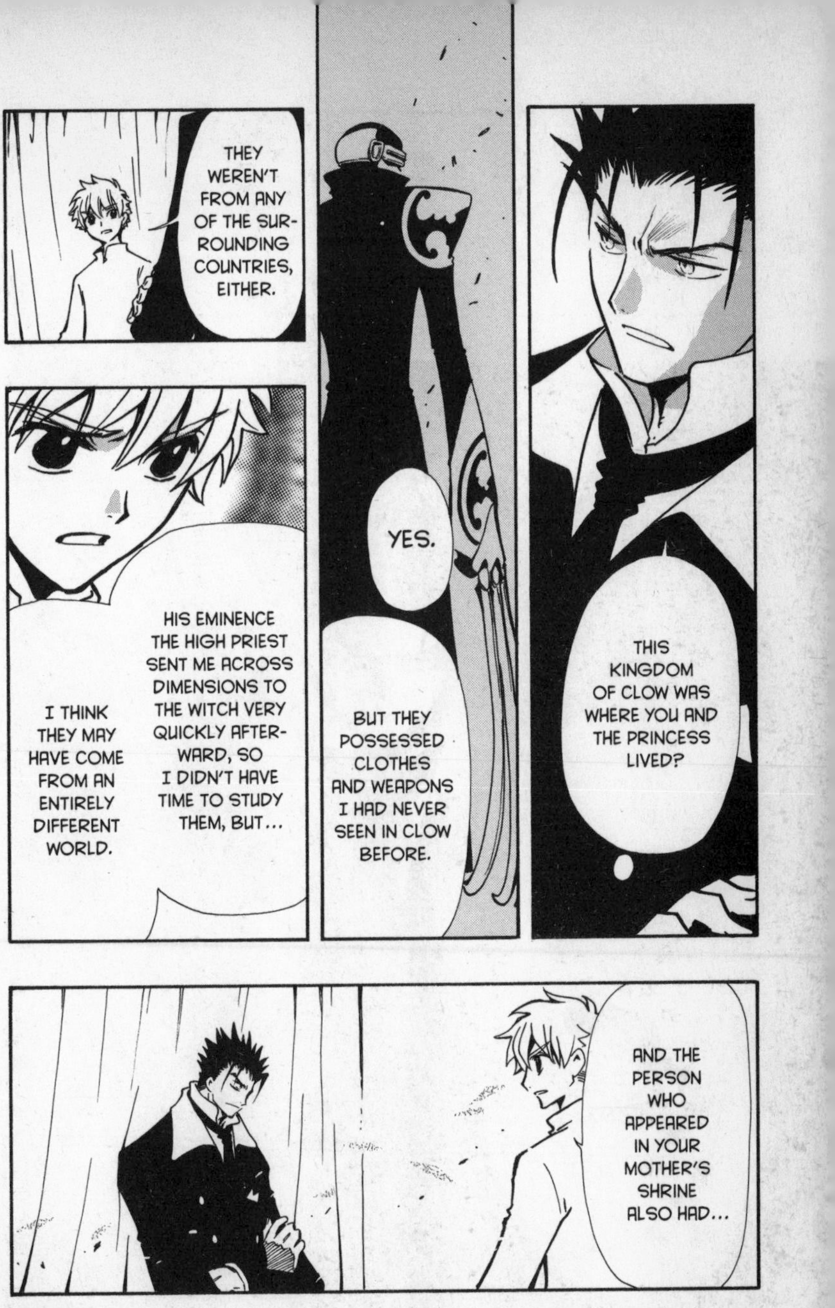
THIS KINGDOM OF CLOW WAS WHERE YOU AND THE PRINCESS LIVED?
YES.
BUT THEY POSSESSED CLOTHES AND WEAPONS I HAD NEVER SEEN IN CLOW BEFORE.
THEY WEREN'T FROM ANY OF THE SUR-ROUNDING COUNTRIES, EITHER.
HIS EMINENCE THE HIGH PRIEST SENT ME ACROSS DIMENSIONS TO THE WITCH VERY QUICKLY AFTER-WARD, SO I DIDN'T HAVE TIME TO STUDY THEM, BUT...
I THINK THEY MAY HAVE COME FROM AN ENTIRELY DIFFERENT WORLD.
AND THE PERSON WHO APPEARED IN YOUR MOTHER'S SHRINE ALSO HAD...

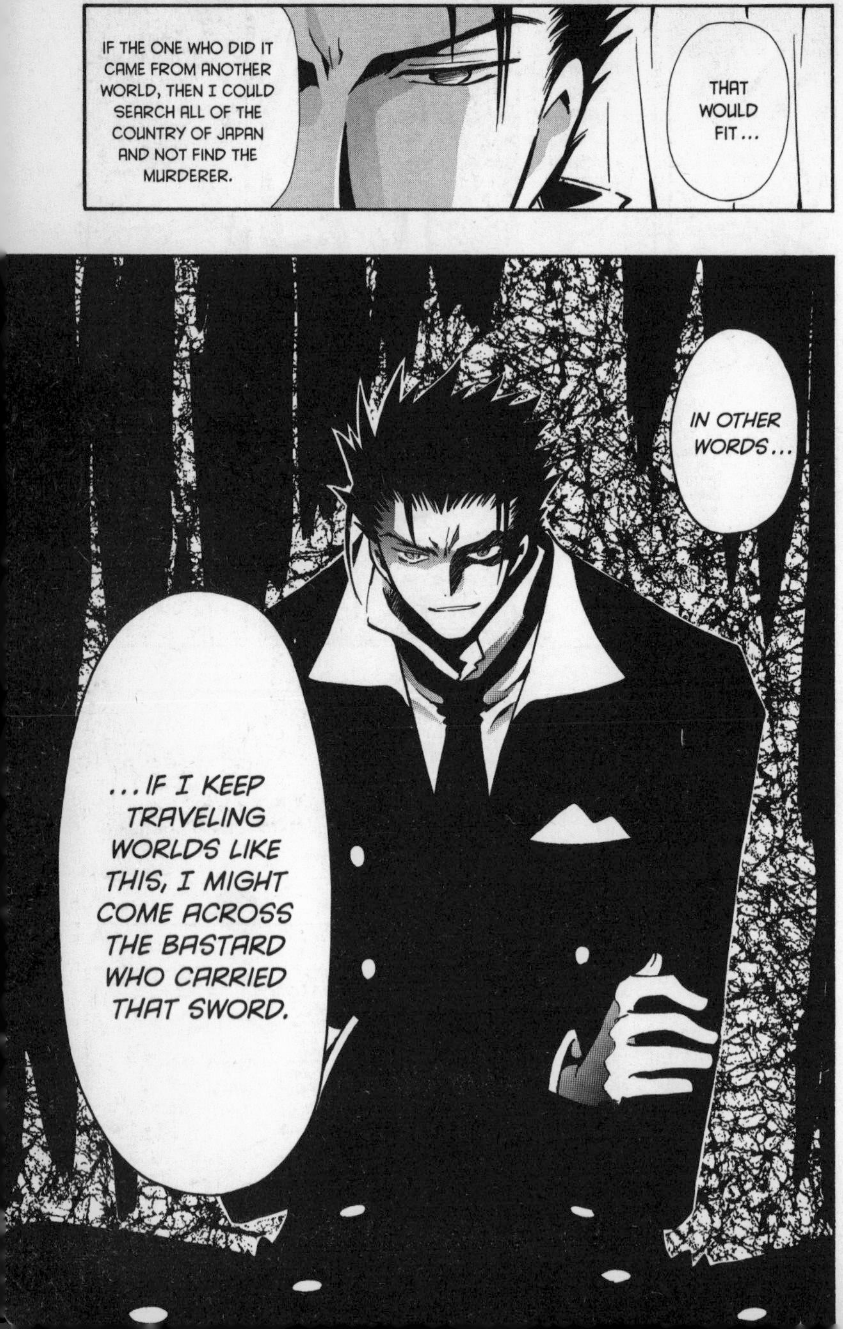
THAT WOULD FIT...
IF THE ONE WHO DID IT CAME FROM ANOTHER WORLD, THEN I COULD SEARCH ALL OF THE COUNTRY OF JAPAN AND NOT FIND THE MURDERER.
IN OTHER WORDS...
...IF I KEEP TRAVELING WORLDS LIKE THIS, I MIGHT COME ACROSS THE BASTARD WHO CARRIED THAT SWORD.

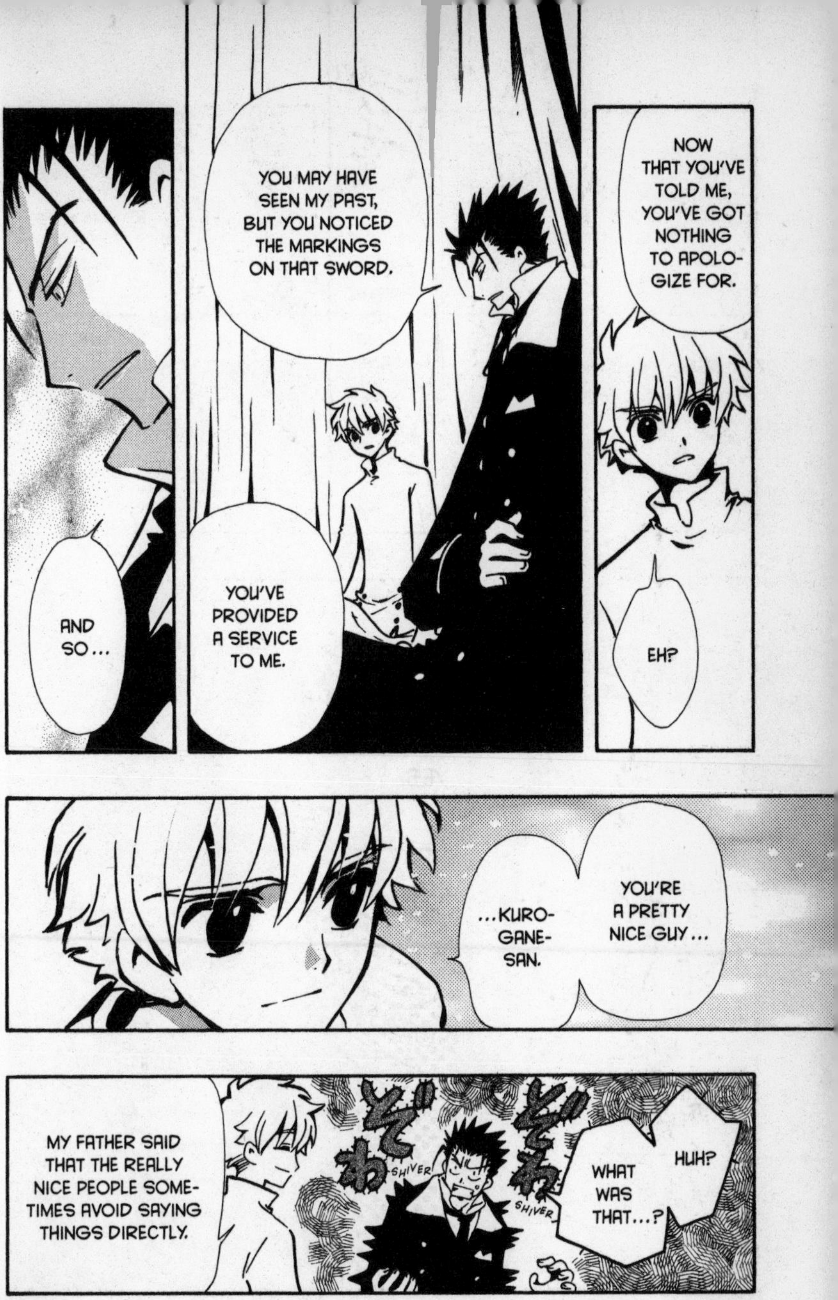
NOW THAT YOU'VE TOLD ME, YOU'VE GOT NOTHING TO APOLOGIZE FOR.
EH?
YOU MAY HAVE SEEN MY PAST, BUT YOU NOTICED THE MARKINGS ON THAT SWORD.
YOU'VE PROVIDED A SERVICE TO ME.
AND SO...
YOU'RE A PRETTY NICE GUY...
...KURO-GANE-SAN.
HUH?
WHAT WAS THAT...?
ぞわ
SHIVER
ぞわ
SHIVER
MY FATHER SAID THAT THE REALLY NICE PEOPLE SOME-TIMES AVOID SAYING THINGS DIRECTLY.

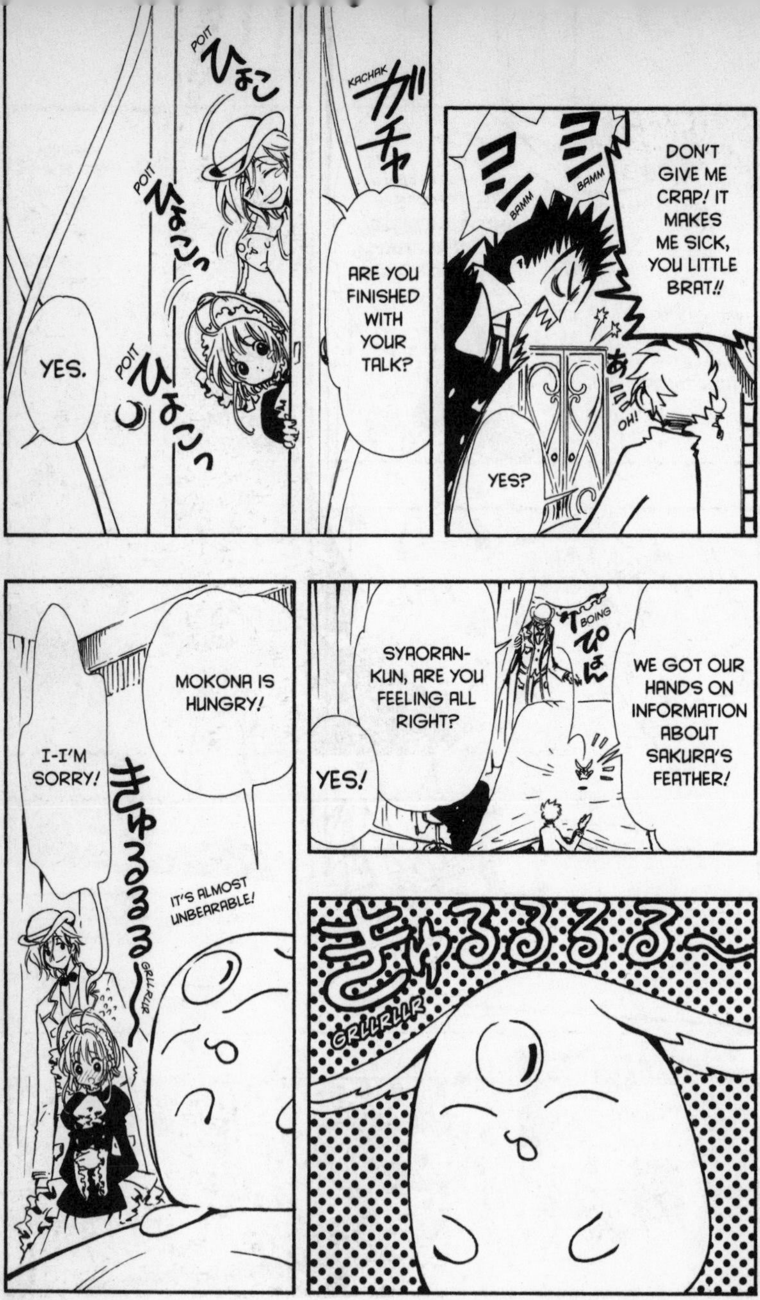
DON'T GIVE ME CRAP! IT MAKES ME SICK, YOU LITTLE BRAT!!
ヨシ
BAMM
ヨシ
BAMM
あ
OH!
YES?
ガチャ
KACHAK
ARE YOU FINISHED WITH YOUR TALK?
ひょこ
POIT
ひょこっ
POIT
ひょこっ
POIT
YES.
WE GOT OUR HANDS ON INFORMATION ABOUT SAKURA'S FEATHER!
ぴょん
BOING
SYAORAN-KUN, ARE YOU FEELING ALL RIGHT?
YES!
きゅるるるる～
GRLLRLLR
MOKONA IS HUNGRY!
I-I'M SORRY!
きゅるるる～
GRLLRLLR
IT'S ALMOST UNBEARABLE!

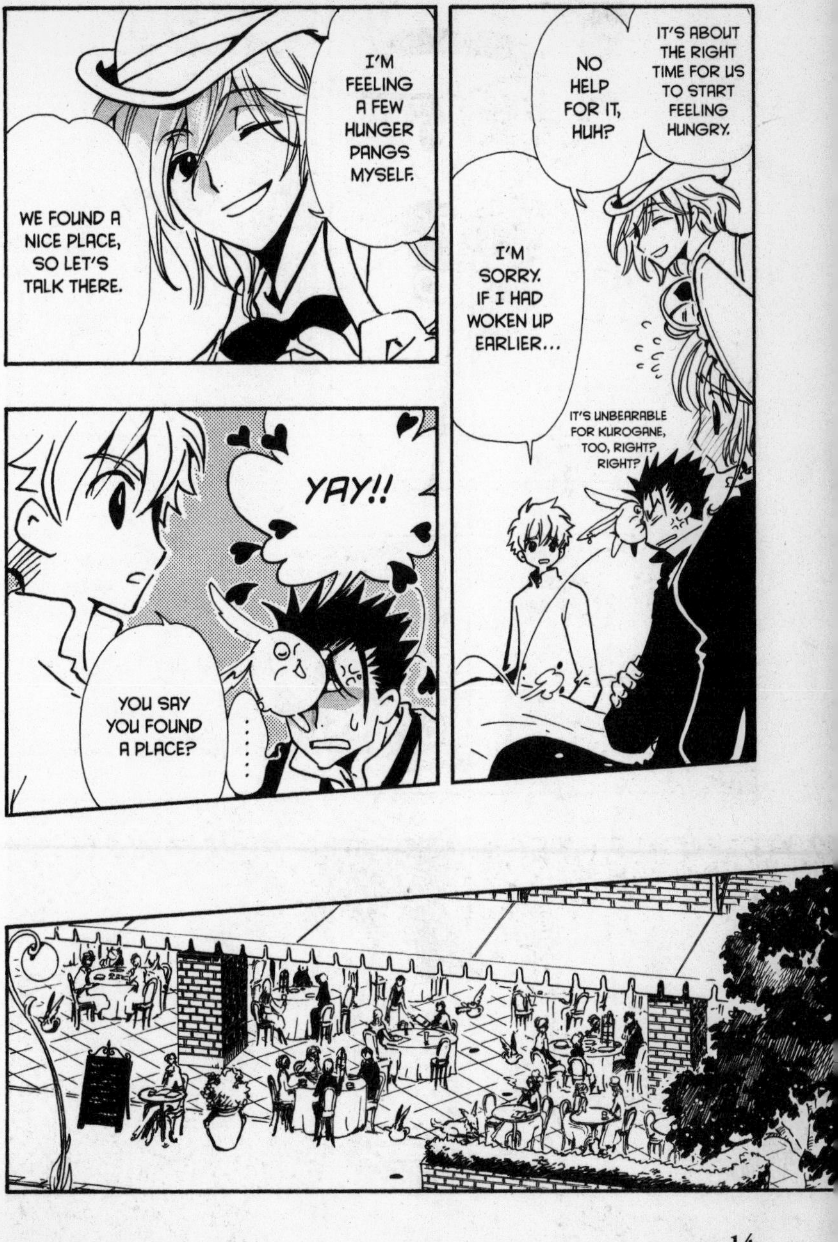
IT'S ABOUT THE RIGHT TIME FOR US TO START FEELING HUNGRY.
NO HELP FOR IT, HUH?
I'M SORRY. IF I HAD WOKEN UP EARLIER...
IT'S UNBEARABLE FOR KUROGANE, TOO, RIGHT? RIGHT?
I'M FEELING A FEW HUNGER PANGS MYSELF.
WE FOUND A NICE PLACE, SO LET'S TALK THERE.
YAY!!
......
YOU SAY YOU FOUND A PLACE?

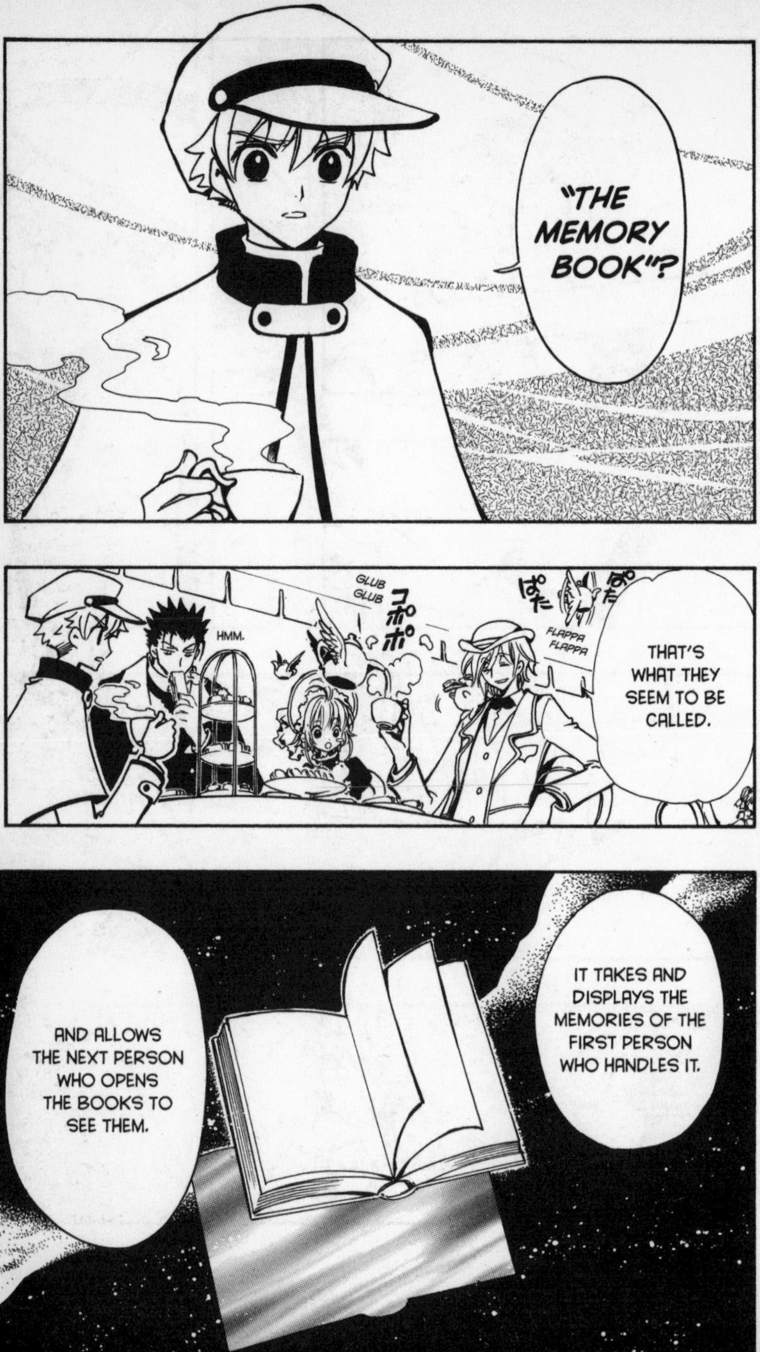
"THE MEMORY BOOK"?
THAT'S WHAT THEY SEEM TO BE CALLED.
ぱたぱた
FLAPPA FLAPPA
コポポ
GLUB GLUB
HMM.
IT TAKES AND DISPLAYS THE MEMORIES OF THE FIRST PERSON WHO HANDLES IT.
AND ALLOWS THE NEXT PERSON WHO OPENS THE BOOKS TO SEE THEM.

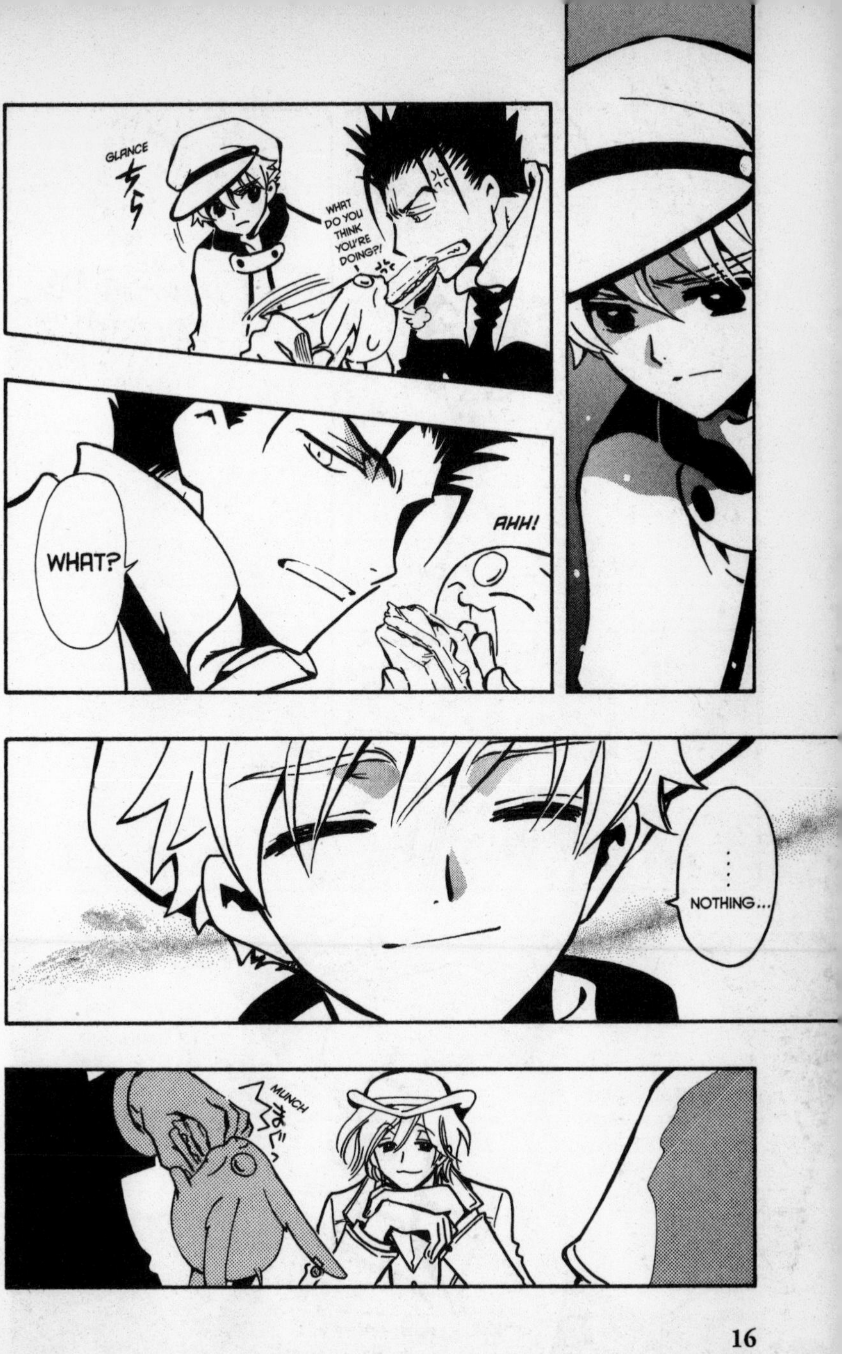
WHAT DO YOU THINK YOU'RE DOING?!
GLANCE
AHH!
WHAT?
...NOTHING...
MUNCH

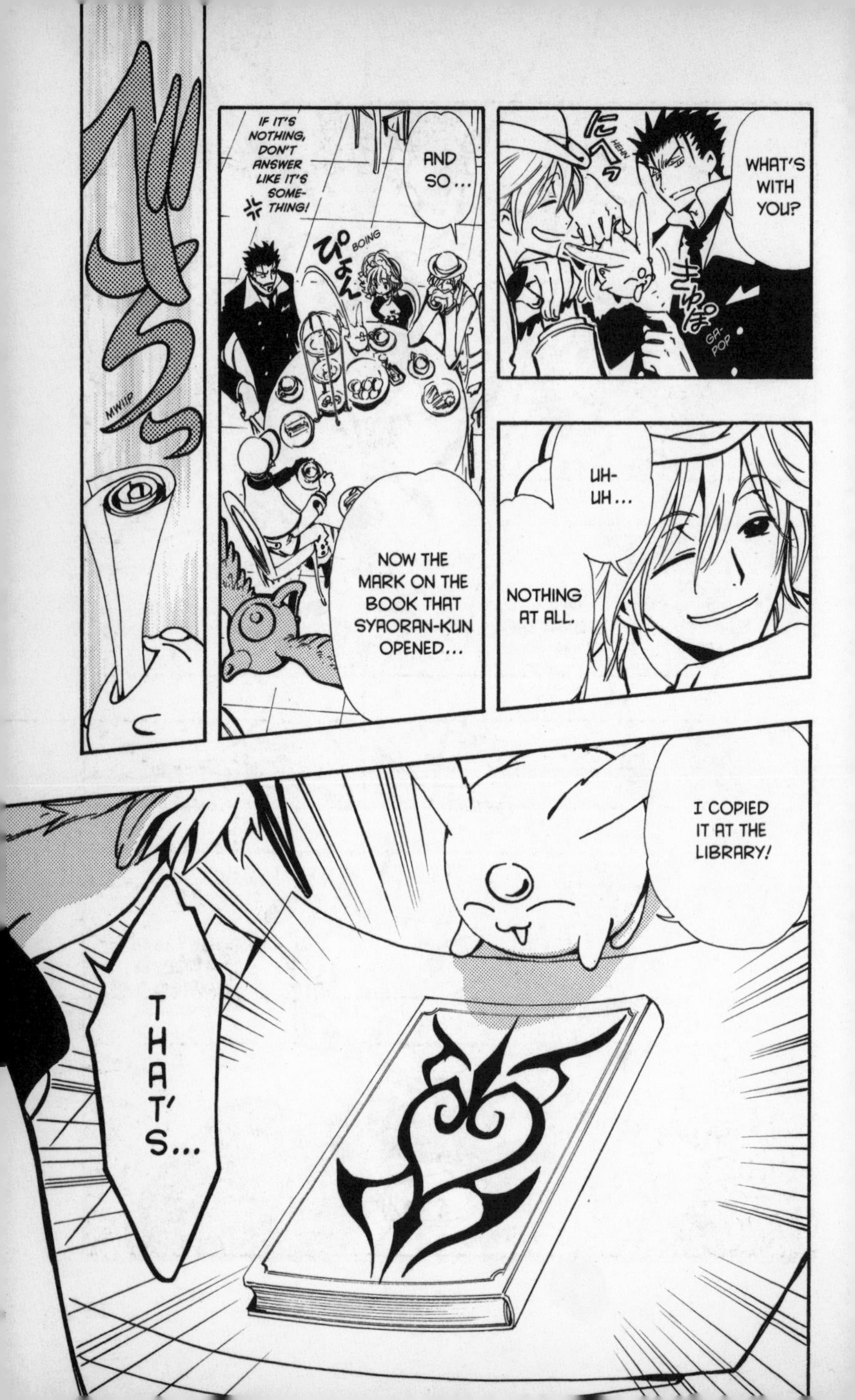
HENN
WHAT'S WITH YOU?
GA-POP
UH-UH...
NOTHING AT ALL.
IF IT'S NOTHING, DON'T ANSWER LIKE IT'S SOME-THING!
AND SO...
BOING
NOW THE MARK ON THE BOOK THAT SYAORAN-KUN OPENED...
MWIIP
I COPIED IT AT THE LIBRARY!
THAT'S...

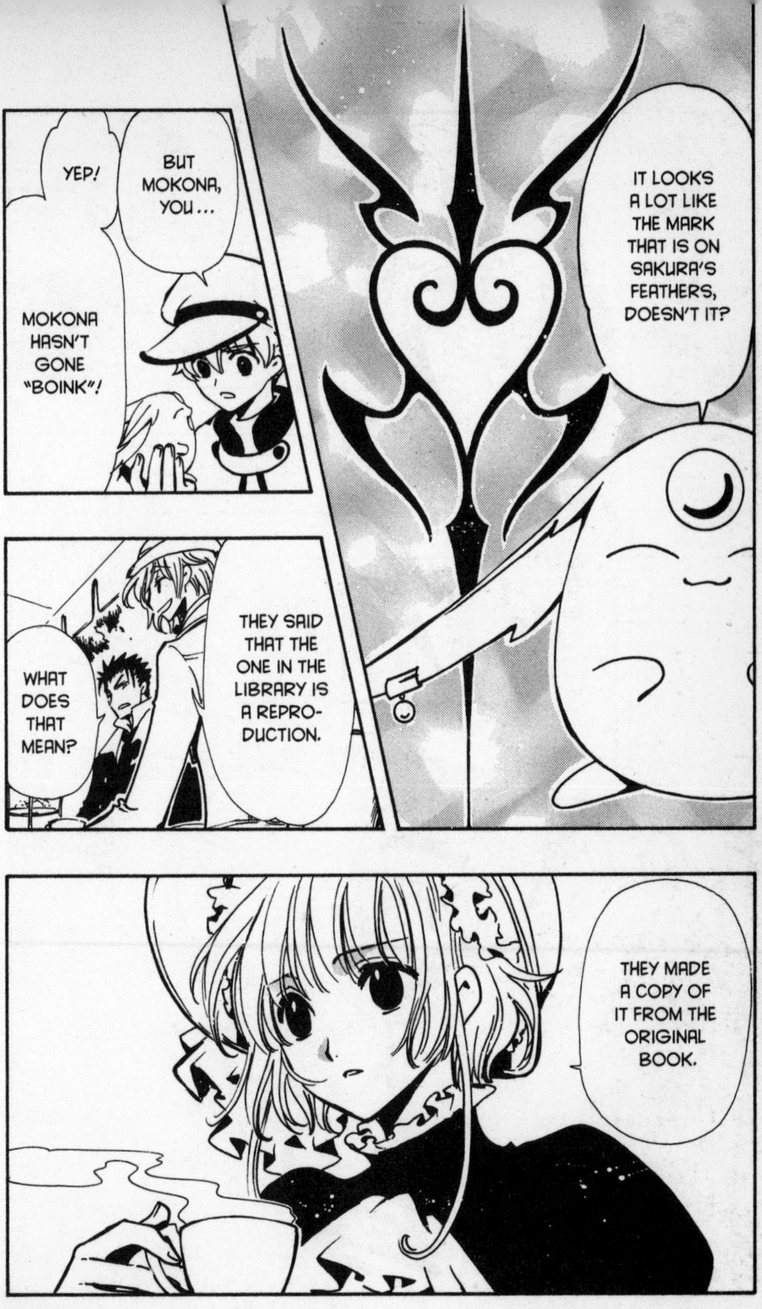
IT LOOKS A LOT LIKE THE MARK THAT IS ON SAKURA'S FEATHERS, DOESN'T IT?
BUT MOKONA, YOU...
YEP!
MOKONA HASN'T GONE "BOINK"!
THEY SAID THAT THE ONE IN THE LIBRARY IS A REPRO-DUCTION.
WHAT DOES THAT MEAN?
THEY MADE A COPY OF IT FROM THE ORIGINAL BOOK.

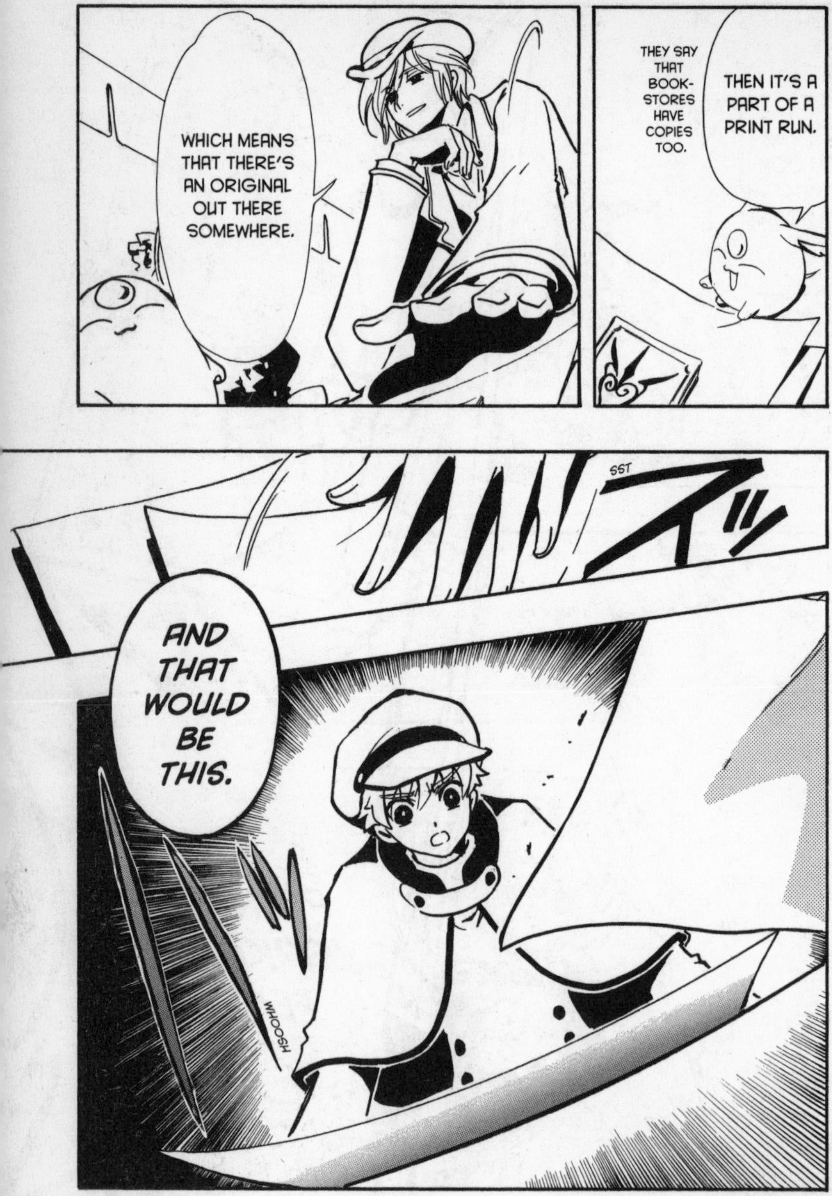
THEN IT'S A PART OF A PRINT RUN.
THEY SAY THAT BOOK-STORES HAVE COPIES TOO.
WHICH MEANS THAT THERE'S AN ORIGINAL OUT THERE SOMEWHERE.
SST
AND THAT WOULD BE THIS.
WHOOSH

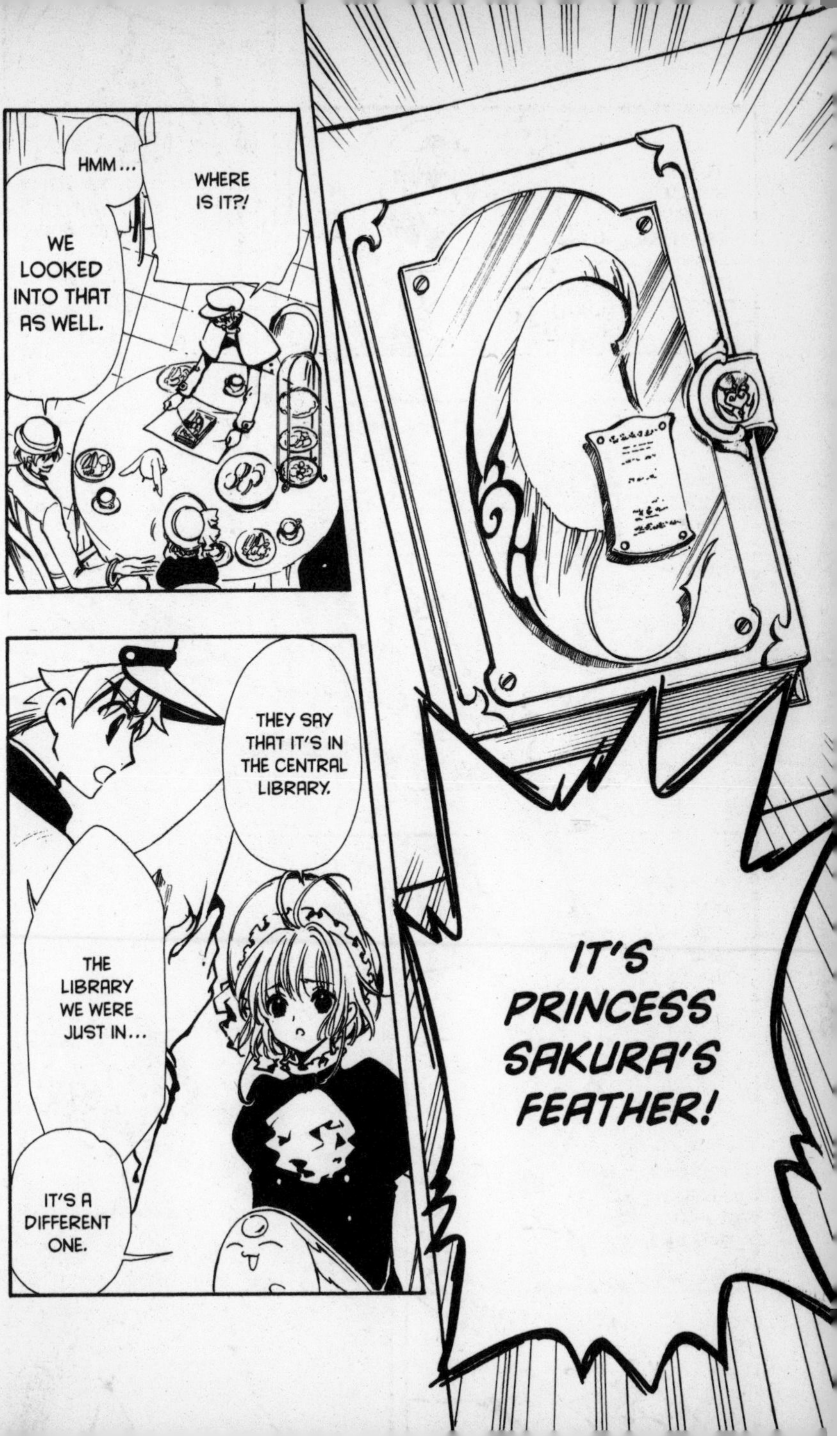
IT'S PRINCESS SAKURA'S FEATHER!
WHERE IS IT?!
HMM...
WE LOOKED INTO THAT AS WELL.
THEY SAY THAT IT'S IN THE CENTRAL LIBRARY.
THE LIBRARY WE WERE JUST IN...
IT'S A DIFFERENT ONE.

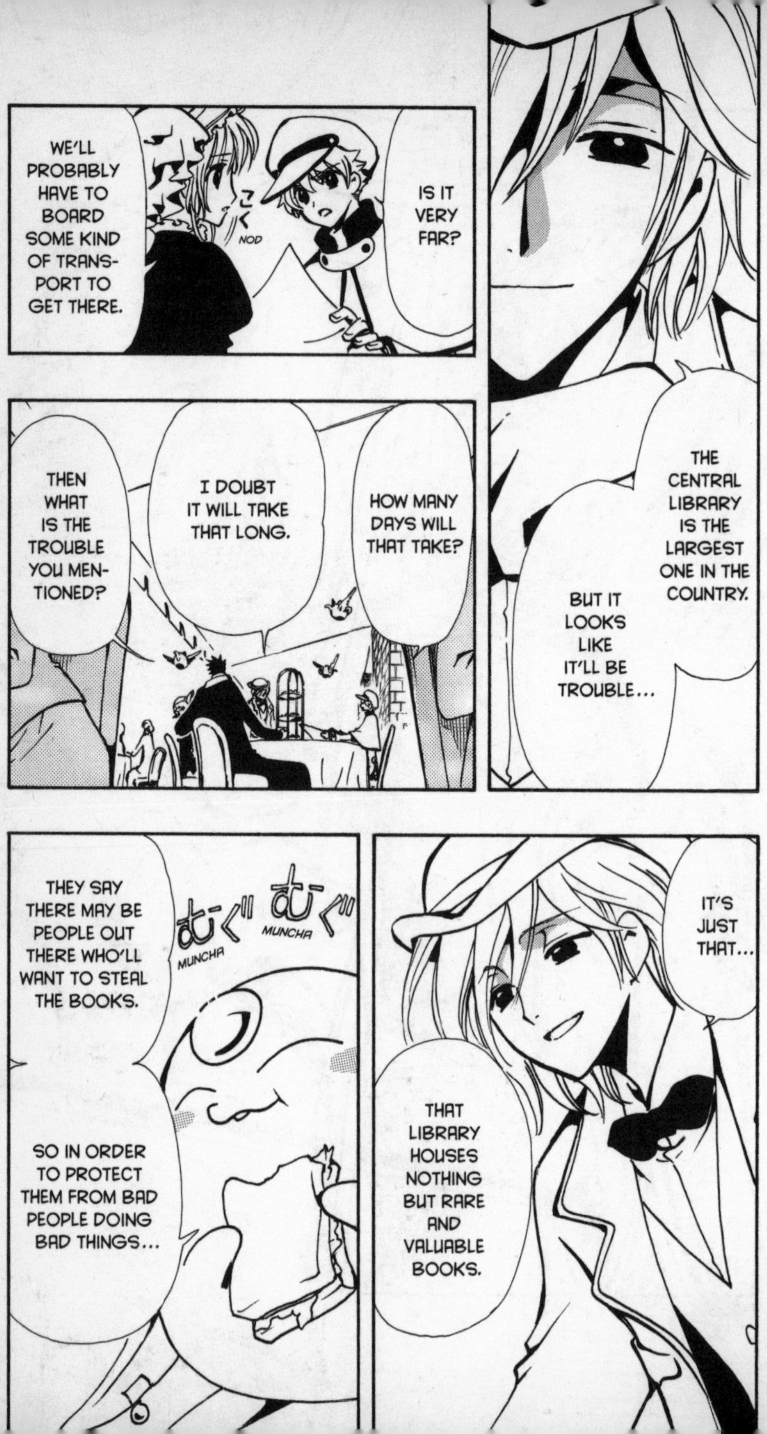
THE CENTRAL LIBRARY IS THE LARGEST ONE IN THE COUNTRY.
BUT IT LOOKS LIKE IT'LL BE TROUBLE...
IS IT VERY FAR?
こく
NOD
WE'LL PROBABLY HAVE TO BOARD SOME KIND OF TRANS-PORT TO GET THERE.
HOW MANY DAYS WILL THAT TAKE?
I DOUBT IT WILL TAKE THAT LONG.
THEN WHAT IS THE TROUBLE YOU MEN-TIONED?
IT'S JUST THAT...
THAT LIBRARY HOUSES NOTHING BUT RARE AND VALUABLE BOOKS.
むぐ
MUNCHA
むぐ
MUNCHA
THEY SAY THERE MAY BE PEOPLE OUT THERE WHO'LL WANT TO STEAL THE BOOKS.
SO IN ORDER TO PROTECT THEM FROM BAD PEOPLE DOING BAD THINGS...

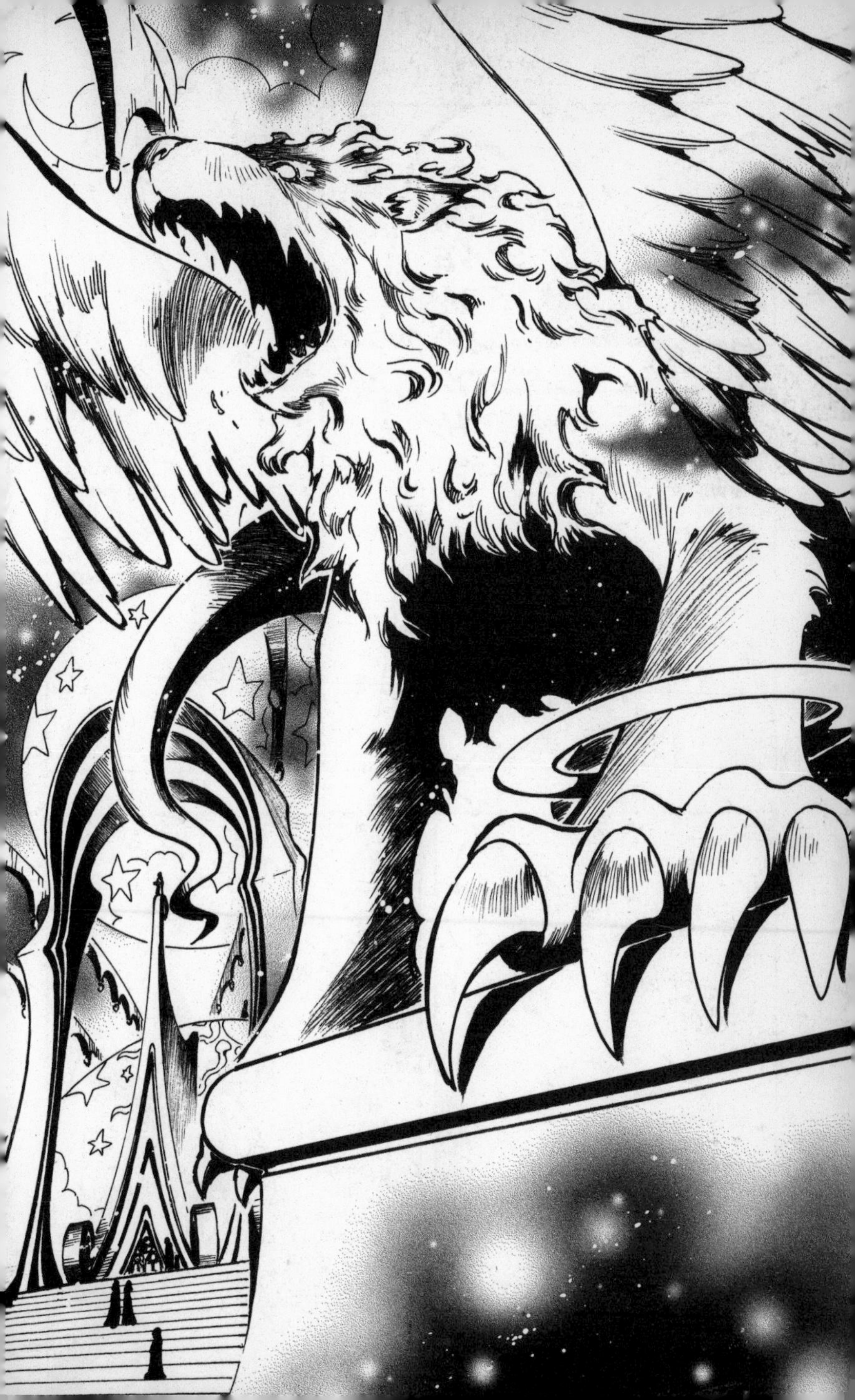

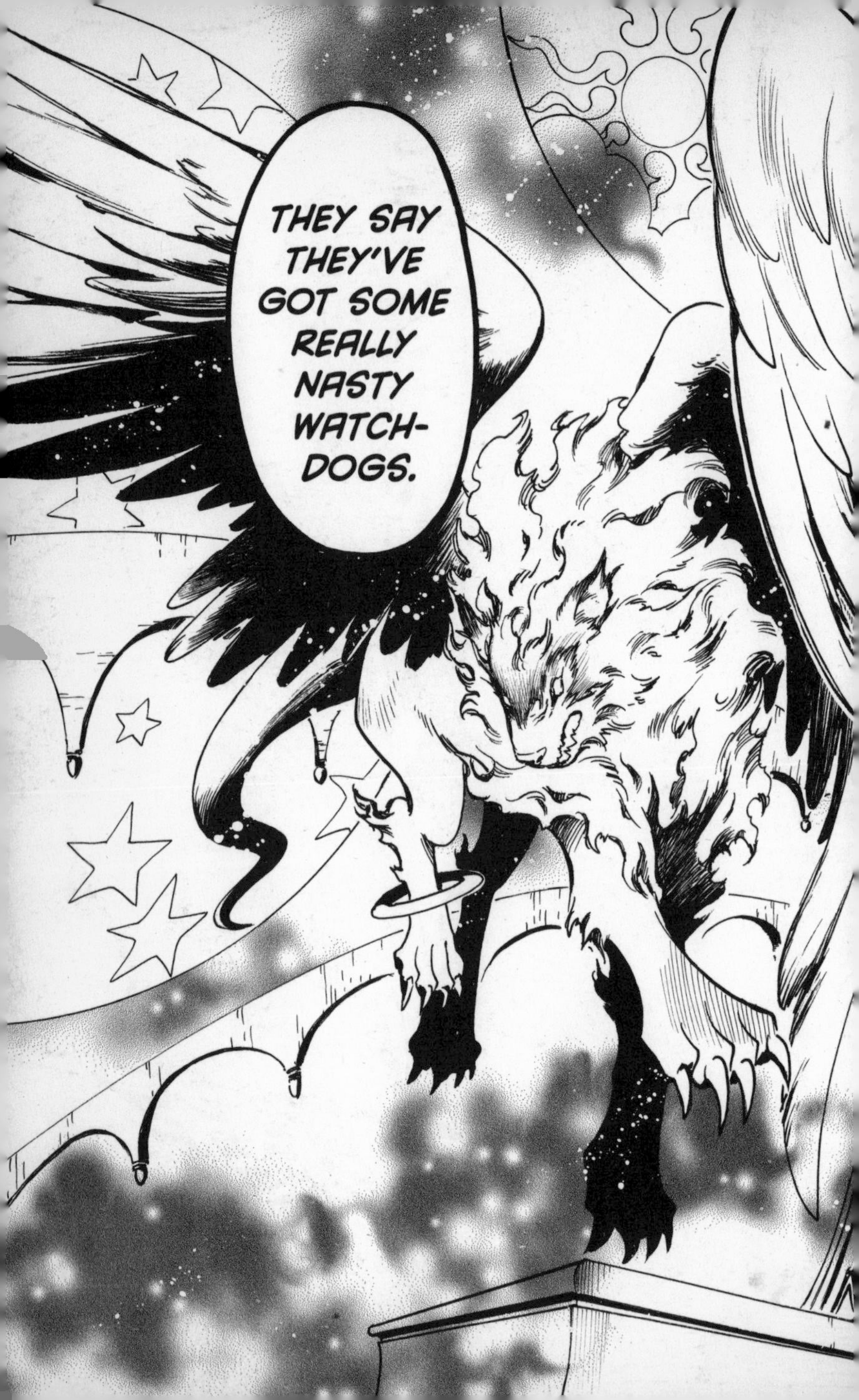
THEY SAY THEY'VE GOT SOME REALLY NASTY WATCH-DOGS.

ツバサ

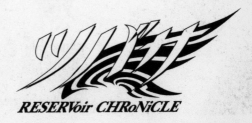

RESERVoir CHRoNiCLE

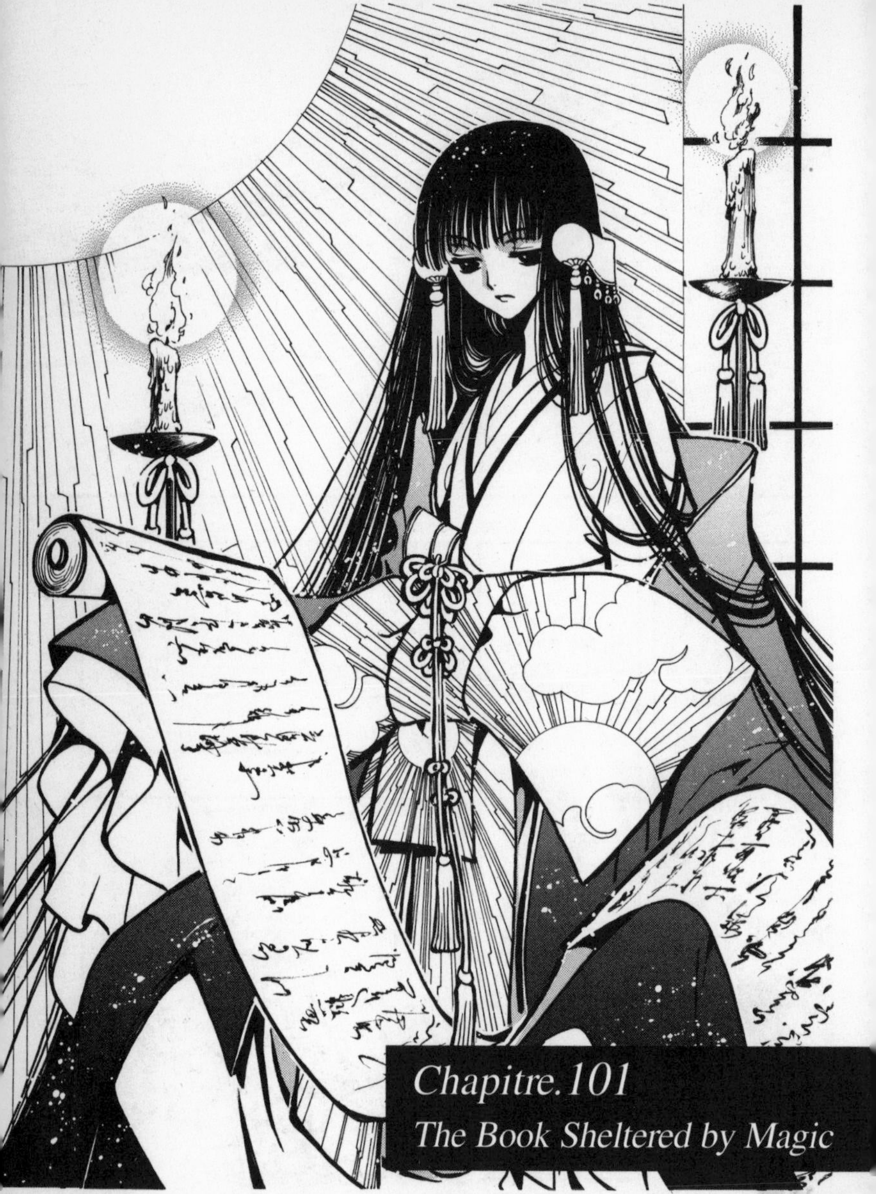
Chapitre.101
The Book Sheltered by Magic

I'M SORRY, KIDS! DADDY JUST DOESN'T BRING IN THE MONEY LIKE HE SHOULD!

AND IT SEEMS THERE ARE ALL SORTS OF SEATS AVAILABLE.

BUT WE DON'T HAVE MUCH MONEY, SO...

WOW! WE'RE FLYING THROUGH THE AIR!

IT'S AMAZING!

SO THIS IS FLYING BY MAGIC, TOO, HUH?

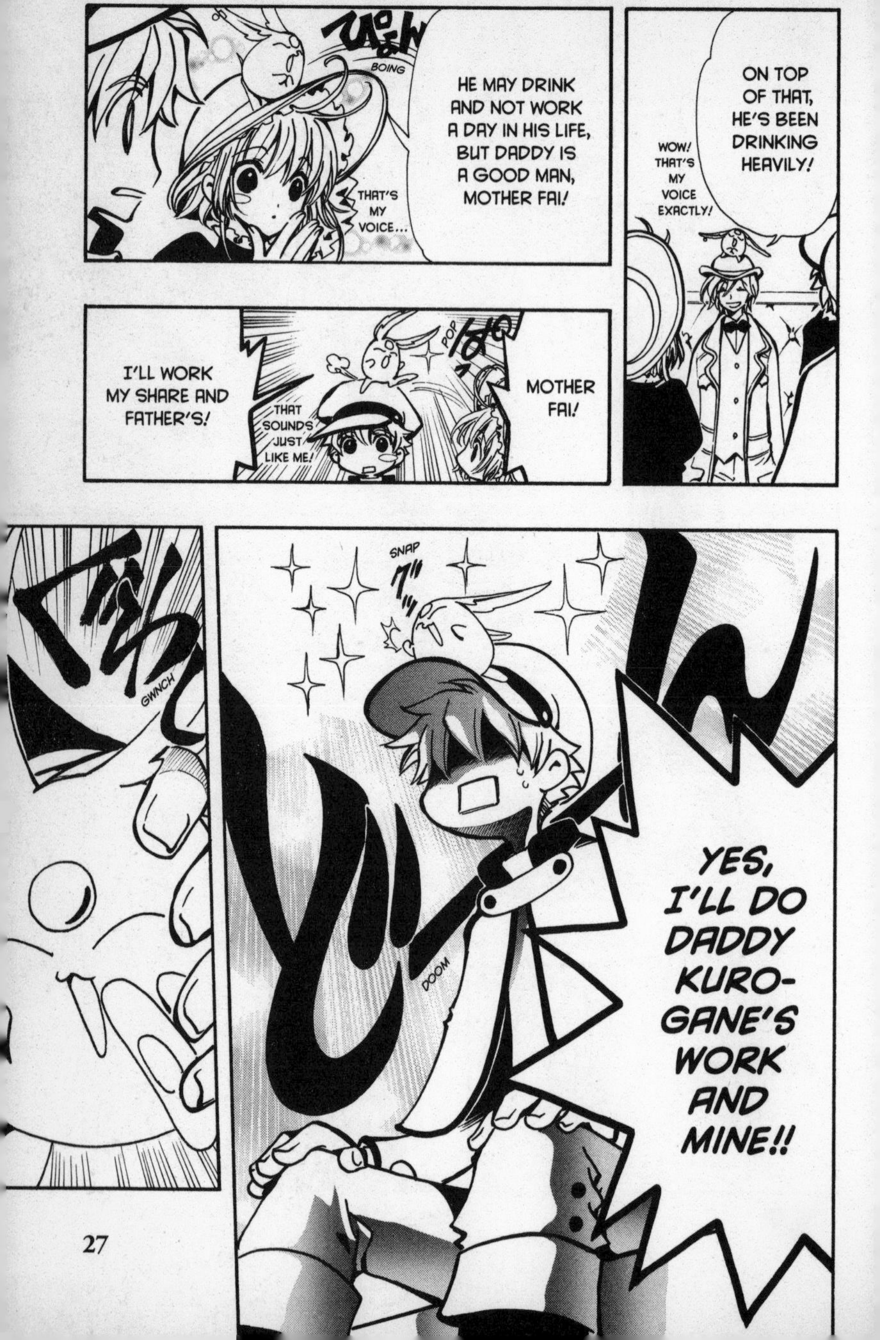
ON TOP OF THAT, HE'S BEEN DRINKING HEAVILY!
WOW! THAT'S MY VOICE EXACTLY!
BOING
HE MAY DRINK AND NOT WORK A DAY IN HIS LIFE, BUT DADDY IS A GOOD MAN, MOTHER FAI!
THAT'S MY VOICE...
MOTHER FAI!
POP
THAT SOUNDS JUST LIKE ME!
I'LL WORK MY SHARE AND FATHER'S!
SNAP
YES, I'LL DO DADDY KURO-GANE'S WORK AND MINE!!
DOOM
GWNCH

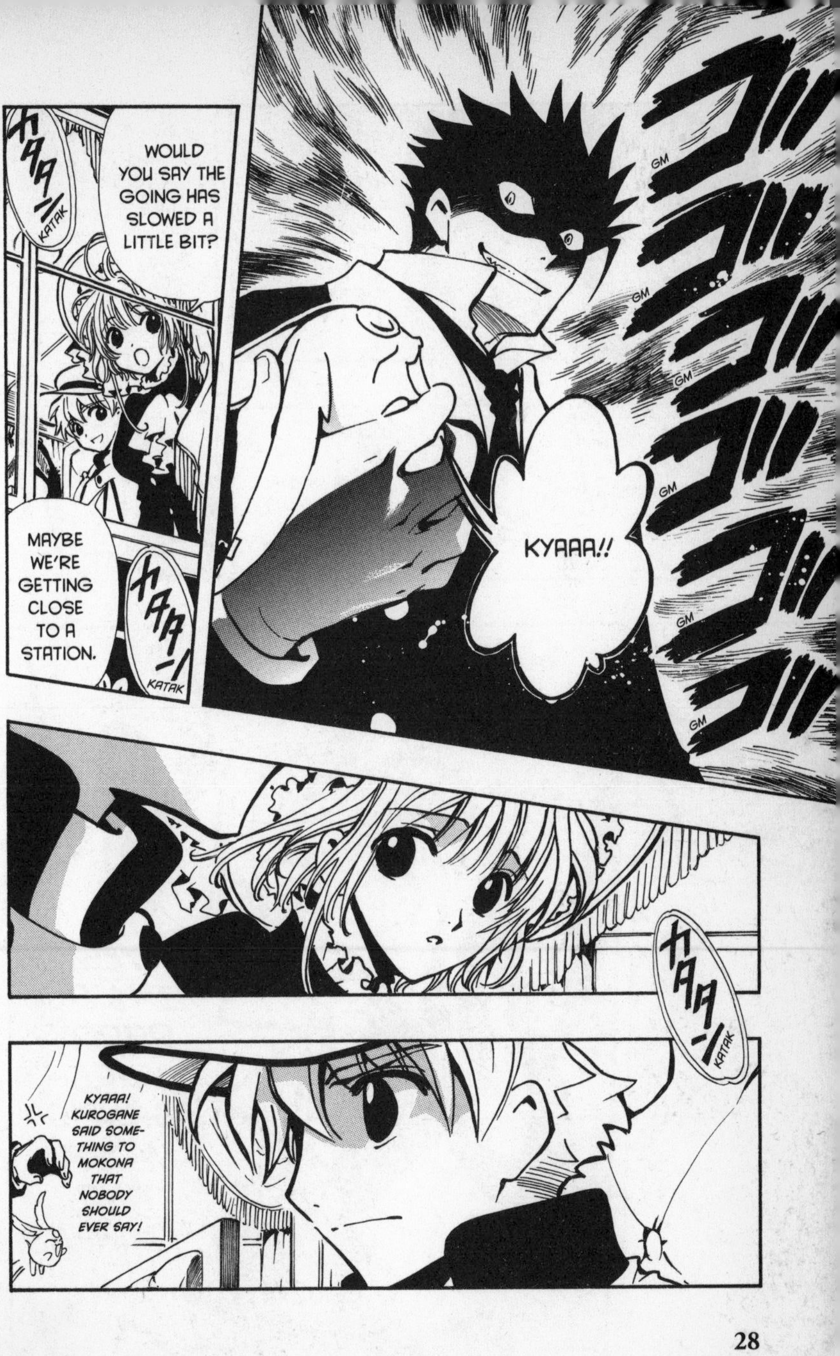
GM
GM
GM
GM
GM
GM
KYAAA!!
WOULD YOU SAY THE GOING HAS SLOWED A LITTLE BIT?
KATAK
MAYBE WE'RE GETTING CLOSE TO A STATION.
KATAK
KATAK
KYAAA! KUROGANE SAID SOMETHING TO MOKONA THAT NOBODY SHOULD EVER SAY!

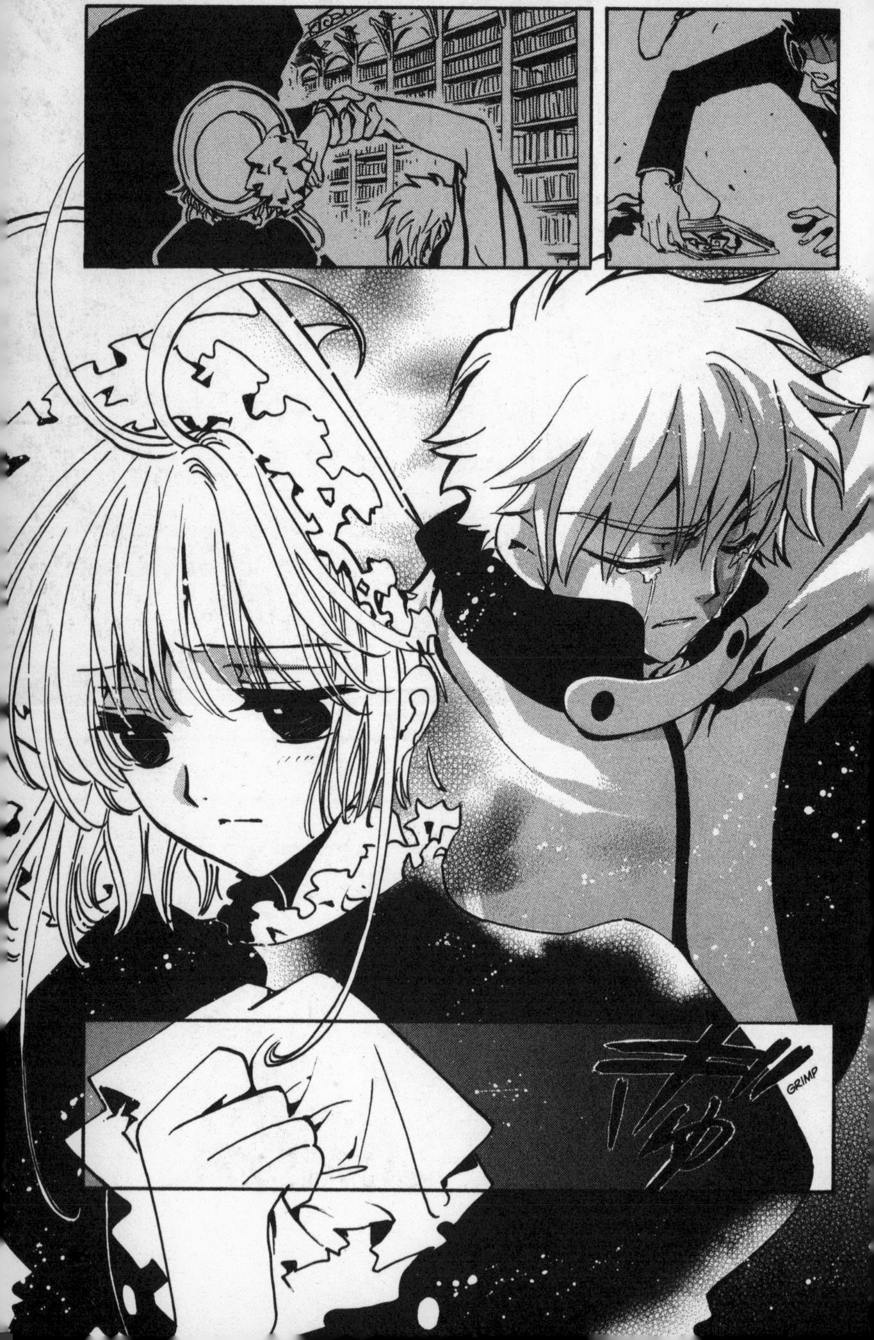
GRIMP

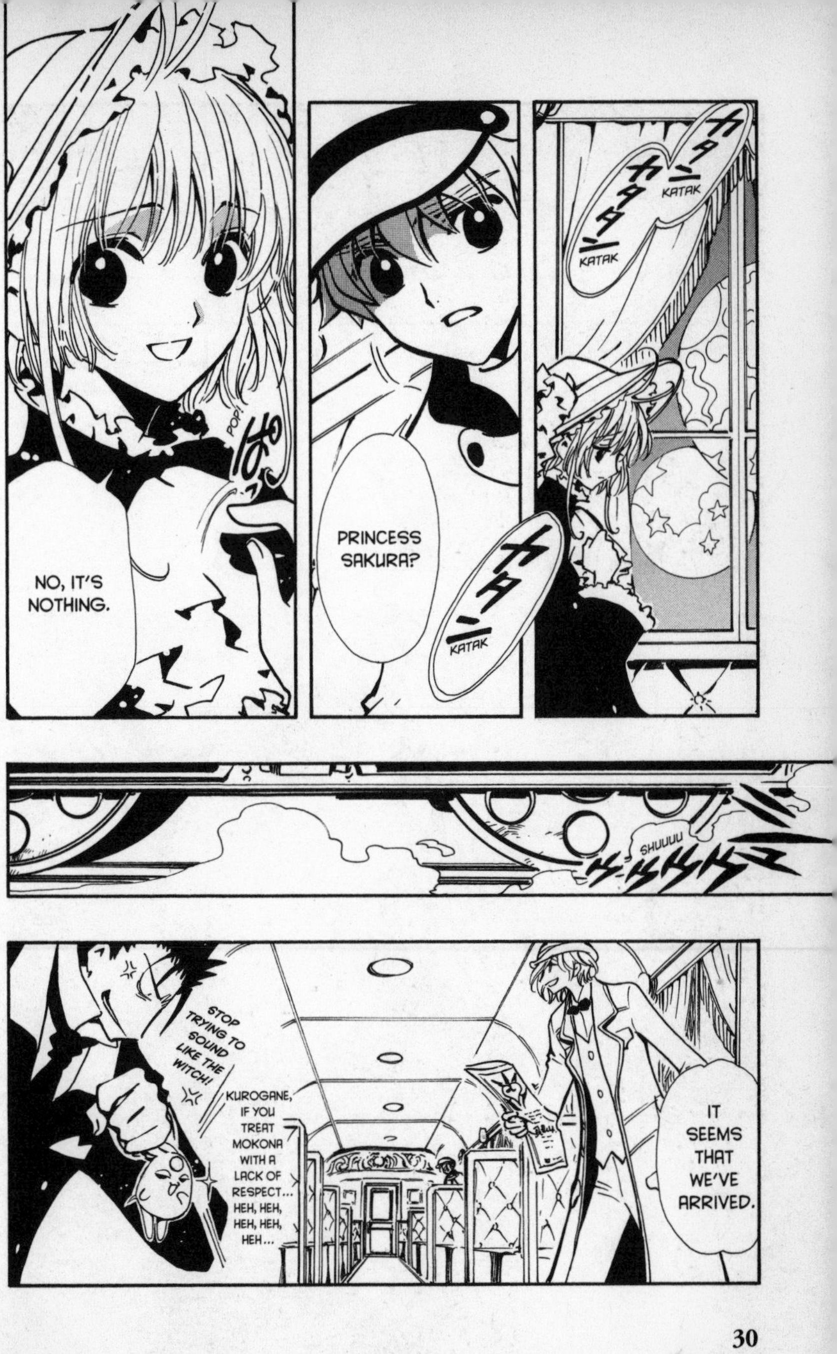

カタン
KATAK
カタン
KATAK
カタン
KATAK
PRINCESS SAKURA?
POP!
NO, IT'S NOTHING.
SHUUUU
IT SEEMS THAT WE'VE ARRIVED.
KUROGANE, IF YOU TREAT MOKONA WITH A LACK OF RESPECT... HEH, HEH, HEH, HEH, HEH...
STOP TRYING TO SOUND LIKE THE WITCH!

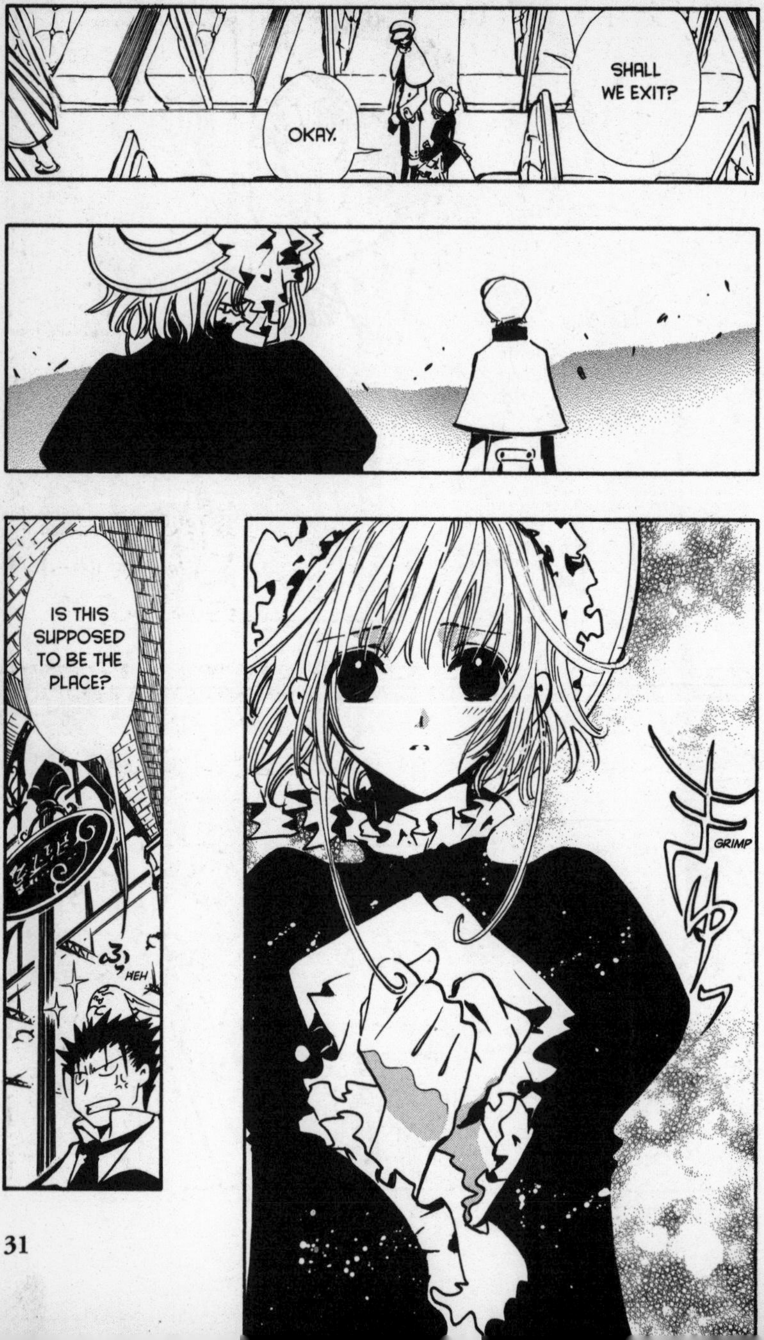
SHALL WE EXIT?
OKAY.
GRIMP
IS THIS SUPPOSED TO BE THE PLACE?
HEH

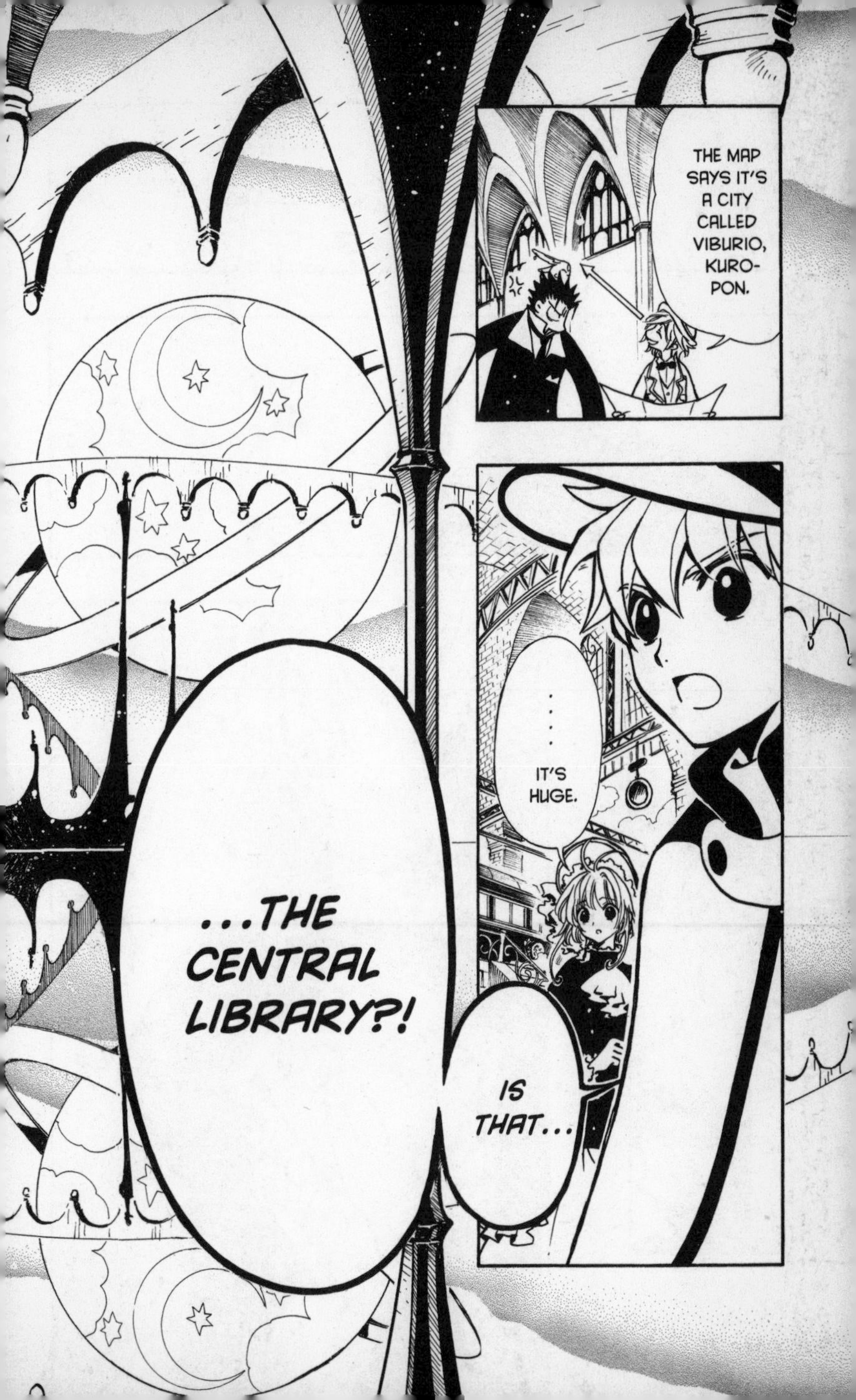
THE MAP SAYS IT'S A CITY CALLED VIBURIO, KURO-PON.
.... IT'S HUGE.
IS THAT...
...THE CENTRAL LIBRARY?!

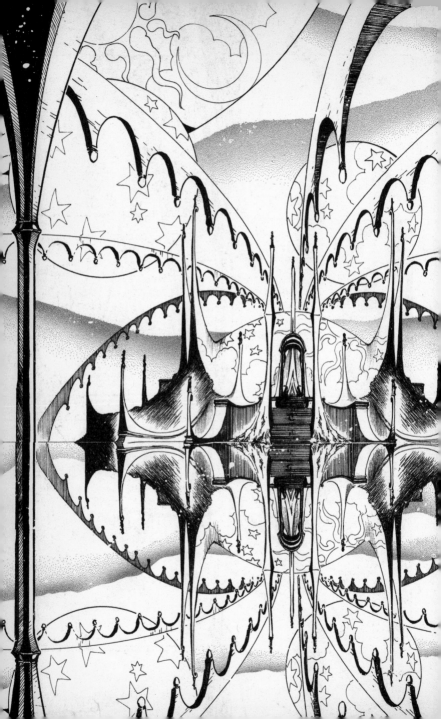

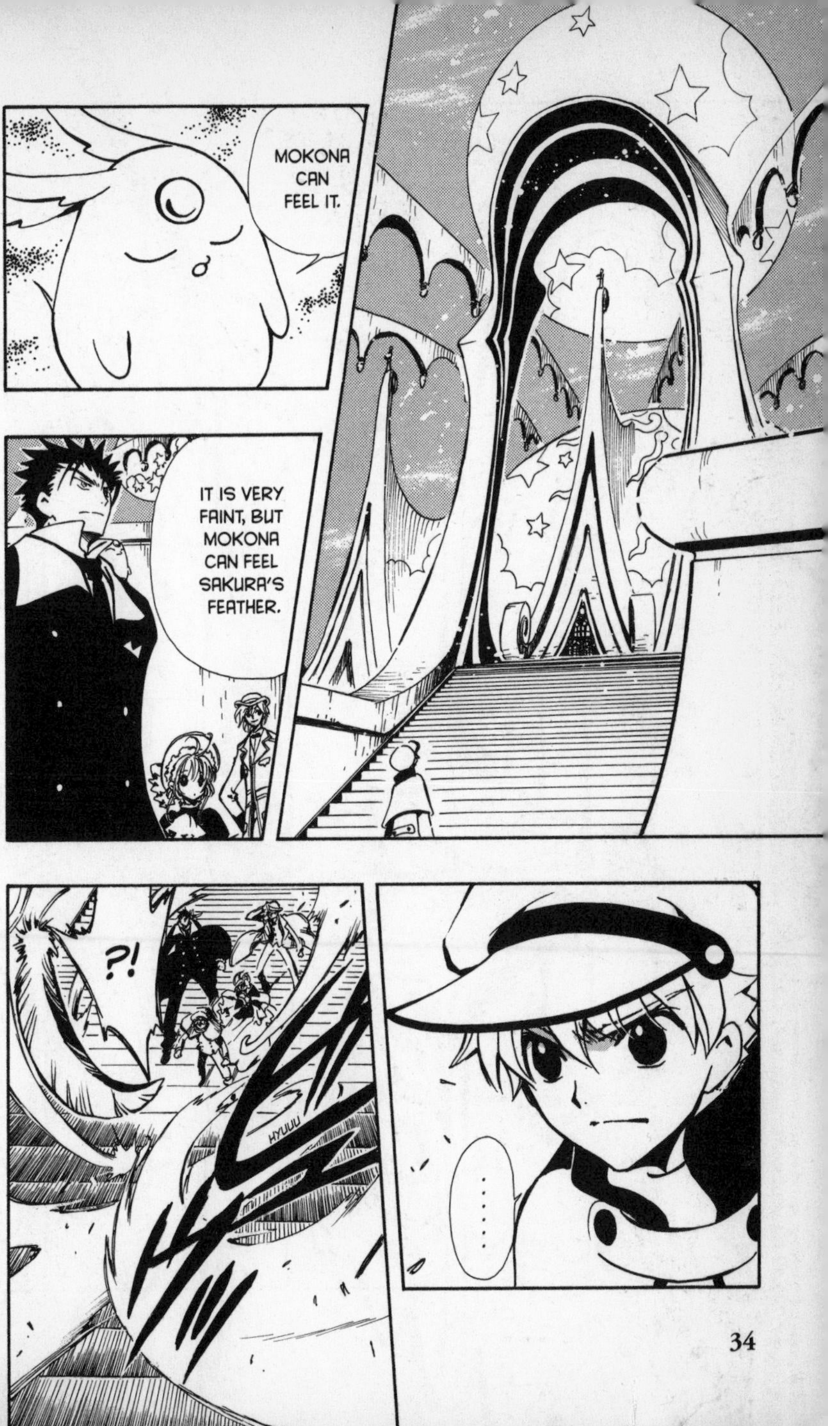
MOKONA CAN FEEL IT.
IT IS VERY FAINT, BUT MOKONA CAN FEEL SAKURA'S FEATHER.
......
?!
HYUUU

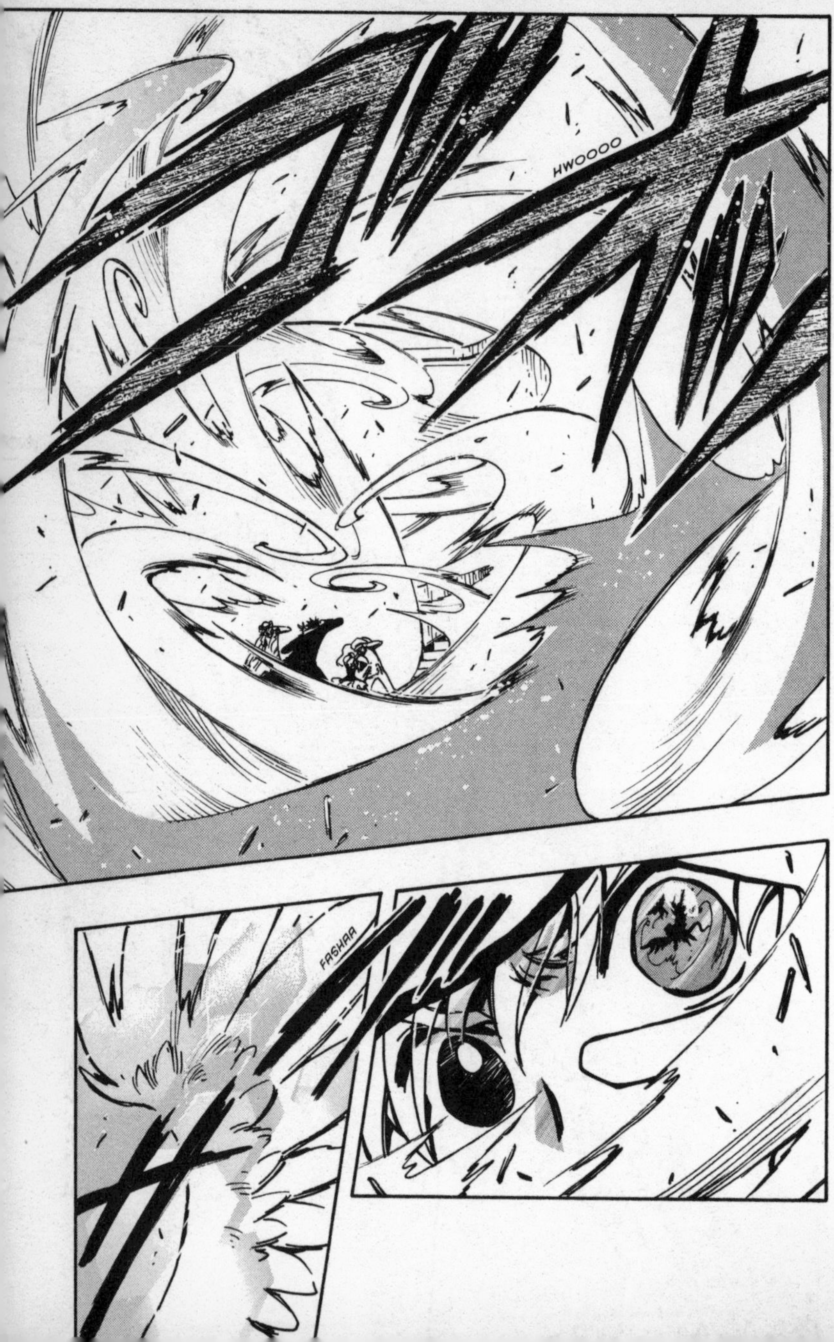
HWOOOO
FASHAA

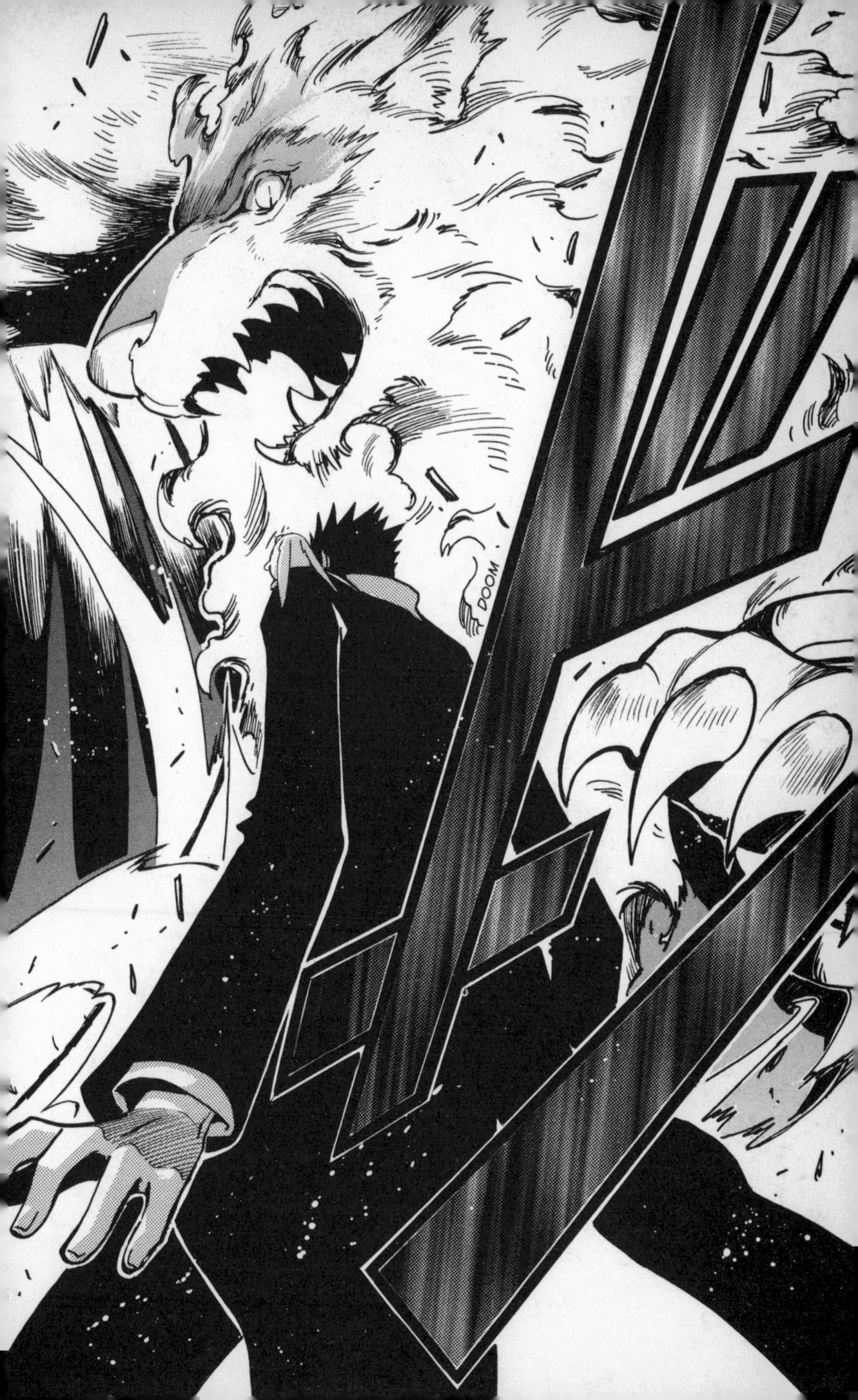
DOOM

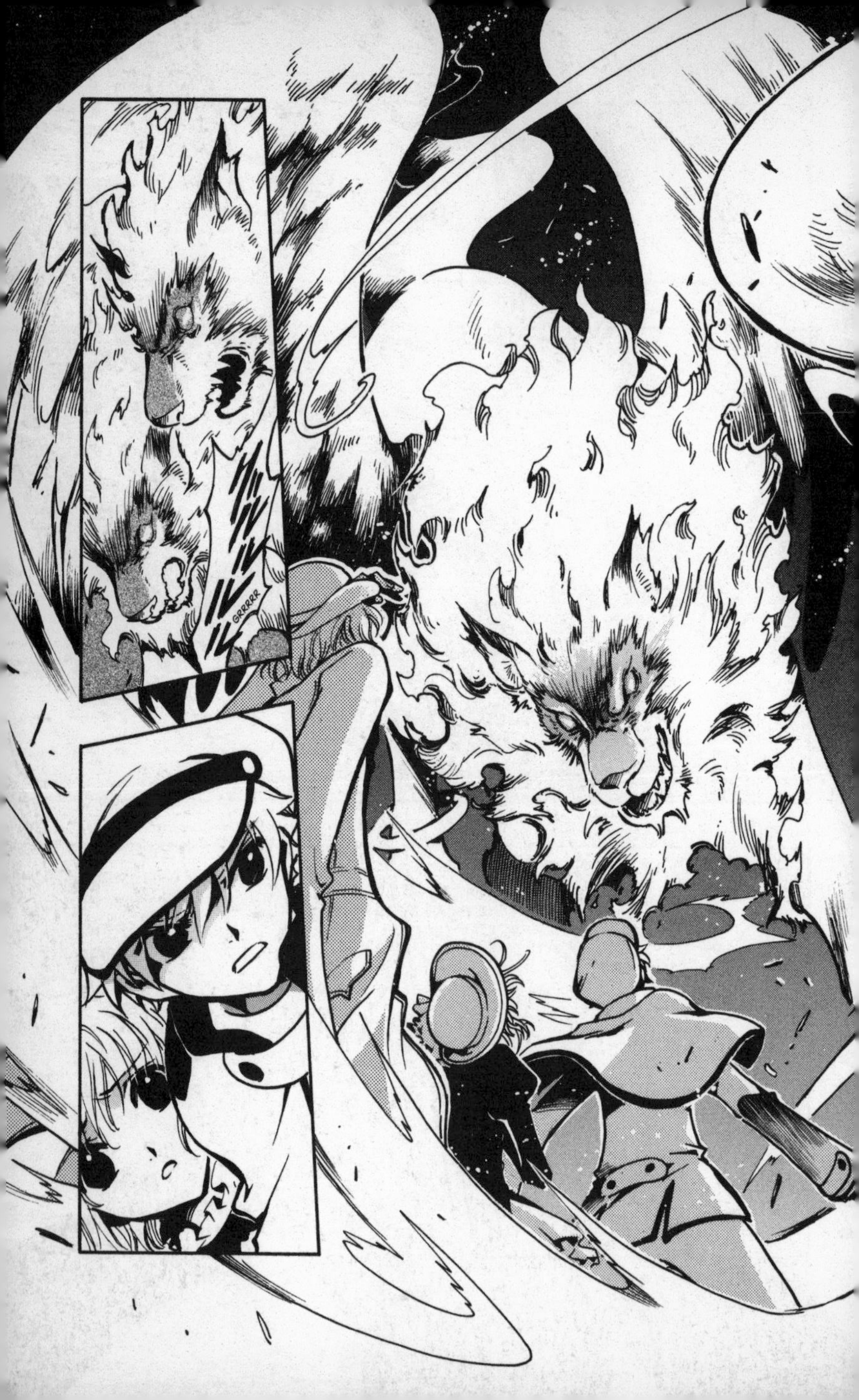
GRRRRR

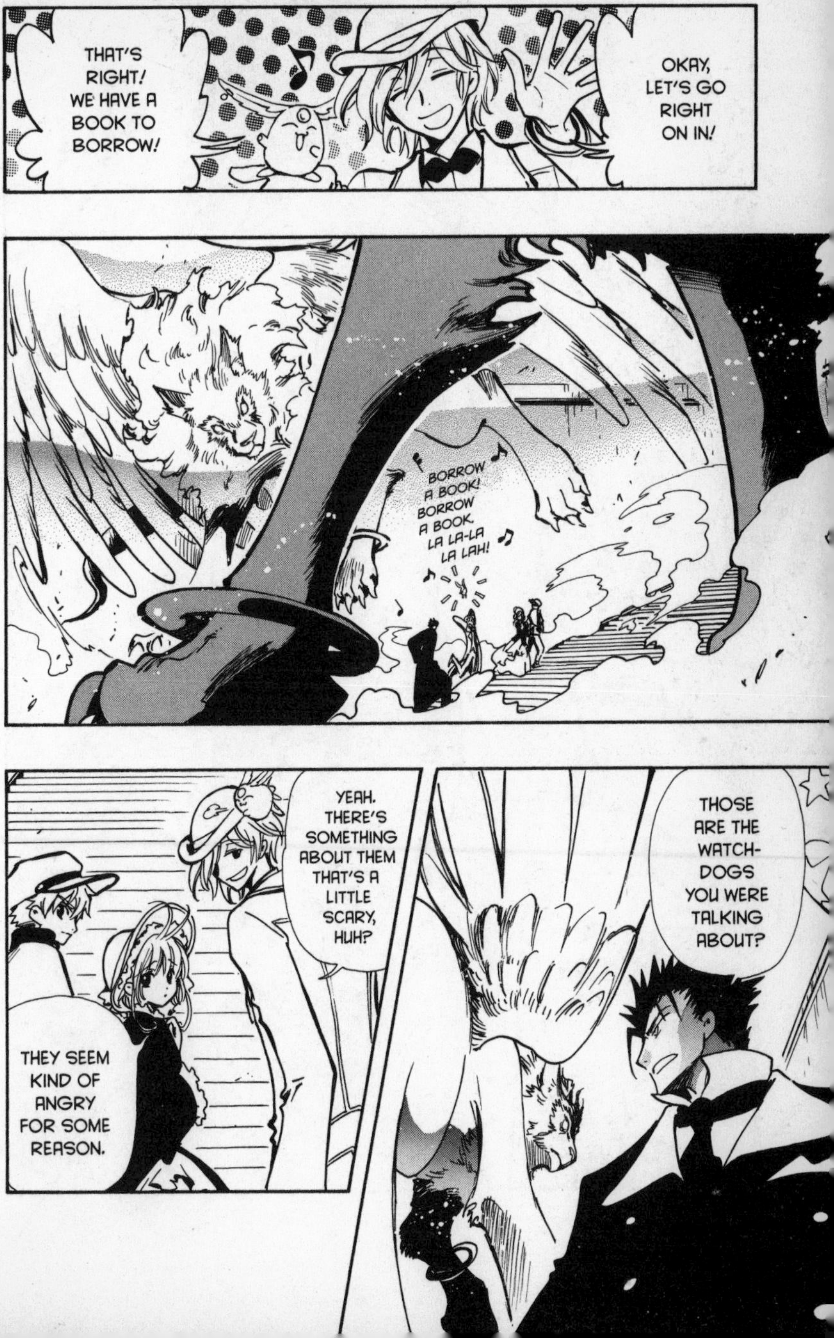
OKAY, LET'S GO RIGHT ON IN!
THAT'S RIGHT! WE HAVE A BOOK TO BORROW!
BORROW A BOOK! BORROW A BOOK. LA LA-LA LA LAH!
THOSE ARE THE WATCH-DOGS YOU WERE TALKING ABOUT?
YEAH. THERE'S SOMETHING ABOUT THEM THAT'S A LITTLE SCARY, HUH?
THEY SEEM KIND OF ANGRY FOR SOME REASON.

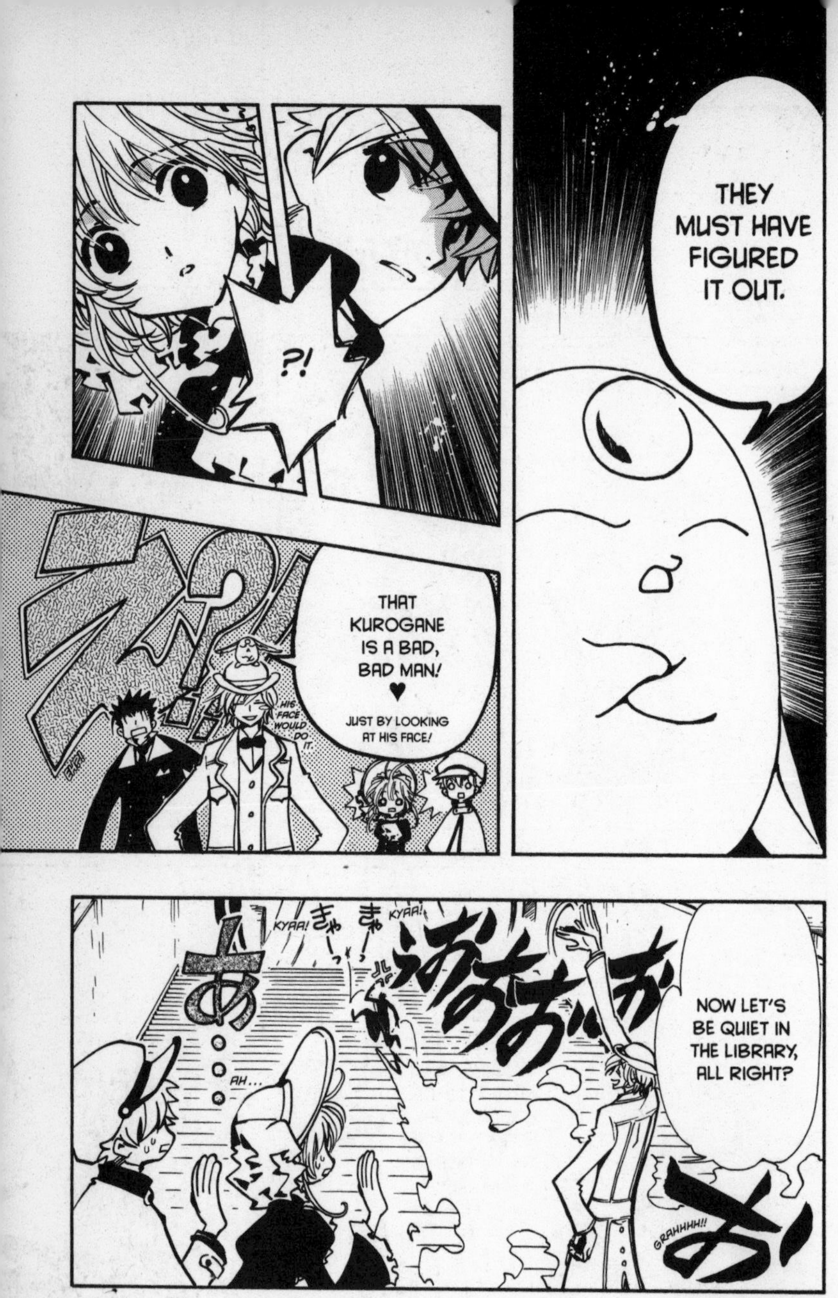
THEY MUST HAVE FIGURED IT OUT.
?!
THAT KUROGANE IS A BAD, BAD MAN! ♥
JUST BY LOOKING AT HIS FACE!
HIS FACE WOULD DO IT.
NOW LET'S BE QUIET IN THE LIBRARY, ALL RIGHT?
KYAA!
KYAA!
GRAHHHH!!
AH...

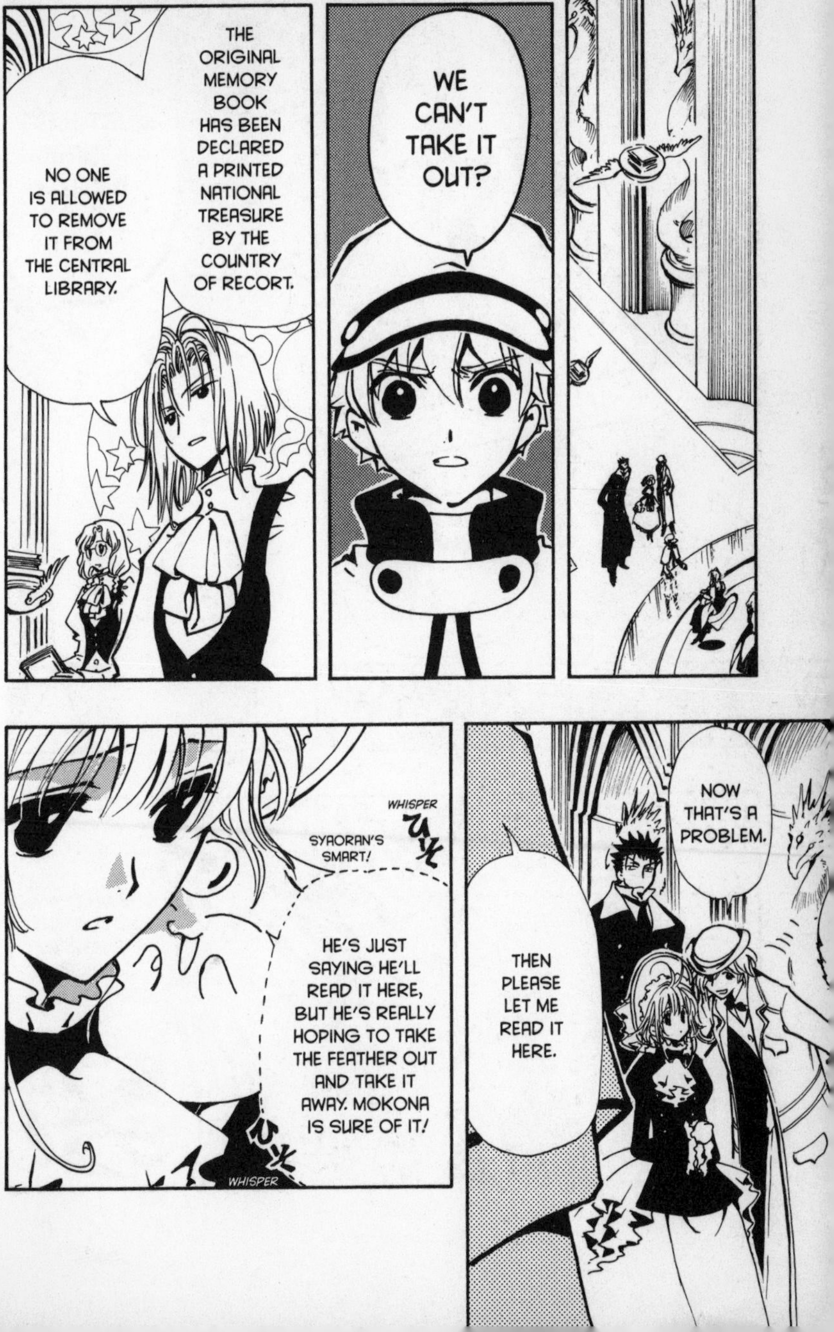
WE CAN'T TAKE IT OUT?
THE ORIGINAL MEMORY BOOK HAS BEEN DECLARED A PRINTED NATIONAL TREASURE BY THE COUNTRY OF RECORT.
NO ONE IS ALLOWED TO REMOVE IT FROM THE CENTRAL LIBRARY.
NOW THAT'S A PROBLEM.
THEN PLEASE LET ME READ IT HERE.
WHISPER
SYAORAN'S SMART!
HE'S JUST SAYING HE'LL READ IT HERE, BUT HE'S REALLY HOPING TO TAKE THE FEATHER OUT AND TAKE IT AWAY. MOKONA IS SURE OF IT!
WHISPER

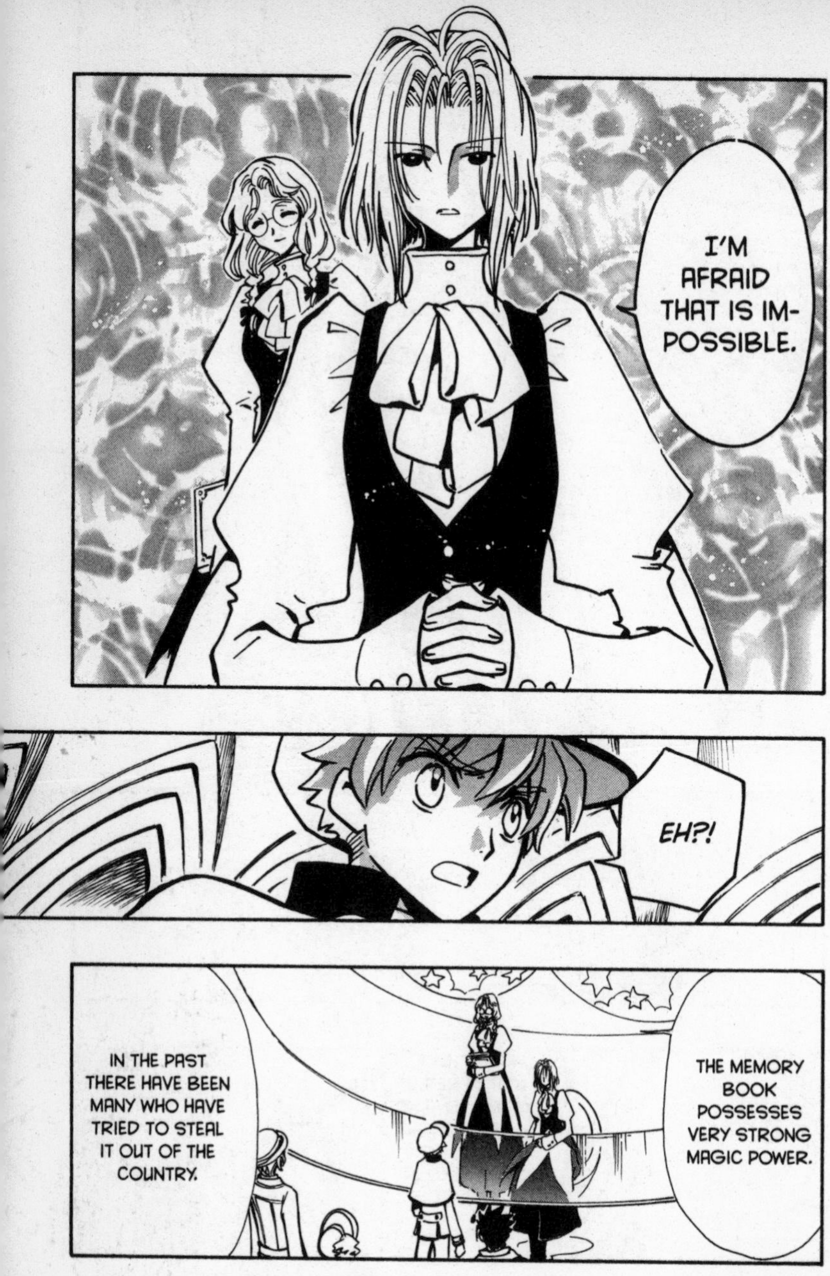
I'M AFRAID THAT IS IM- POSSIBLE.
EH?!
THE MEMORY BOOK POSSESSES VERY STRONG MAGIC POWER.
IN THE PAST THERE HAVE BEEN MANY WHO HAVE TRIED TO STEAL IT OUT OF THE COUNTRY.

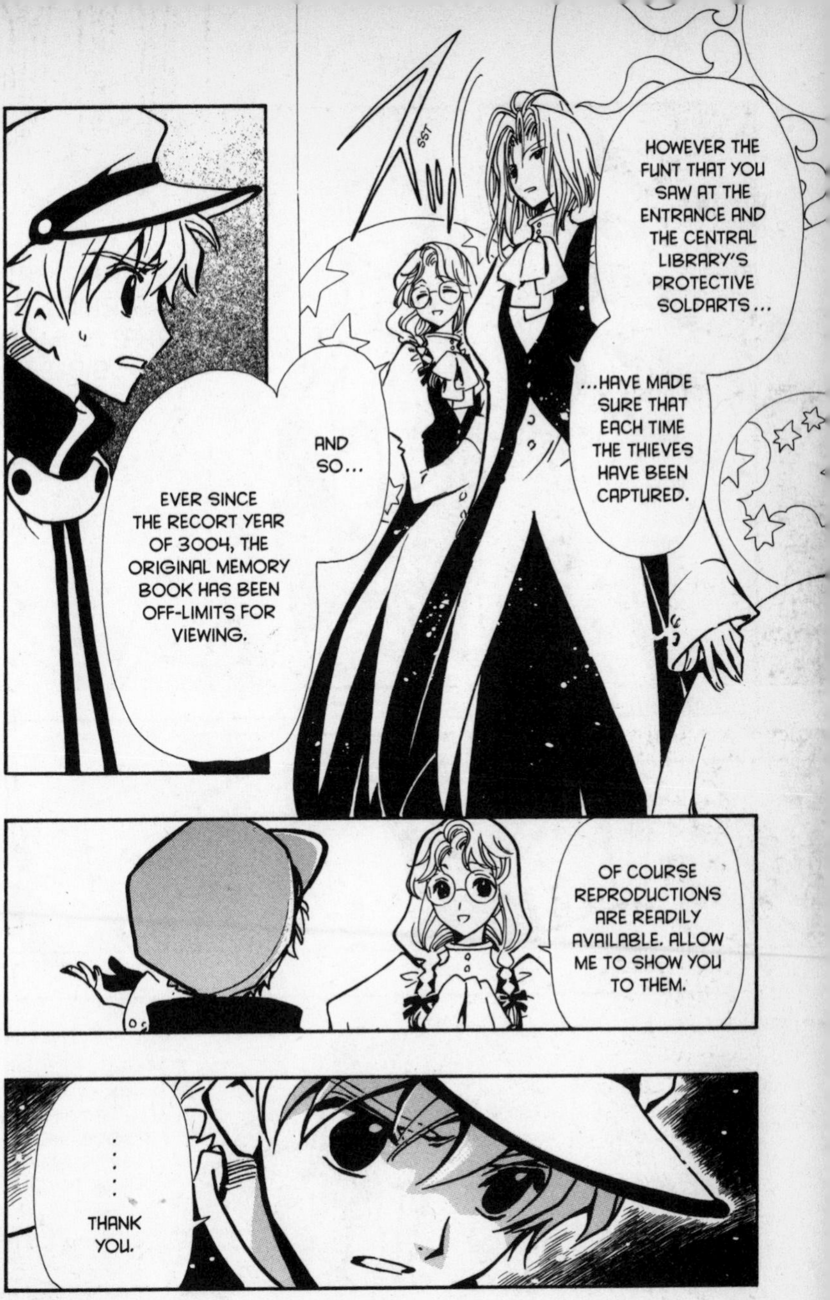
SST
HOWEVER THE FUNT THAT YOU SAW AT THE ENTRANCE AND THE CENTRAL LIBRARY'S PROTECTIVE SOLDARTS...
...HAVE MADE SURE THAT EACH TIME THE THIEVES HAVE BEEN CAPTURED.
AND SO...
EVER SINCE THE RECORT YEAR OF 3004, THE ORIGINAL MEMORY BOOK HAS BEEN OFF-LIMITS FOR VIEWING.
OF COURSE REPRODUCTIONS ARE READILY AVAILABLE. ALLOW ME TO SHOW YOU TO THEM.
.....
THANK YOU.

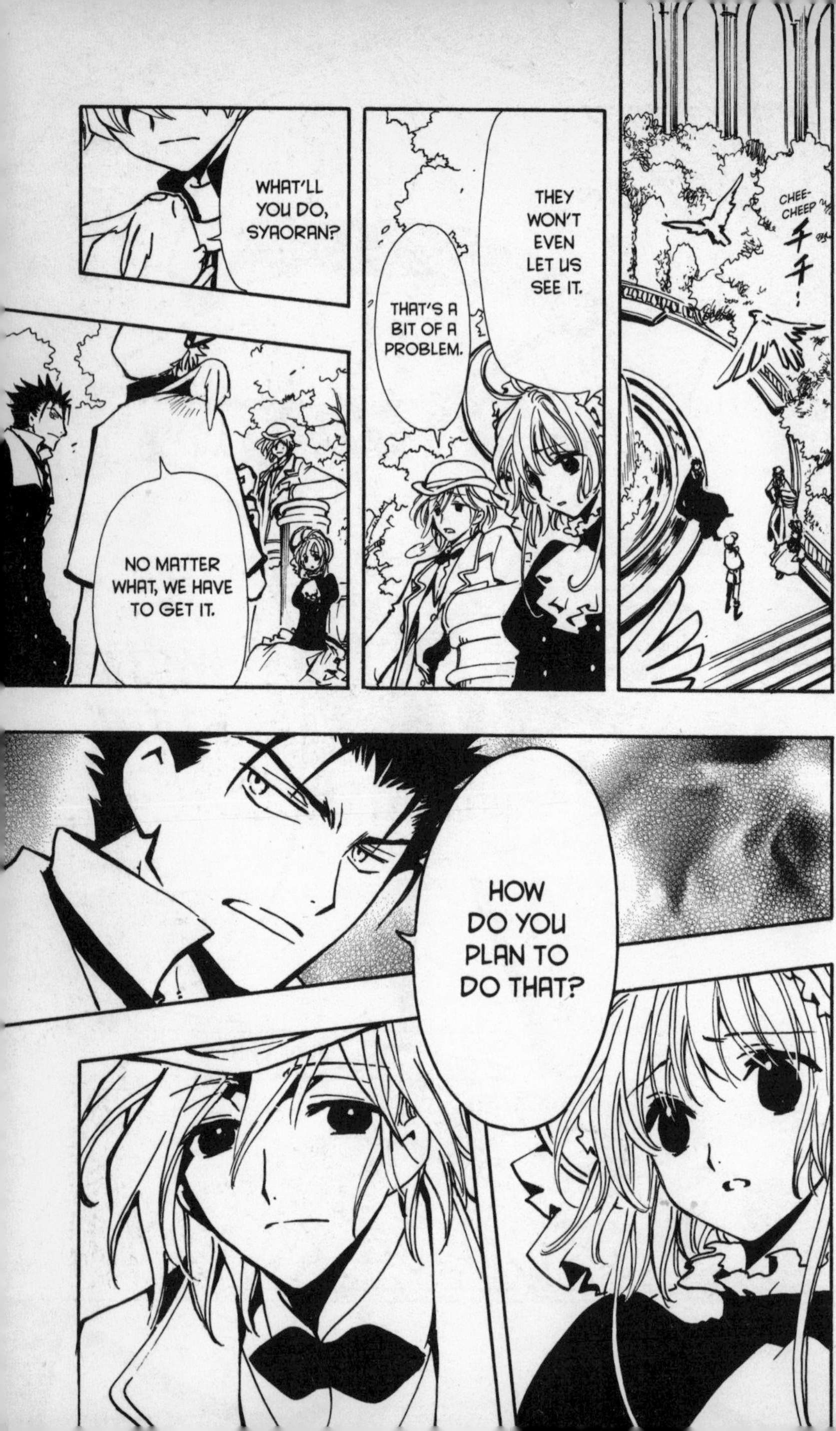
CHEE-CHEEP
チチ!
THEY WON'T EVEN LET US SEE IT.
THAT'S A BIT OF A PROBLEM.
WHAT'LL YOU DO, SYAORAN?
NO MATTER WHAT, WE HAVE TO GET IT.
HOW DO YOU PLAN TO DO THAT?

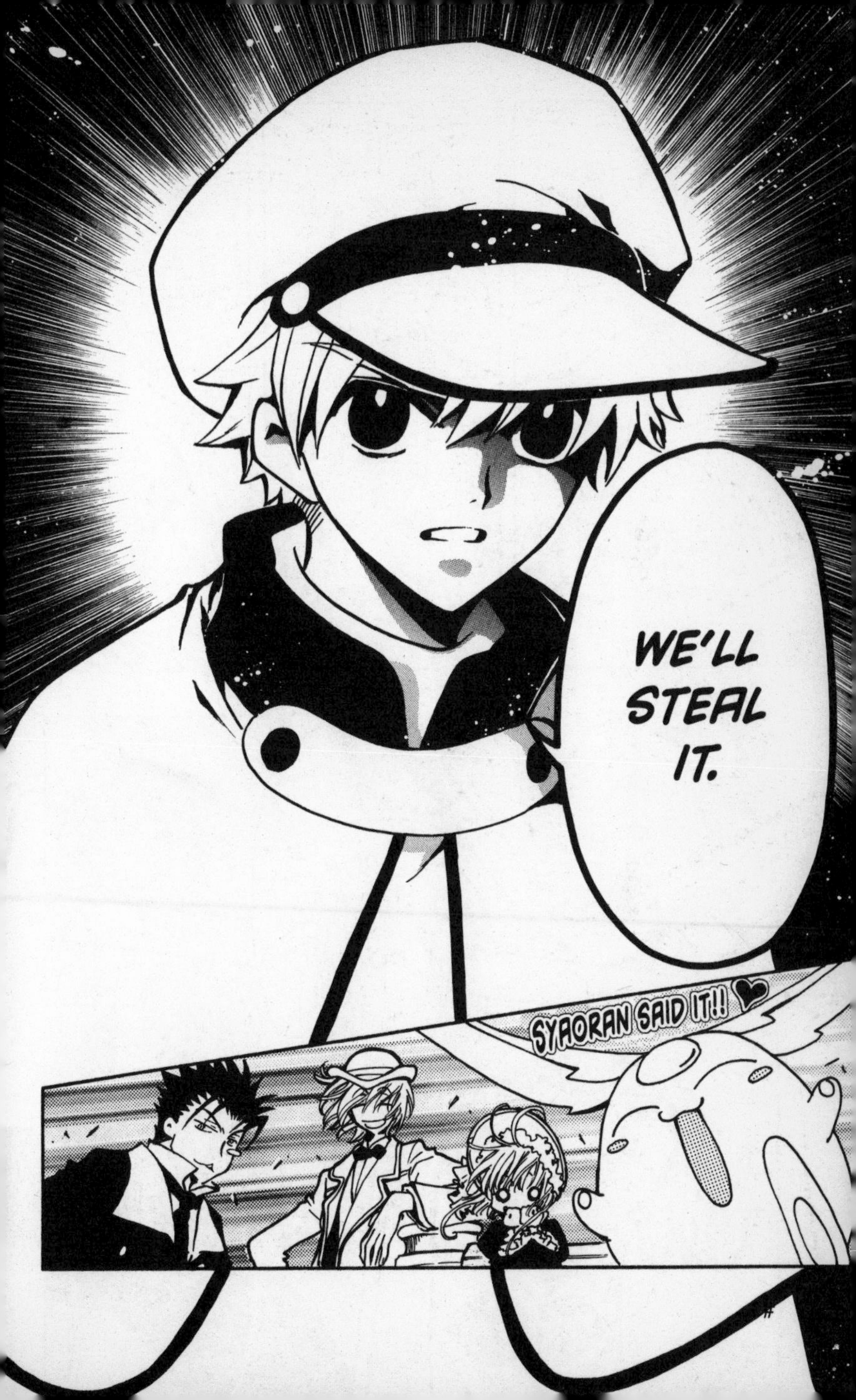
WE'LL STEAL IT.
SYAORAN SAID IT!! ♥

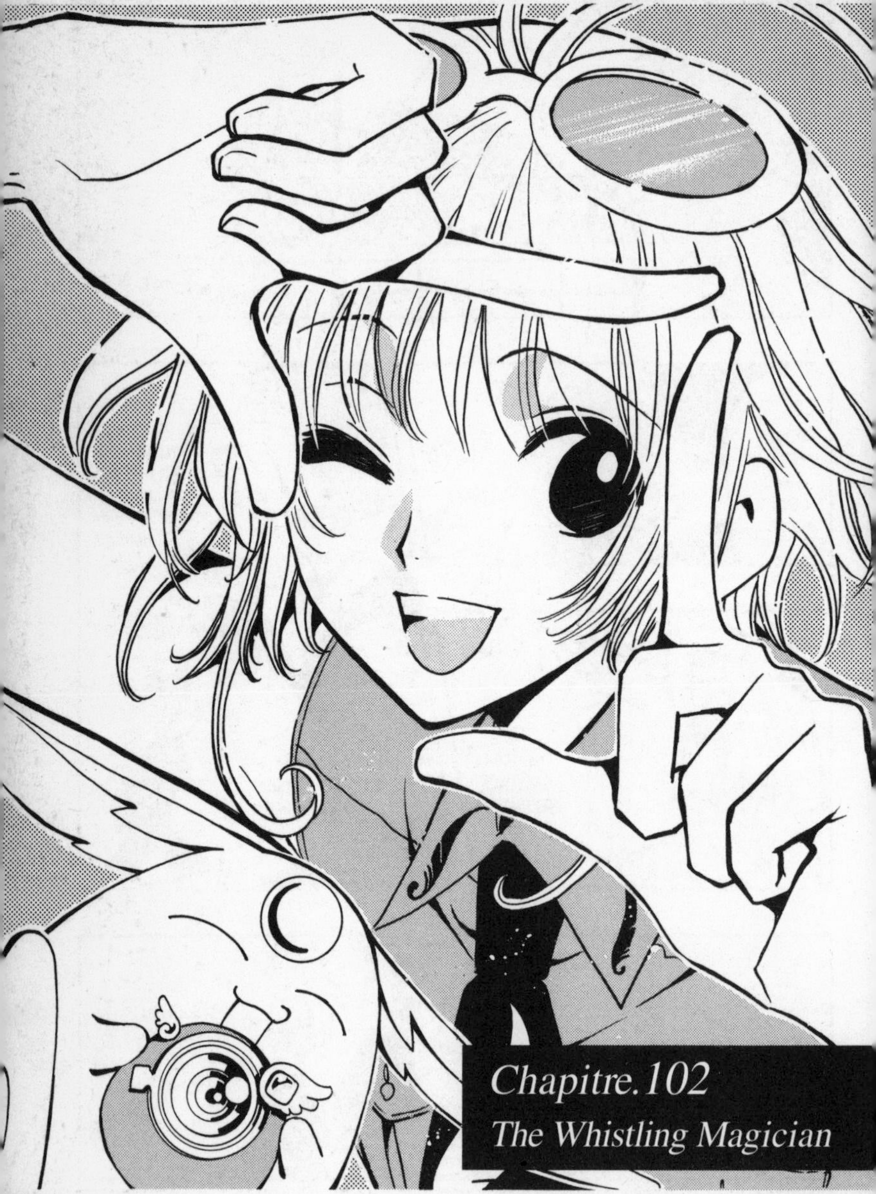
Chapitre.102
The Whistling Magician

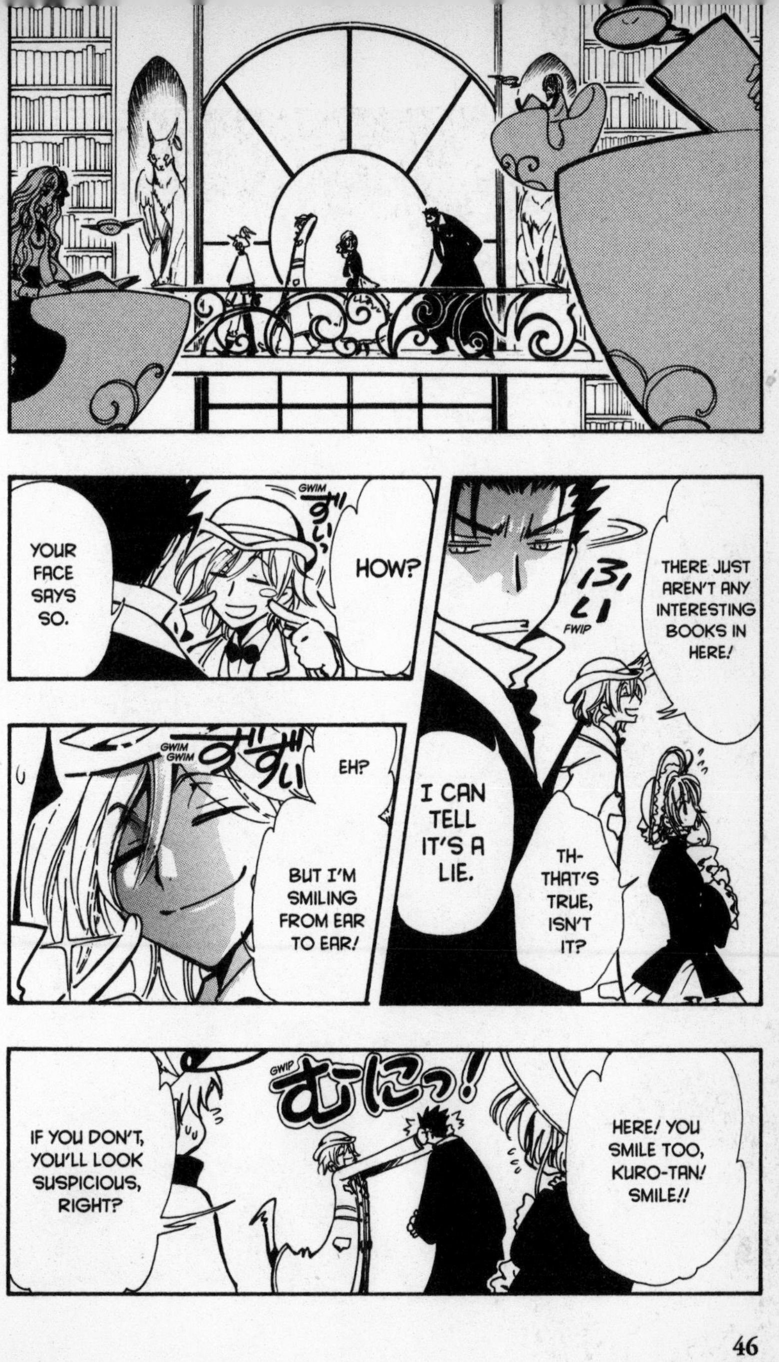
THERE JUST AREN'T ANY INTERESTING BOOKS IN HERE!
ふい
FWIP
TH-THAT'S TRUE, ISN'T IT?
I CAN TELL IT'S A LIE.
ずい
GWIM
HOW?
YOUR FACE SAYS SO.
ずずい
GWIM GWIM
EH?
BUT I'M SMILING FROM EAR TO EAR!
HERE! YOU SMILE TOO, KURO-TAN! SMILE!!
むにっ!
GWIP
IF YOU DON'T, YOU'LL LOOK SUSPICIOUS, RIGHT?

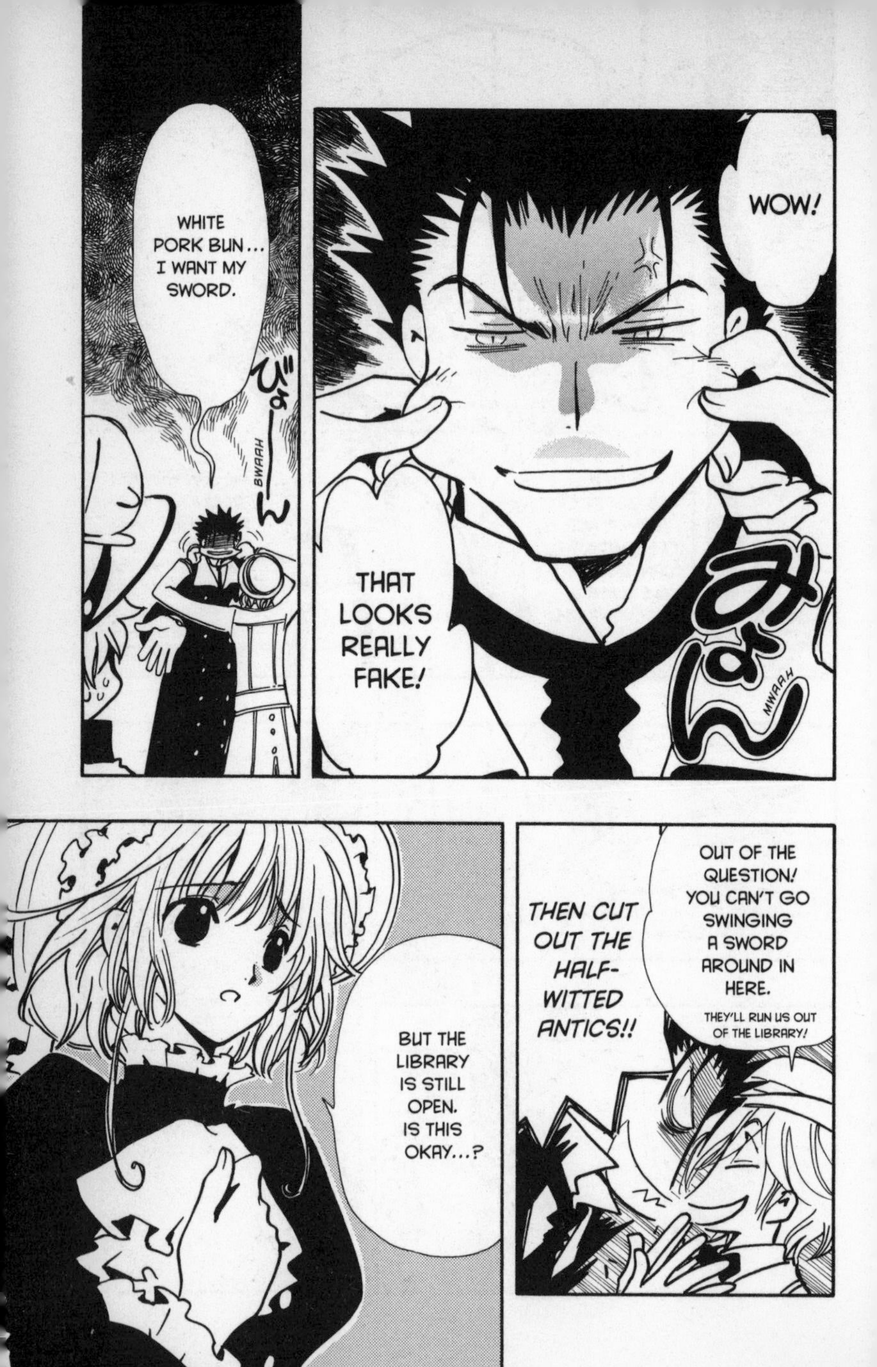
WOW!
みょん
MWAAH
THAT LOOKS REALLY FAKE!
WHITE PORK BUN... I WANT MY SWORD.
びょーん
BWAAH
OUT OF THE QUESTION! YOU CAN'T GO SWINGING A SWORD AROUND IN HERE.
THEY'LL RUN US OUT OF THE LIBRARY!
THEN CUT OUT THE HALF-WITTED ANTICS!!
BUT THE LIBRARY IS STILL OPEN. IS THIS OKAY...?

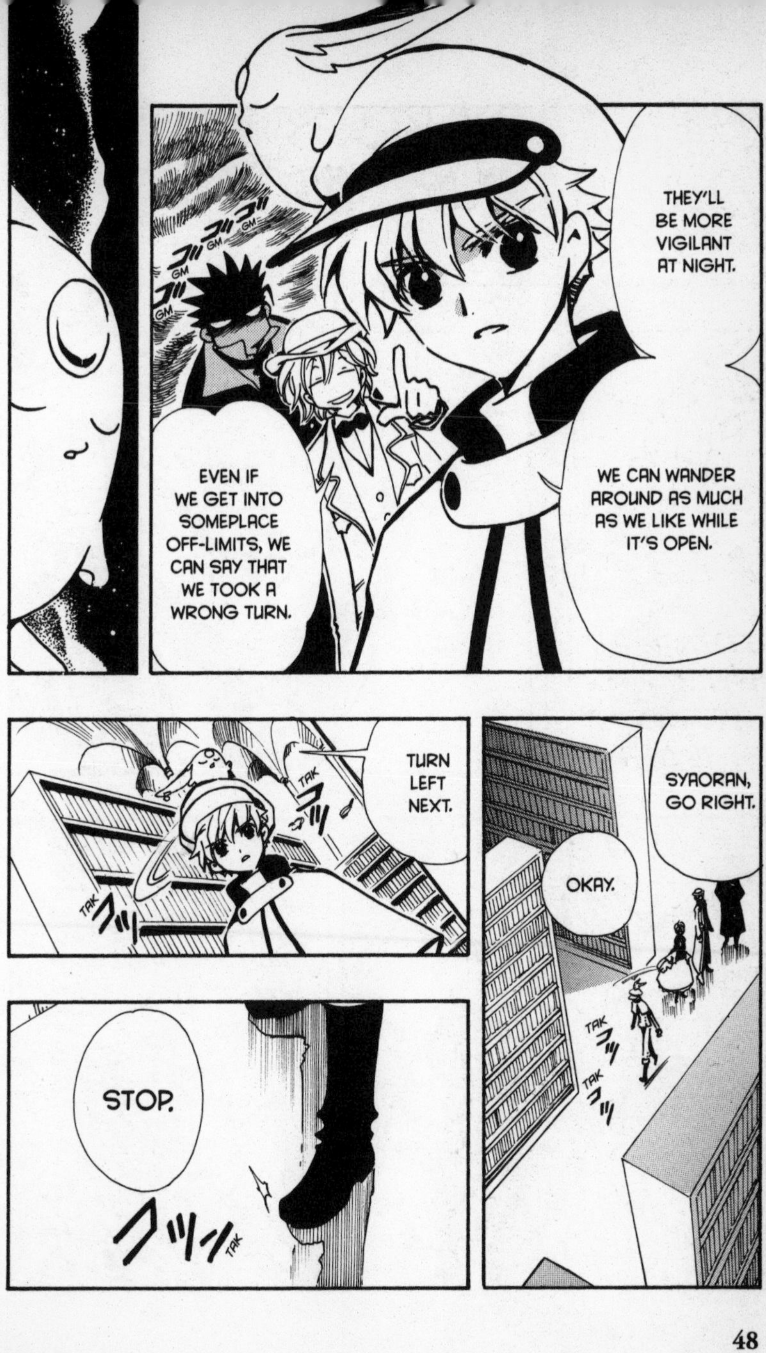
THEY'LL BE MORE VIGILANT AT NIGHT.
WE CAN WANDER AROUND AS MUCH AS WE LIKE WHILE IT'S OPEN.
GM GM GM GM
EVEN IF WE GET INTO SOMEPLACE OFF-LIMITS, WE CAN SAY THAT WE TOOK A WRONG TURN.
SYAORAN, GO RIGHT.
OKAY.
TAK
TAK
TURN LEFT NEXT.
TAK
TAK
STOP.
TAK

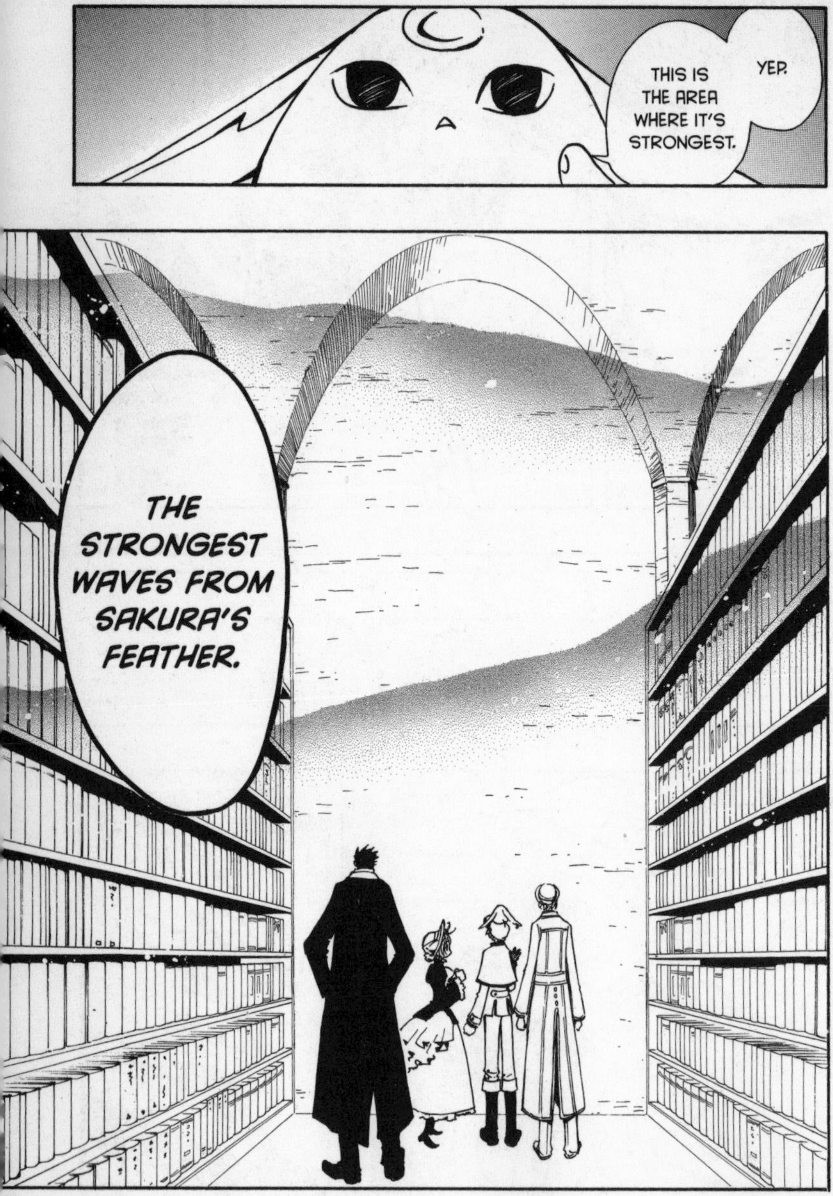
YEP.
THIS IS THE AREA WHERE IT'S STRONGEST.
THE STRONGEST WAVES FROM SAKURA'S FEATHER.

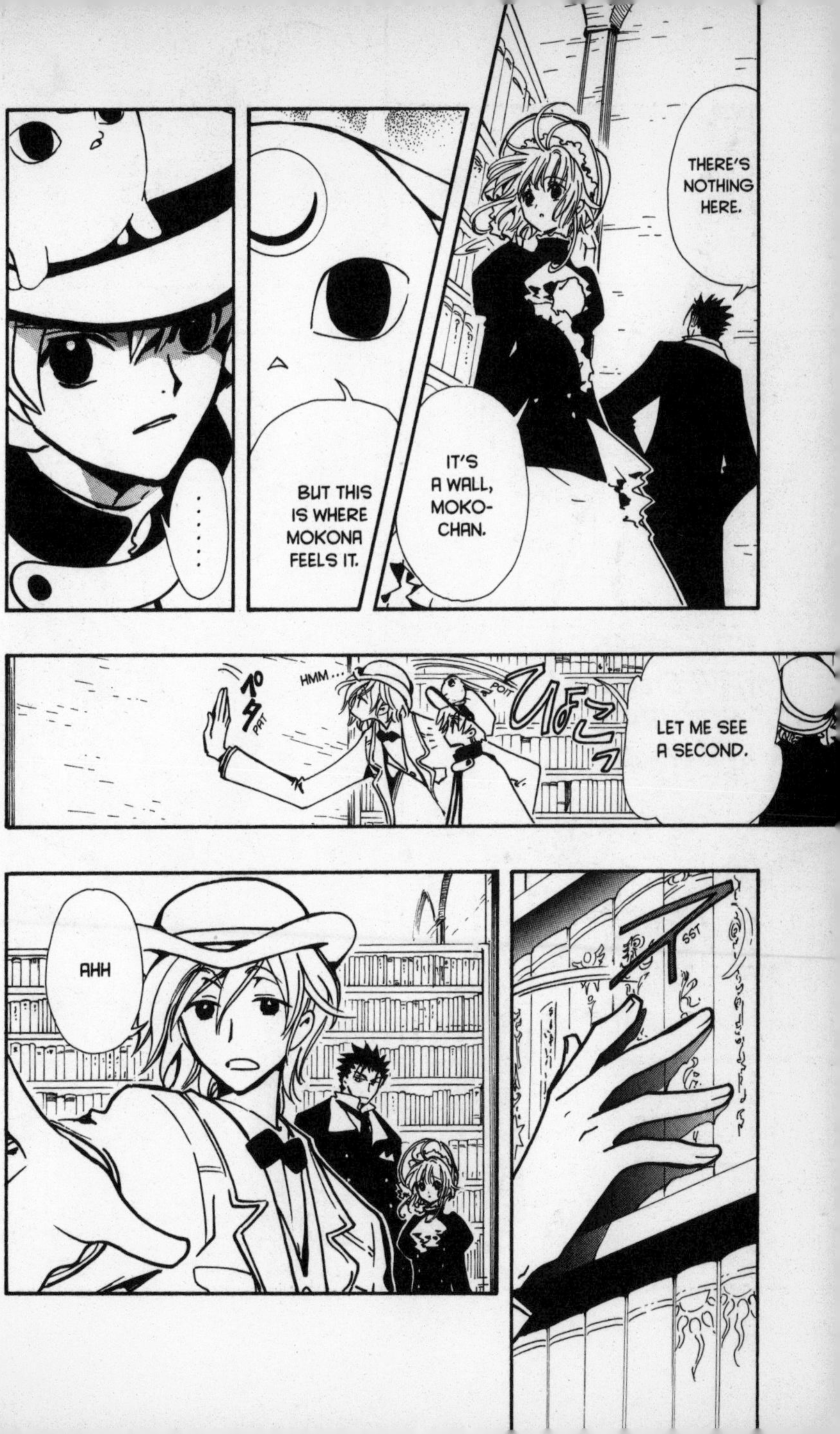
THERE'S NOTHING HERE.
IT'S A WALL, MOKO-CHAN.
BUT THIS IS WHERE MOKONA FEELS IT.
......
LET ME SEE A SECOND.
POIT
HMM...
PAT
SST
AHH

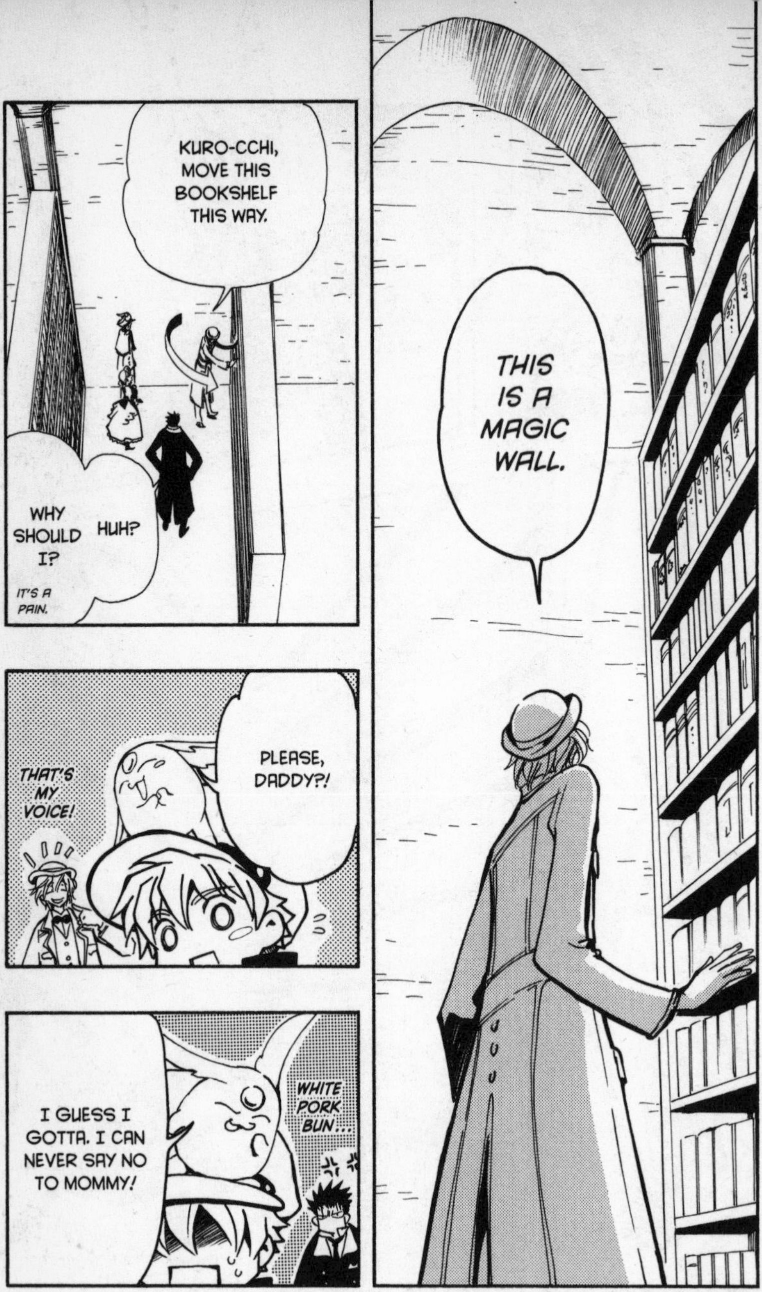
THIS IS A MAGIC WALL.
KURO-CCHI, MOVE THIS BOOKSHELF THIS WAY.
HUH?
WHY SHOULD I?
IT'S A PAIN.
PLEASE, DADDY?!
THAT'S MY VOICE!
I GUESS I GOTTA. I CAN NEVER SAY NO TO MOMMY!
WHITE PORK BUN...

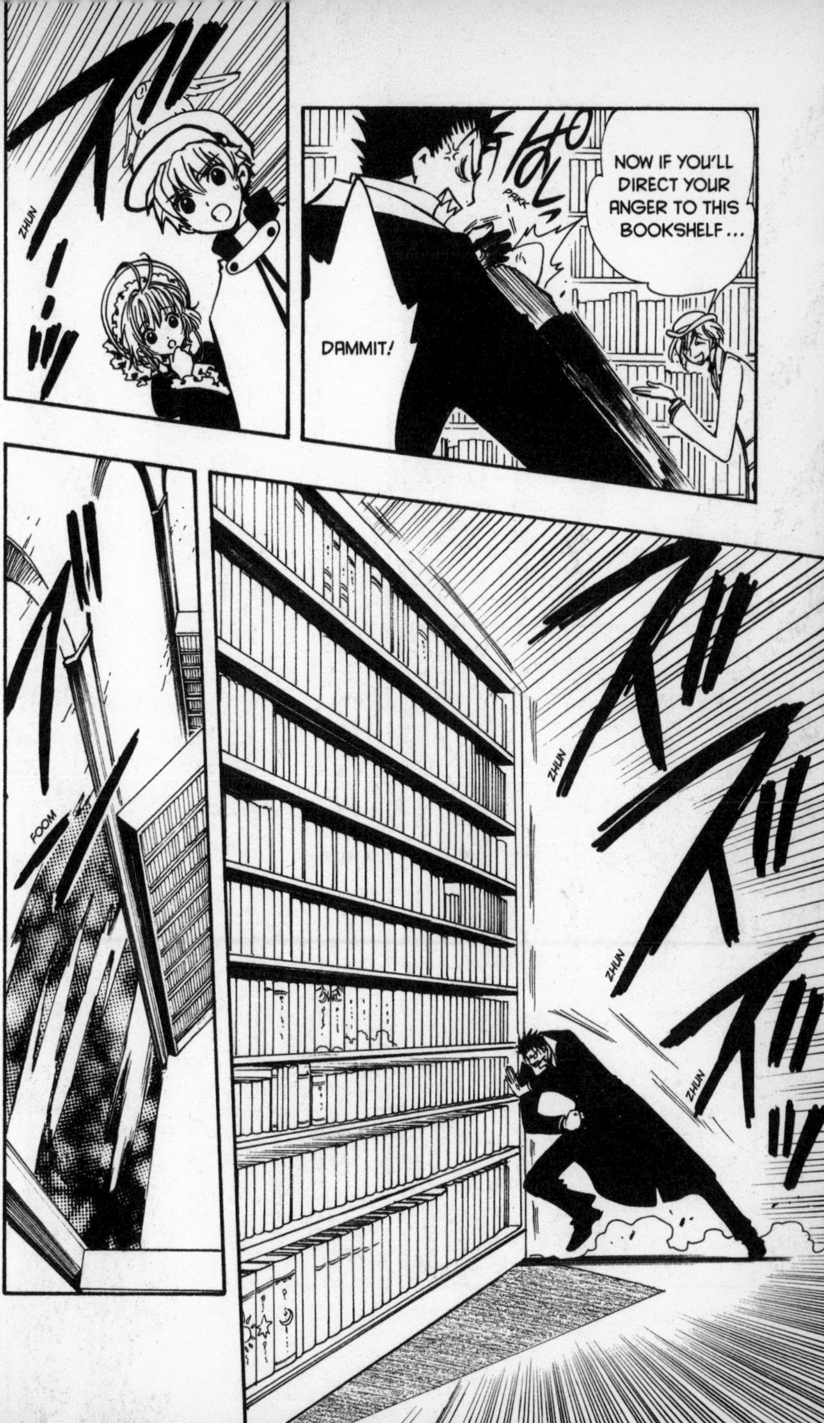
NOW IF YOU'LL DIRECT YOUR ANGER TO THIS BOOKSHELF...
PAKK
DAMMIT!
ZHUN
ZHUN
ZHUN
ZHUN
FOOM

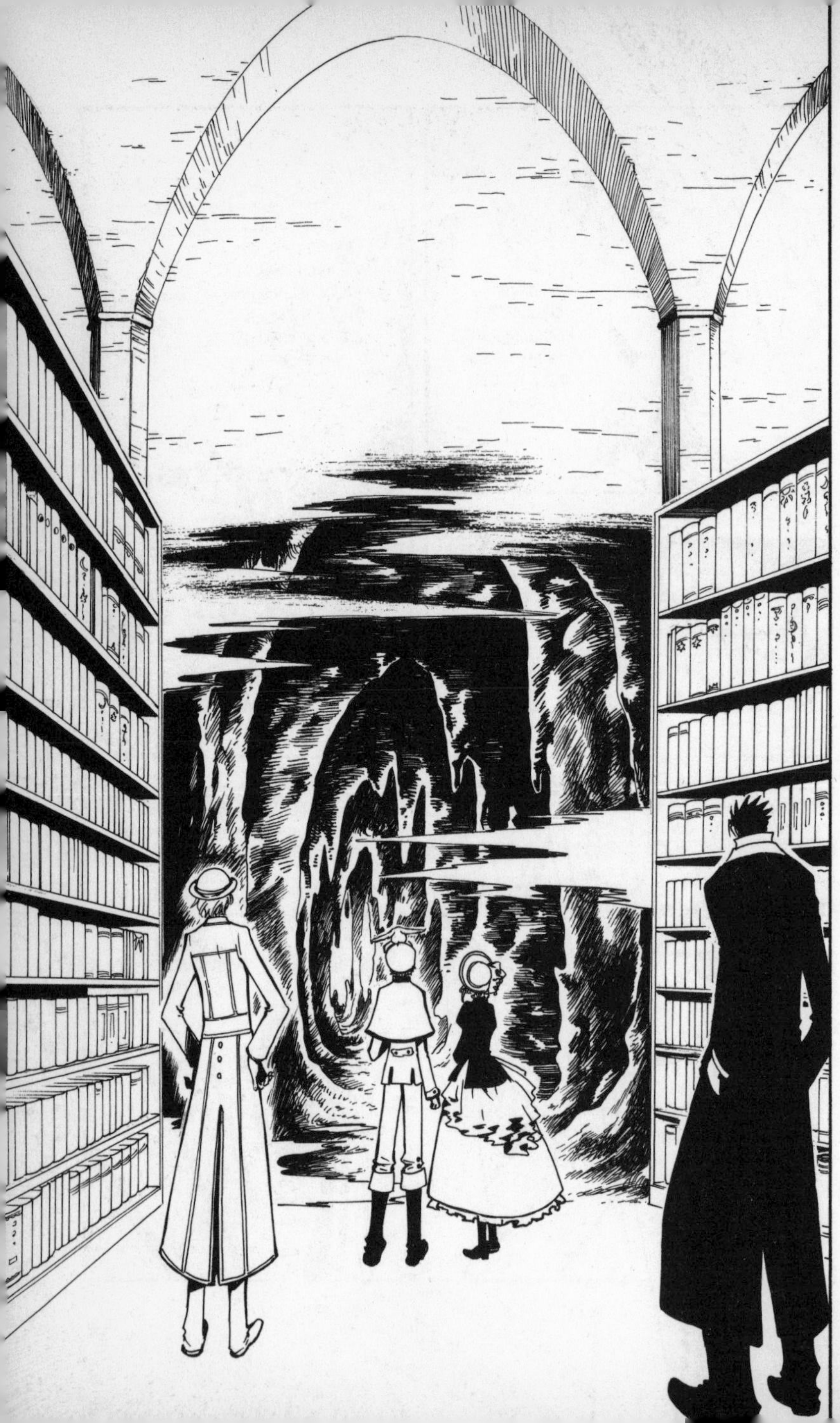

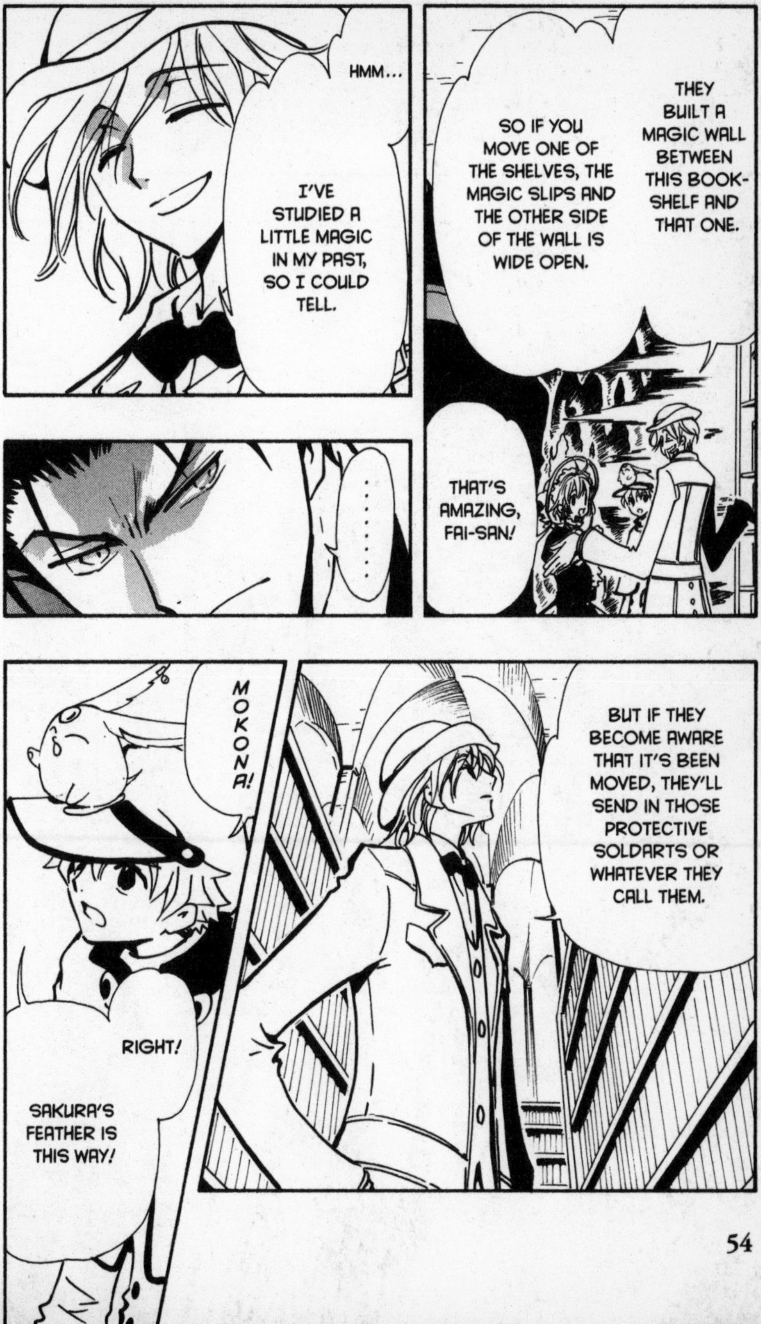
THEY BUILT A MAGIC WALL BETWEEN THIS BOOK-SHELF AND THAT ONE.
SO IF YOU MOVE ONE OF THE SHELVES, THE MAGIC SLIPS AND THE OTHER SIDE OF THE WALL IS WIDE OPEN.
THAT'S AMAZING, FAI-SAN!
HMM...
I'VE STUDIED A LITTLE MAGIC IN MY PAST, SO I COULD TELL.
......
BUT IF THEY BECOME AWARE THAT IT'S BEEN MOVED, THEY'LL SEND IN THOSE PROTECTIVE SOLDARTS OR WHATEVER THEY CALL THEM.
MOKONA!
RIGHT!
SAKURA'S FEATHER IS THIS WAY!

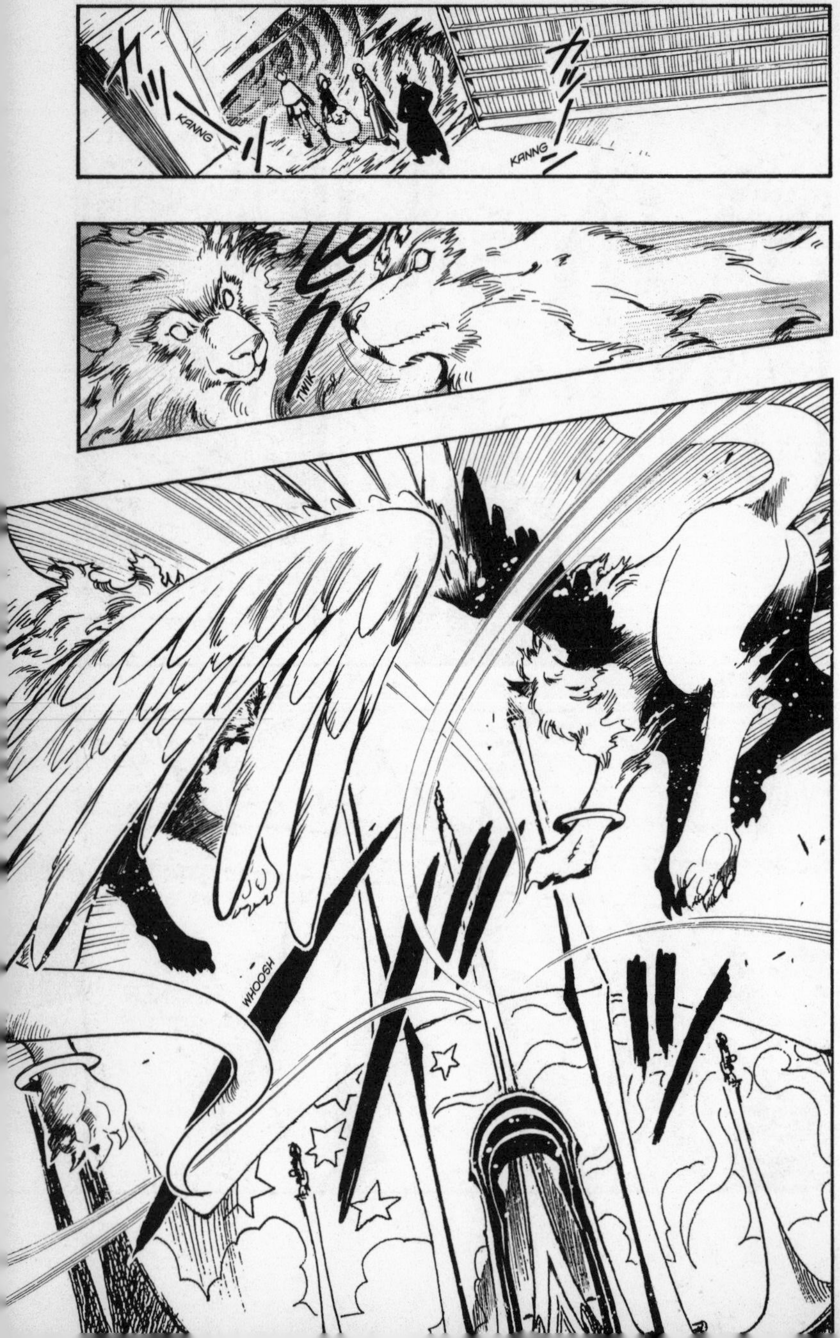
KANNG
KANNG
TWIK
WHOOSH

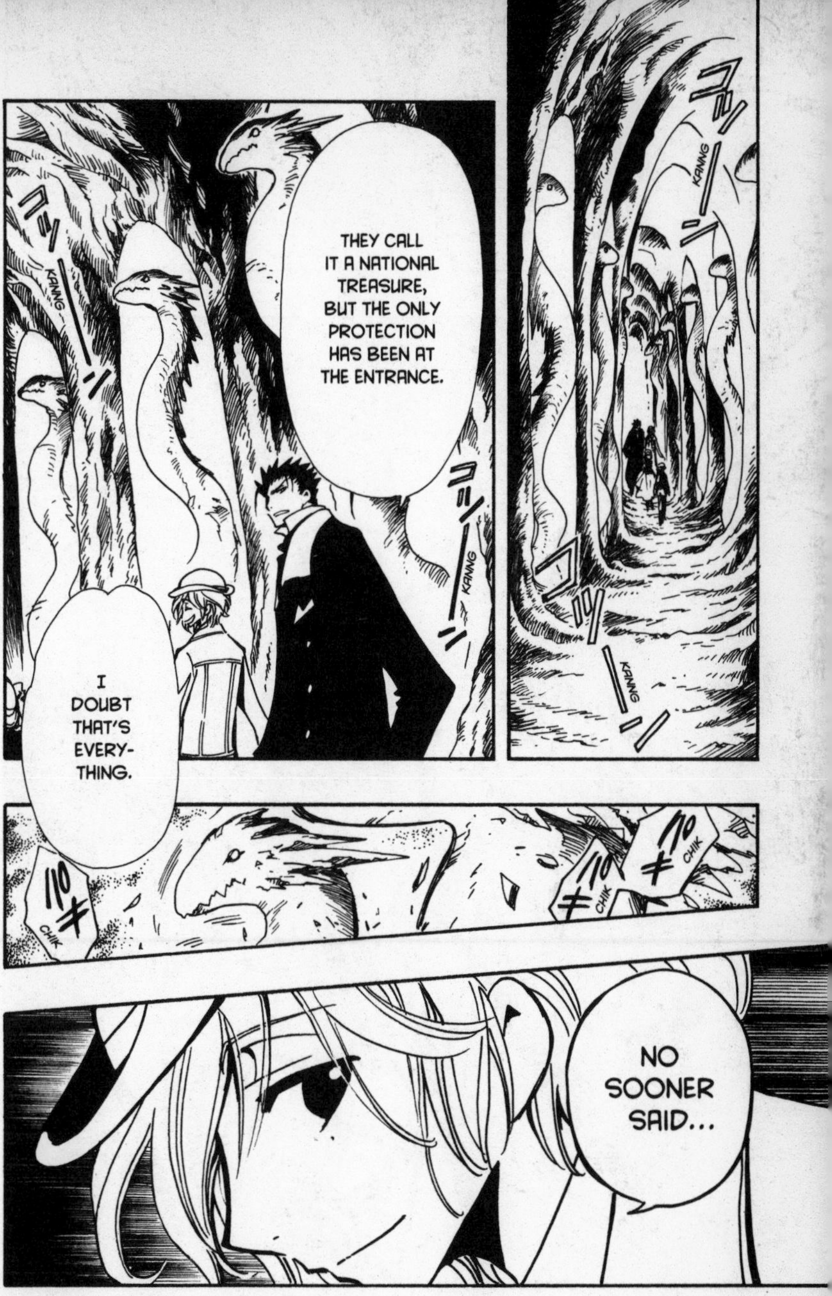
KANNG
KANNG
THEY CALL IT A NATIONAL TREASURE, BUT THE ONLY PROTECTION HAS BEEN AT THE ENTRANCE.
KANNG
KANNG
I DOUBT THAT'S EVERY-THING.
CHIK
CHIK
CHIK
NO SOONER SAID...

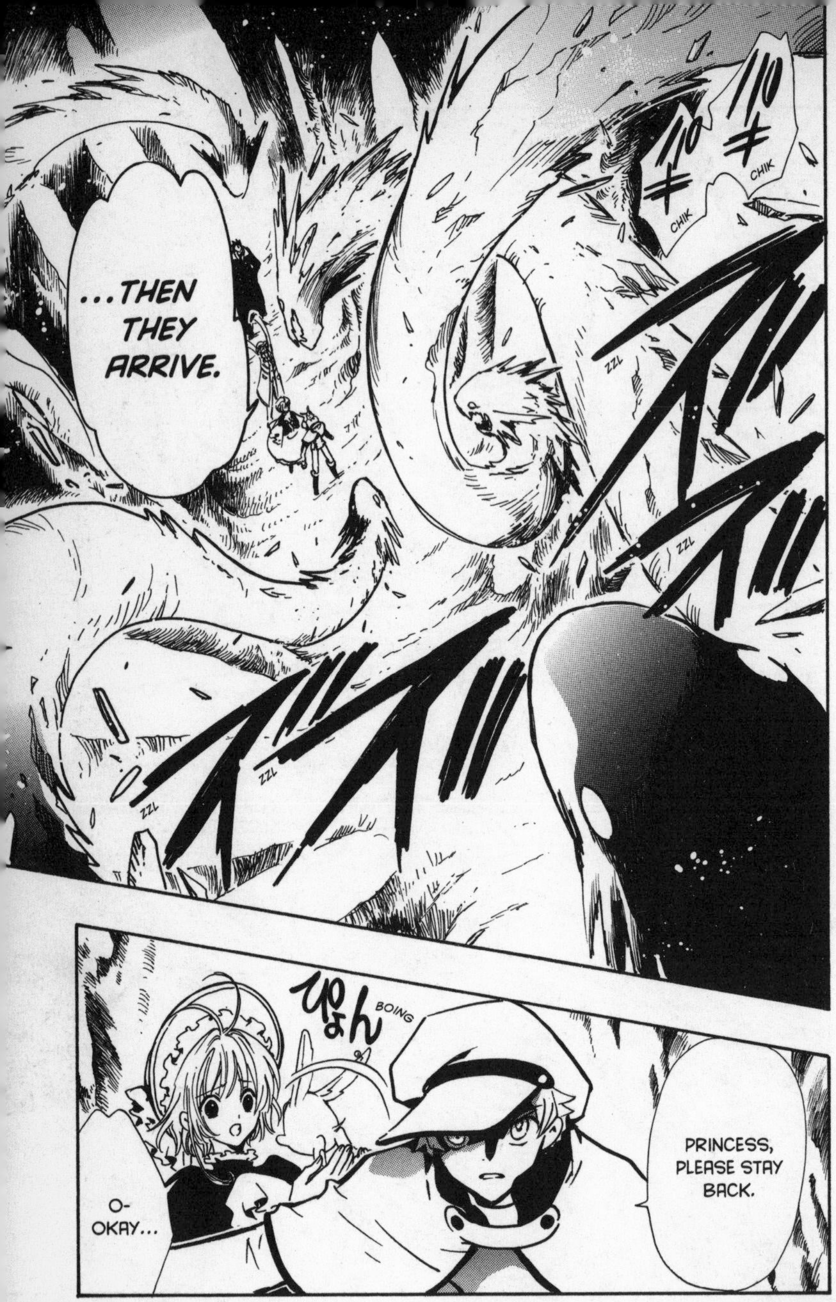
...THEN THEY ARRIVE.
CHIK
CHIK
ZZL
ZZL
ZZL
ZZL
PRINCESS, PLEASE STAY BACK.
ぴょん
BOING
O- OKAY...

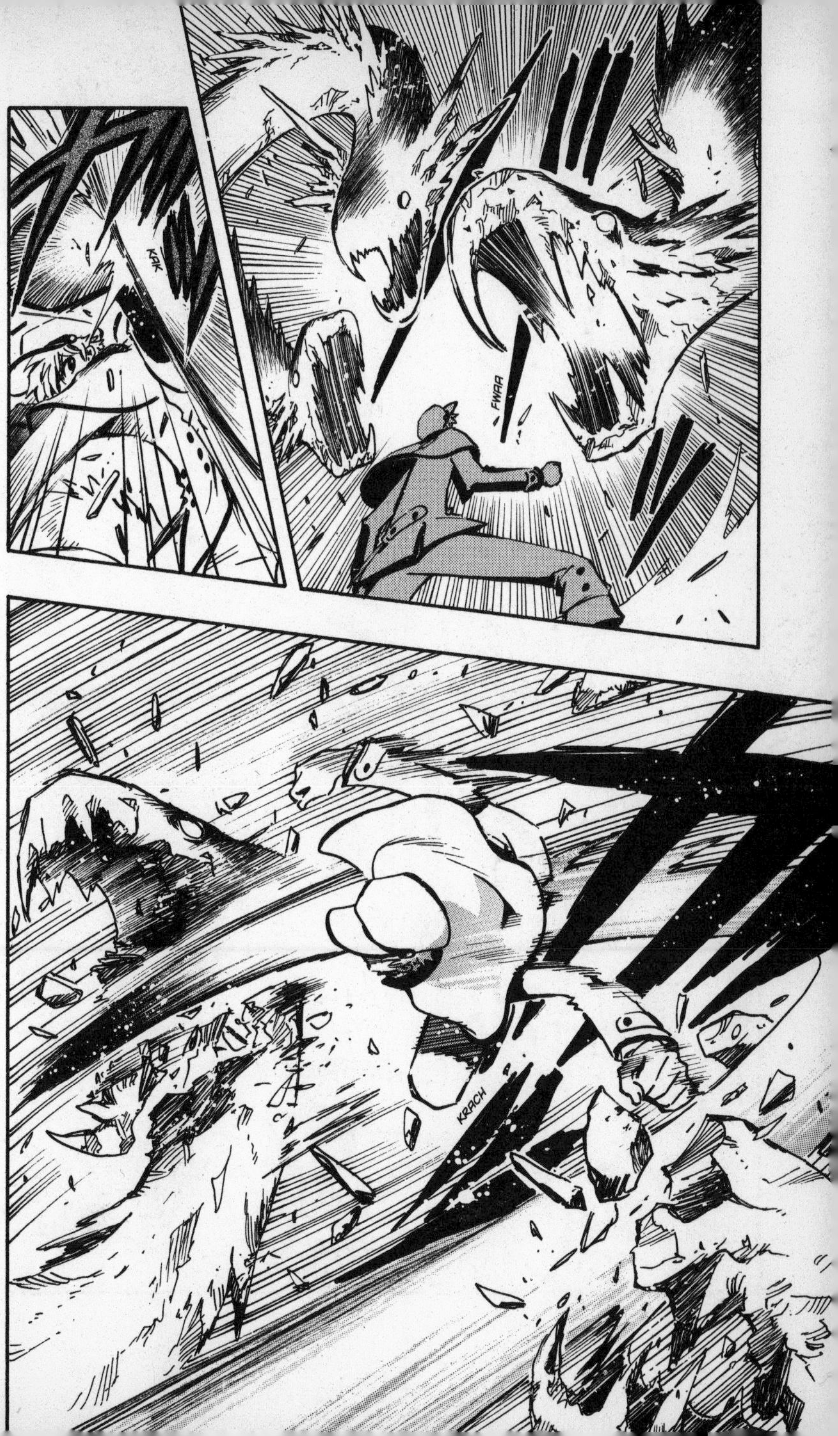
FWAA
KAK
KRACH

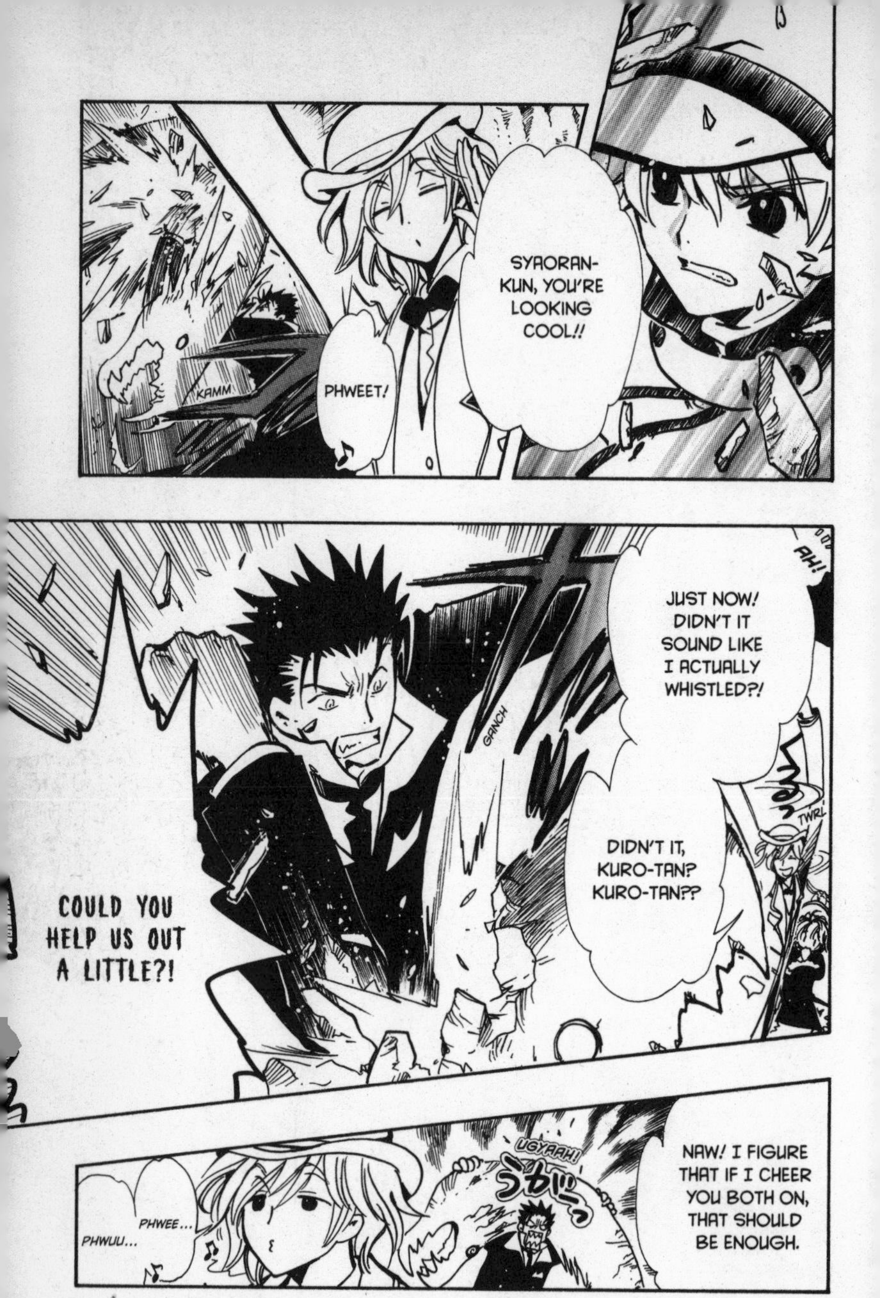
SYAORAN-KUN, YOU'RE LOOKING COOL!!
PHWEET!
KAMM
AH!
JUST NOW! DIDN'T IT SOUND LIKE I ACTUALLY WHISTLED?!
TWRL
DIDN'T IT, KURO-TAN? KURO-TAN??
GANCH
COULD YOU HELP US OUT A LITTLE?!
NAW! I FIGURE THAT IF I CHEER YOU BOTH ON, THAT SHOULD BE ENOUGH.
UGYAAH!
PHWEE...
PHWUU...

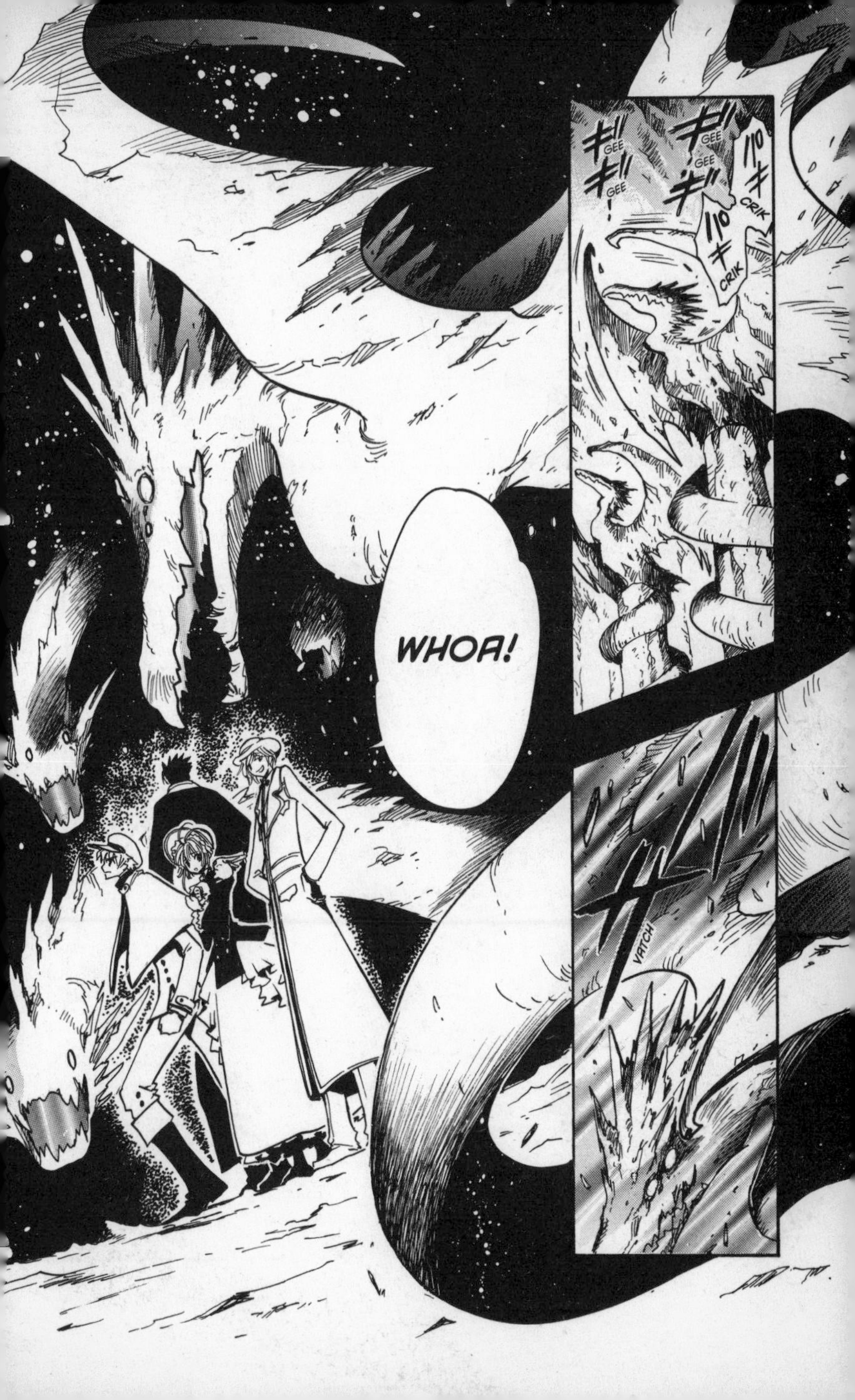
GEE GEE
GEE GEE
CRIK CRIK
VATCH
WHOA!

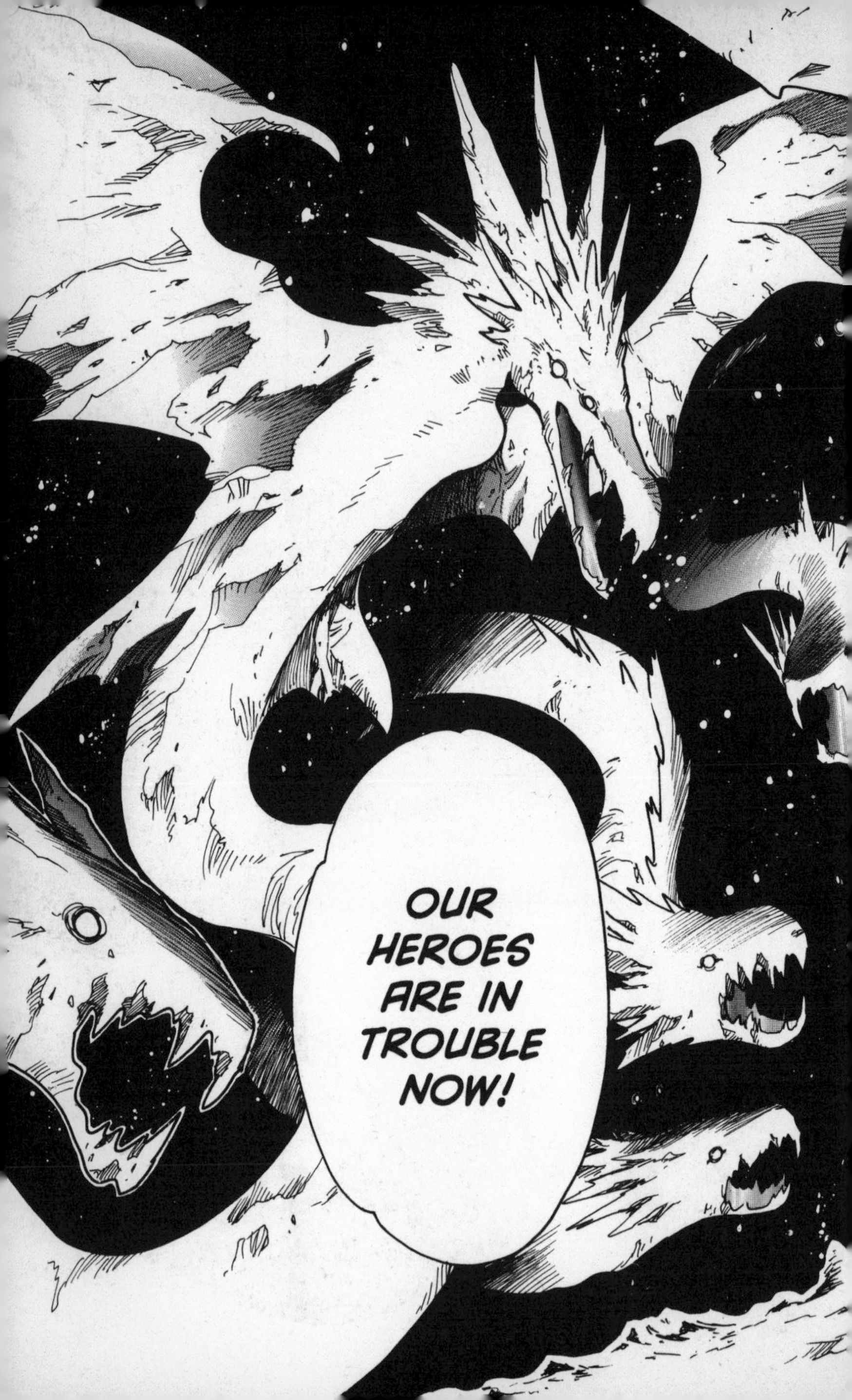
OUR HEROES ARE IN TROUBLE NOW!

ツバサ

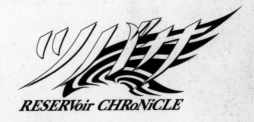

RESERVoir CHRoNiCLE

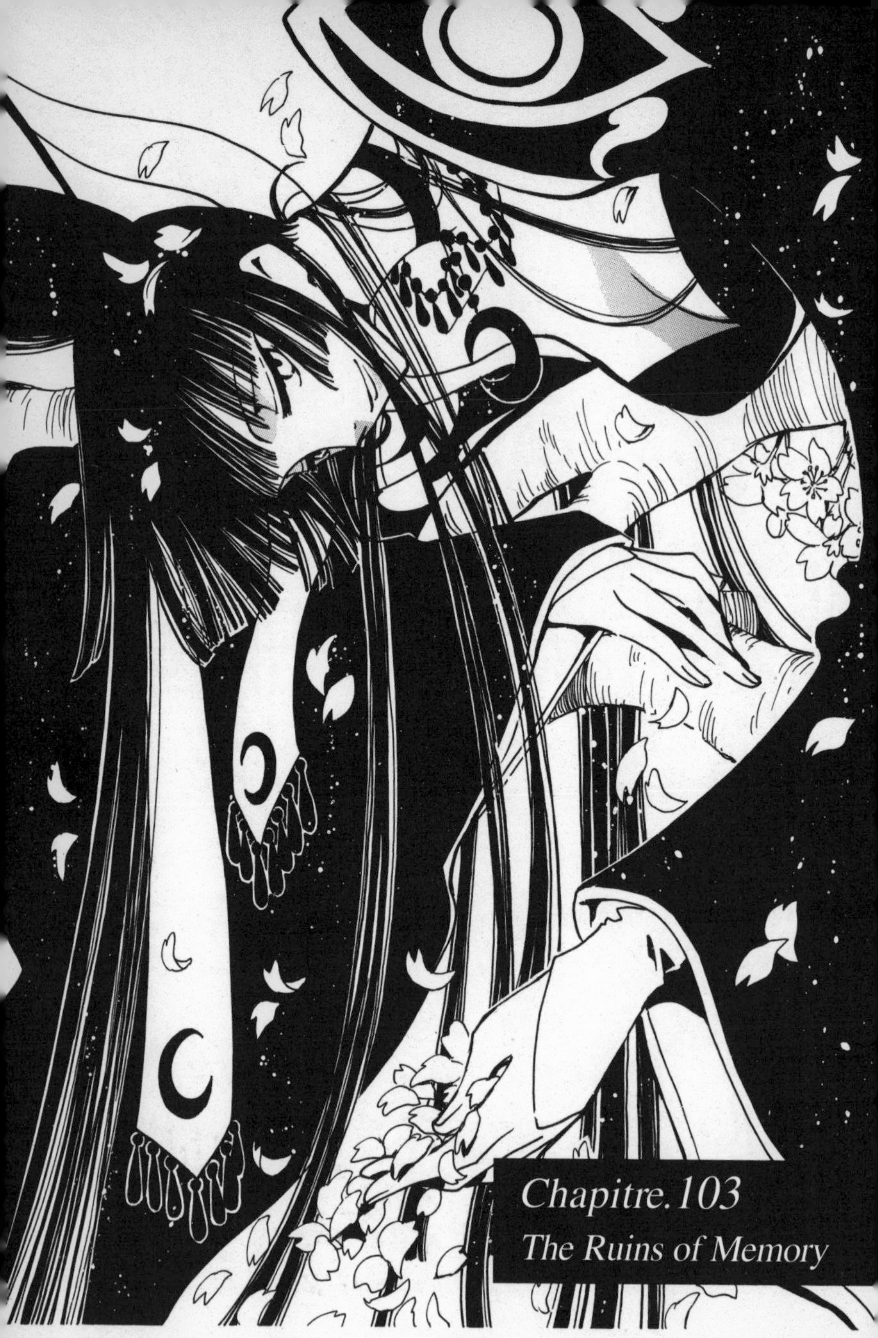
Chapitre.103
The Ruins of Memory

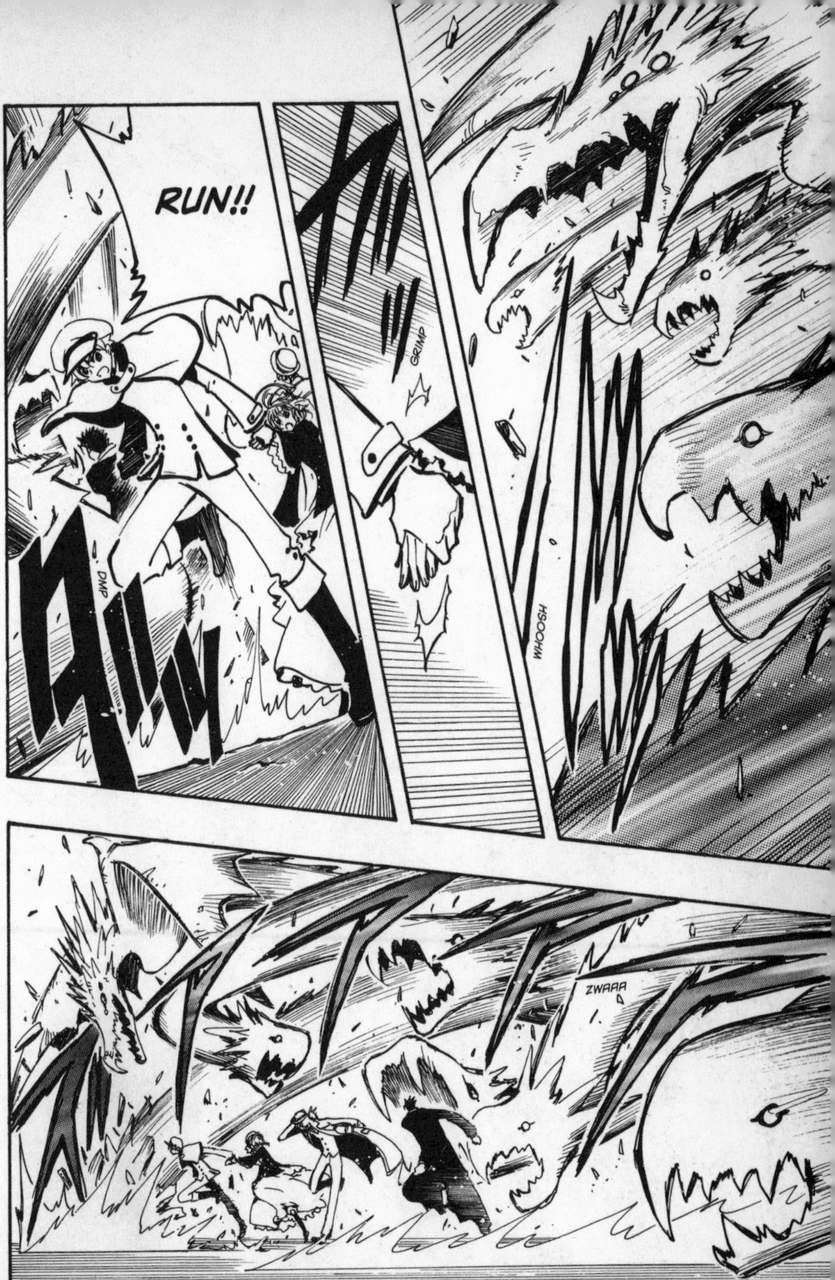
WHOOSH
GRIMP
RUN!!
DMP
ZWAAA

...RUNNING WILL GET US WHERE WE WANT TO GO FASTER.

BUT I DON'T SEE WHERE WE'LL BE ABLE TO STOP RUNNING.

IT'S TRUE. RATHER THAN TAKING THEM ON...

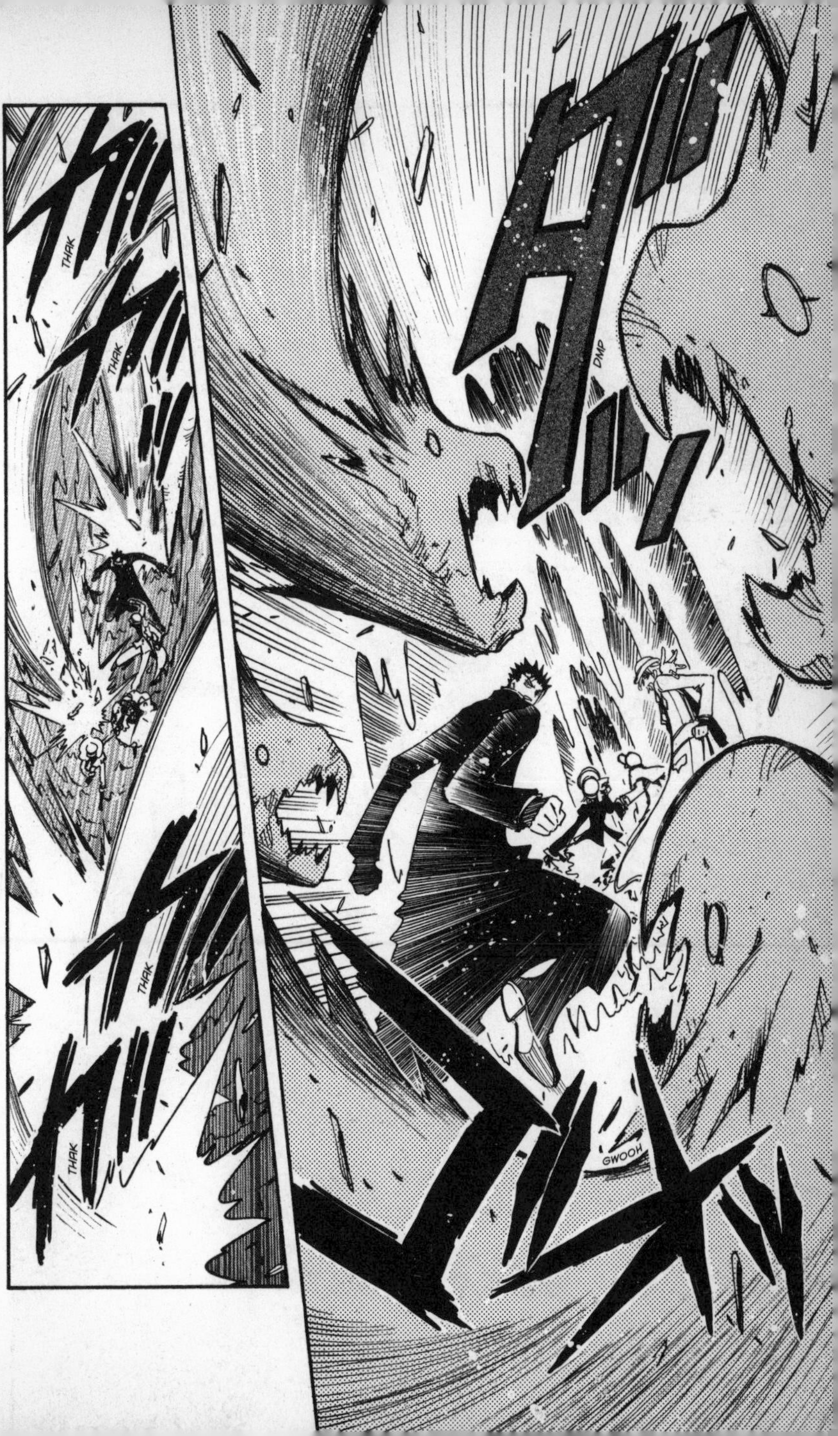
DMP
GWOOH
THAK
THAK
THAK
THAK

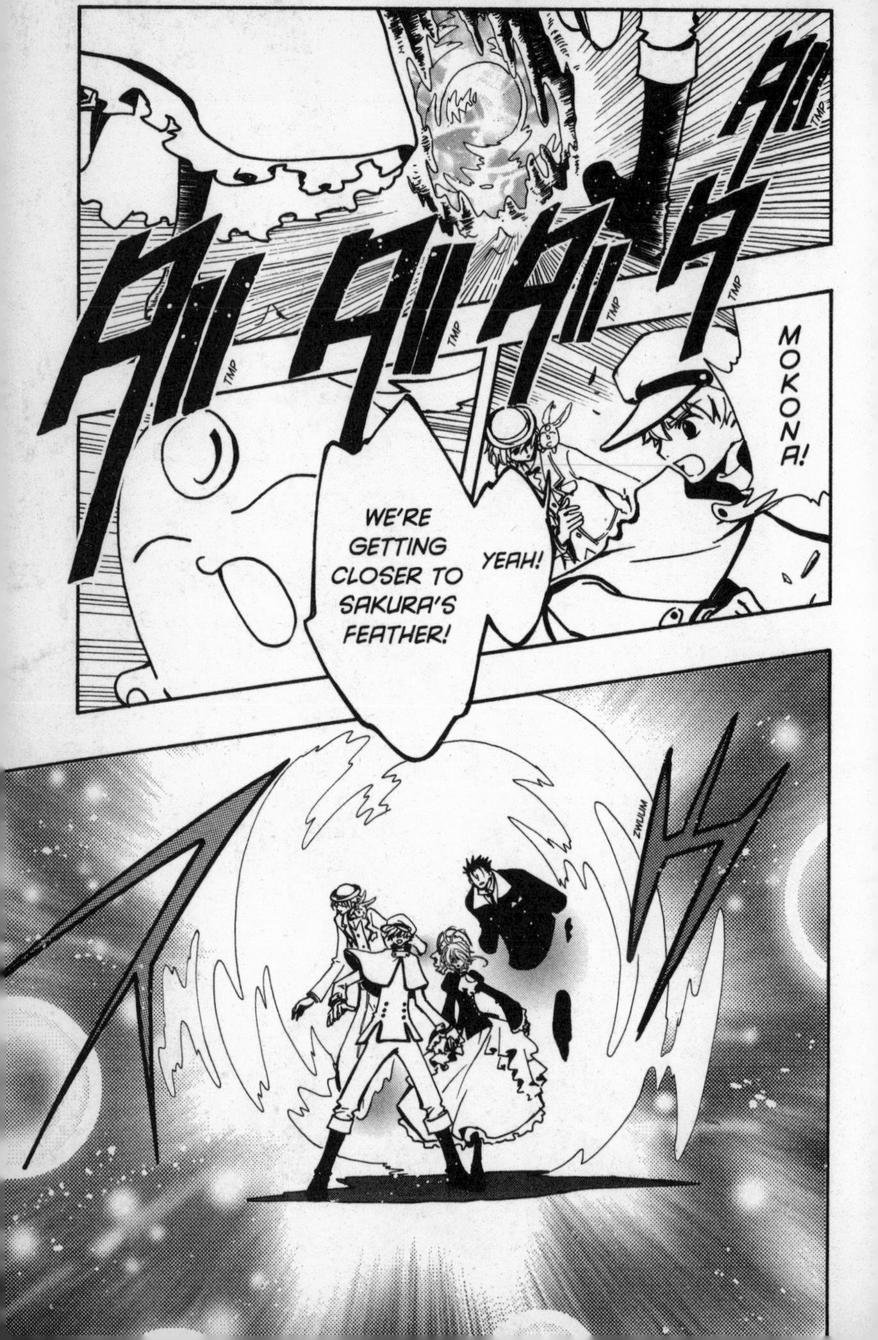
TMP
TMP
TMP
TMP
TMP
MOKONA!
YEAH!
WE'RE GETTING CLOSER TO SAKURA'S FEATHER!
ZWUUM

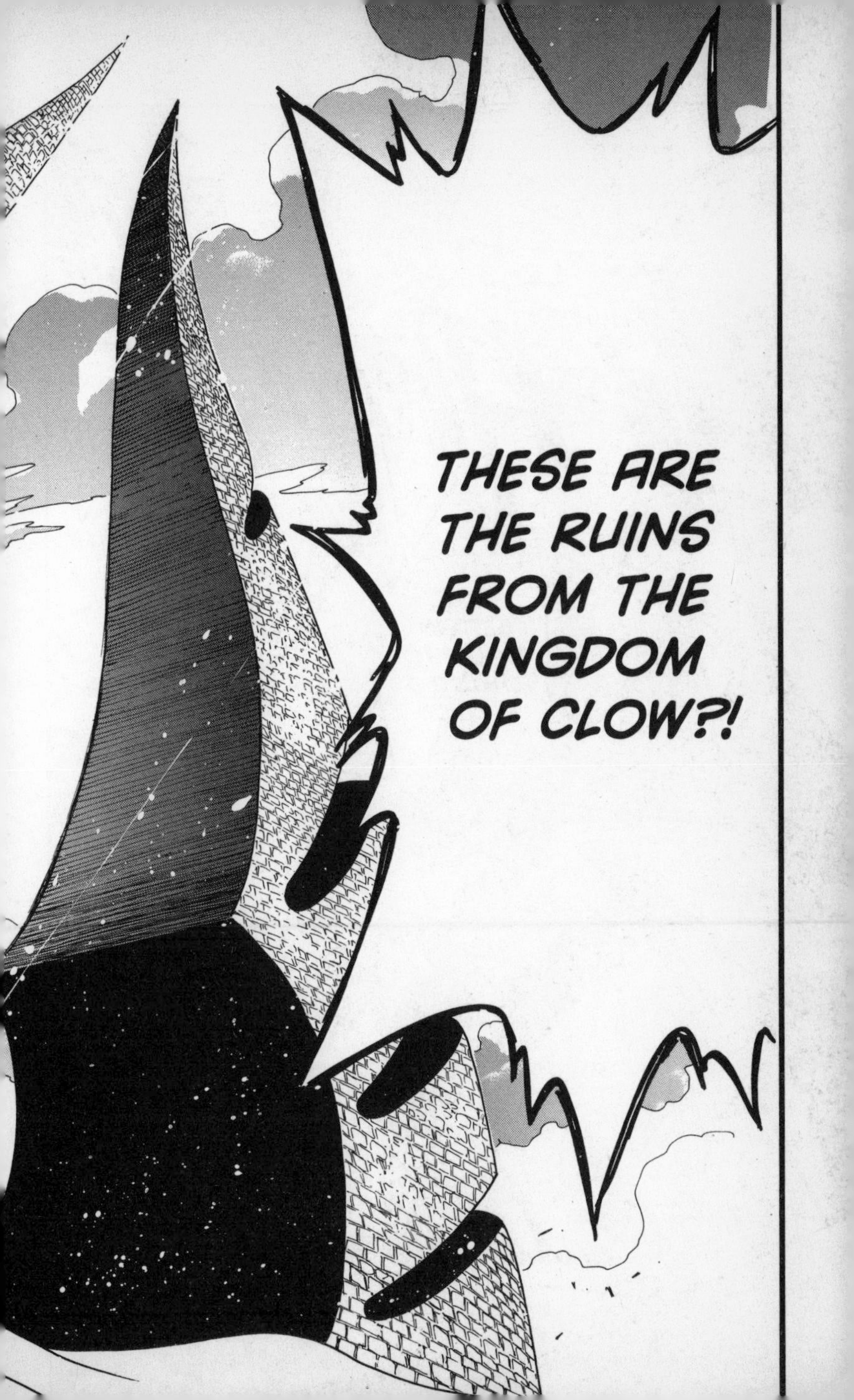
THESE ARE THE RUINS FROM THE KINGDOM OF CLOW?!

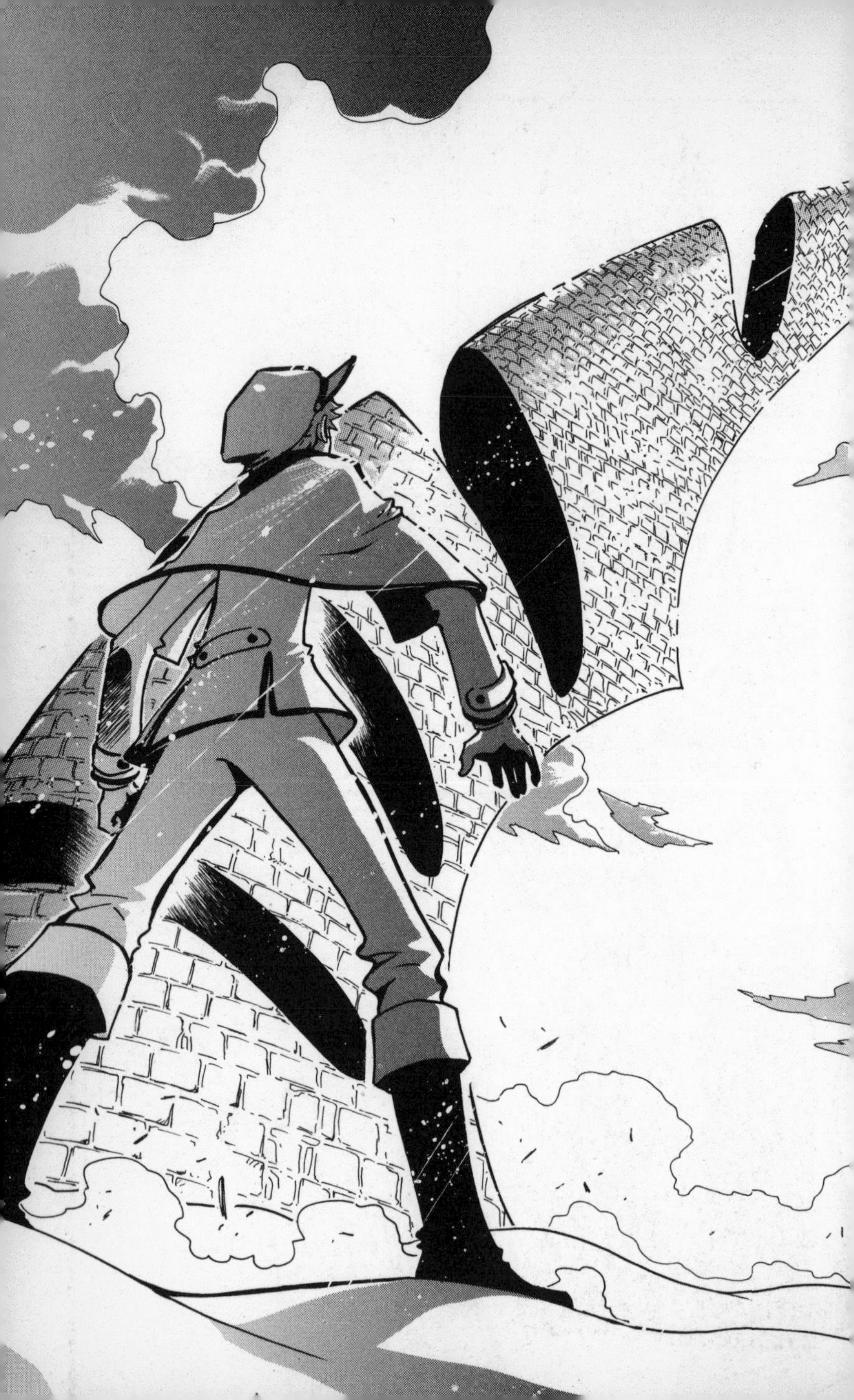

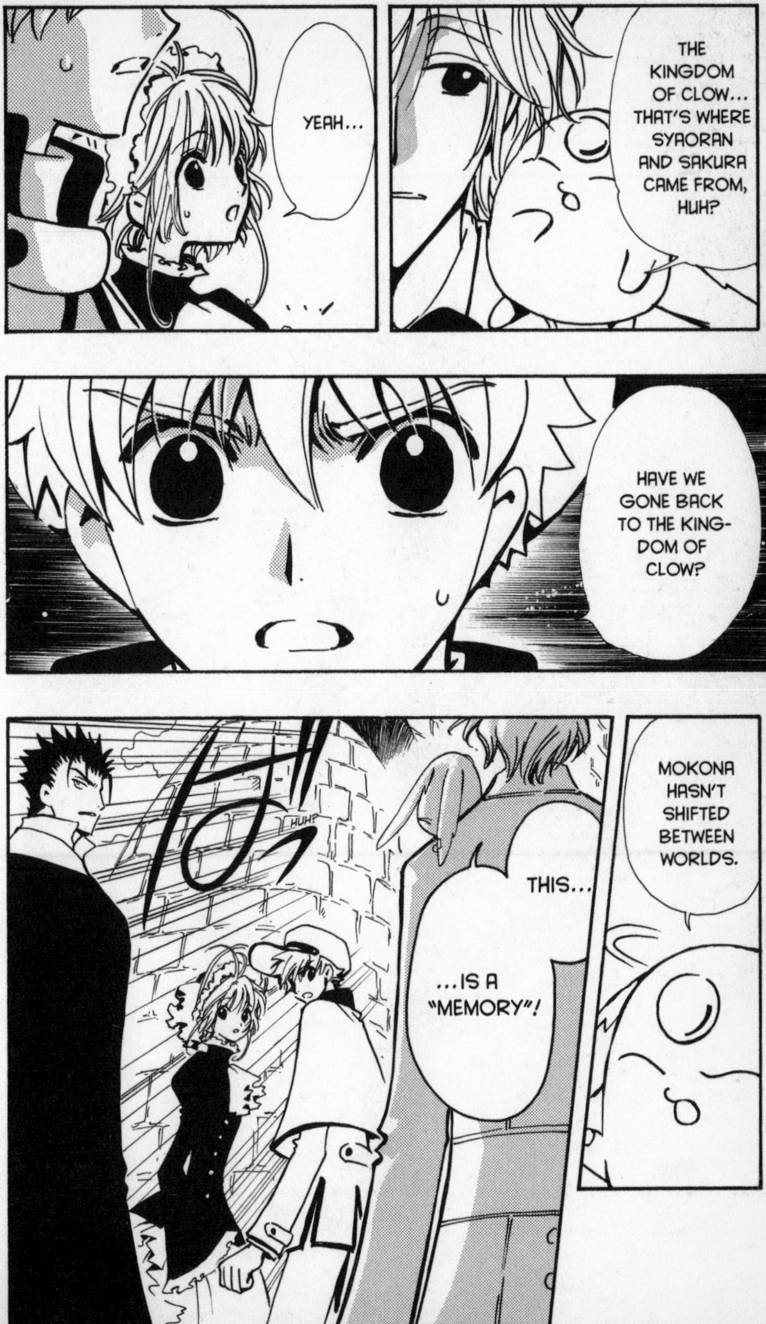
THE KINGDOM OF CLOW... THAT'S WHERE SYAORAN AND SAKURA CAME FROM, HUH?
YEAH...
HAVE WE GONE BACK TO THE KING-DOM OF CLOW?
MOKONA HASN'T SHIFTED BETWEEN WORLDS.
THIS...
...IS A "MEMORY"!
HUH?

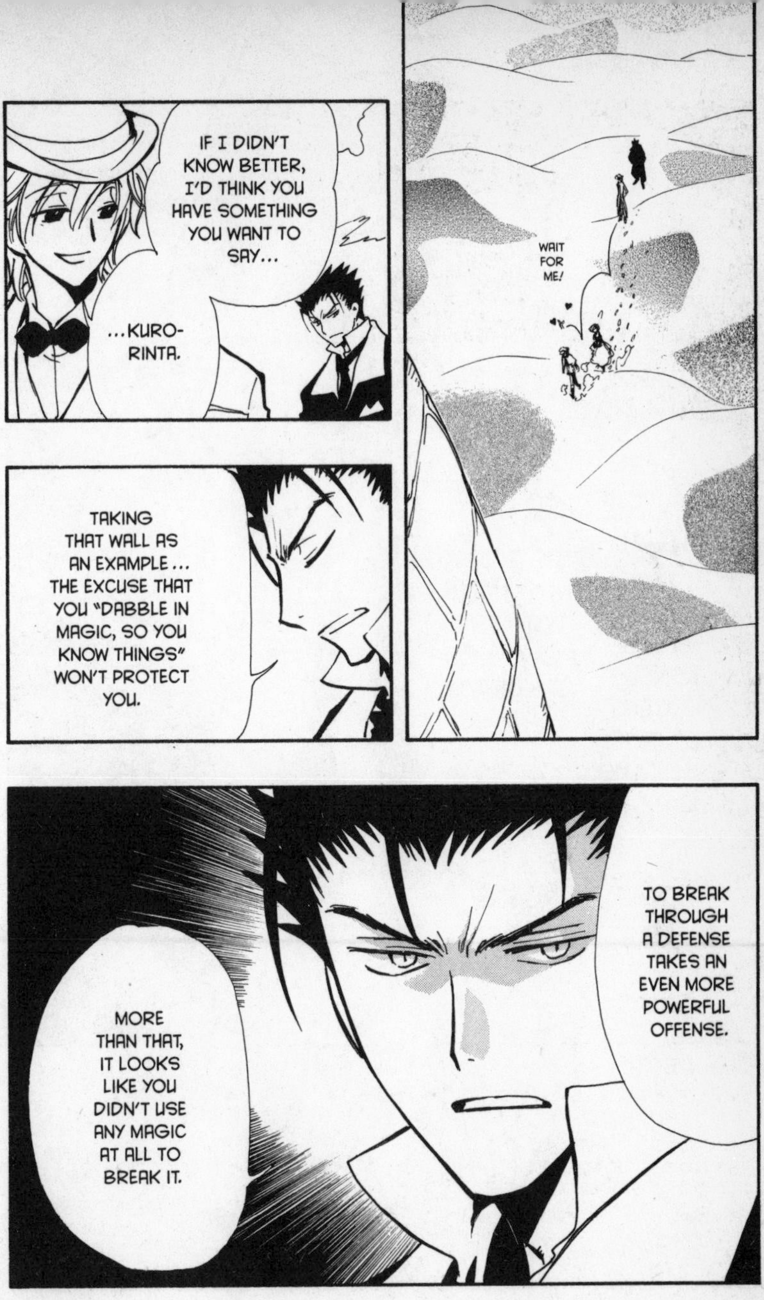
WAIT FOR ME!
IF I DIDN'T KNOW BETTER, I'D THINK YOU HAVE SOMETHING YOU WANT TO SAY...
...KURO-RINTA.
TAKING THAT WALL AS AN EXAMPLE... THE EXCUSE THAT YOU "DABBLE IN MAGIC, SO YOU KNOW THINGS" WON'T PROTECT YOU.
TO BREAK THROUGH A DEFENSE TAKES AN EVEN MORE POWERFUL OFFENSE.
MORE THAN THAT, IT LOOKS LIKE YOU DIDN'T USE ANY MAGIC AT ALL TO BREAK IT.

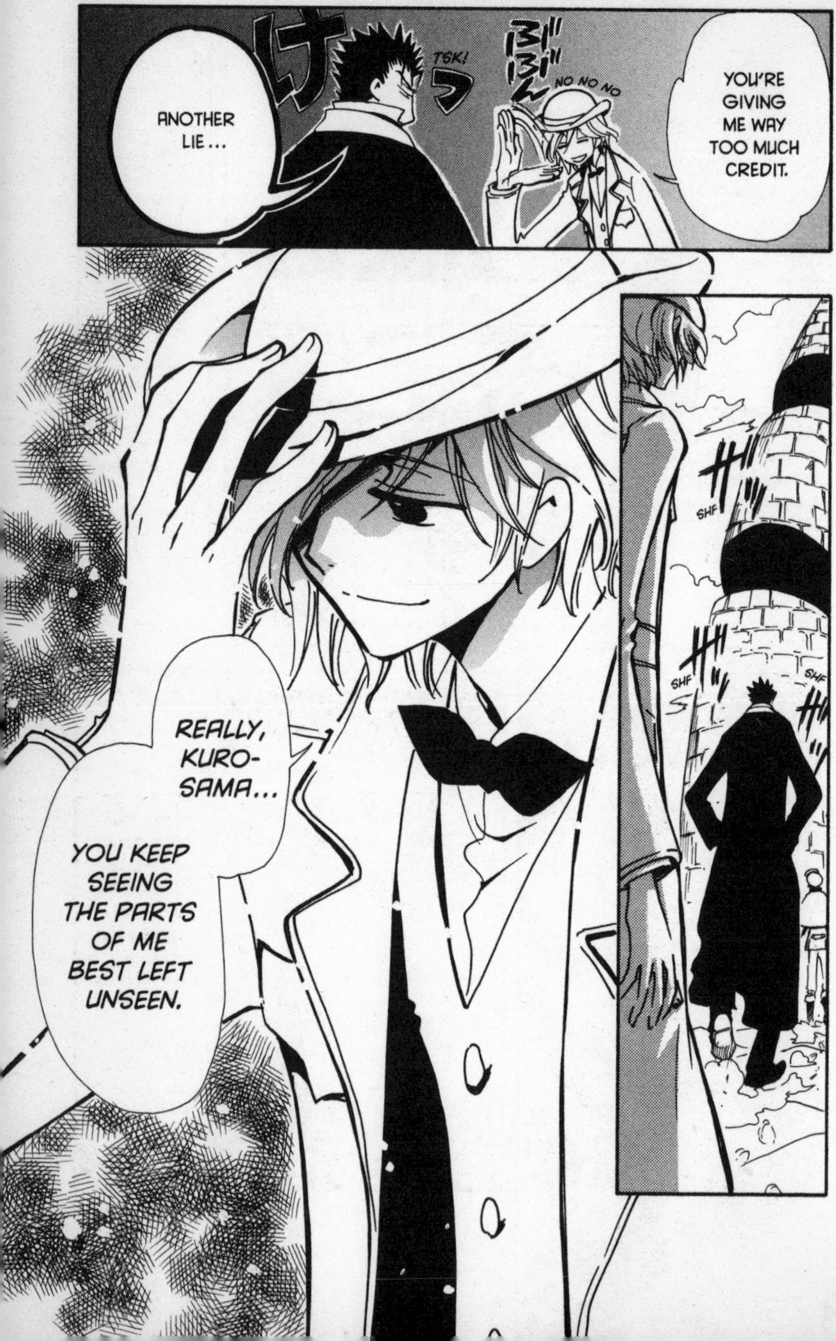
YOU'RE GIVING ME WAY TOO MUCH CREDIT.
ぶんぶん
NO NO NO
けっ
TSK!
ANOTHER LIE...
SHF
SHF
SHF
REALLY, KURO-SAMA...
YOU KEEP SEEING THE PARTS OF ME BEST LEFT UNSEEN.

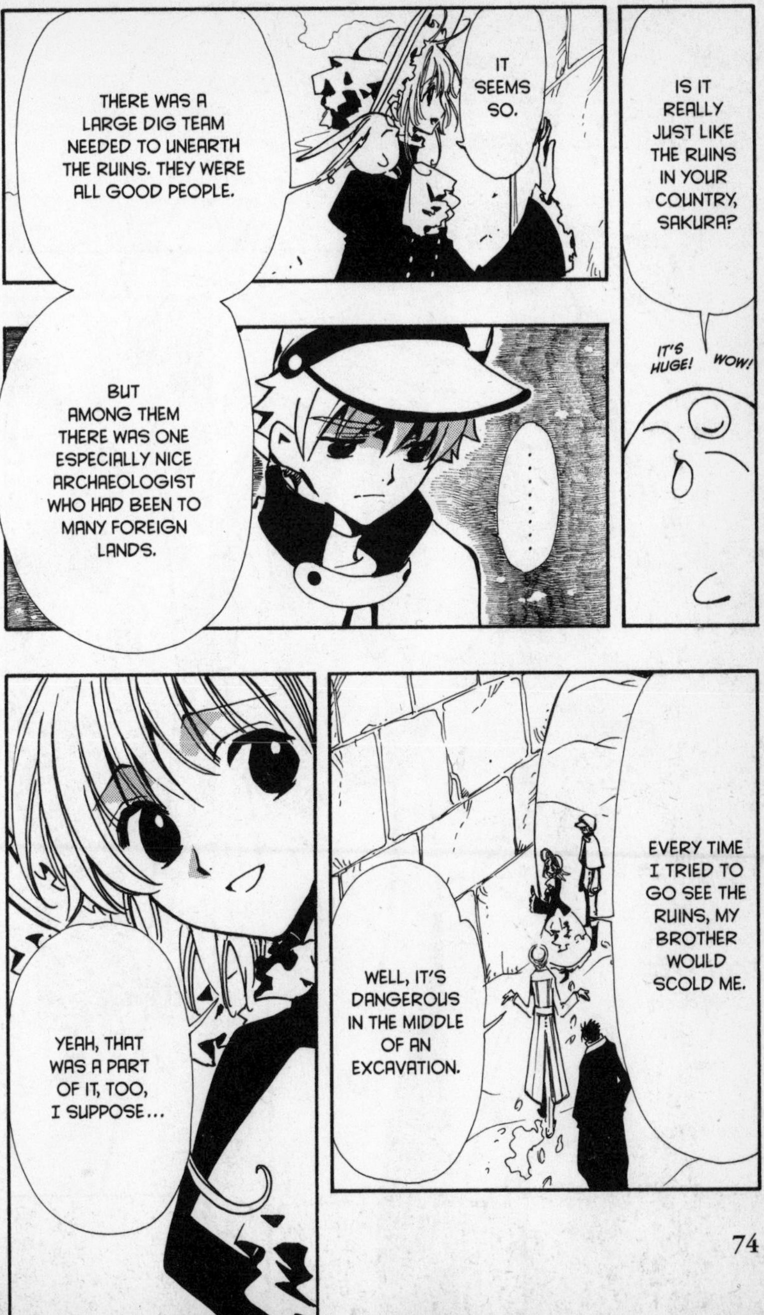

IS IT REALLY JUST LIKE THE RUINS IN YOUR COUNTRY, SAKURA?
IT'S HUGE!
WOW!
IT SEEMS SO.
THERE WAS A LARGE DIG TEAM NEEDED TO UNEARTH THE RUINS. THEY WERE ALL GOOD PEOPLE.
BUT AMONG THEM THERE WAS ONE ESPECIALLY NICE ARCHAEOLOGIST WHO HAD BEEN TO MANY FOREIGN LANDS.
....
EVERY TIME I TRIED TO GO SEE THE RUINS, MY BROTHER WOULD SCOLD ME.
WELL, IT'S DANGEROUS IN THE MIDDLE OF AN EXCAVATION.
YEAH, THAT WAS A PART OF IT, TOO, I SUPPOSE...

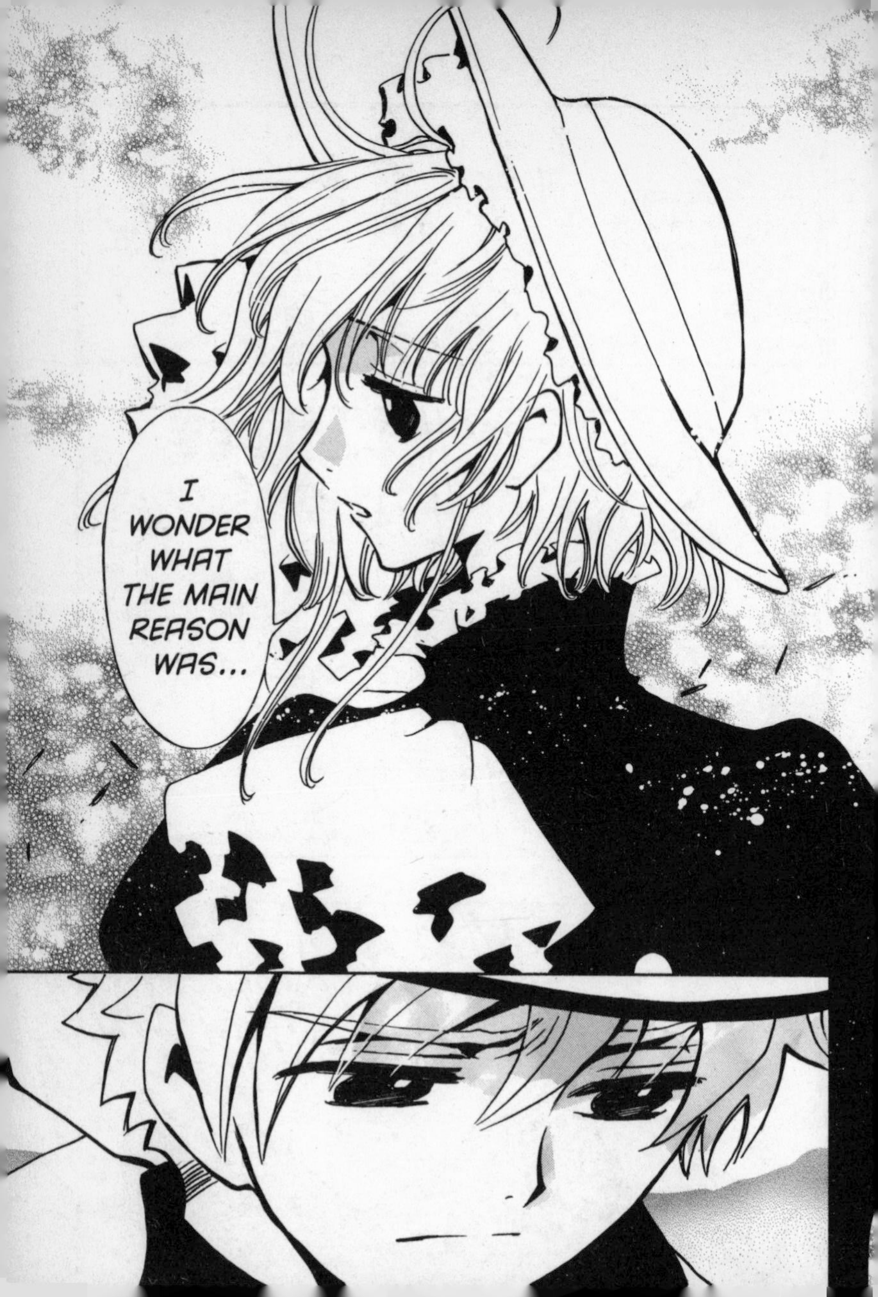
I WONDER WHAT THE MAIN REASON WAS...

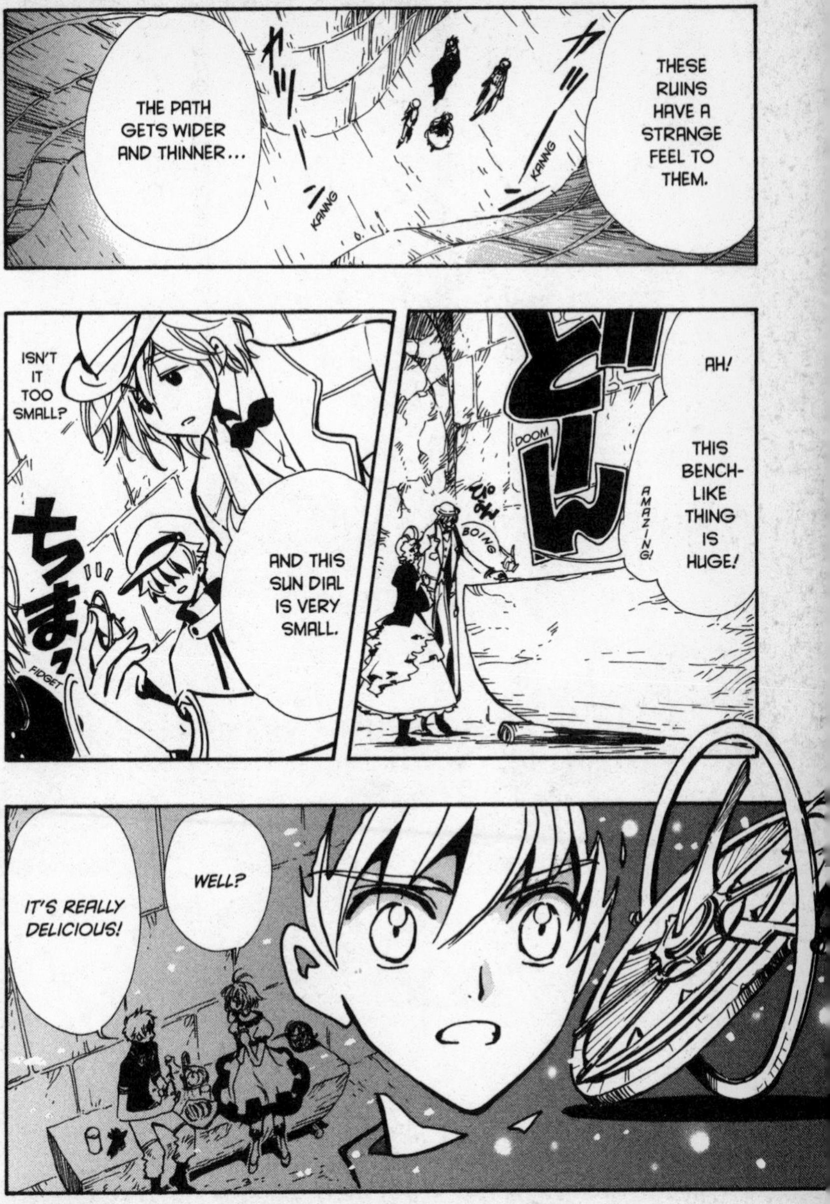
THESE RUINS HAVE A STRANGE FEEL TO THEM.
KANNG
KANNG
THE PATH GETS WIDER AND THINNER...
AH!
THIS BENCH-LIKE THING IS HUGE!
DOOM
AMAZING!
BOING
AND THIS SUN DIAL IS VERY SMALL.
ISN'T IT TOO SMALL?
FIDGET
WELL?
IT'S REALLY DELICIOUS!

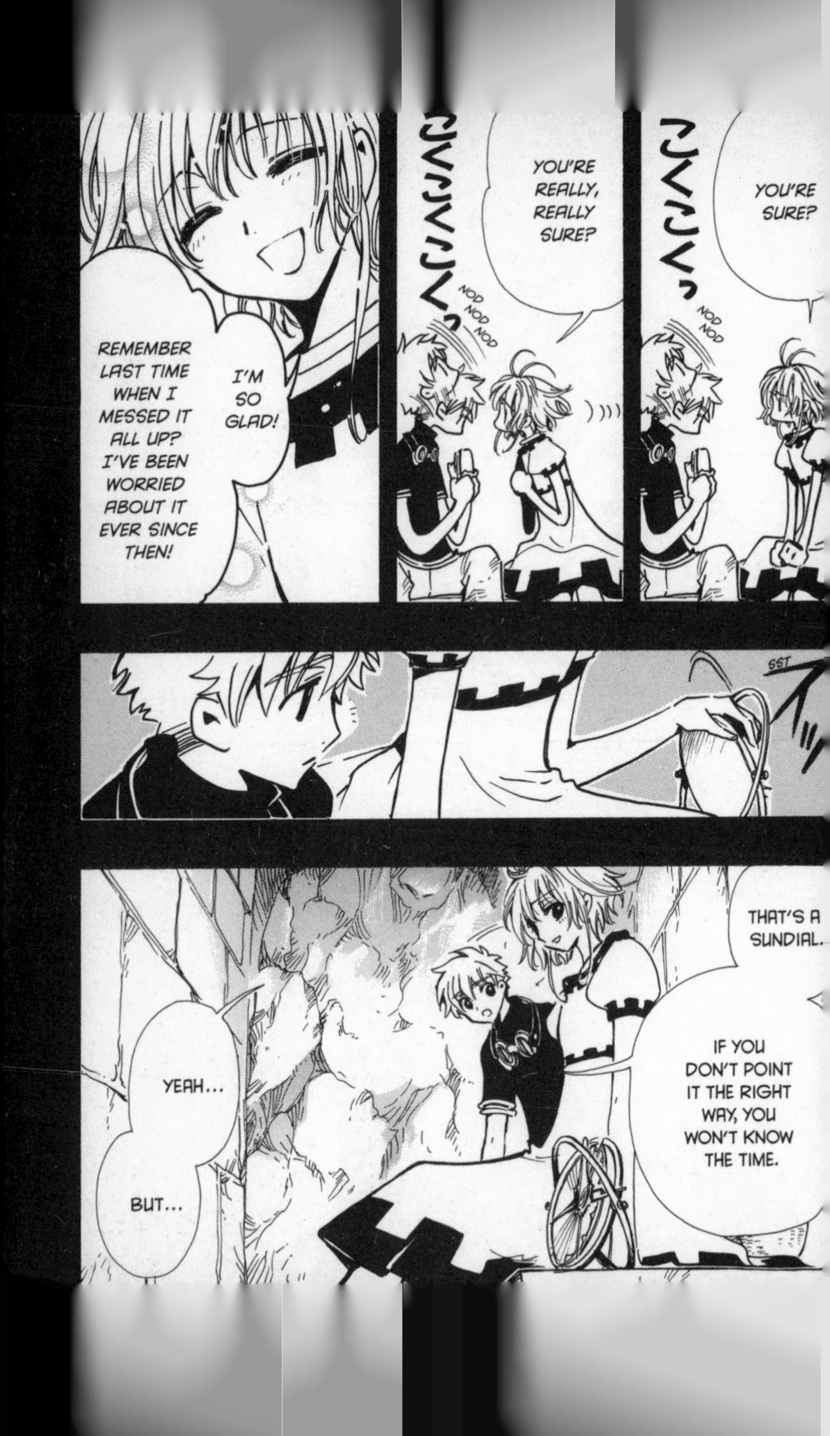
YOU'RE SURE?
こくこくっ
NOD NOD
YOU'RE REALLY, REALLY SURE?
こくこくこくっ
NOD NOD NOD
I'M SO GLAD!
REMEMBER LAST TIME WHEN I MESSED IT ALL UP? I'VE BEEN WORRIED ABOUT IT EVER SINCE THEN!
SST
THAT'S A SUNDIAL.
IF YOU DON'T POINT IT THE RIGHT WAY, YOU WON'T KNOW THE TIME.
YEAH...
BUT...

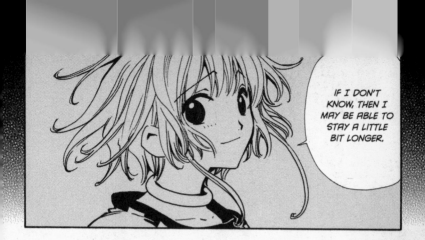

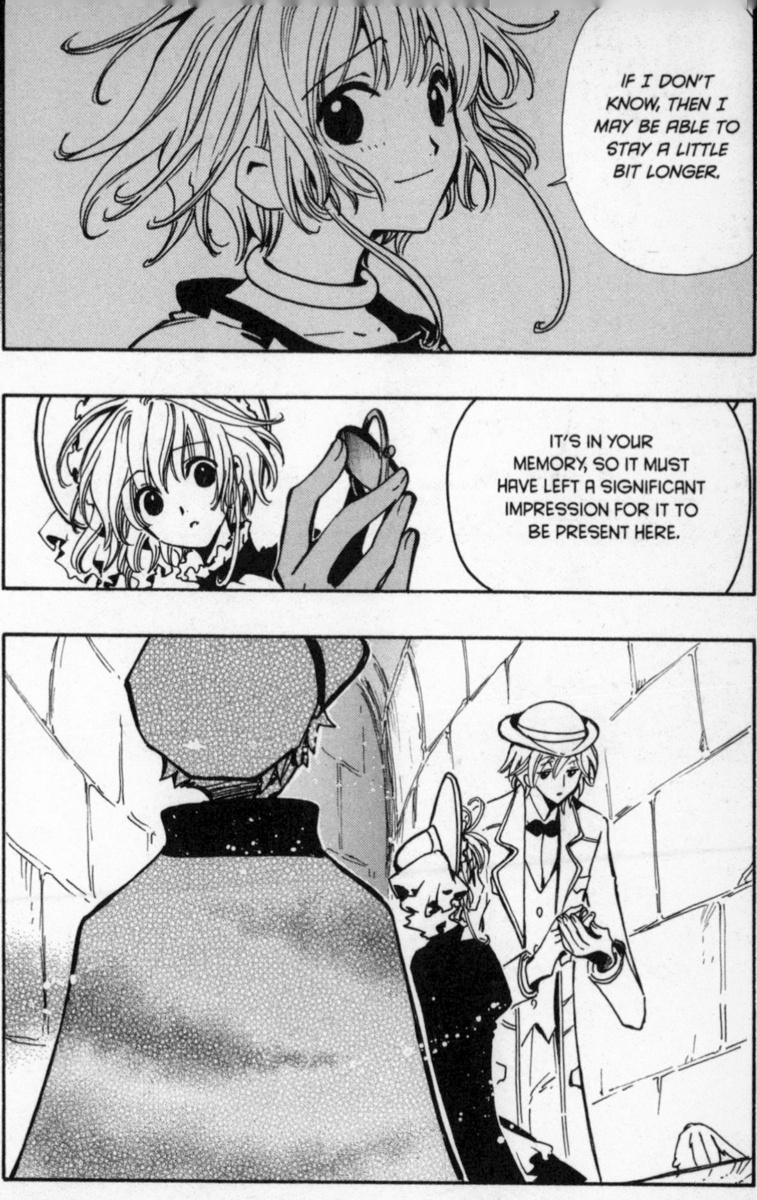
IF I DON'T KNOW, THEN I MAY BE ABLE TO STAY A LITTLE BIT LONGER.
IT'S IN YOUR MEMORY, SO IT MUST HAVE LEFT A SIGNIFICANT IMPRESSION FOR IT TO BE PRESENT HERE.

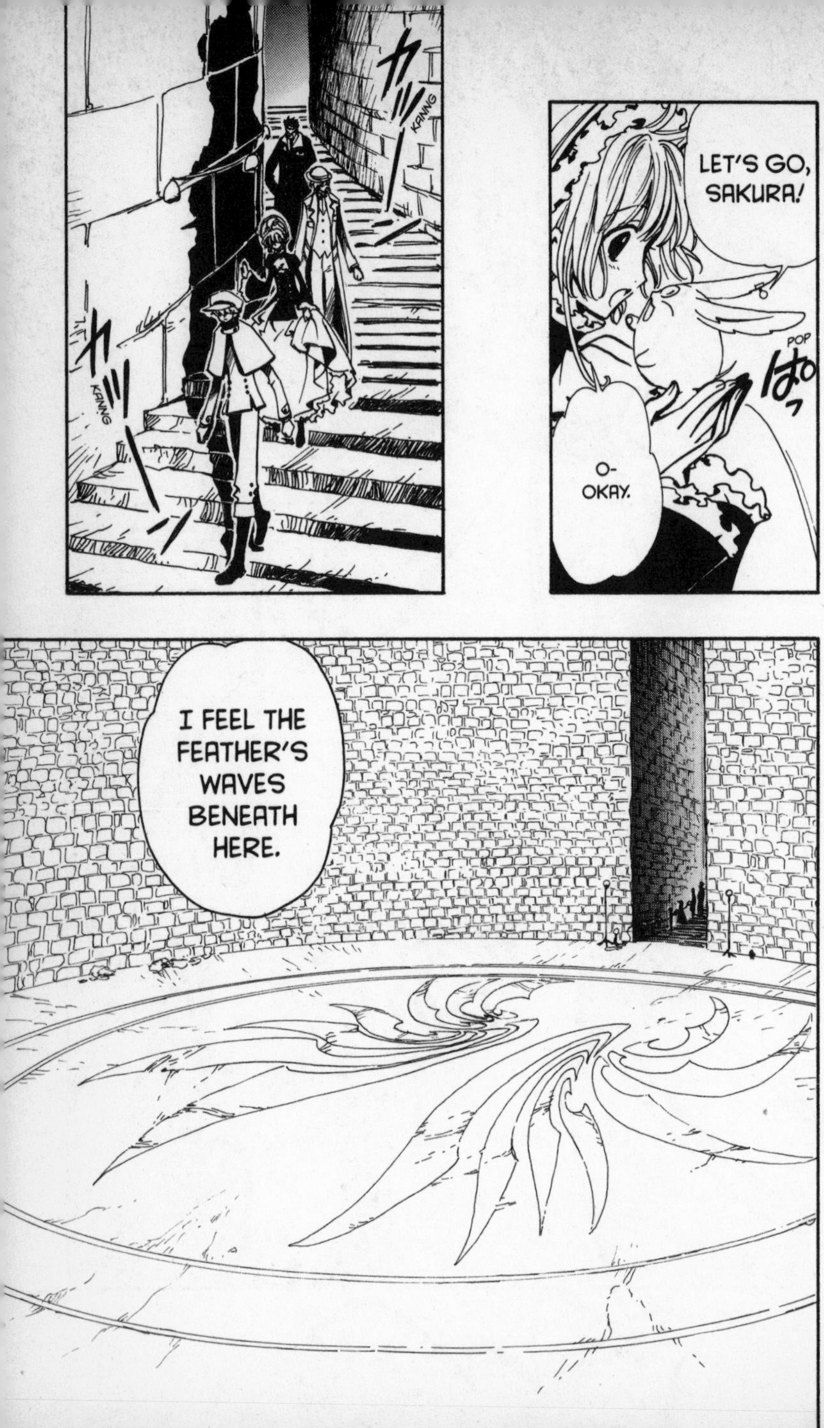
LET'S GO, SAKURA!
POP
ぱっ
O-OKAY.
KANNG
KANNG
I FEEL THE FEATHER'S WAVES BENEATH HERE.

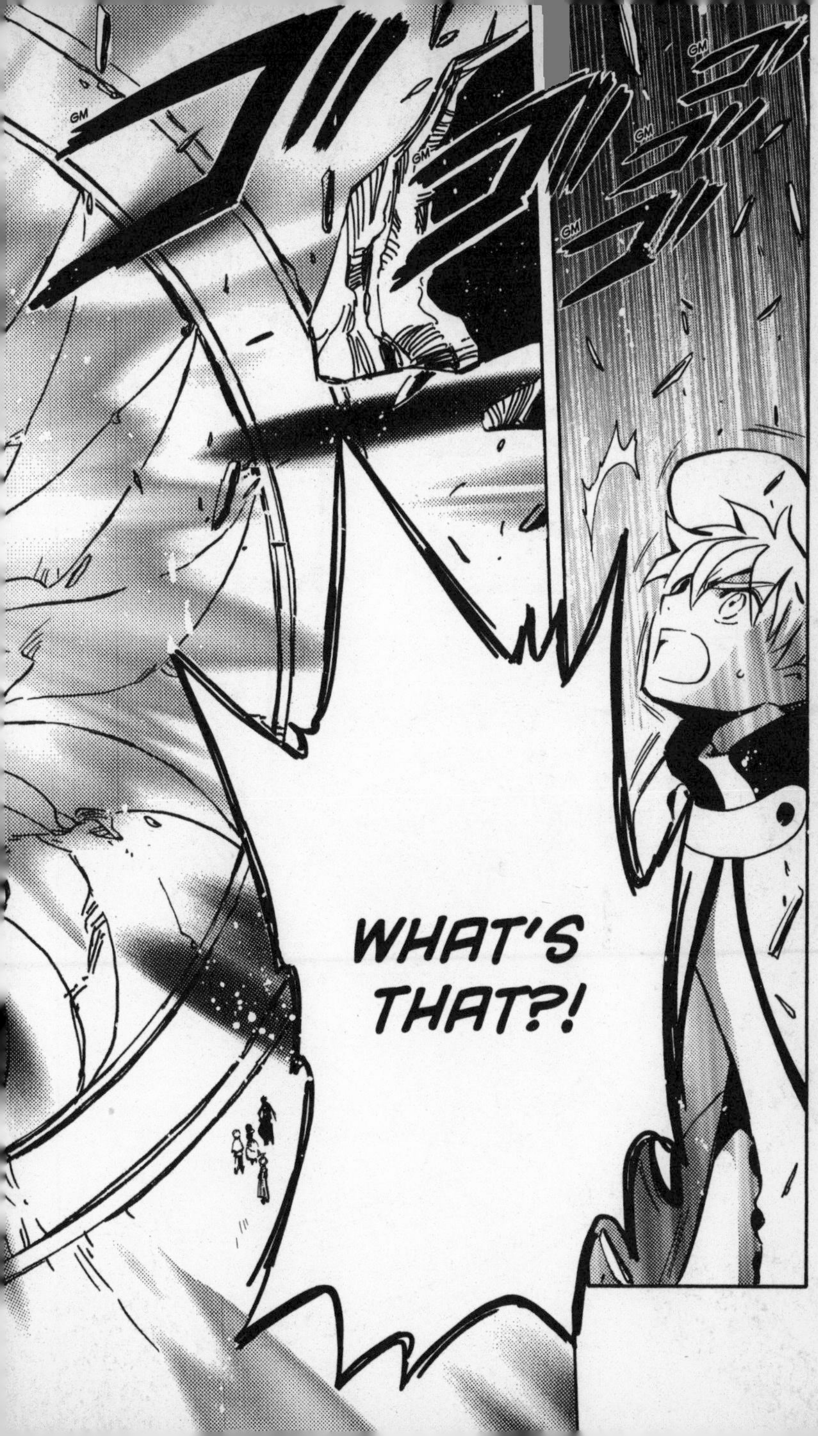
GM
GM
GM
GM
GM
WHAT'S THAT?!

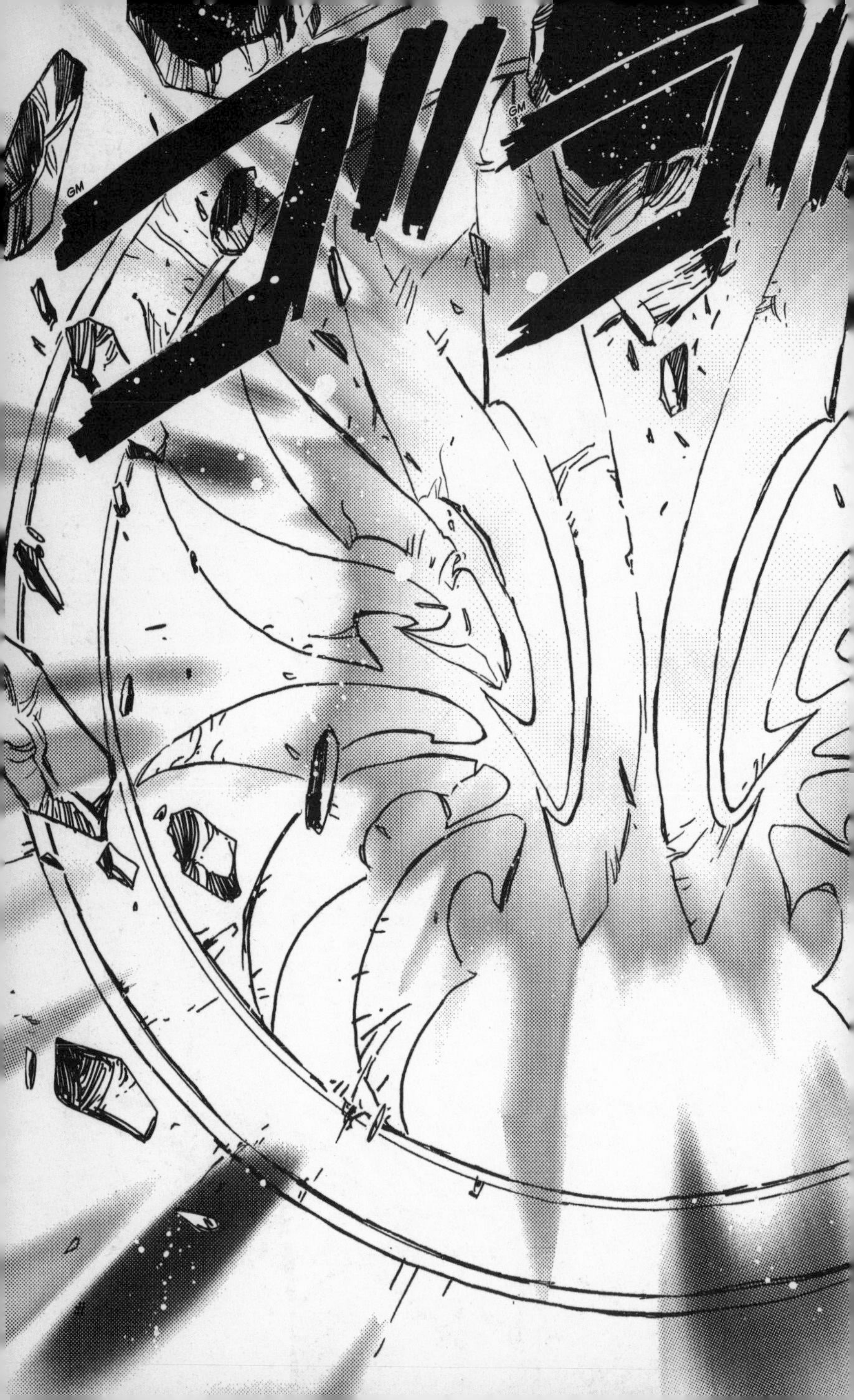
GM
GM

ツバサ

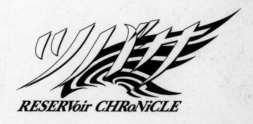

RESERVoir CHRoNiCLE

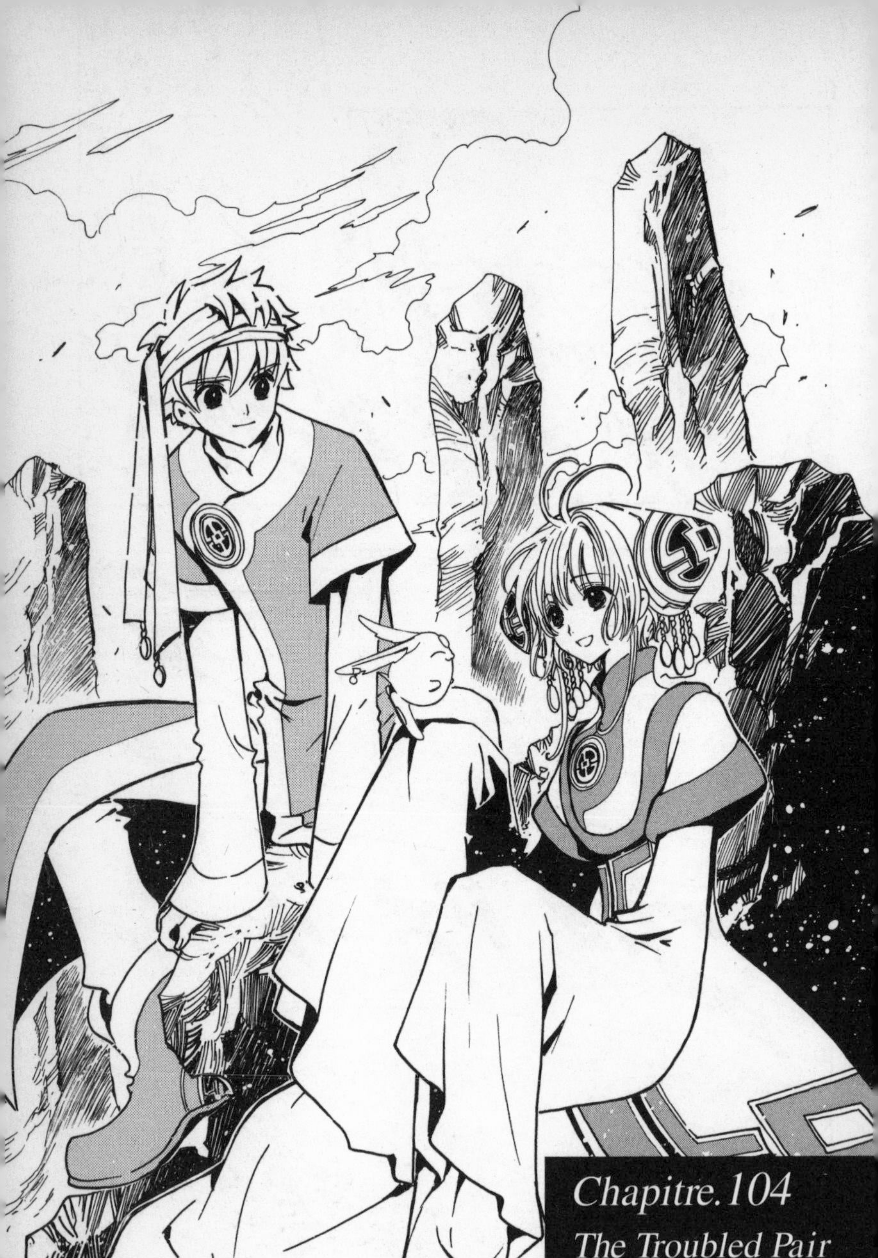

Chapitre.104
The Troubled Pair

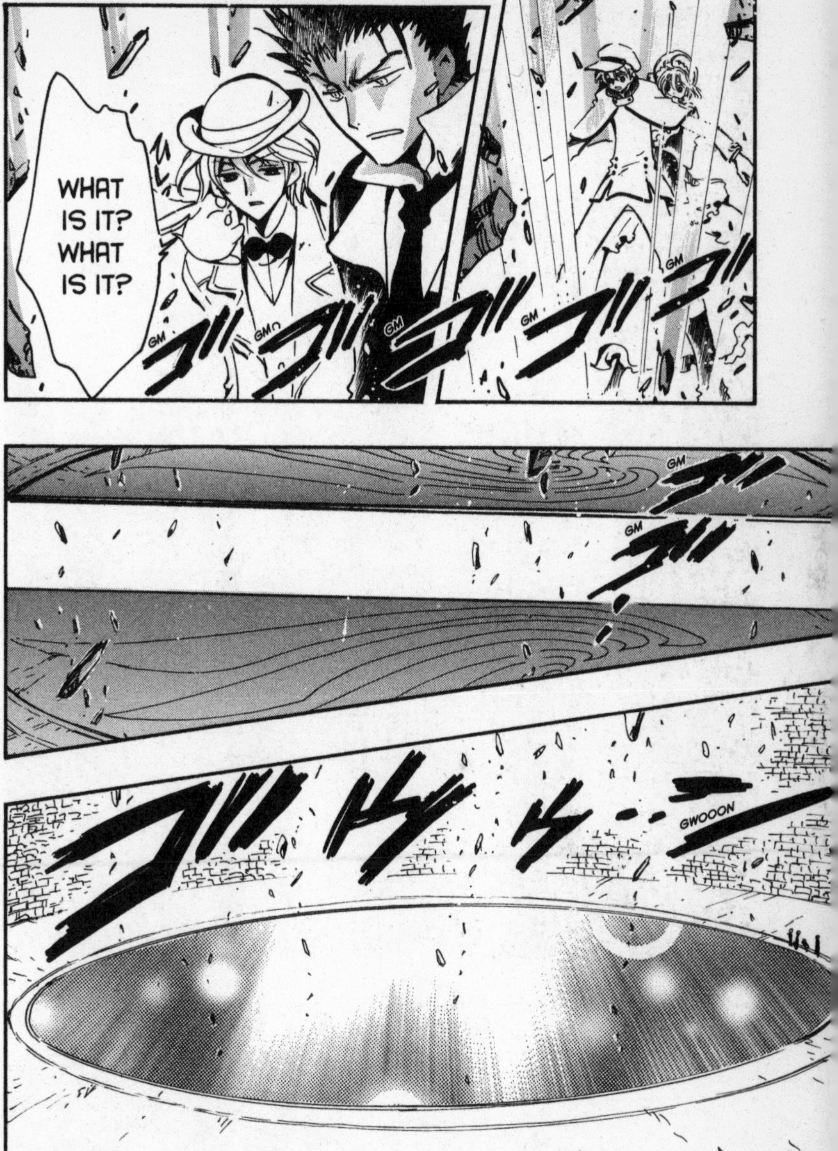

GM
GM
GM
GM
GM
WHAT IS IT? WHAT IS IT?
GM
GM
GWOOON

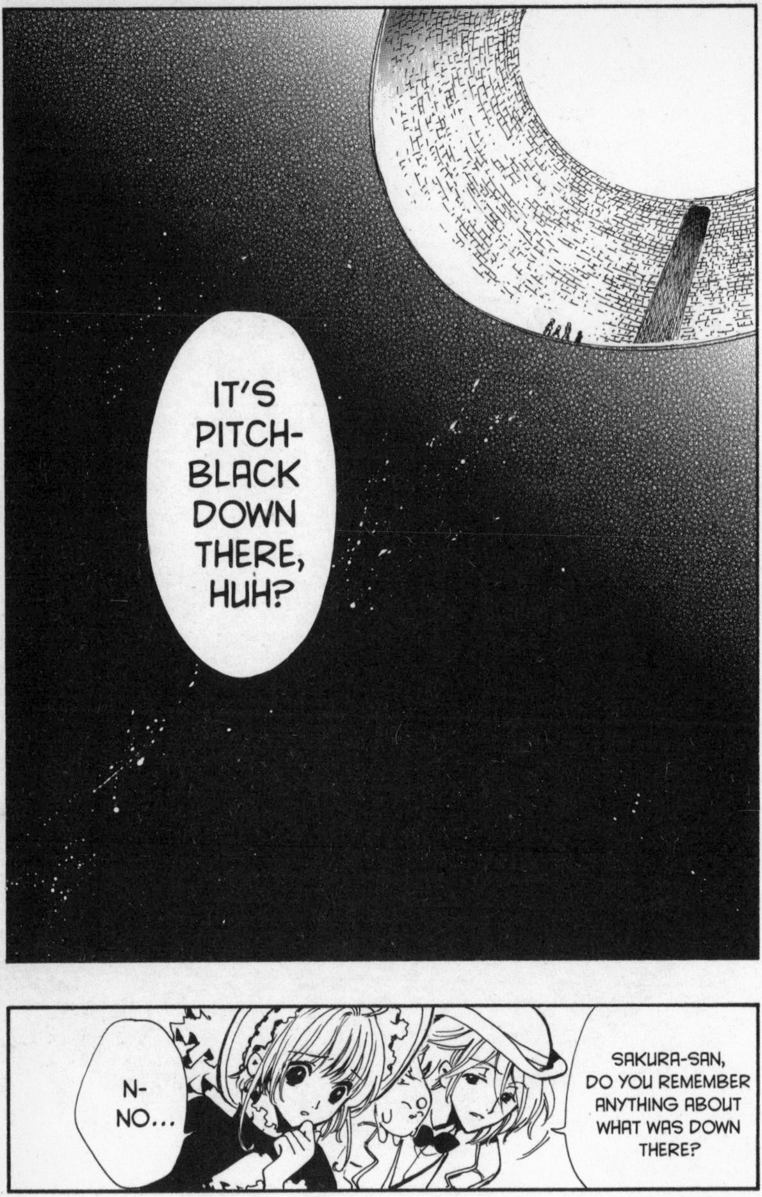
IT'S PITCH-BLACK DOWN THERE, HUH?
SAKURA-SAN, DO YOU REMEMBER ANYTHING ABOUT WHAT WAS DOWN THERE?
N-NO...

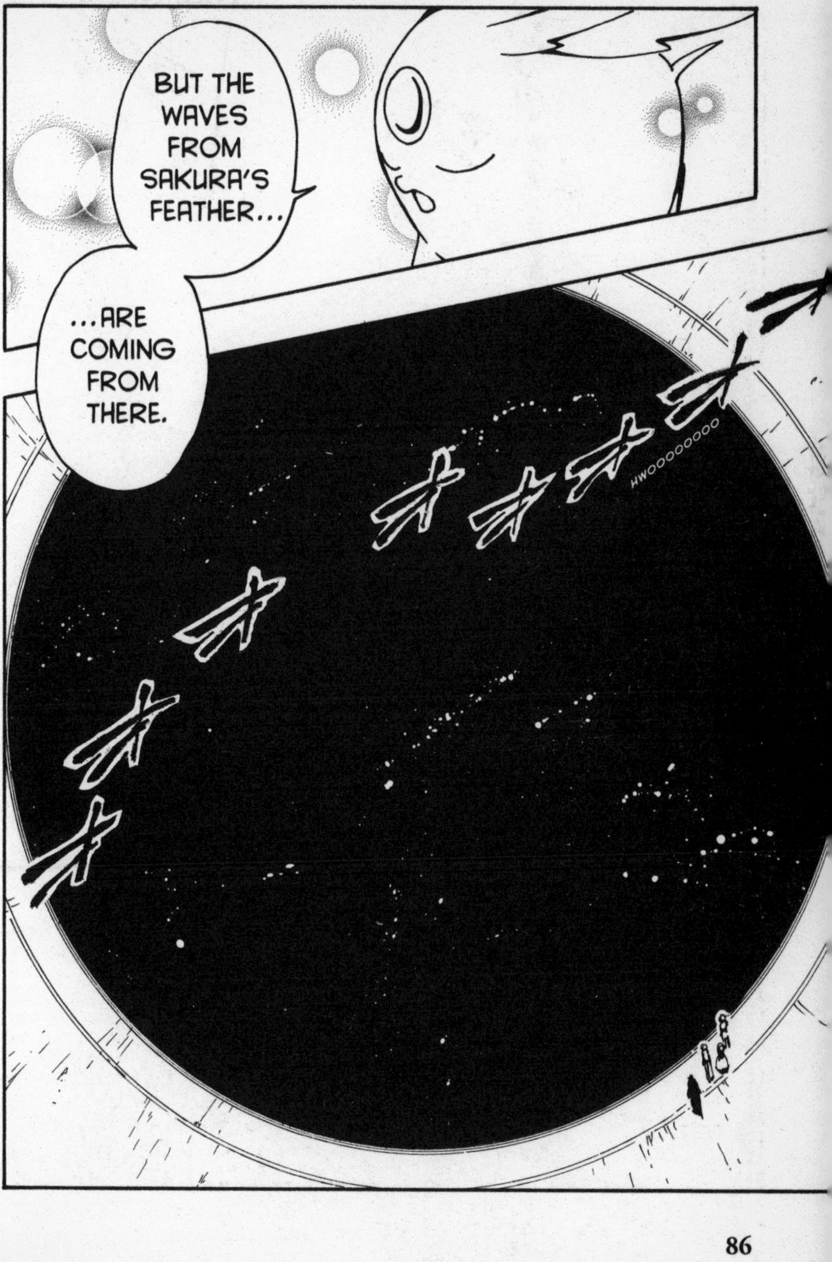
BUT THE WAVES FROM SAKURA'S FEATHER...
...ARE COMING FROM THERE.
HWOOOOOOOOO

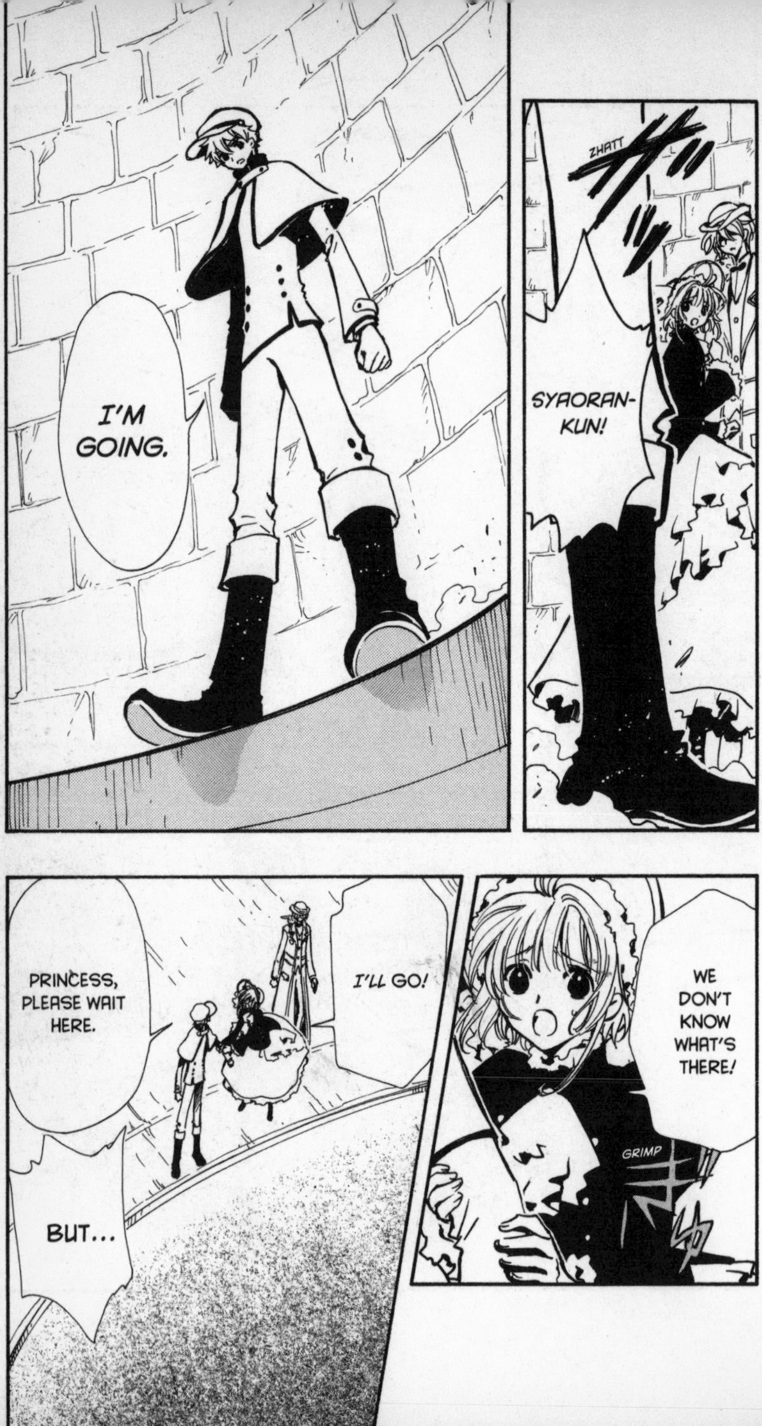
ZHATT
SYAORAN-KUN!
I'M GOING.
WE DON'T KNOW WHAT'S THERE!
GRIMP
I'LL GO!
PRINCESS, PLEASE WAIT HERE.
BUT...

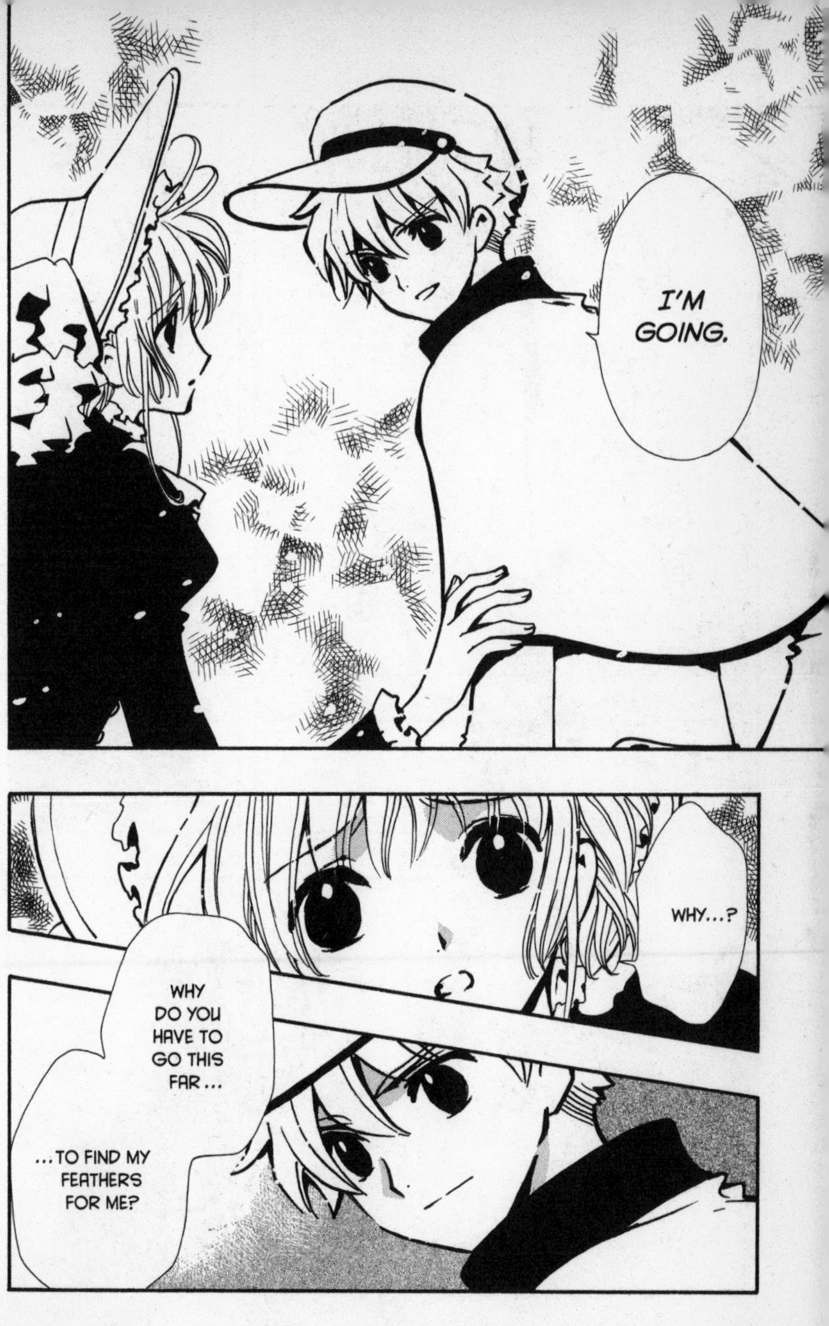
I'M GOING.
WHY...?
WHY DO YOU HAVE TO GO THIS FAR...
...TO FIND MY FEATHERS FOR ME?

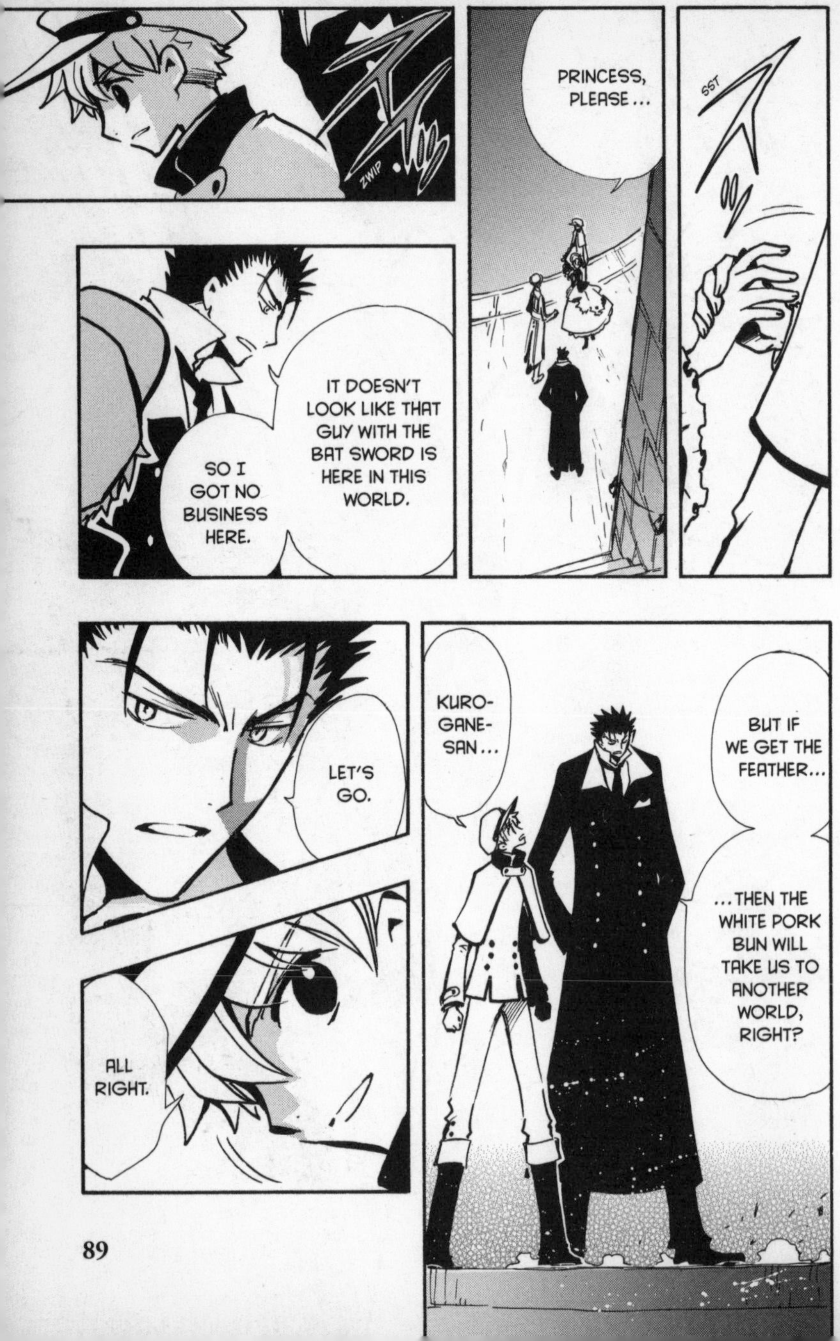
SST
PRINCESS, PLEASE…
ZWIP
IT DOESN'T LOOK LIKE THAT GUY WITH THE BAT SWORD IS HERE IN THIS WORLD.
SO I GOT NO BUSINESS HERE.
BUT IF WE GET THE FEATHER…
…THEN THE WHITE PORK BUN WILL TAKE US TO ANOTHER WORLD, RIGHT?
KURO-GANE-SAN…
LET'S GO.
ALL RIGHT.

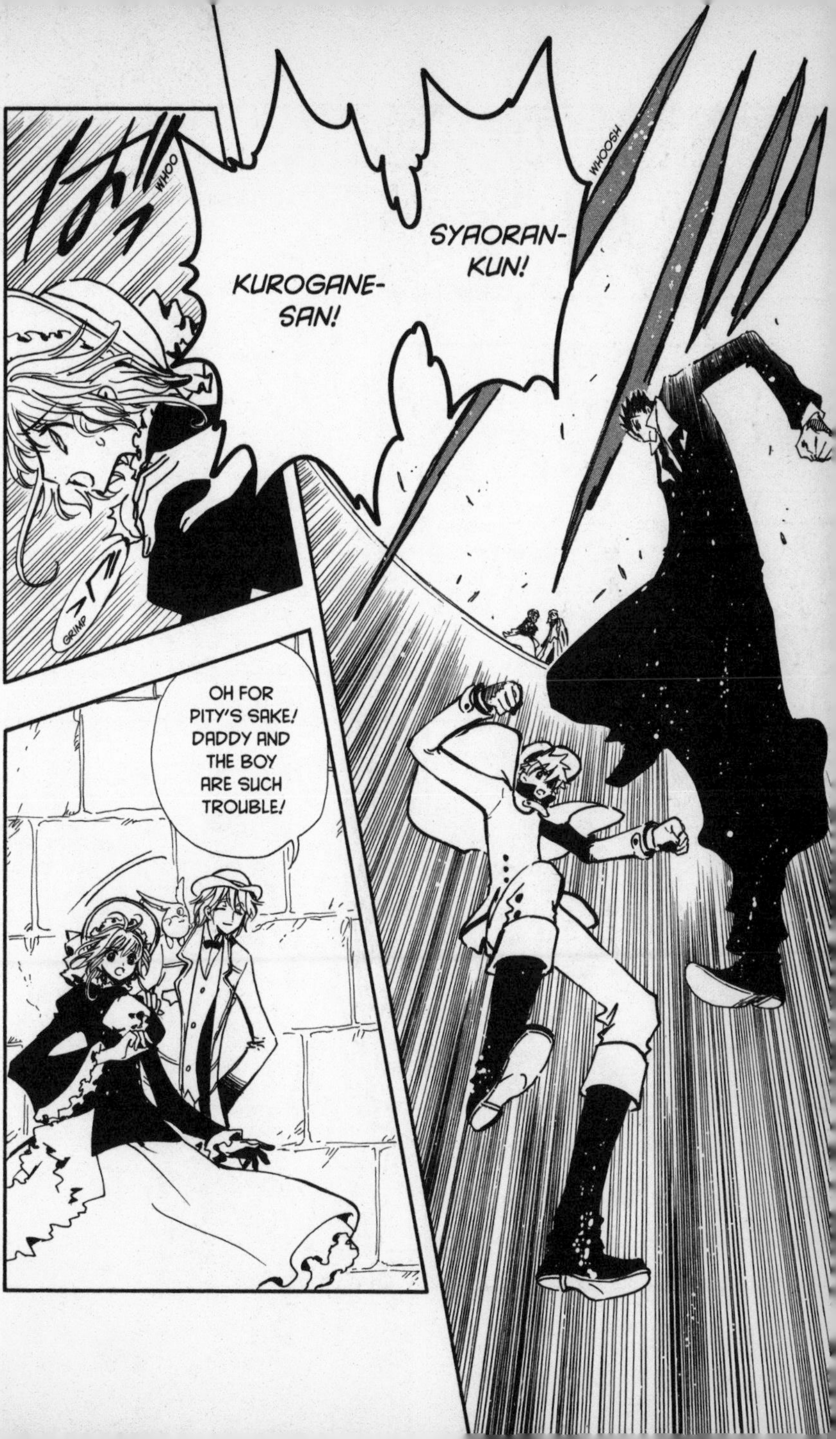
WHOOSH
SYAORAN-KUN!
KUROGANE-SAN!
WHOO
GRIMP
OH FOR PITY'S SAKE! DADDY AND THE BOY ARE SUCH TROUBLE!

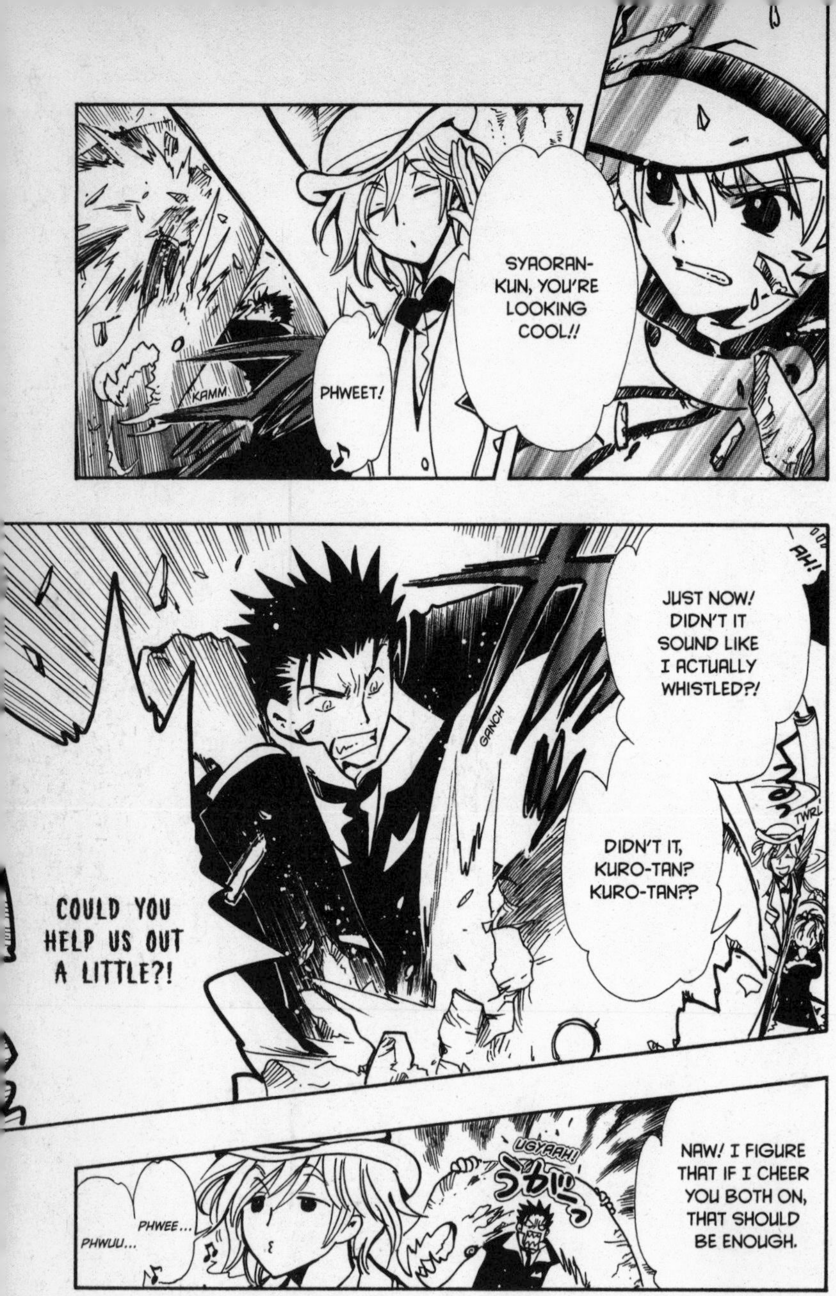
SYAORAN-KUN, YOU'RE LOOKING COOL!!
PHWEET!
KAMM
AH!
JUST NOW! DIDN'T IT SOUND LIKE I ACTUALLY WHISTLED?!
TWRL
DIDN'T IT, KURO-TAN? KURO-TAN??
GANCH
COULD YOU HELP US OUT A LITTLE?!
NAW! I FIGURE THAT IF I CHEER YOU BOTH ON, THAT SHOULD BE ENOUGH.
UGYAAH!
PHWEE...
PHWUU...

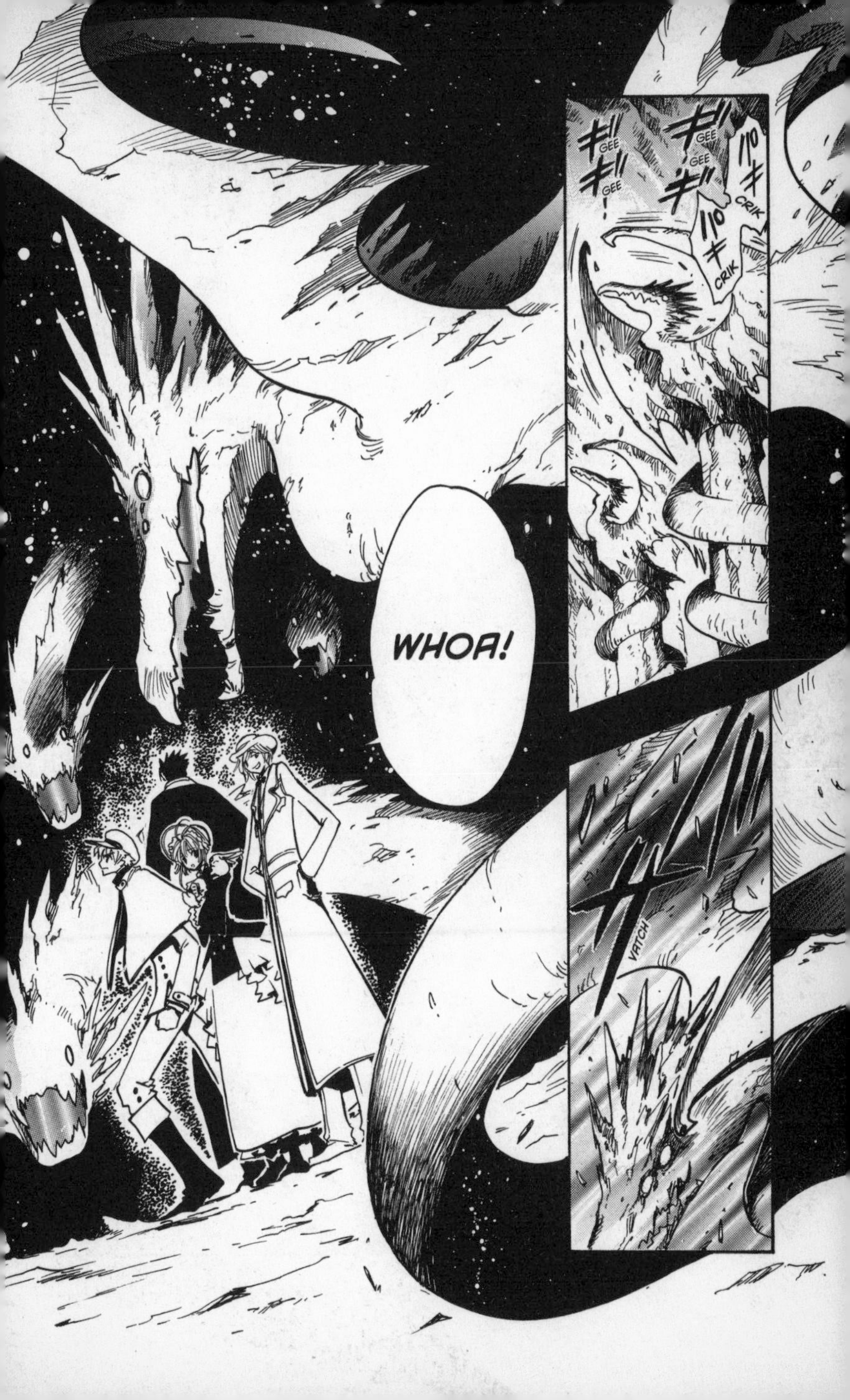
GEE GEE
GEE
CRIK
CRIK
VATCH
WHOA!

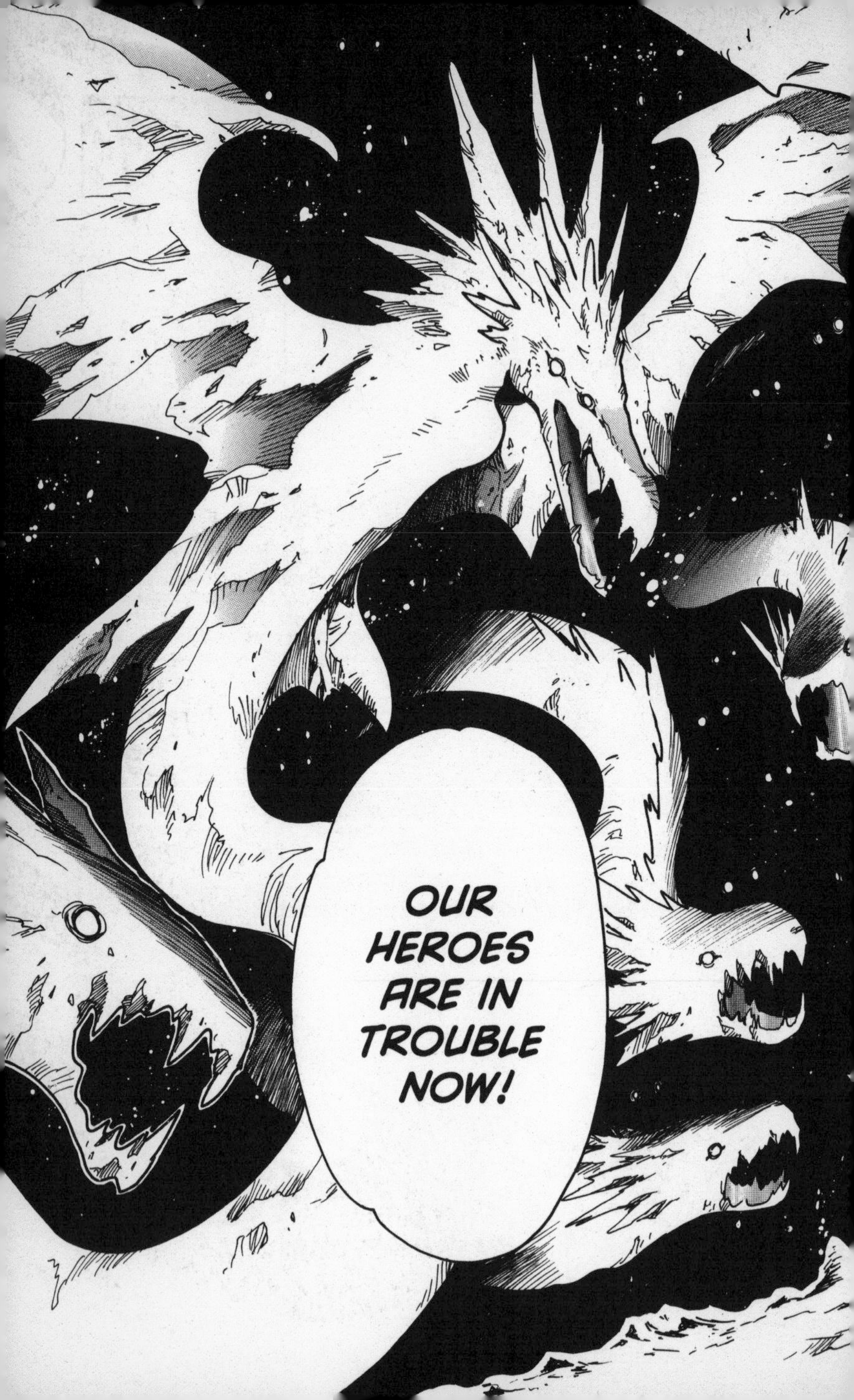
OUR HEROES ARE IN TROUBLE NOW!

ツバサ
RESERVoir CHRoNiCLE

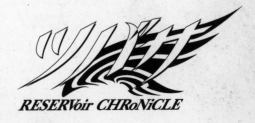

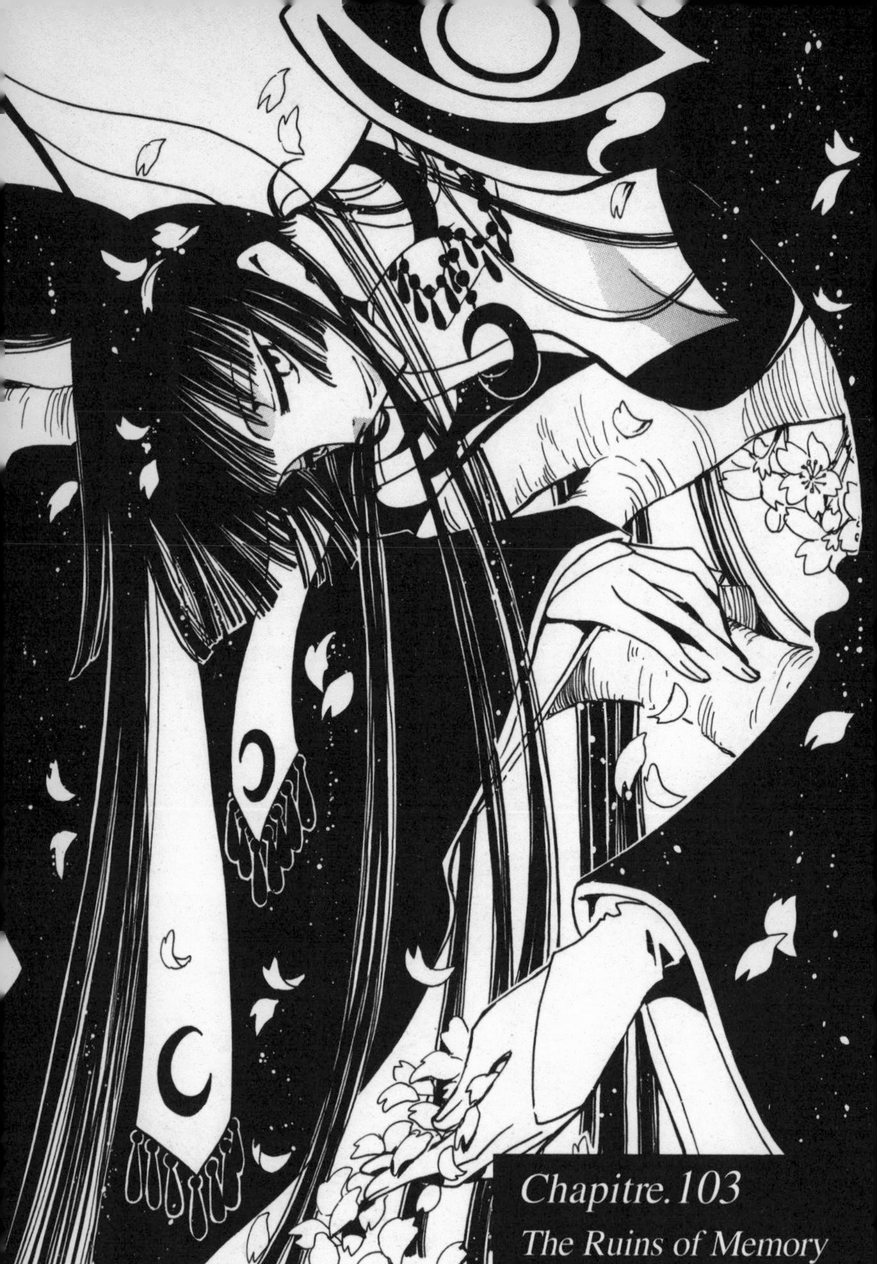
Chapitre.103
The Ruins of Memory

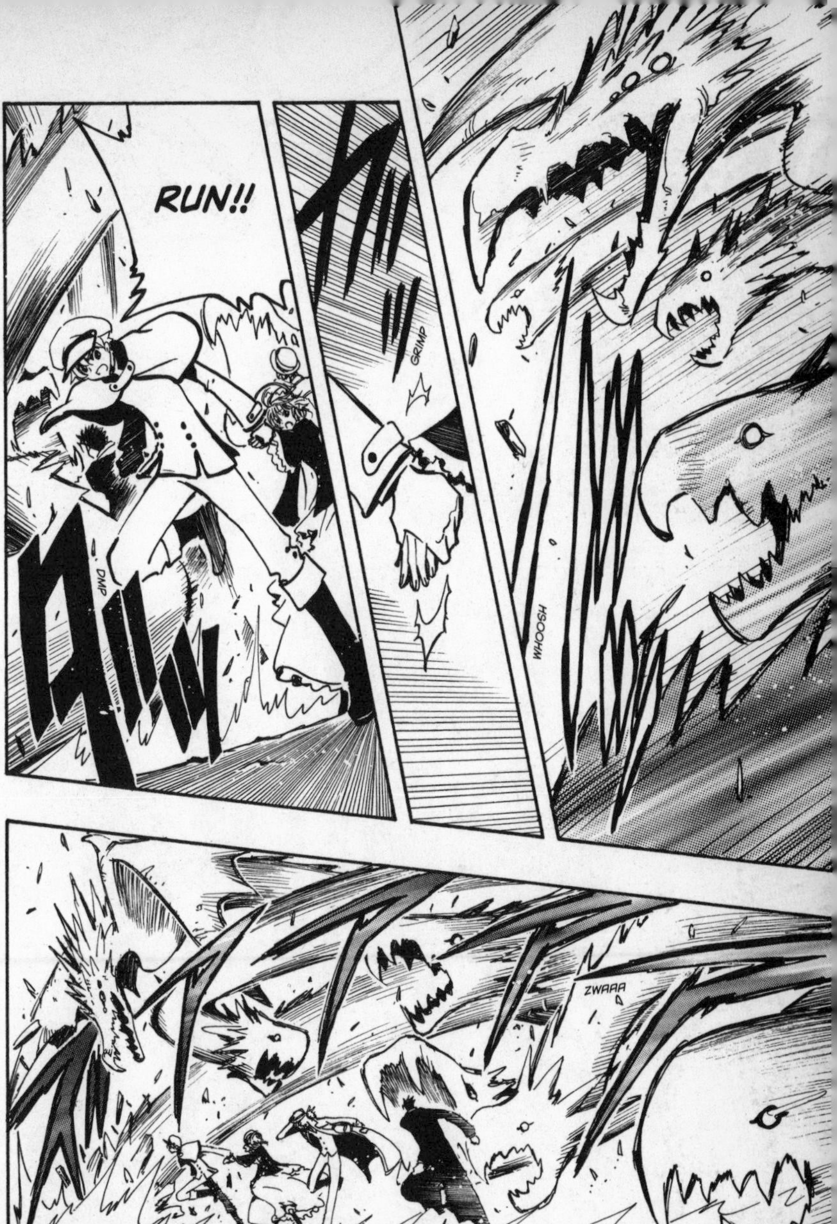
WHOOSH
GRIMP
RUN!!
DMP
ZWAAA

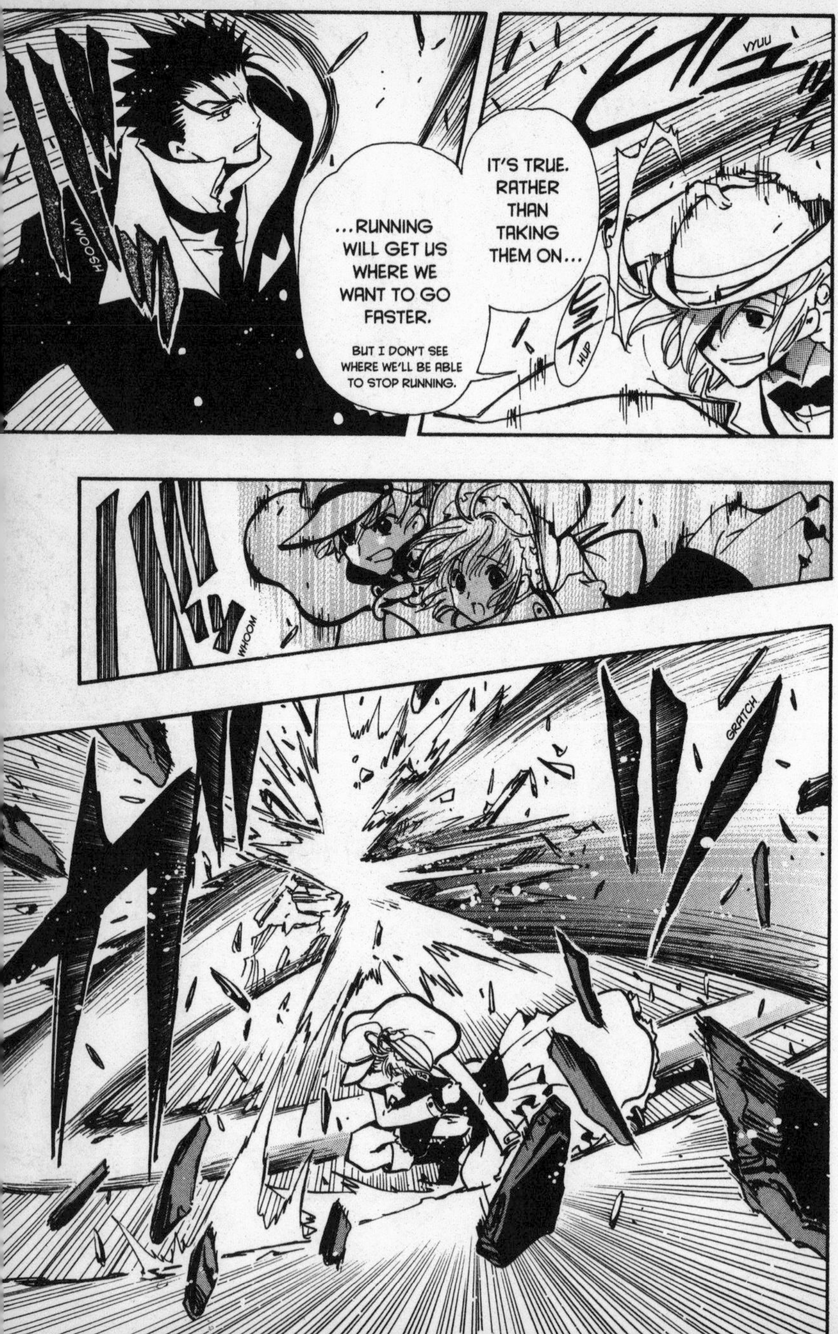
VYUU
IT'S TRUE. RATHER THAN TAKING THEM ON...
HUP
...RUNNING WILL GET US WHERE WE WANT TO GO FASTER.
BUT I DON'T SEE WHERE WE'LL BE ABLE TO STOP RUNNING.
VWOOSH
WHOOM
GRATCH

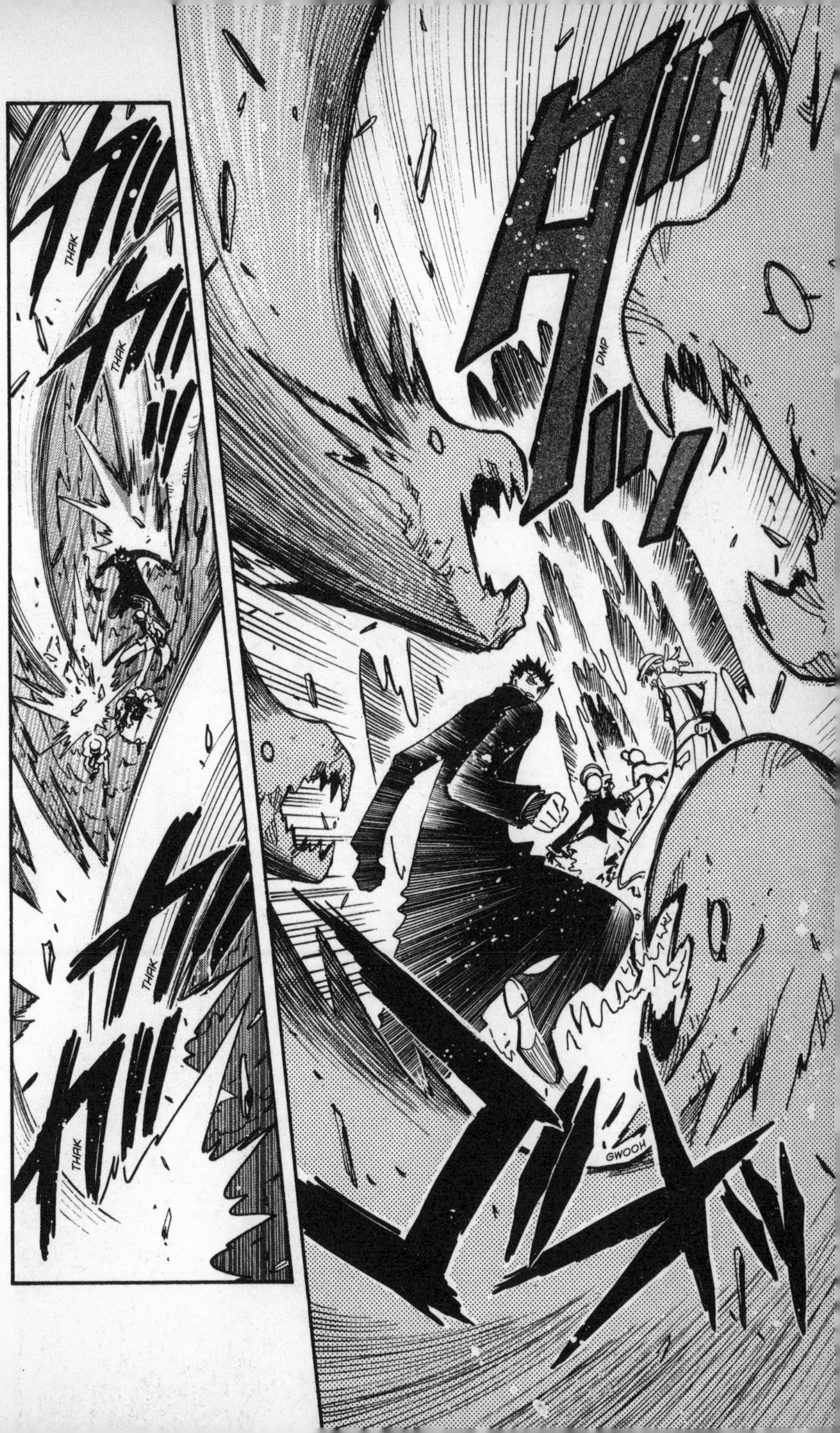
DMP
GWOOH
THAK
THAK
THAK
THAK

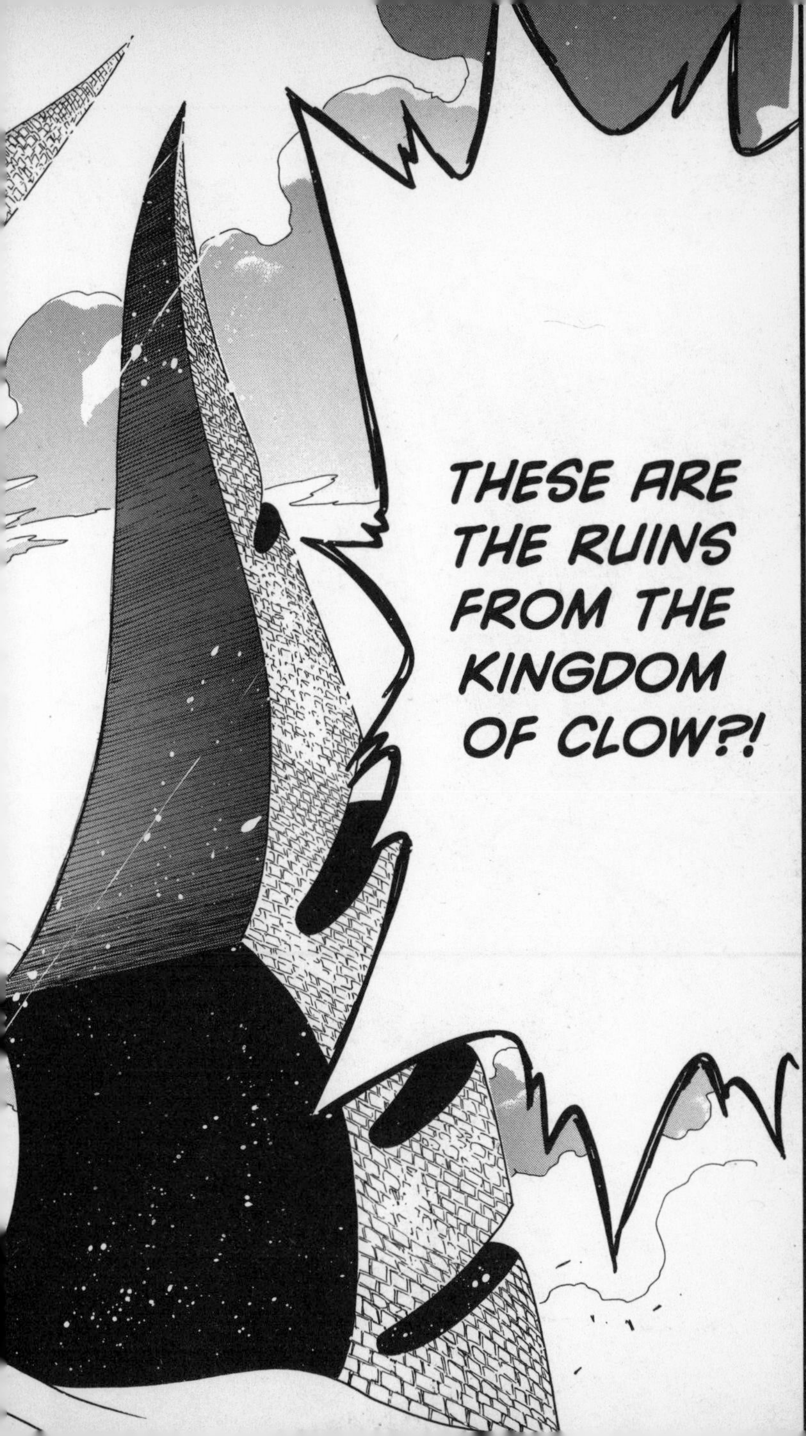
THESE ARE THE RUINS FROM THE KINGDOM OF CLOW?!

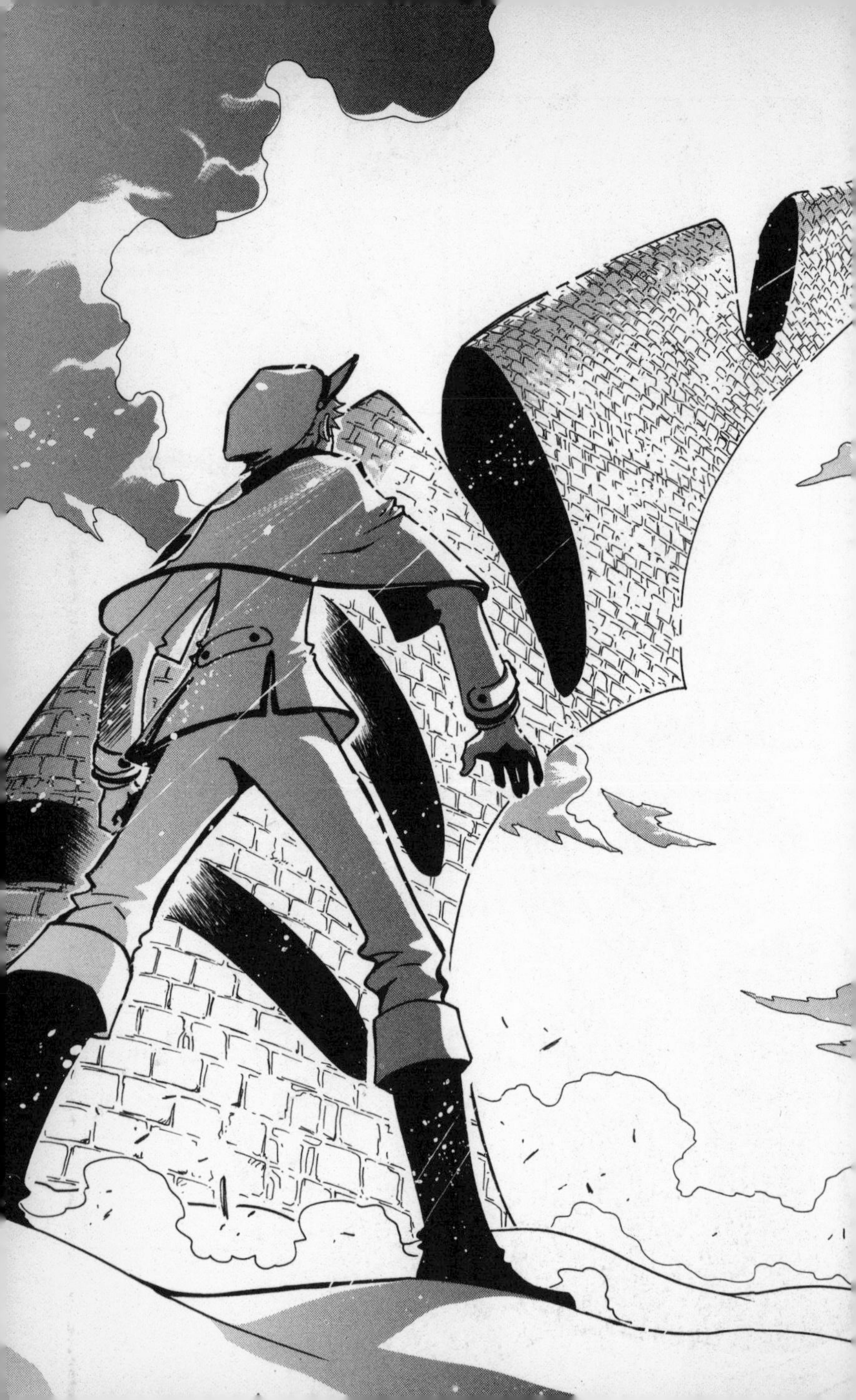

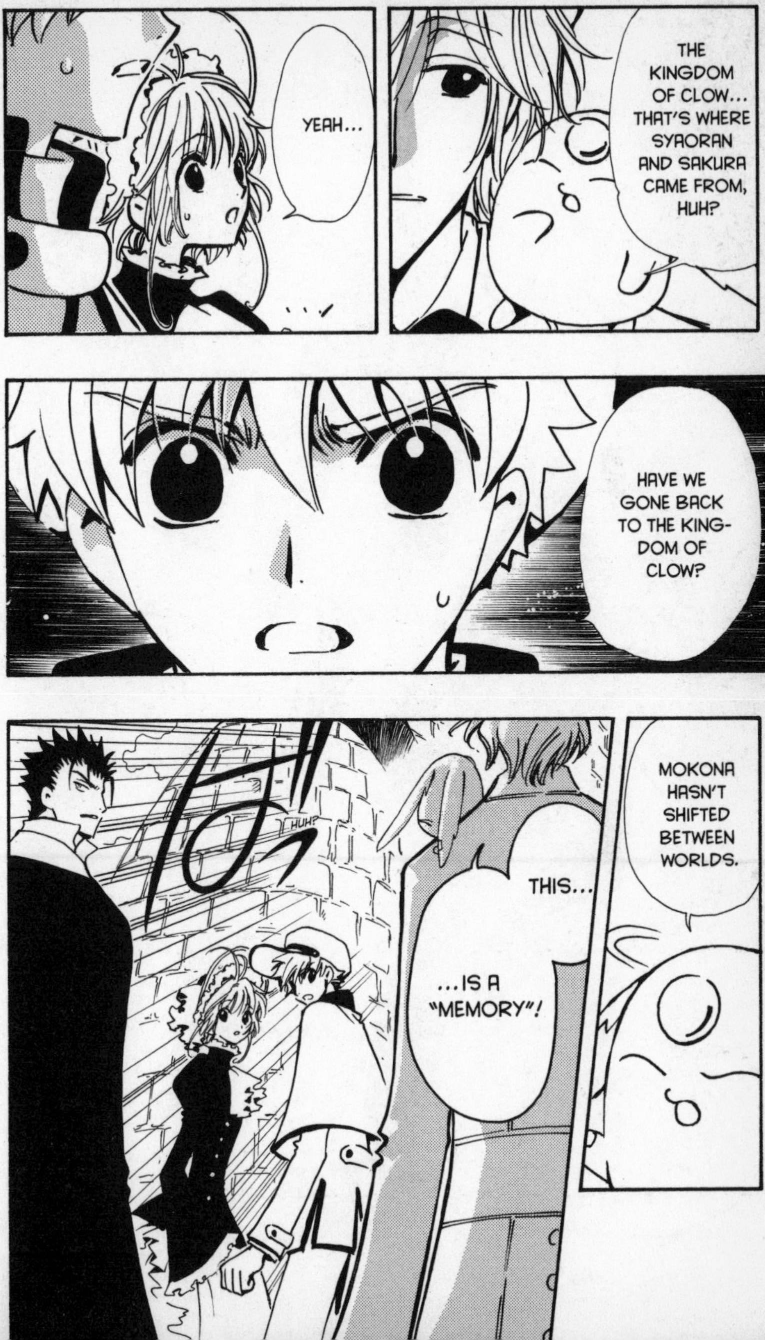
THE KINGDOM OF CLOW... THAT'S WHERE SYAORAN AND SAKURA CAME FROM, HUH?
YEAH...
HAVE WE GONE BACK TO THE KING-DOM OF CLOW?
MOKONA HASN'T SHIFTED BETWEEN WORLDS.
THIS...
...IS A "MEMORY"!
HUH?

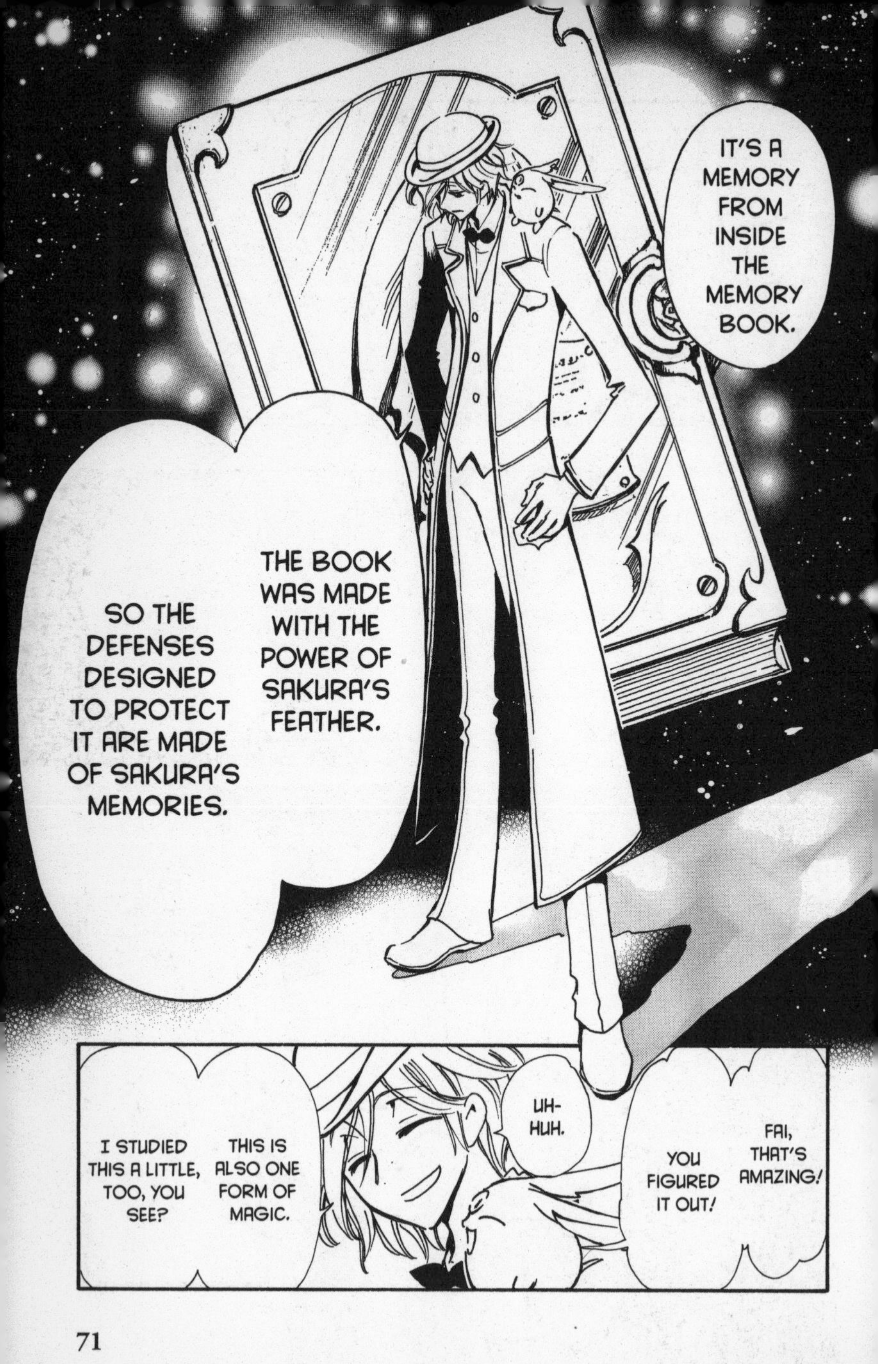
IT'S A MEMORY FROM INSIDE THE MEMORY BOOK.
THE BOOK WAS MADE WITH THE POWER OF SAKURA'S FEATHER.
SO THE DEFENSES DESIGNED TO PROTECT IT ARE MADE OF SAKURA'S MEMORIES.
FAI, THAT'S AMAZING!
YOU FIGURED IT OUT!
UH-HUH.
THIS IS ALSO ONE FORM OF MAGIC.
I STUDIED THIS A LITTLE, TOO, YOU SEE?

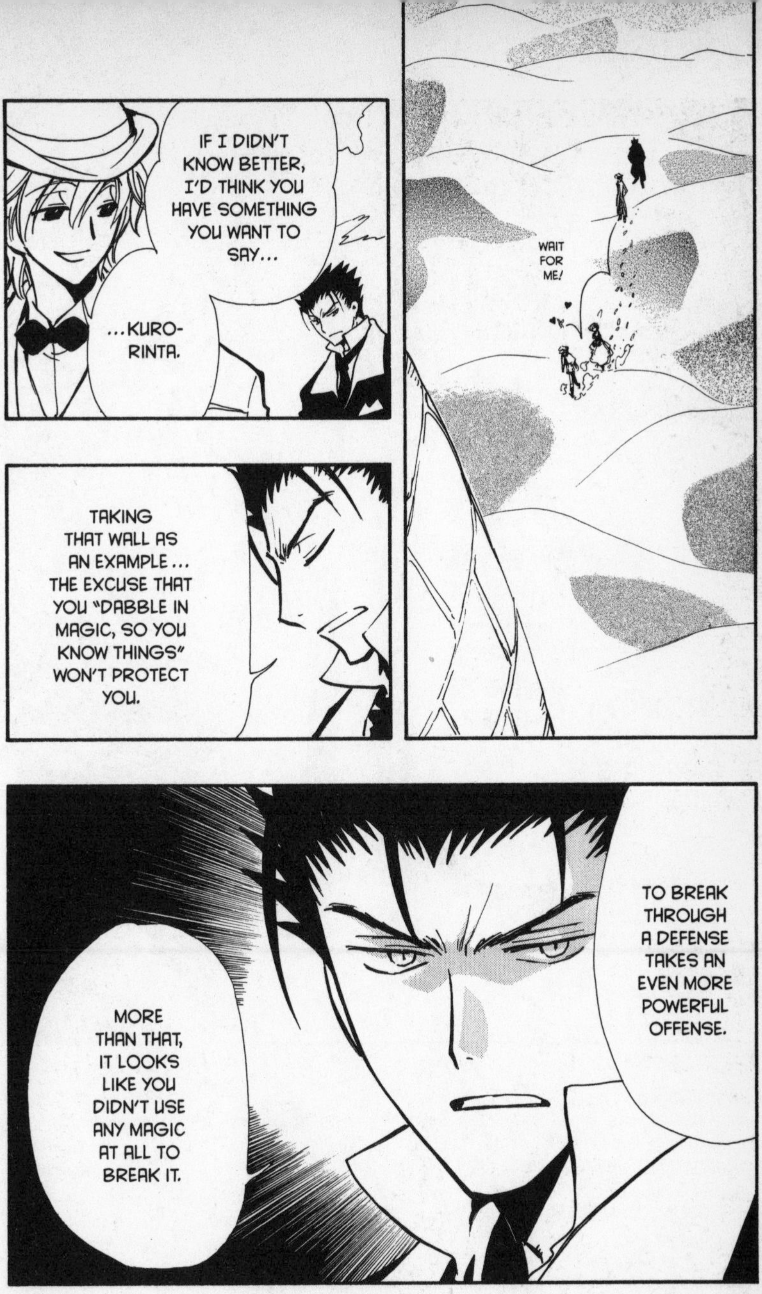
WAIT FOR ME!
IF I DIDN'T KNOW BETTER, I'D THINK YOU HAVE SOMETHING YOU WANT TO SAY...
...KURO-RINTA.
TAKING THAT WALL AS AN EXAMPLE... THE EXCUSE THAT YOU "DABBLE IN MAGIC, SO YOU KNOW THINGS" WON'T PROTECT YOU.
TO BREAK THROUGH A DEFENSE TAKES AN EVEN MORE POWERFUL OFFENSE.
MORE THAN THAT, IT LOOKS LIKE YOU DIDN'T USE ANY MAGIC AT ALL TO BREAK IT.

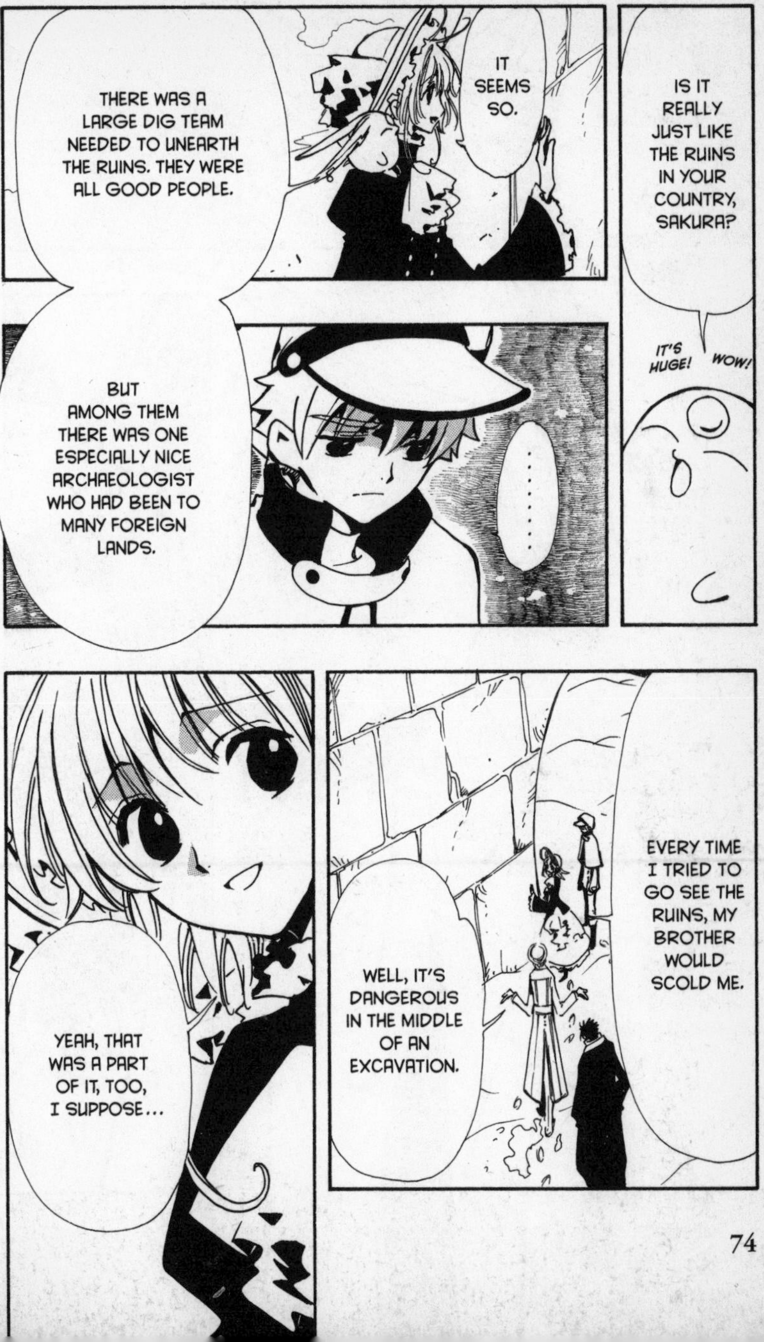
IS IT REALLY JUST LIKE THE RUINS IN YOUR COUNTRY, SAKURA?
WOW!
IT'S HUGE!
IT SEEMS SO.
THERE WAS A LARGE DIG TEAM NEEDED TO UNEARTH THE RUINS. THEY WERE ALL GOOD PEOPLE.
BUT AMONG THEM THERE WAS ONE ESPECIALLY NICE ARCHAEOLOGIST WHO HAD BEEN TO MANY FOREIGN LANDS.
……
EVERY TIME I TRIED TO GO SEE THE RUINS, MY BROTHER WOULD SCOLD ME.
WELL, IT'S DANGEROUS IN THE MIDDLE OF AN EXCAVATION.
YEAH, THAT WAS A PART OF IT, TOO, I SUPPOSE…

THE PATH GETS WIDER AND THINNER...

THESE RUINS HAVE A STRANGE FEEL TO THEM.

ISN'T IT TOO SMALL?

AND THIS SUN DIAL IS VERY SMALL.

AH!

THIS BENCH-LIKE THING IS HUGE!

WELL?

IT'S REALLY DELICIOUS!

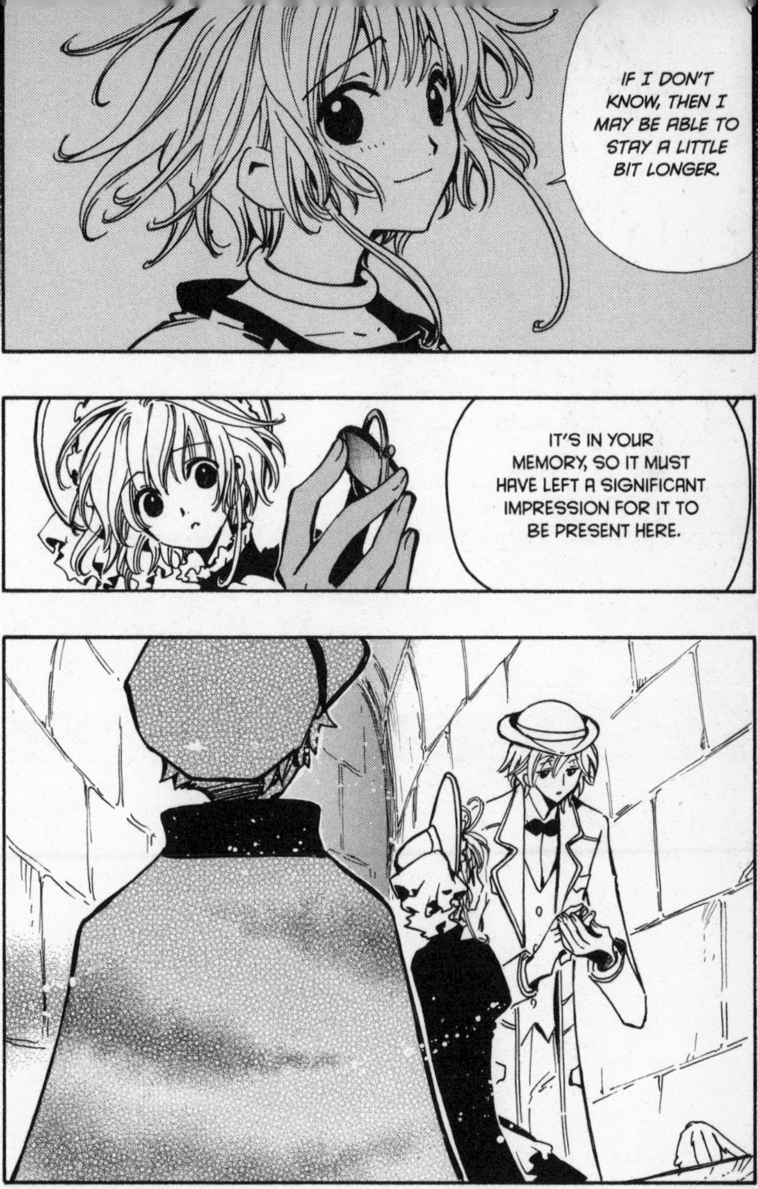
IF I DON'T KNOW, THEN I MAY BE ABLE TO STAY A LITTLE BIT LONGER.
IT'S IN YOUR MEMORY, SO IT MUST HAVE LEFT A SIGNIFICANT IMPRESSION FOR IT TO BE PRESENT HERE.

LET'S GO, SAKURA!

O-OKAY.

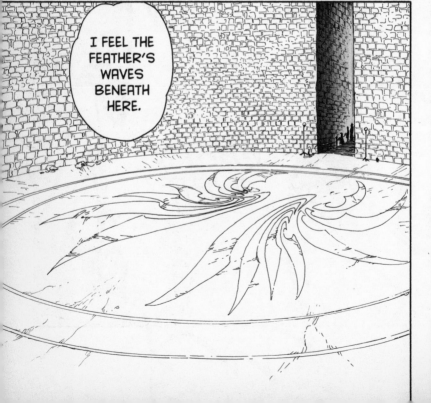

I FEEL THE FEATHER'S WAVES BENEATH HERE.

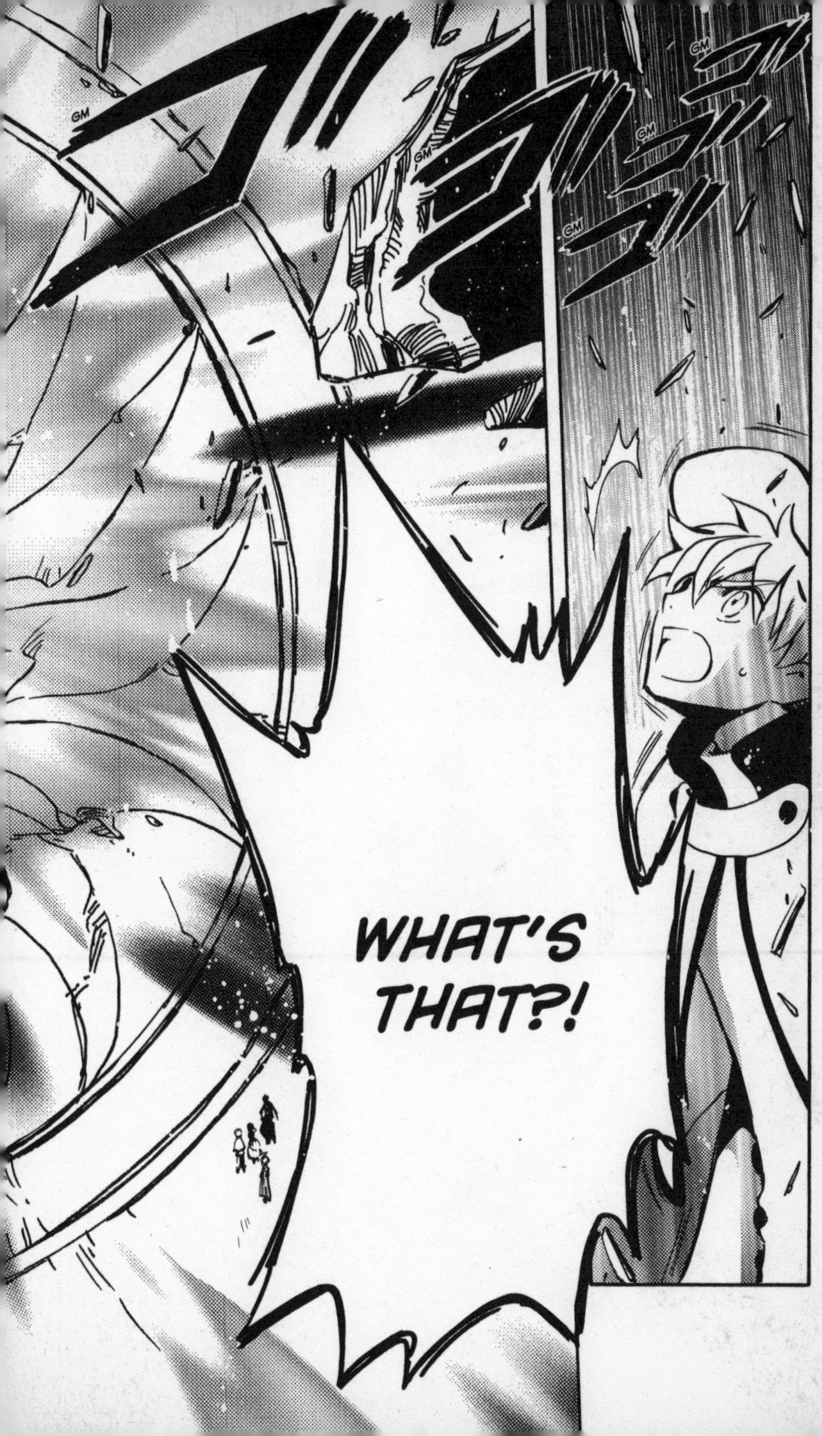
GM
GM
GM
GM
GM
WHAT'S THAT?!

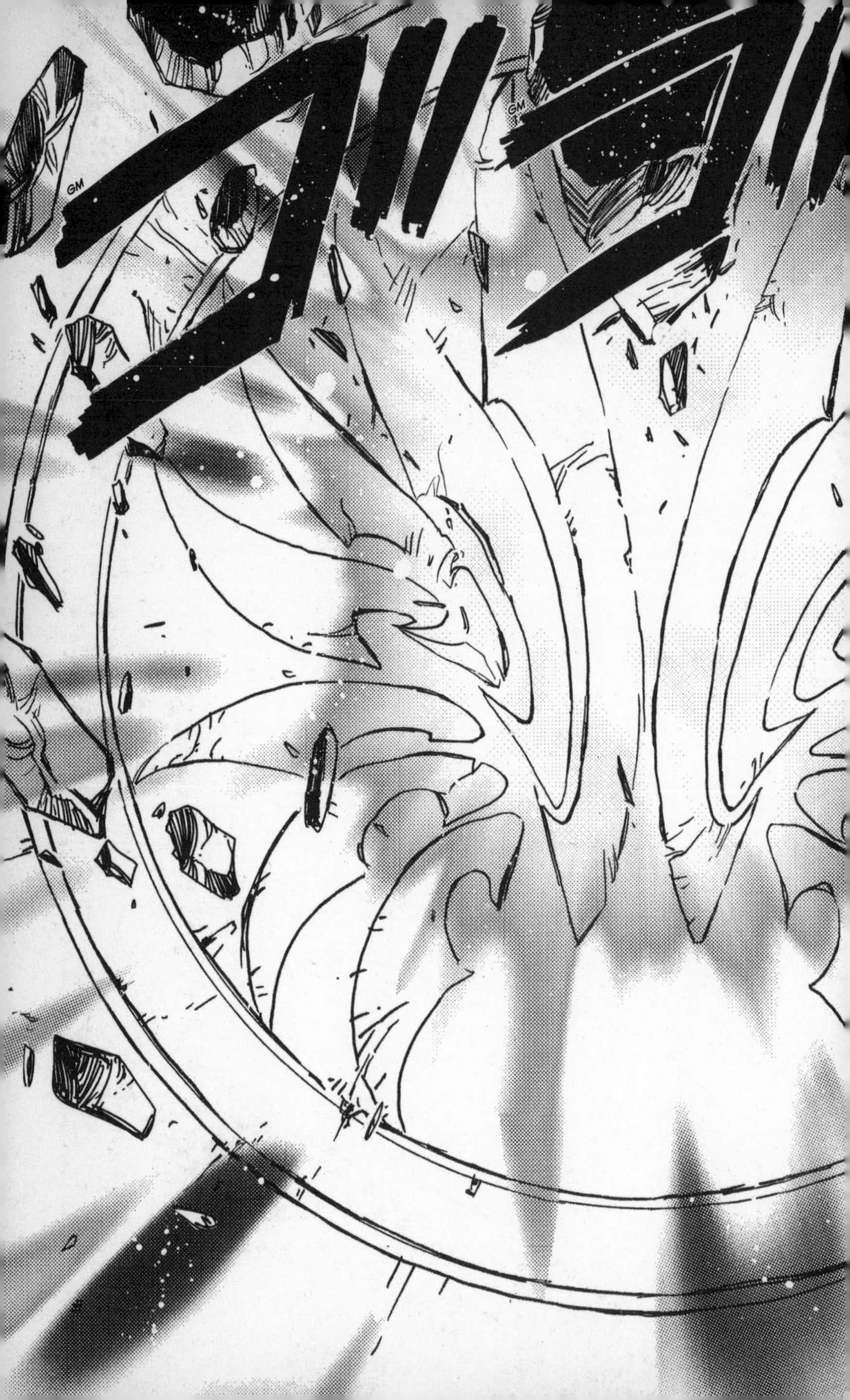

ツバサ

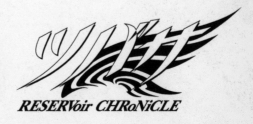

RESERVoir CHRoNiCLE

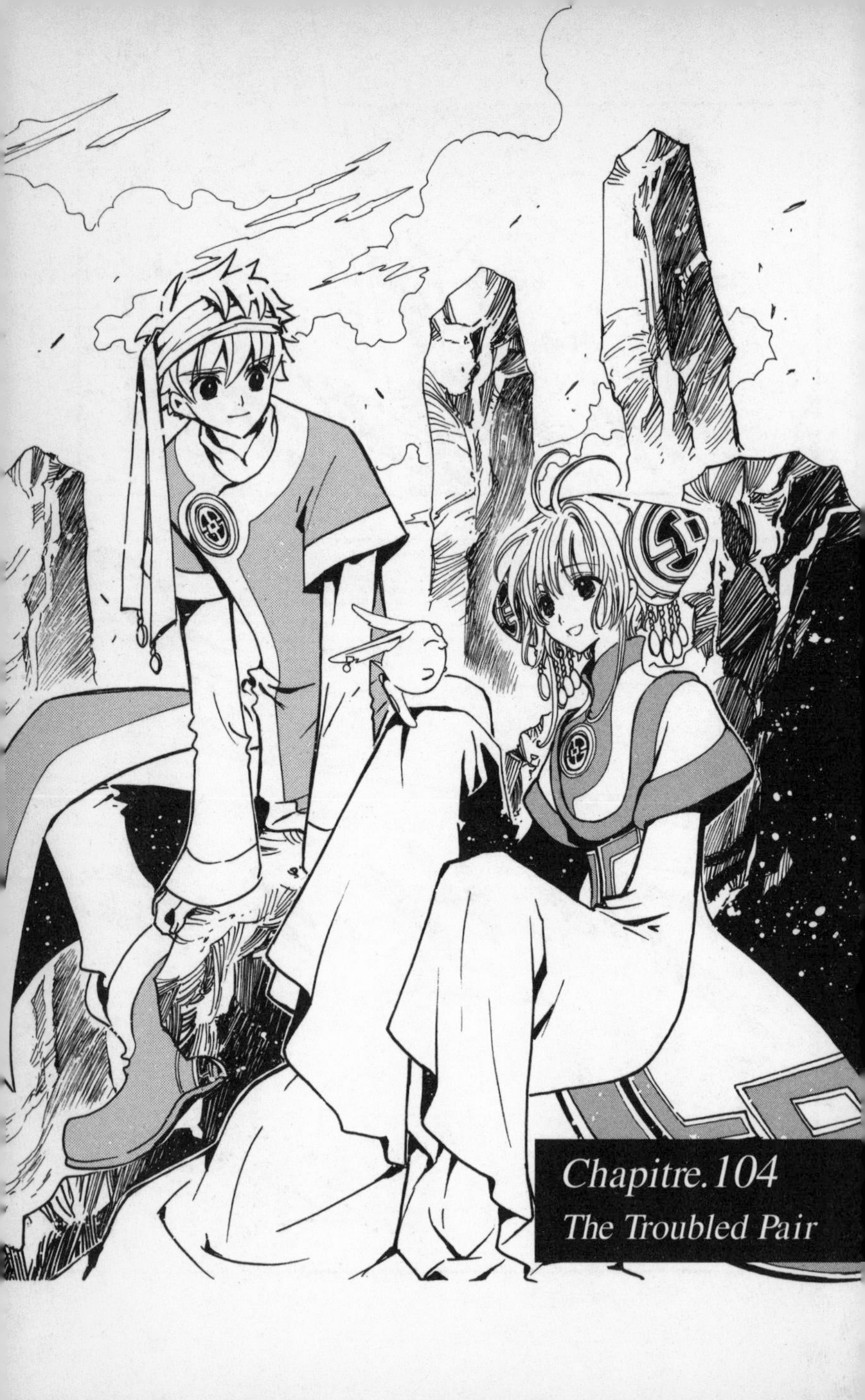
Chapitre.104
The Troubled Pair

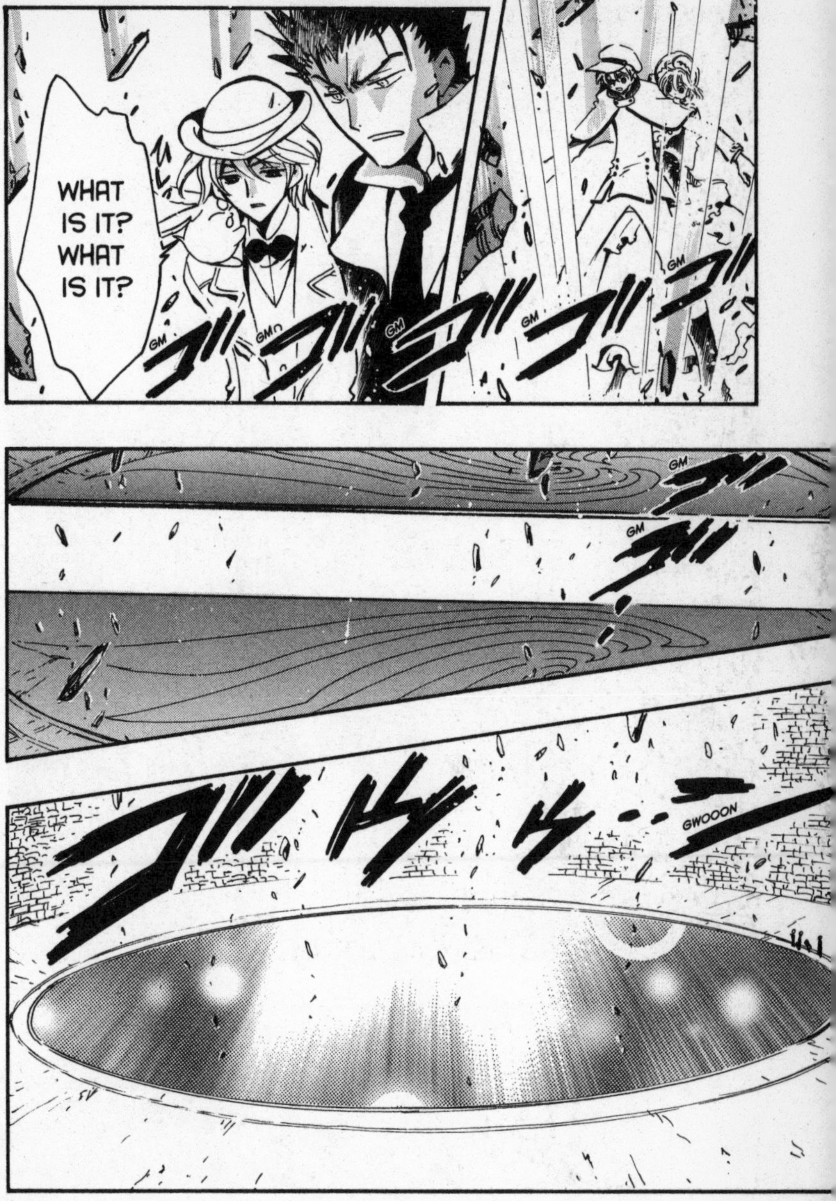
WHAT IS IT? WHAT IS IT?
GM
GM
GM
GM
GM
GM
GM
GWOOON

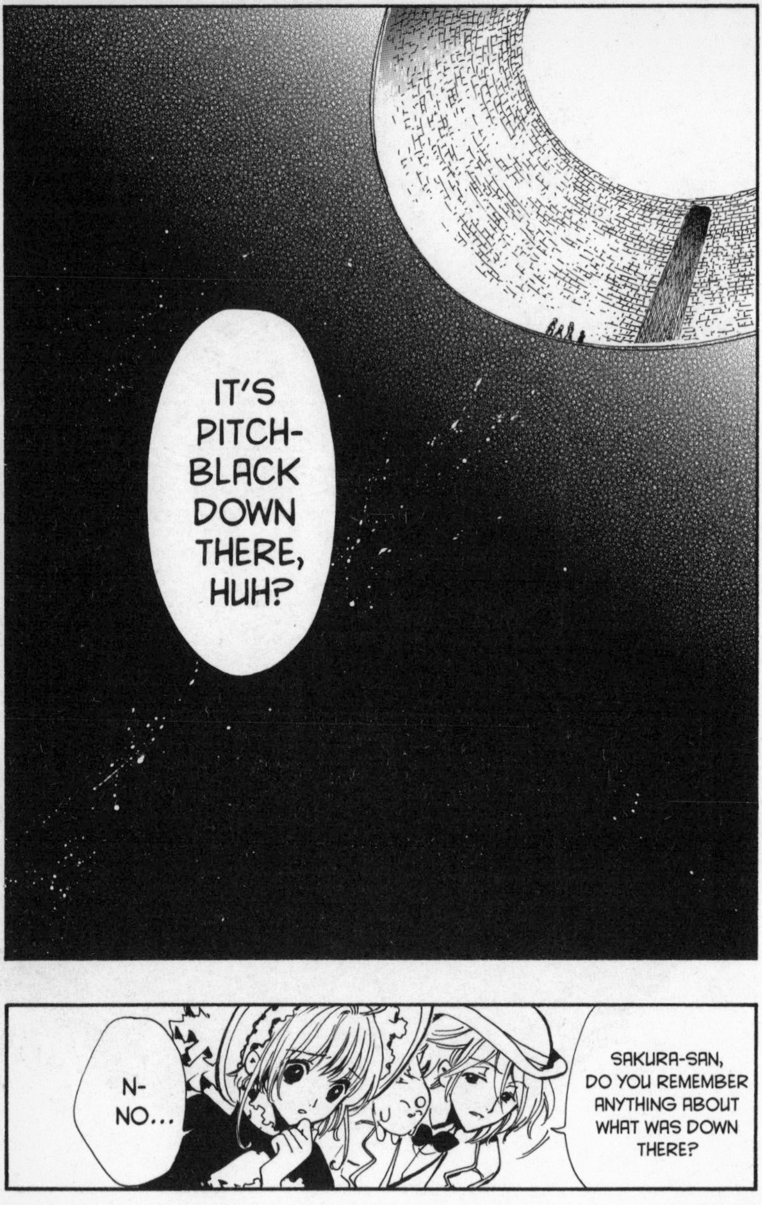
IT'S PITCH-BLACK DOWN THERE, HUH?
SAKURA-SAN, DO YOU REMEMBER ANYTHING ABOUT WHAT WAS DOWN THERE?
N-NO...

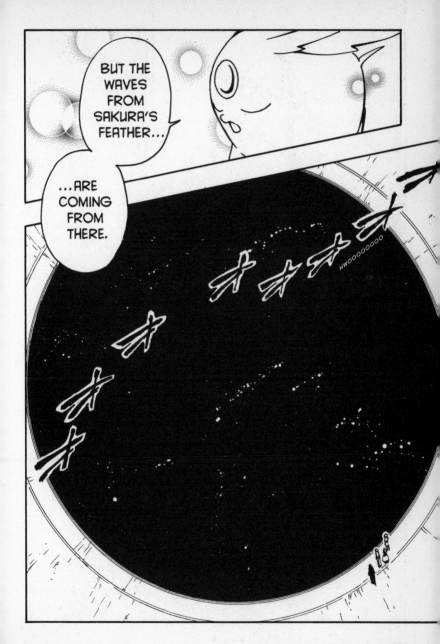

86

I'M GOING.

ZHATT

SYAORAN-KUN!

PRINCESS, PLEASE WAIT HERE.

I'LL GO!

WE DON'T KNOW WHAT'S THERE!

BUT...

GRIMP

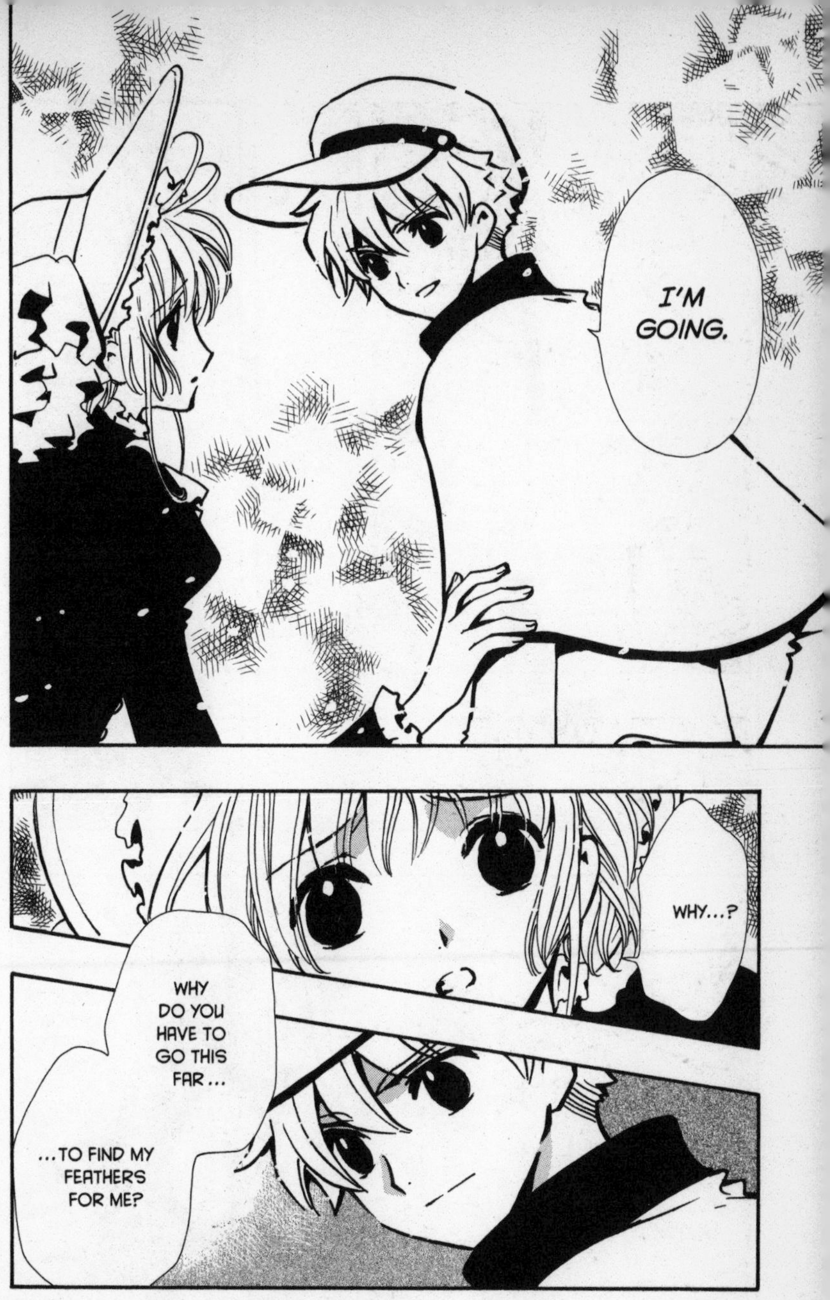
I'M GOING.
WHY...?
WHY DO YOU HAVE TO GO THIS FAR...
...TO FIND MY FEATHERS FOR ME?

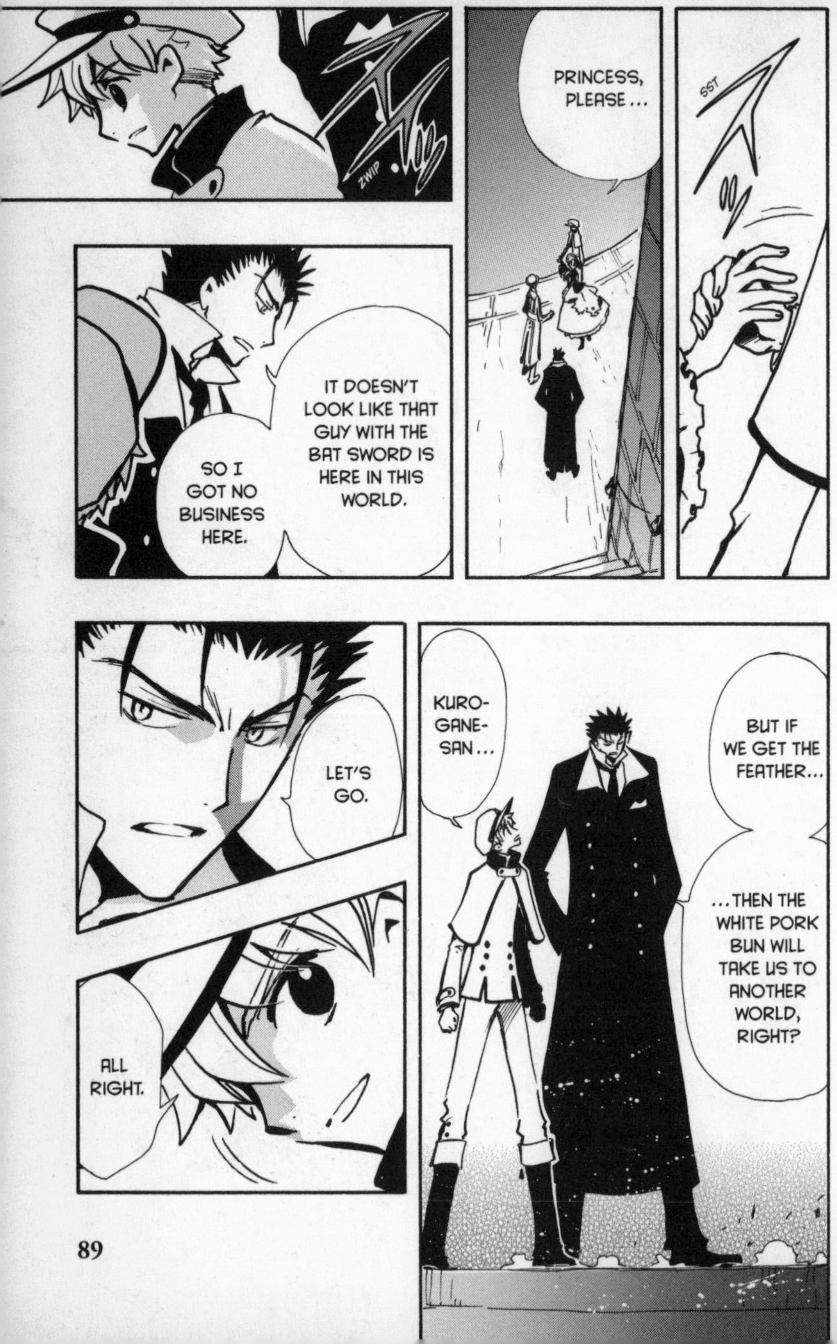

SST
PRINCESS, PLEASE...
ZWIP
IT DOESN'T LOOK LIKE THAT GUY WITH THE BAT SWORD IS HERE IN THIS WORLD.
SO I GOT NO BUSINESS HERE.
KURO-GANE-SAN...
BUT IF WE GET THE FEATHER...
...THEN THE WHITE PORK BUN WILL TAKE US TO ANOTHER WORLD, RIGHT?
LET'S GO.
ALL RIGHT.

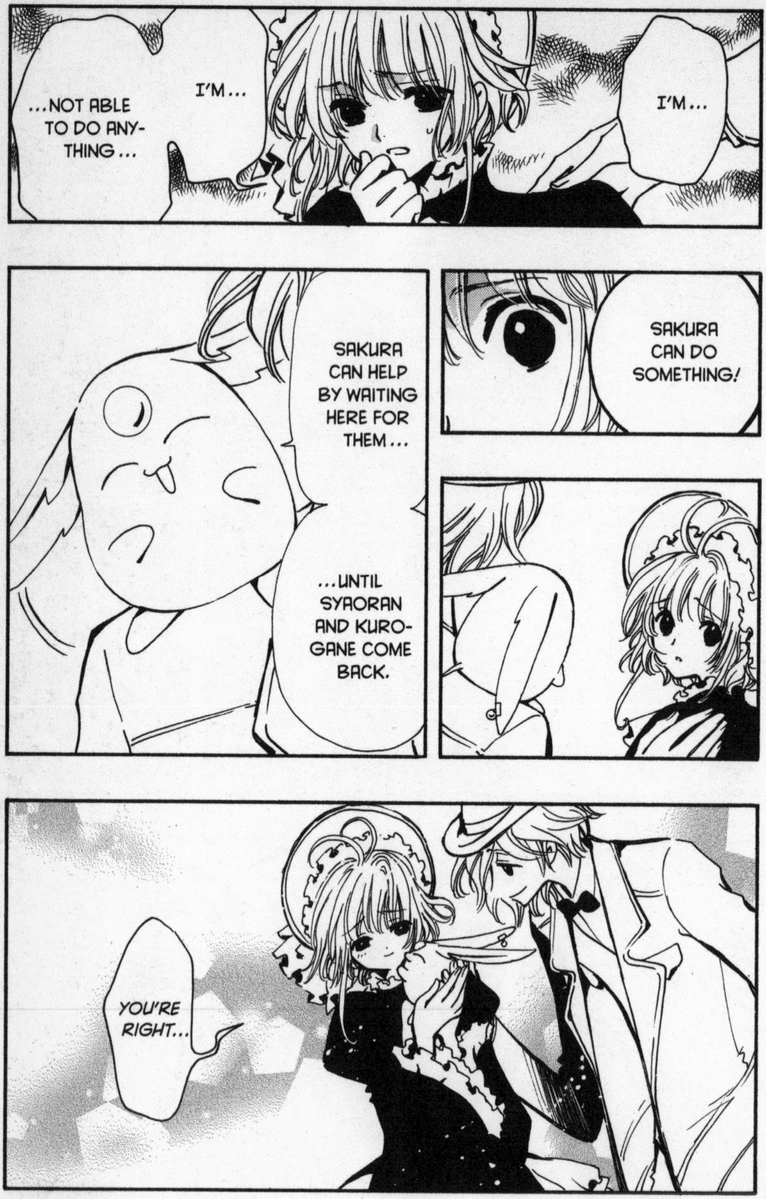
I'M...
I'M...
...NOT ABLE TO DO ANY-THING...
SAKURA CAN DO SOMETHING!
SAKURA CAN HELP BY WAITING HERE FOR THEM...
...UNTIL SYAORAN AND KURO-GANE COME BACK.
YOU'RE RIGHT...

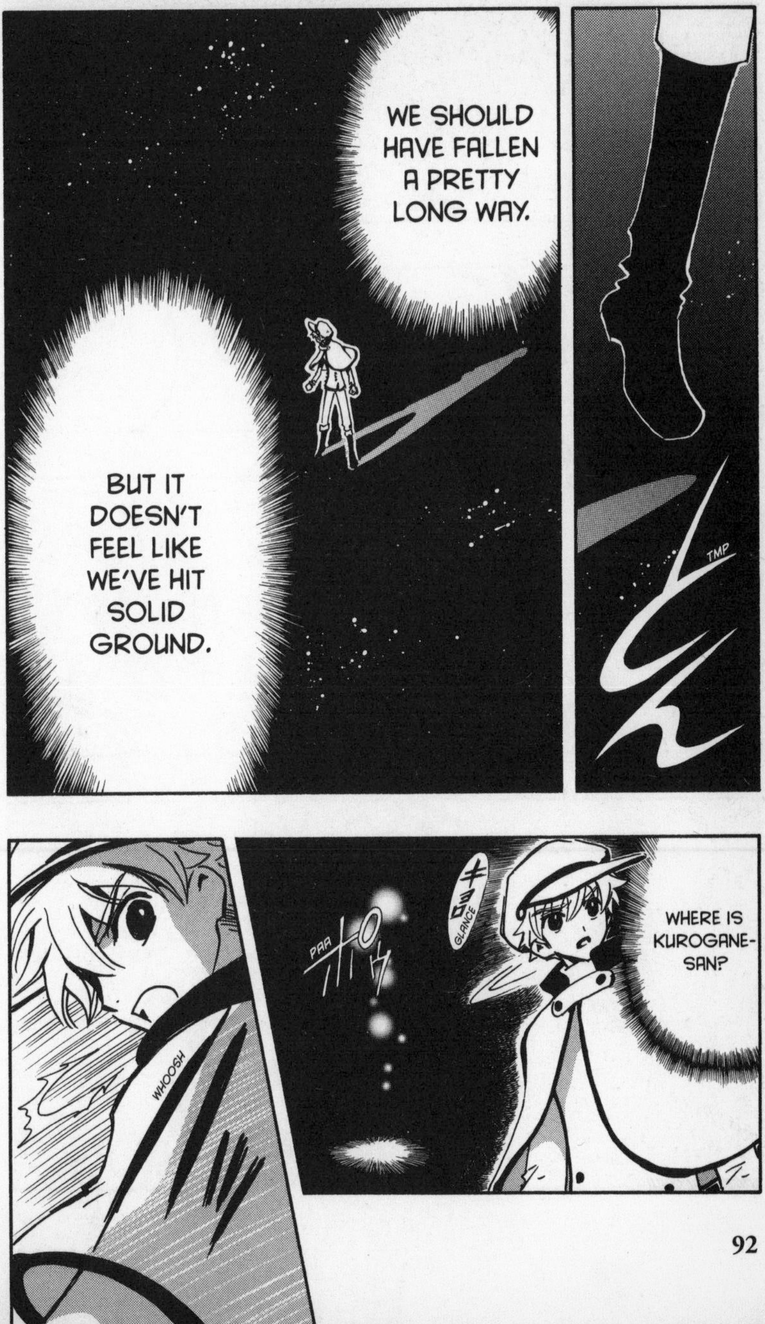
TMP
WE SHOULD HAVE FALLEN A PRETTY LONG WAY.
BUT IT DOESN'T FEEL LIKE WE'VE HIT SOLID GROUND.
WHERE IS KUROGANE-SAN?
GLANCE
PAA
WHOOSH

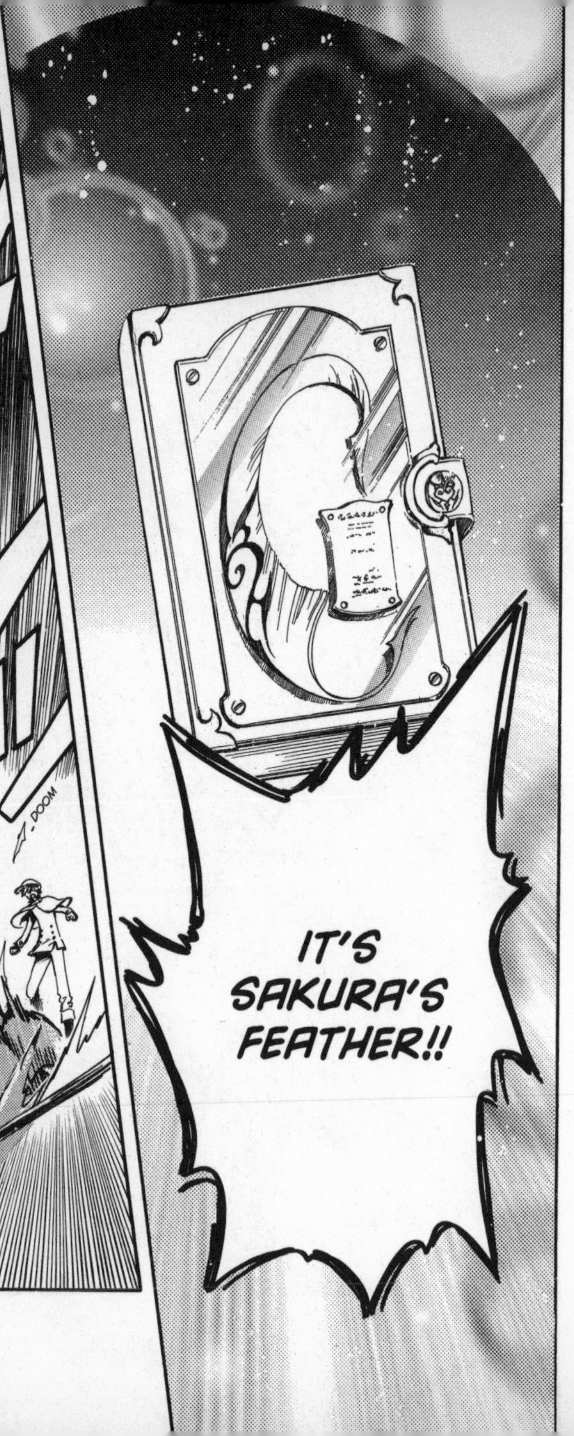
IT'S SAKURA'S FEATHER!!
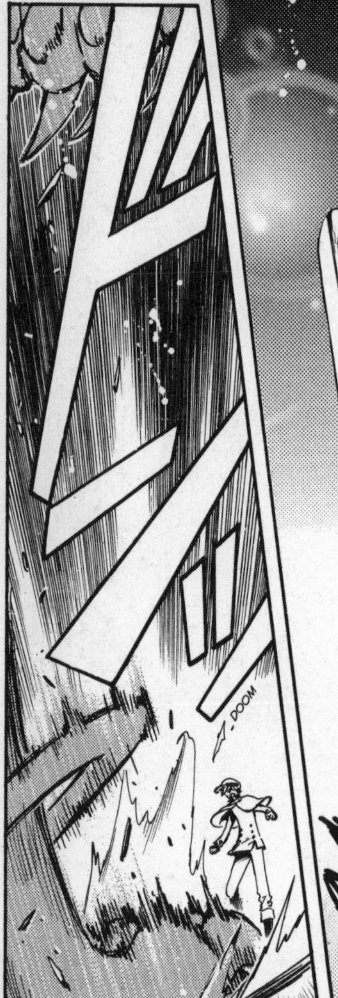
DOOM

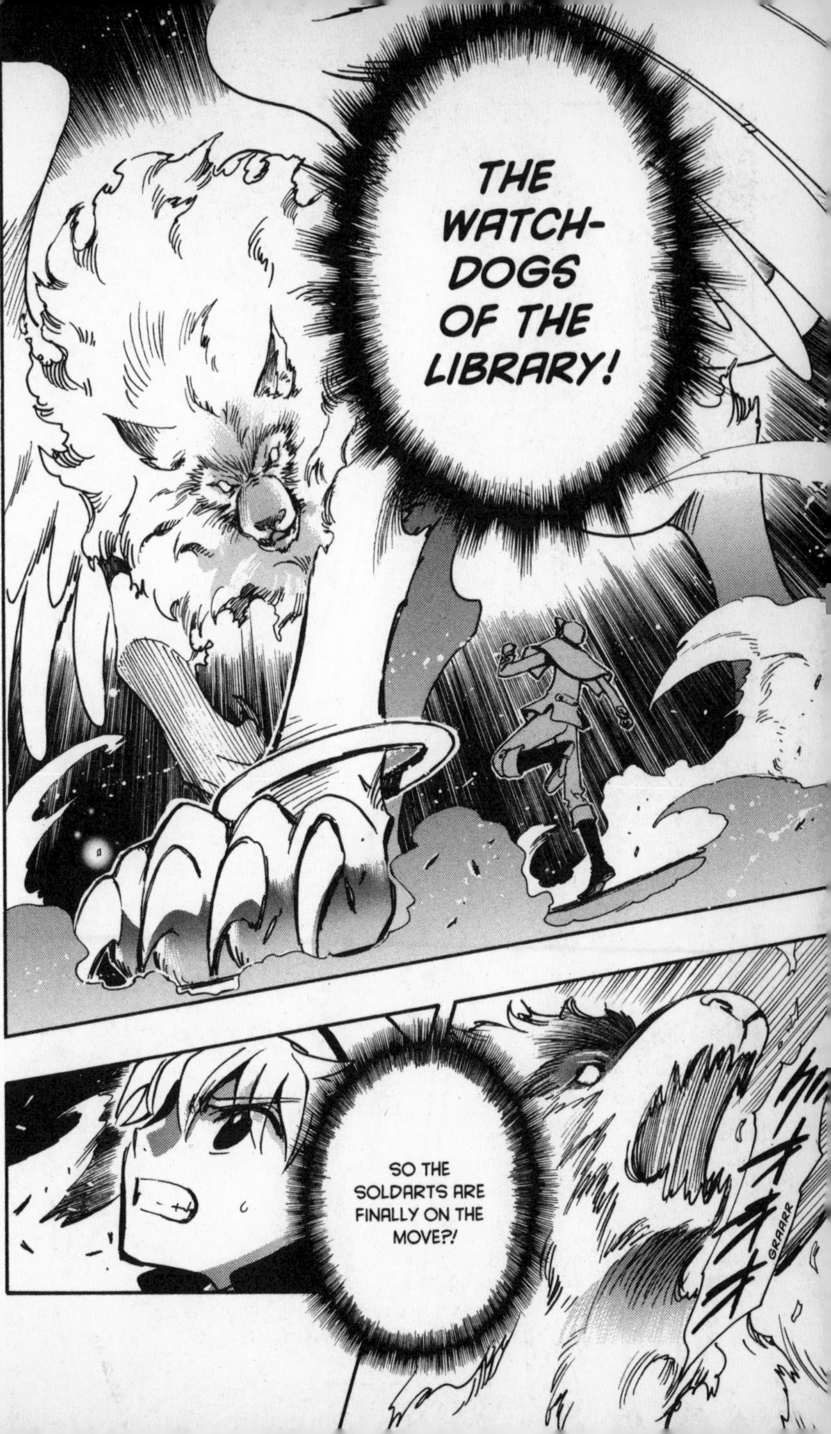
THE WATCH-DOGS OF THE LIBRARY!
GRAARR
SO THE SOLDARTS ARE FINALLY ON THE MOVE?!

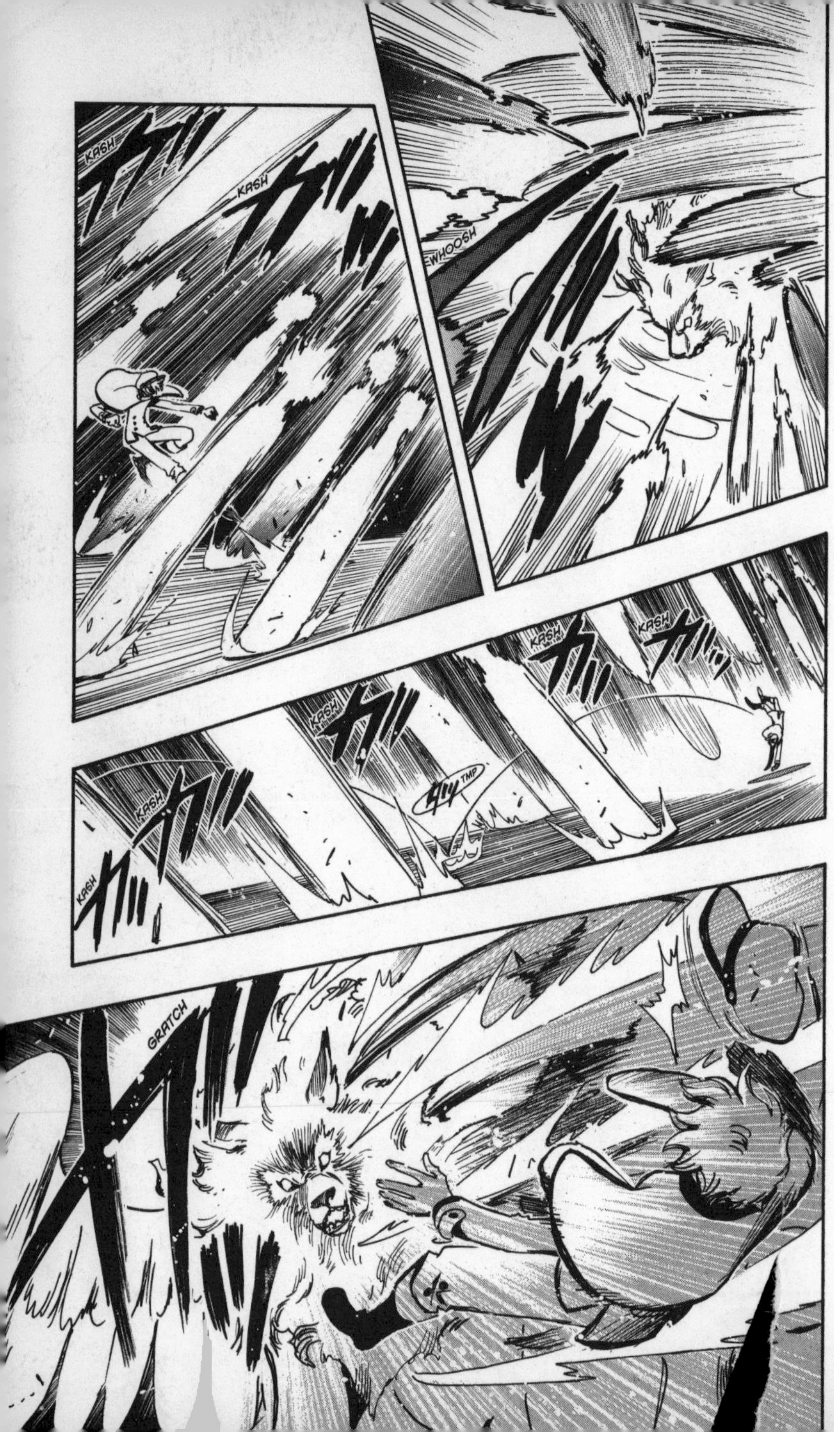
WHOOSH
KASH
KASH
KASH
KASH
KASH
TMP
KASH
KASH
GRATCH

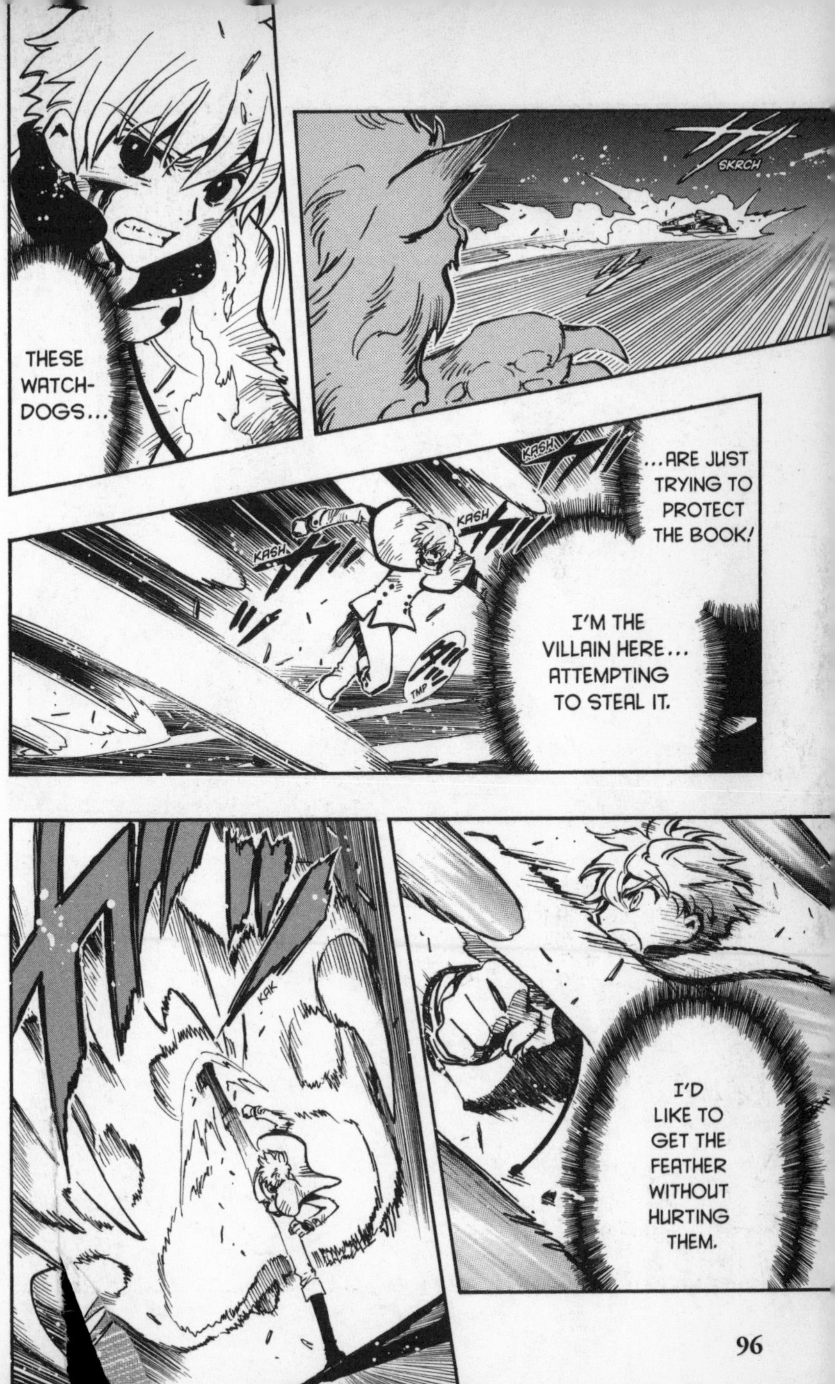
SKRCH
THESE WATCH-DOGS...
KASH
...ARE JUST TRYING TO PROTECT THE BOOK!
KASH
KASH
I'M THE VILLAIN HERE... ATTEMPTING TO STEAL IT.
TMP
I'D LIKE TO GET THE FEATHER WITHOUT HURTING THEM.
KAK

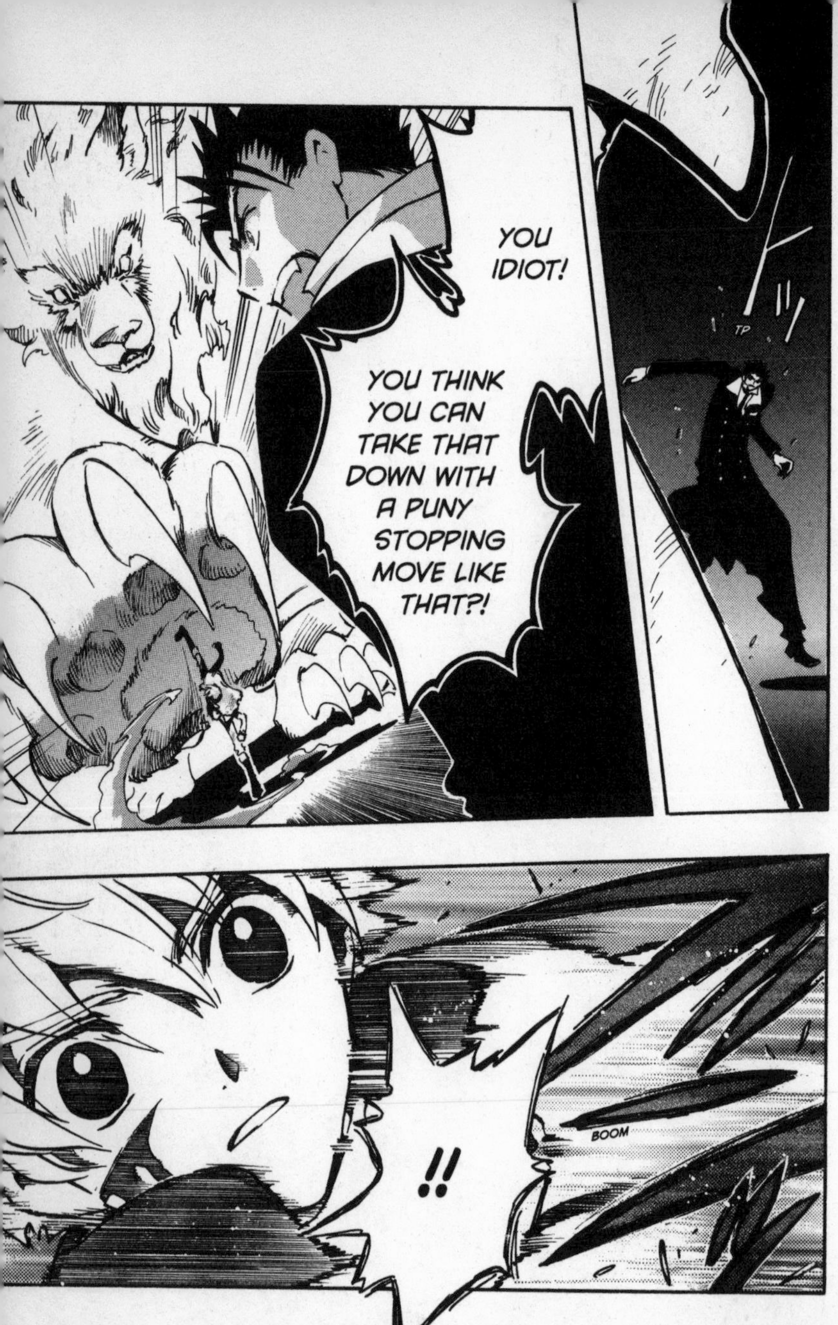
TP
YOU IDIOT!
YOU THINK YOU CAN TAKE THAT DOWN WITH A PUNY STOPPING MOVE LIKE THAT?!
BOOM
!!

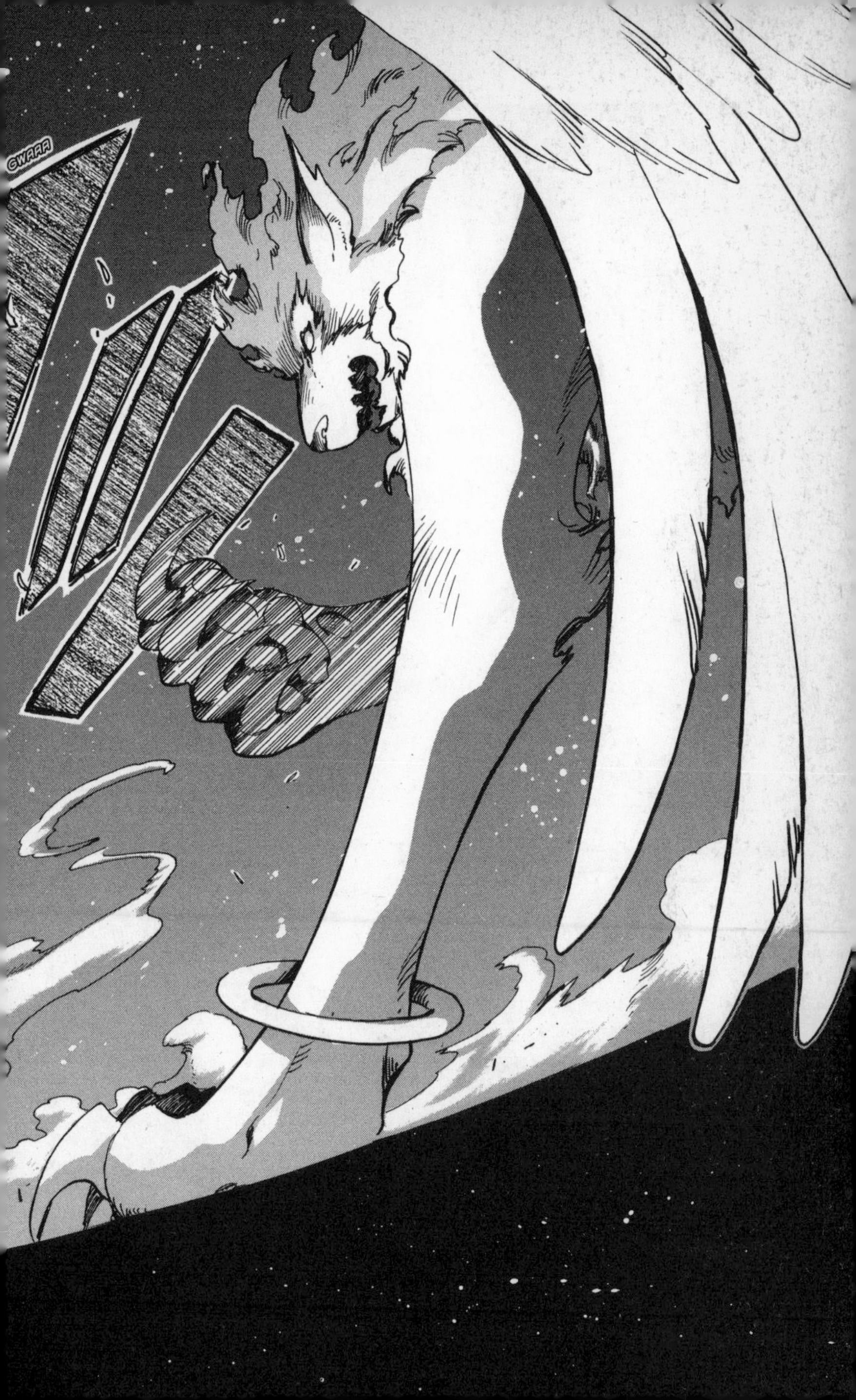
GWAAA

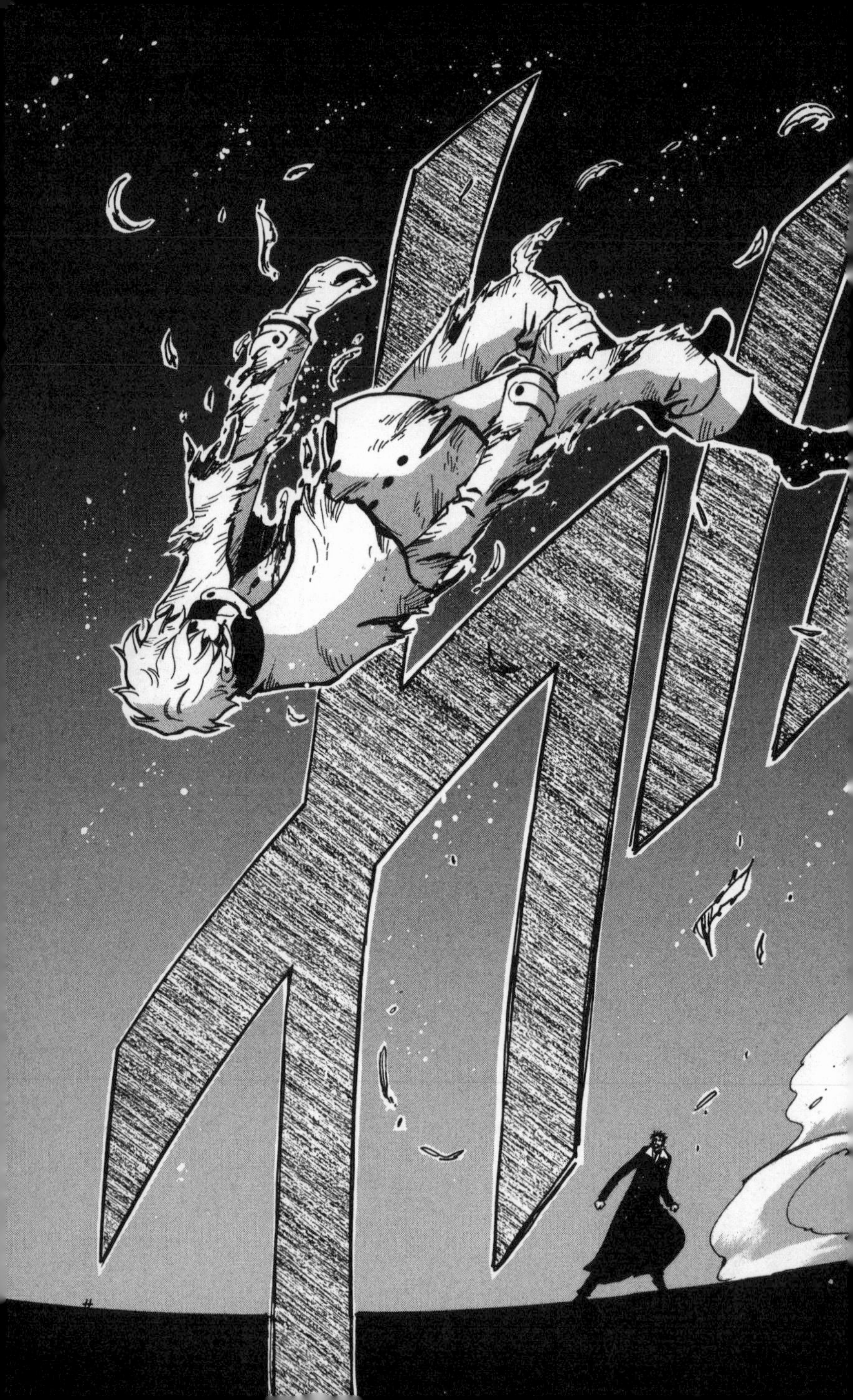

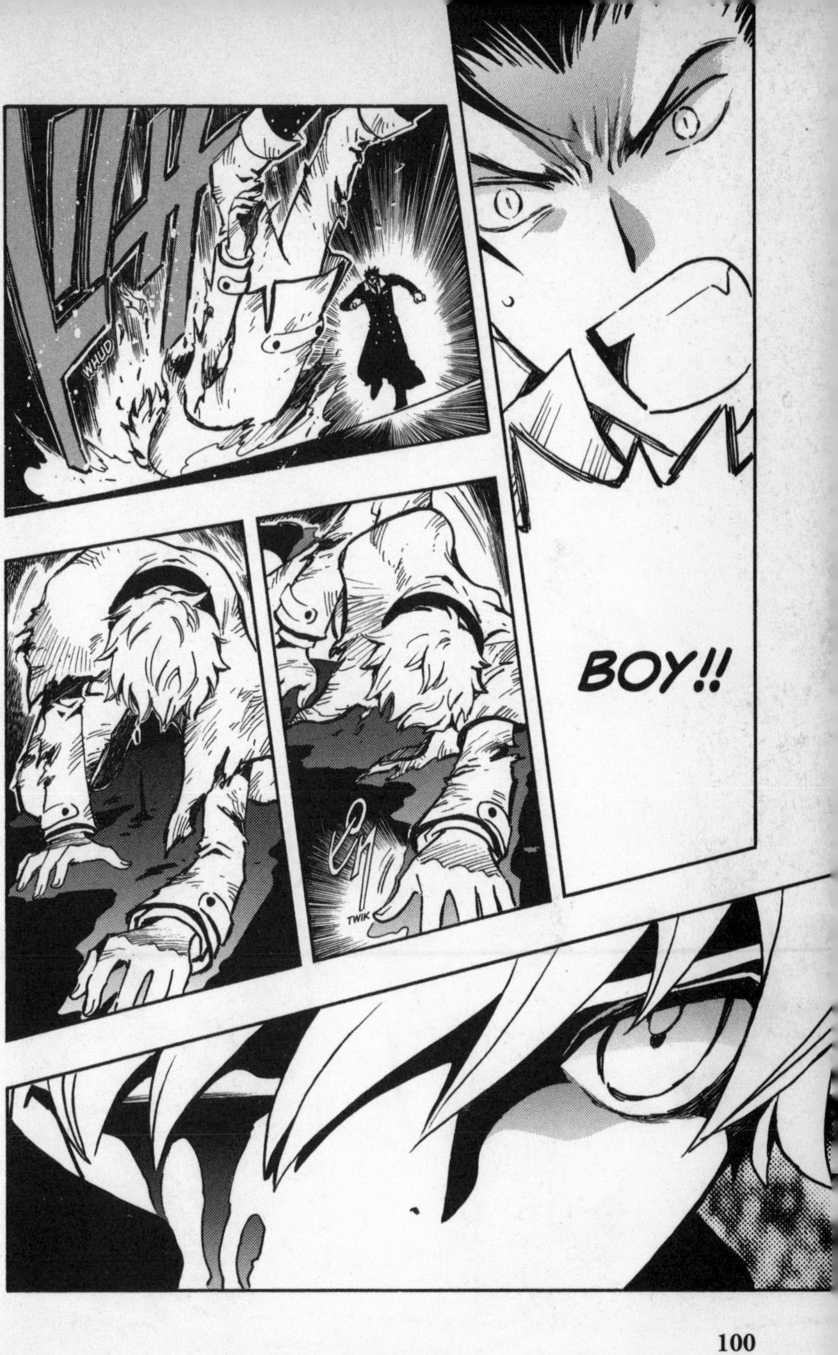
BOY!!
WHUD
TWIK

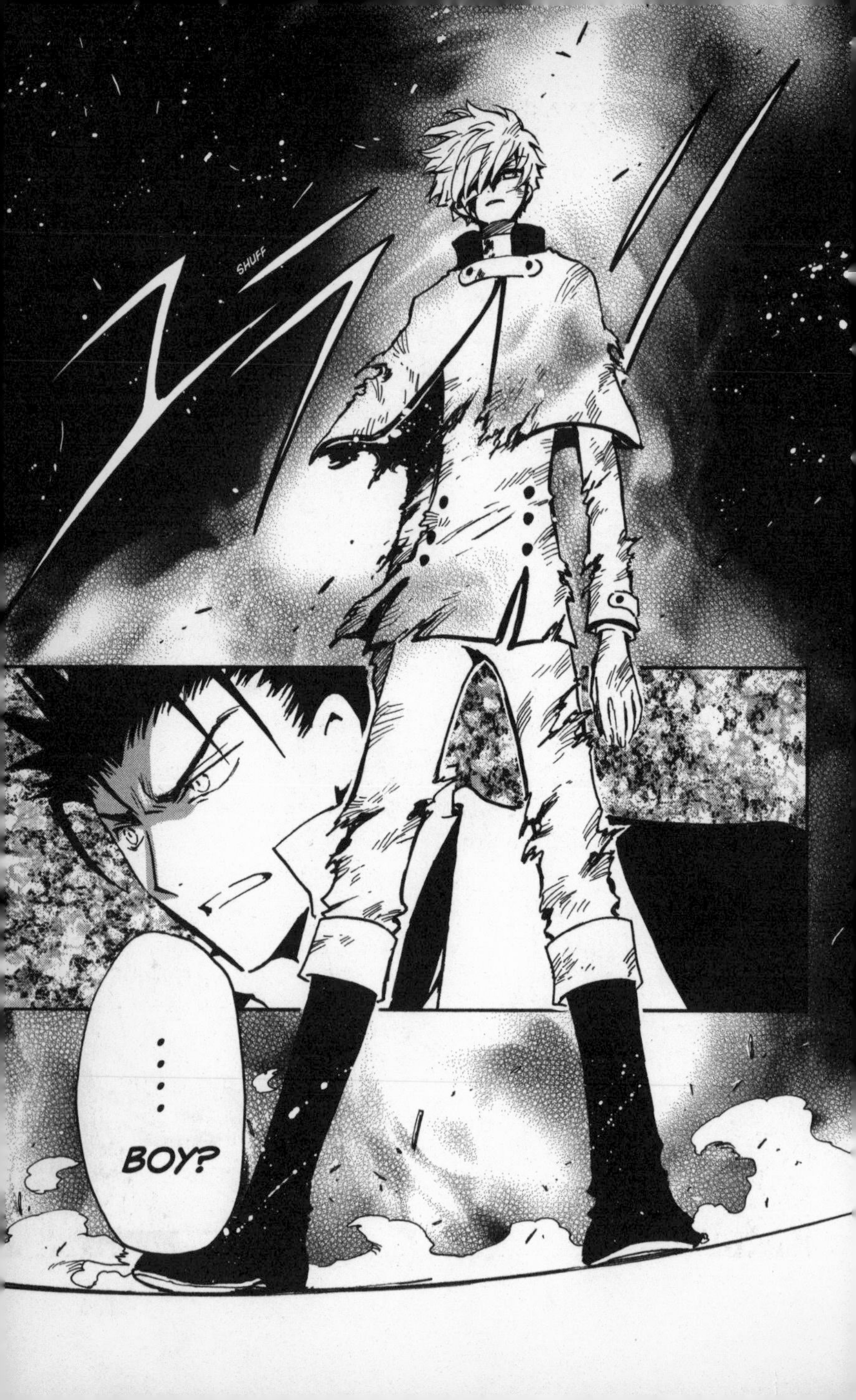
SHUFF
....
BOY?

ツバサ
RESERVoir CHRoNiCLE

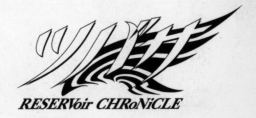

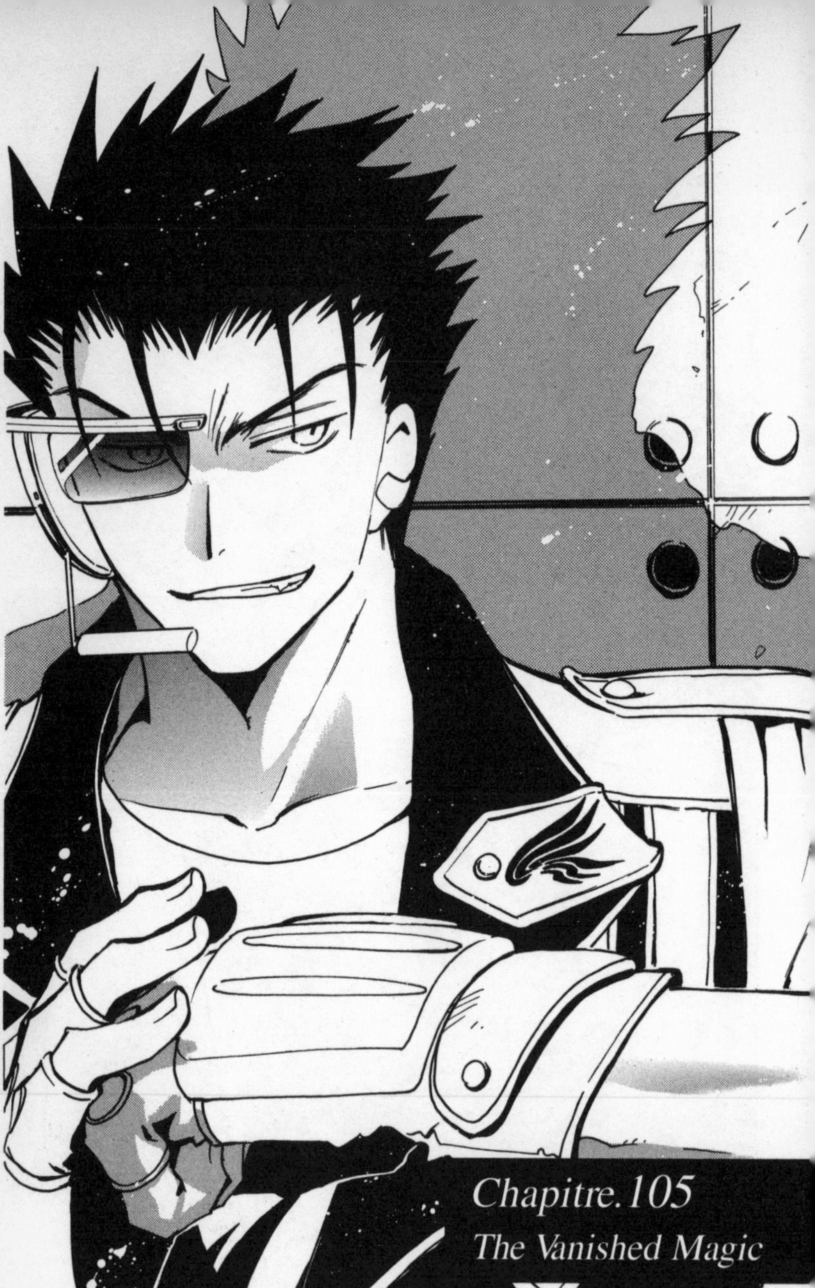
Chapitre. 105
The Vanished Magic

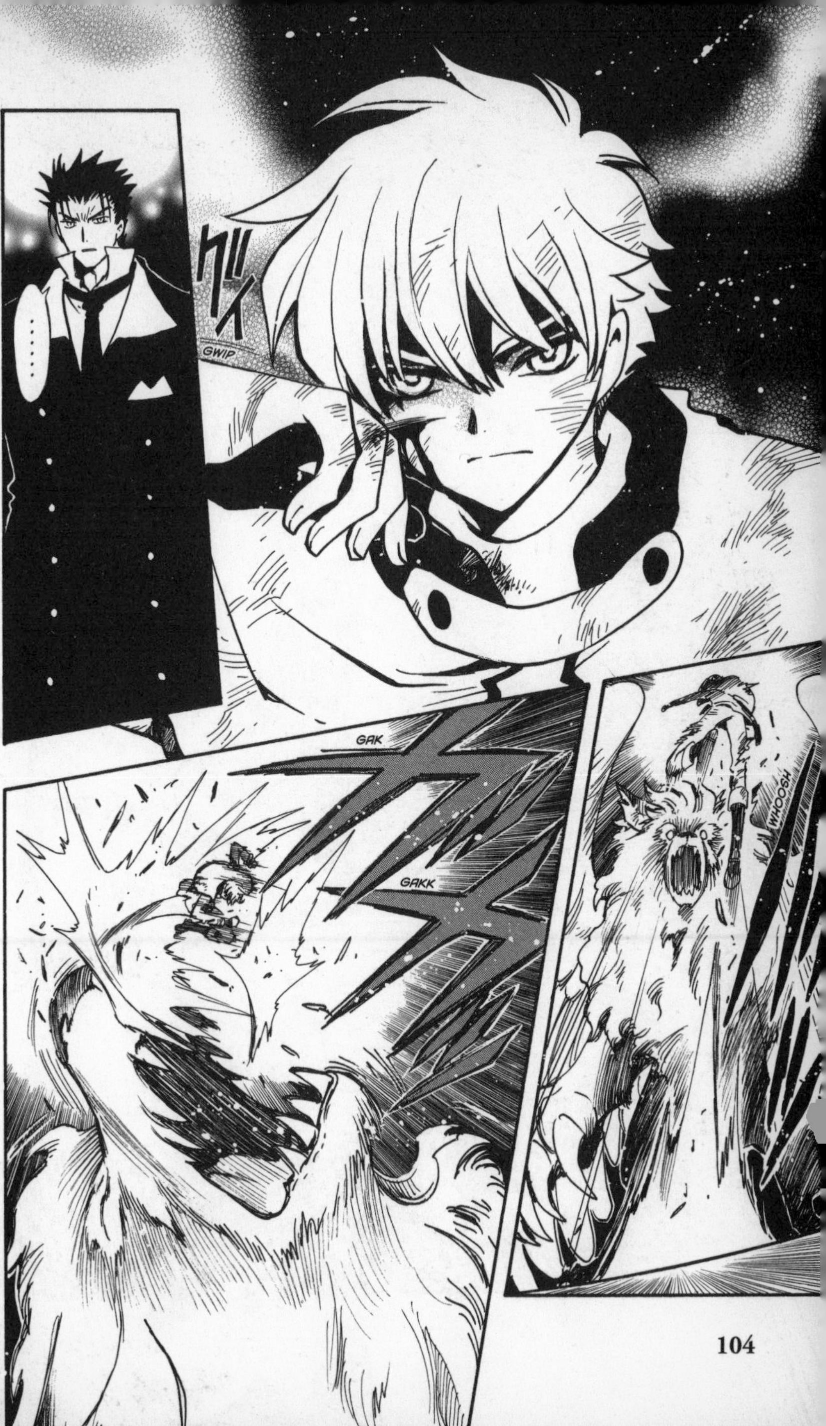
グイ
GWIP
......
WHOOSH
GAK
GAKK

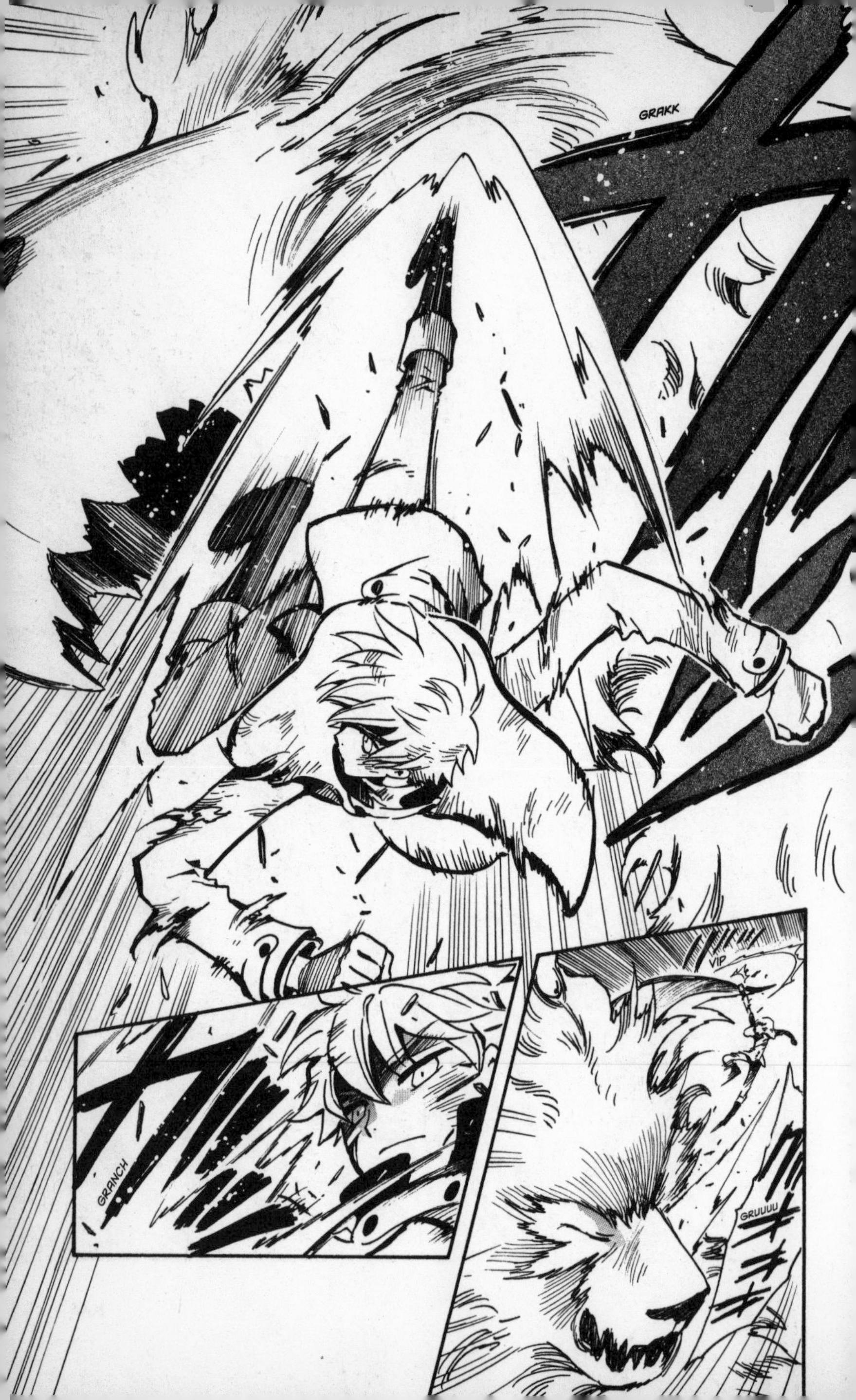
GRAKK
VIP
GRUUUU
GRANCH

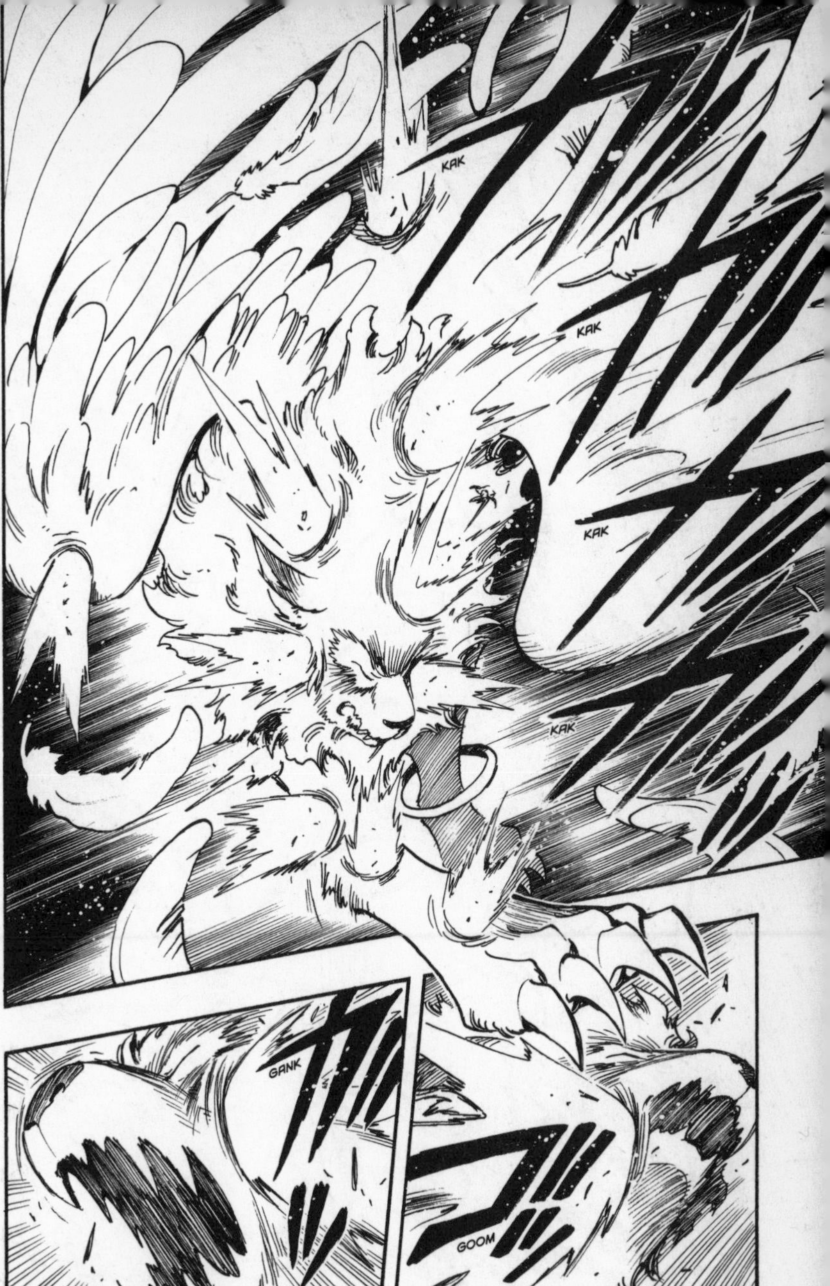
KAK
KAK
KAK
KAK
GOOM
GANK

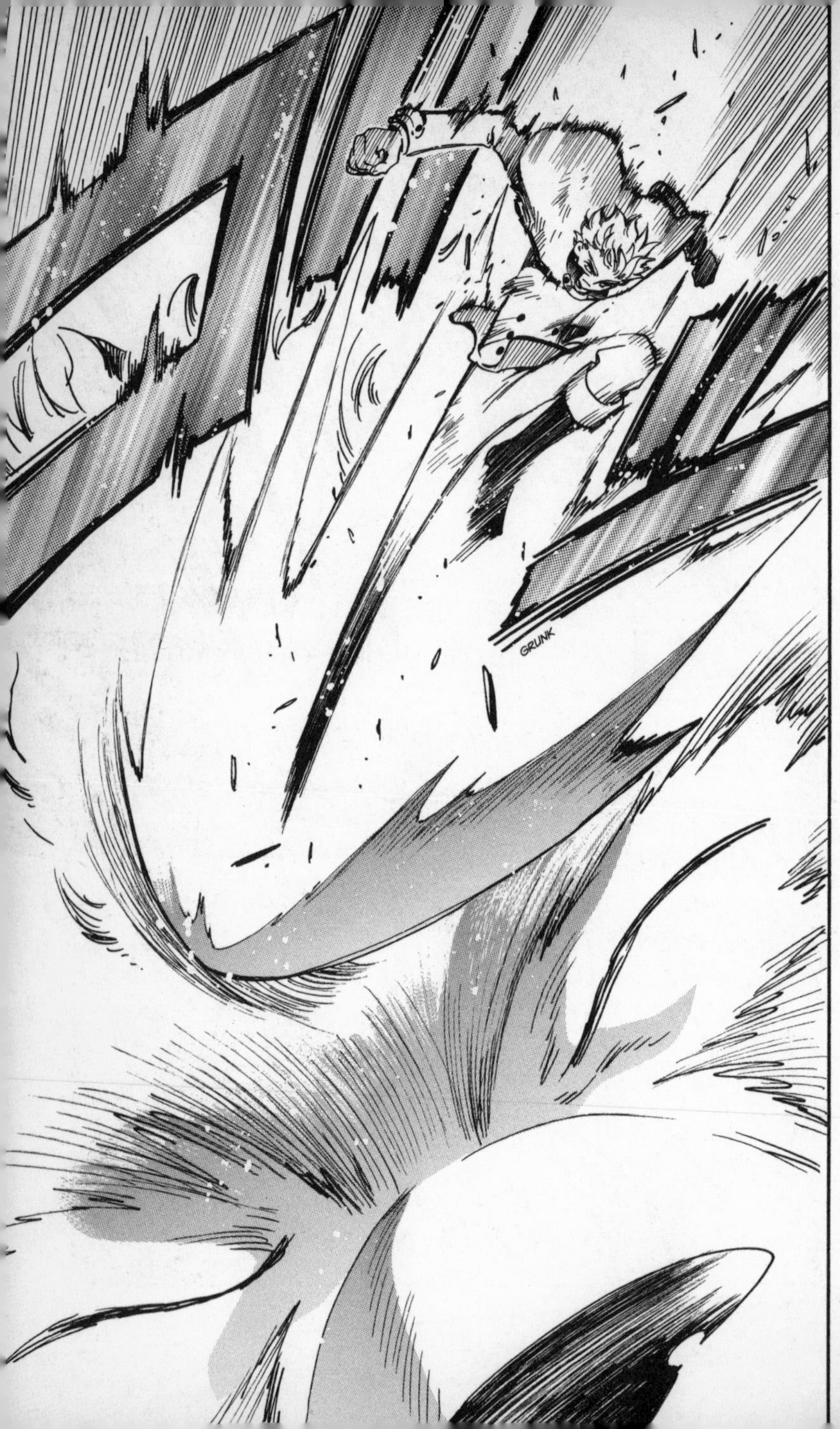
GRUNK

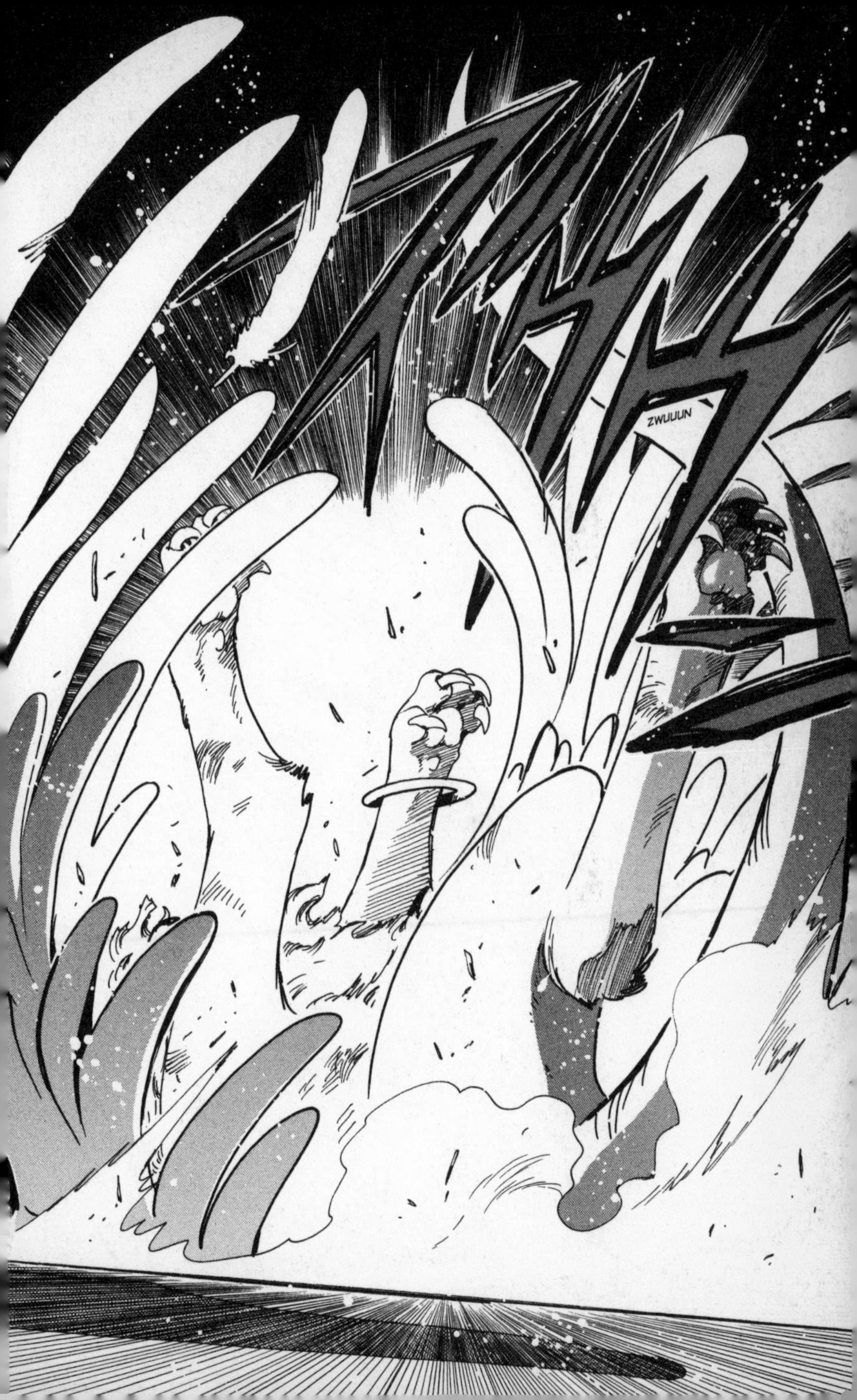
ZWUUUN

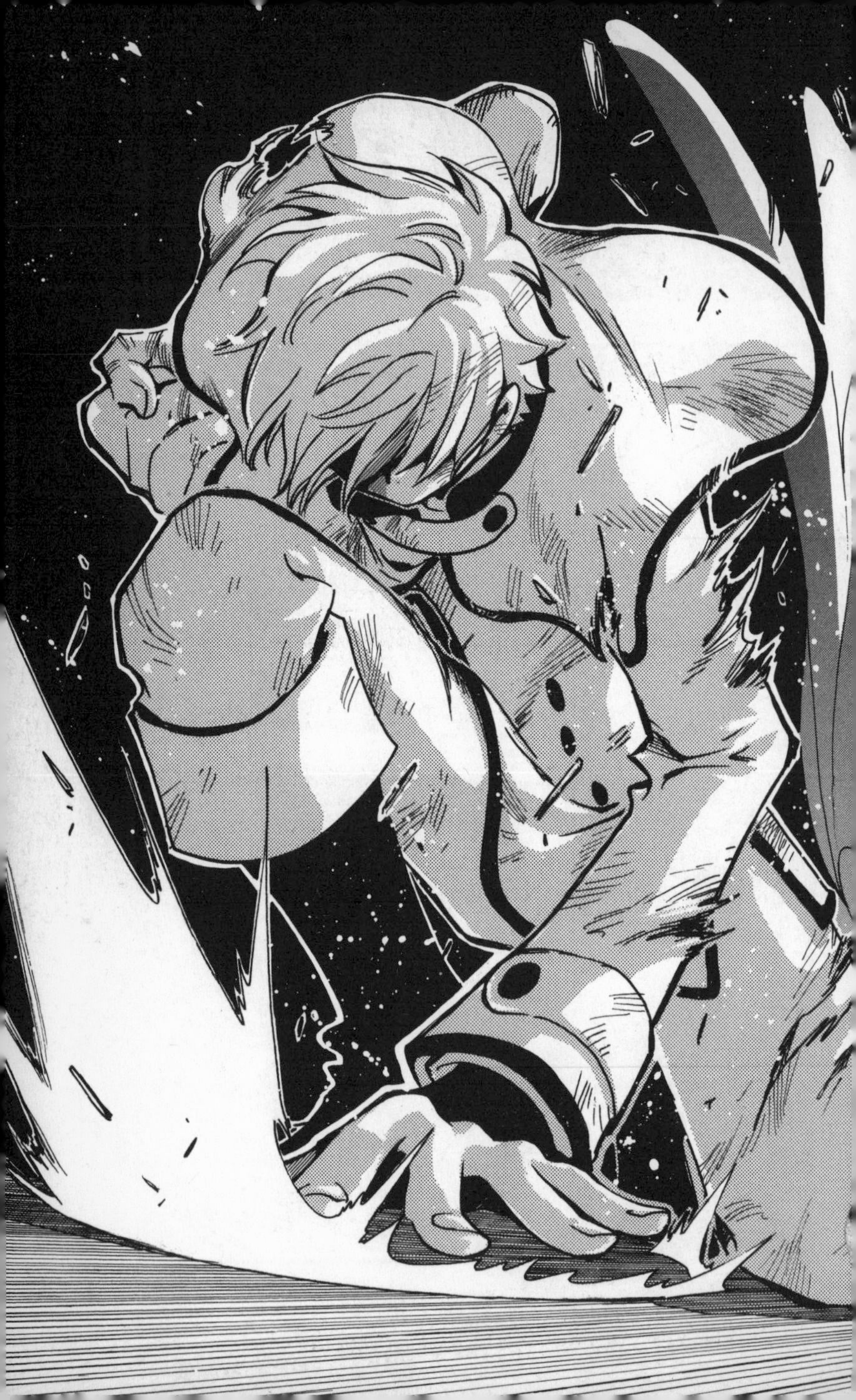

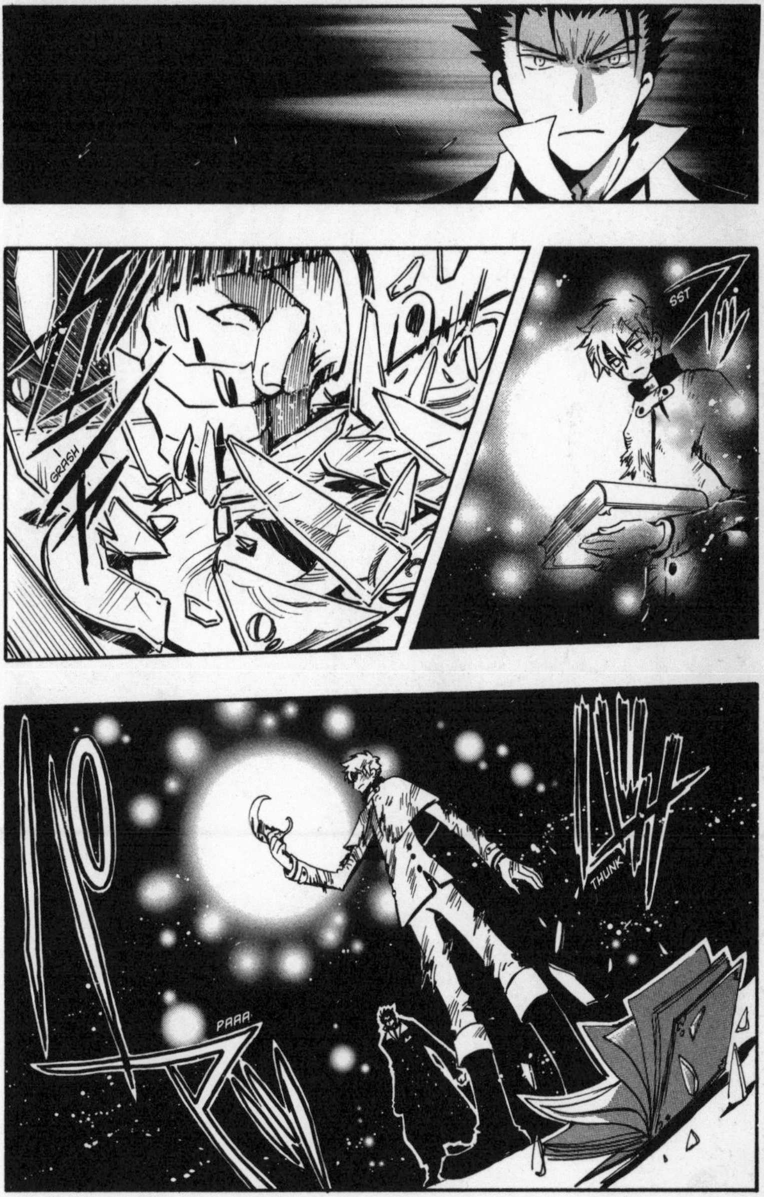
SST
CRASH
THUNK
PAAA

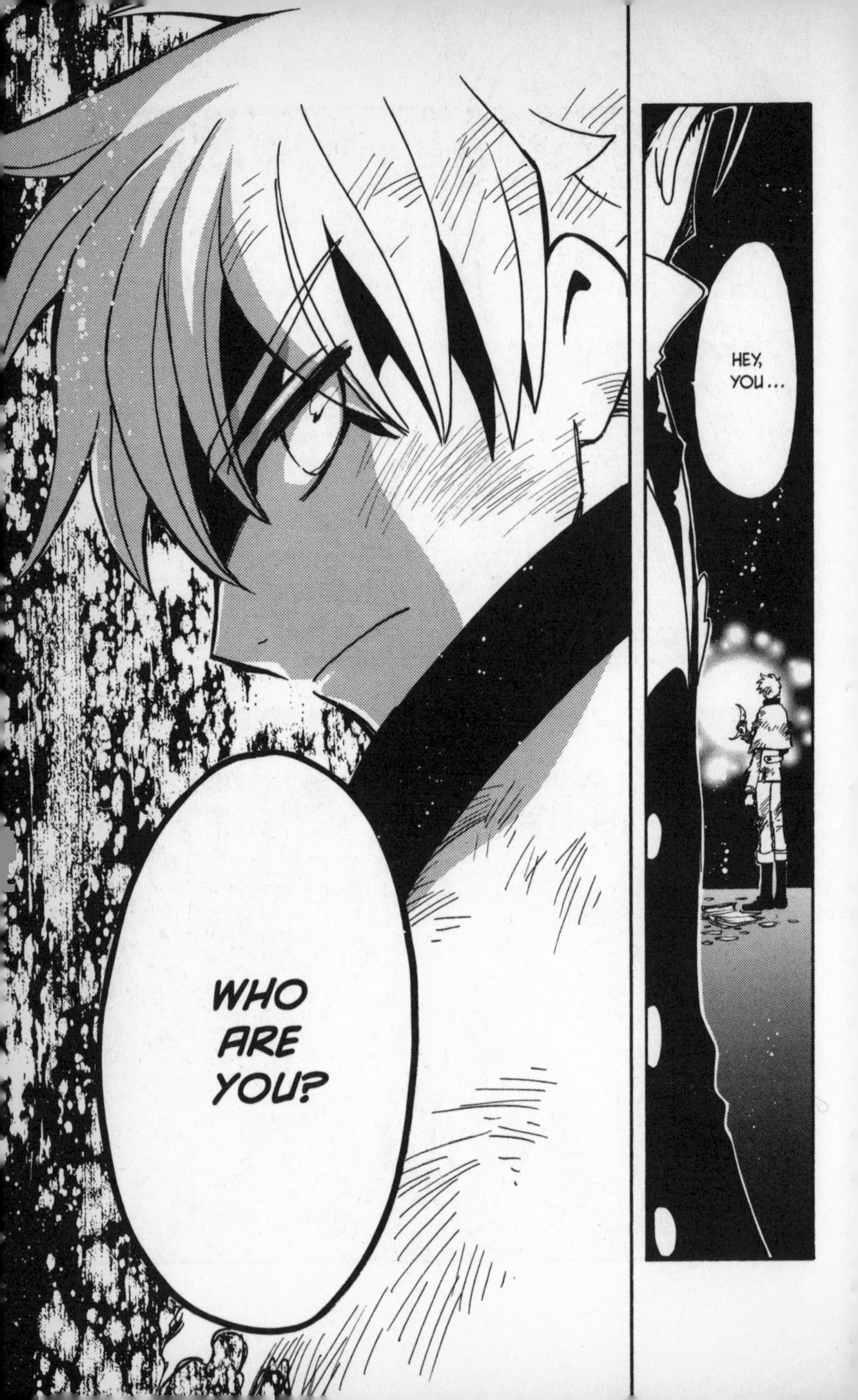
HEY, YOU...
WHO ARE YOU?

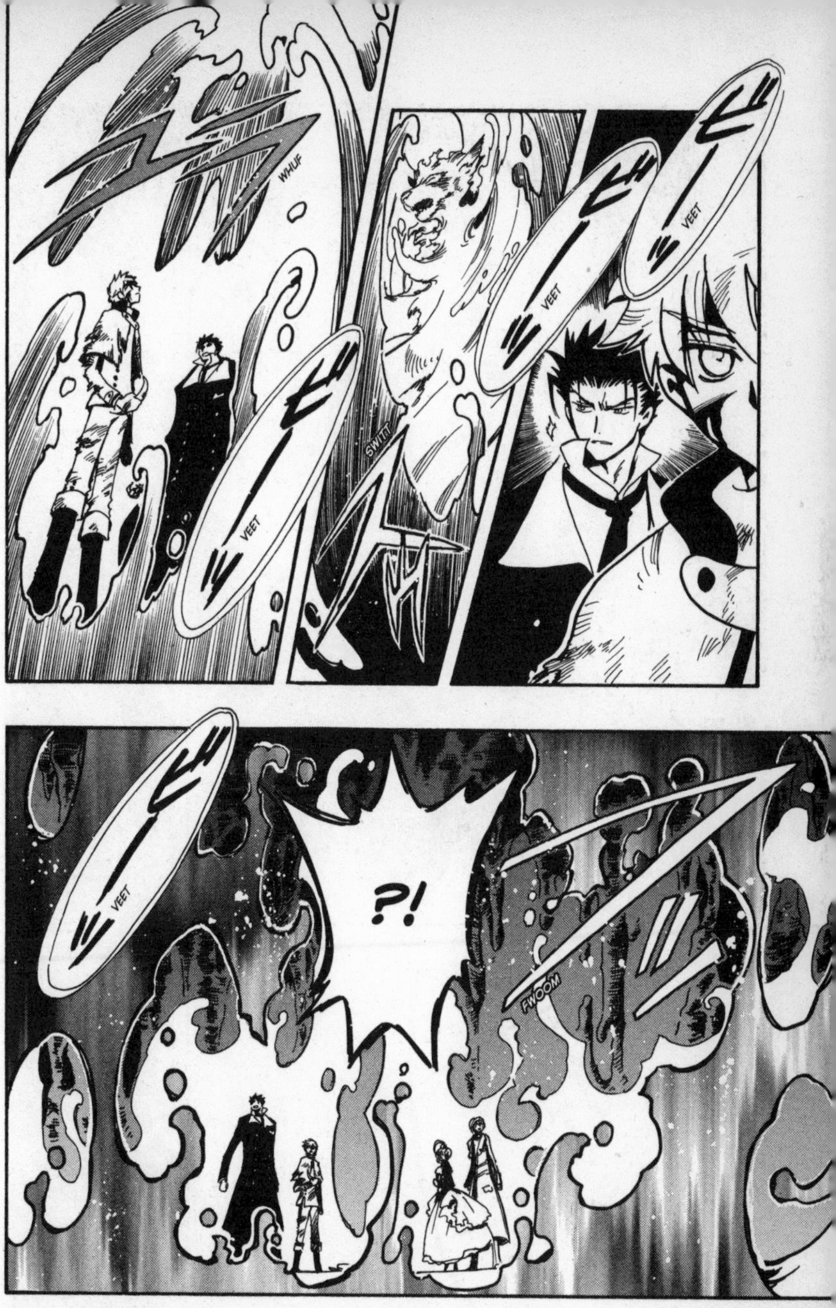
VEET
VEET
SWITT
WHUF
VEET
FWOOM
?!
VEET

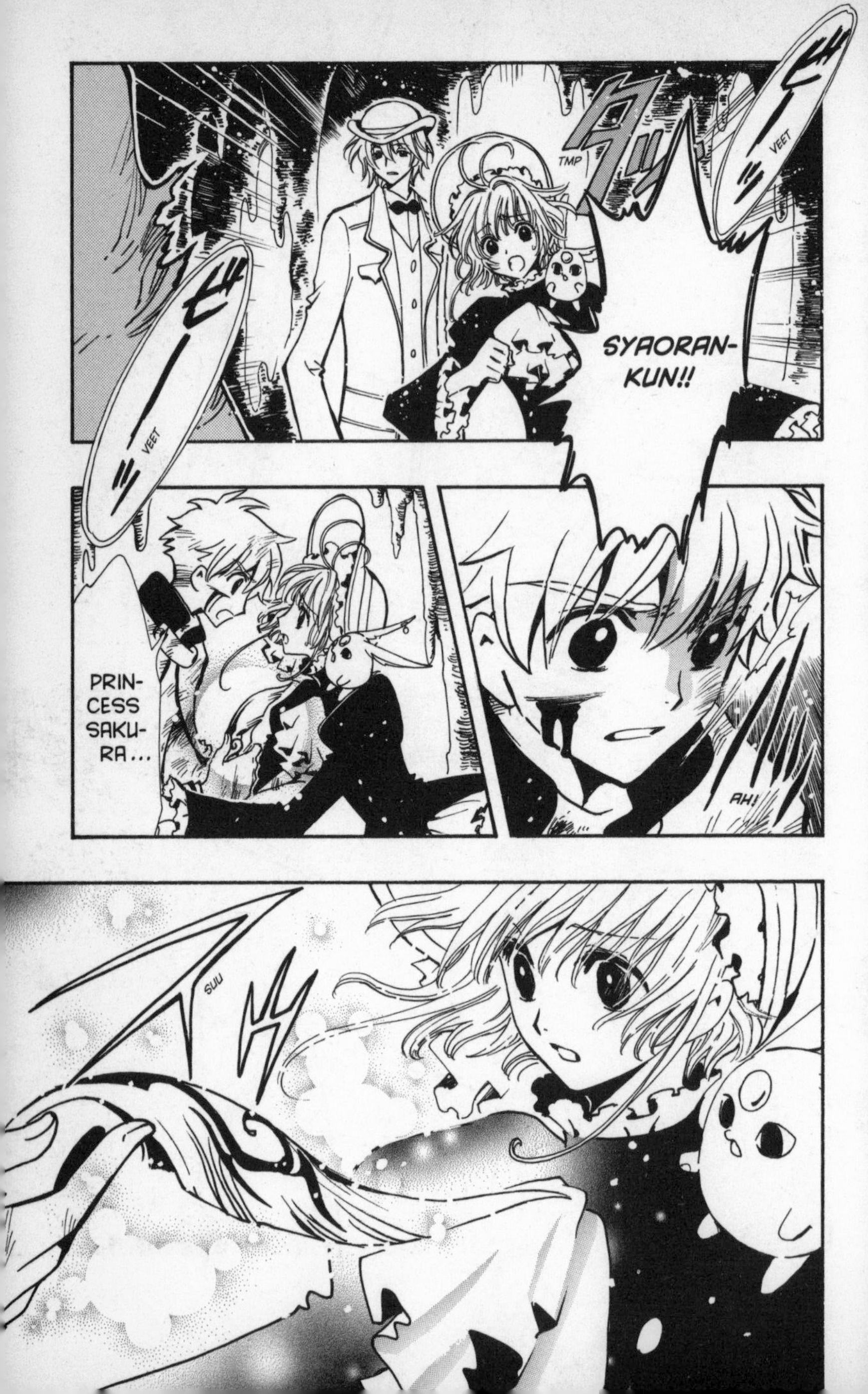
VEET
TMP
SYAORAN-KUN!!
VEET
AH!
PRINCESS SAKURA...
SUU

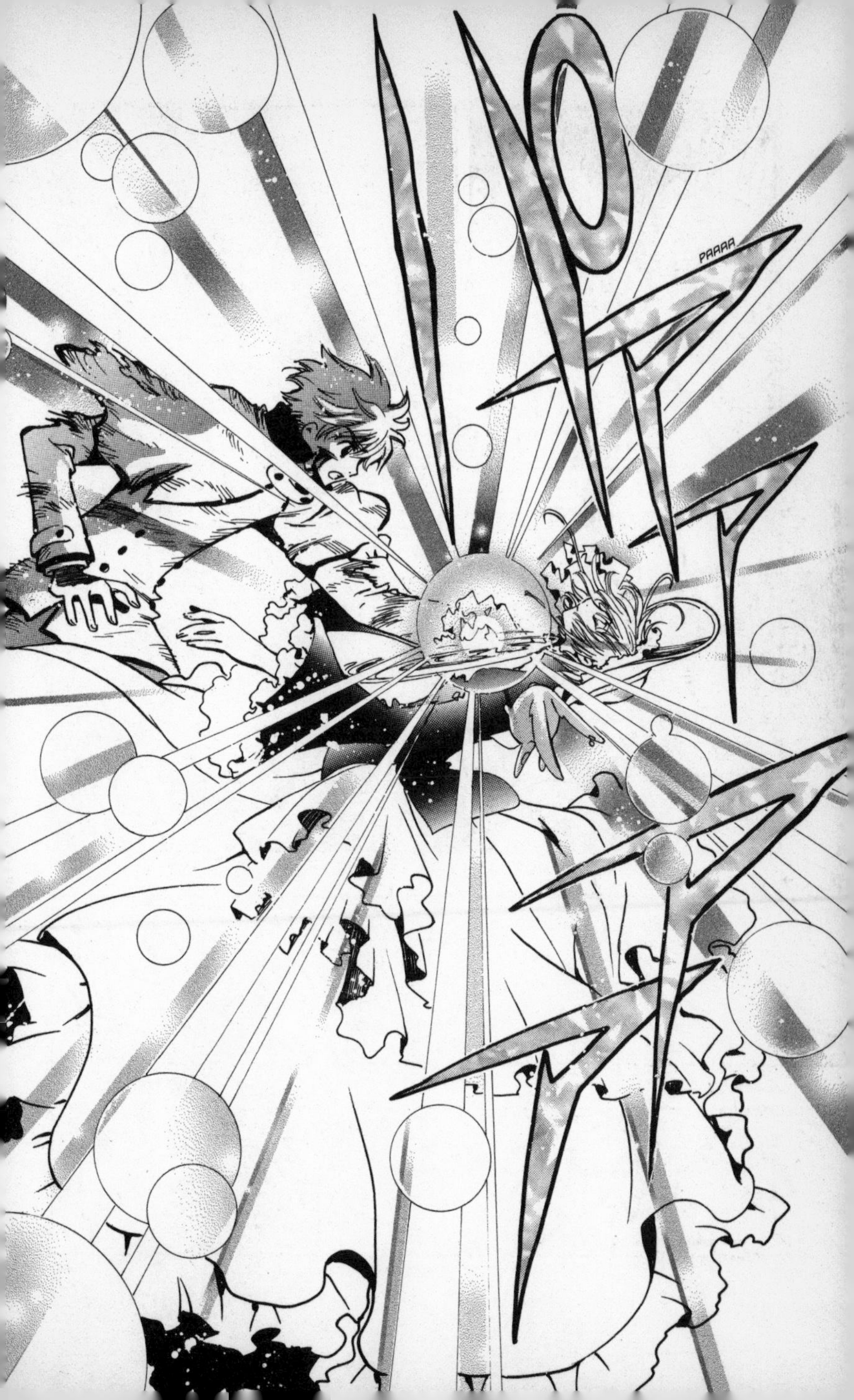
PAAAA

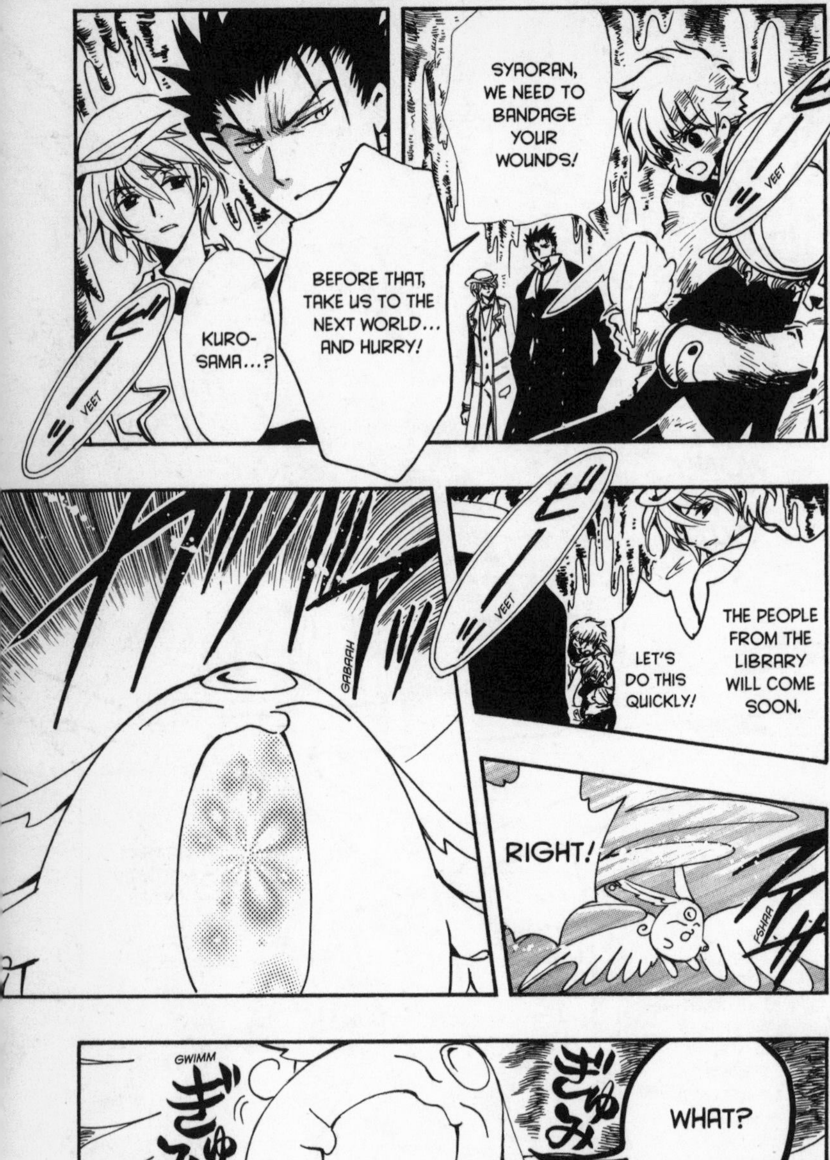
SYAORAN, WE NEED TO BANDAGE YOUR WOUNDS!
VEET
BEFORE THAT, TAKE US TO THE NEXT WORLD... AND HURRY!
KURO-SAMA...?
VEET
THE PEOPLE FROM THE LIBRARY WILL COME SOON.
LET'S DO THIS QUICKLY!
VEET
FSHAA
RIGHT!
GABAAH
WHAT?
ぎゅみ
GWIMM
ぎゅみ
GWIMM

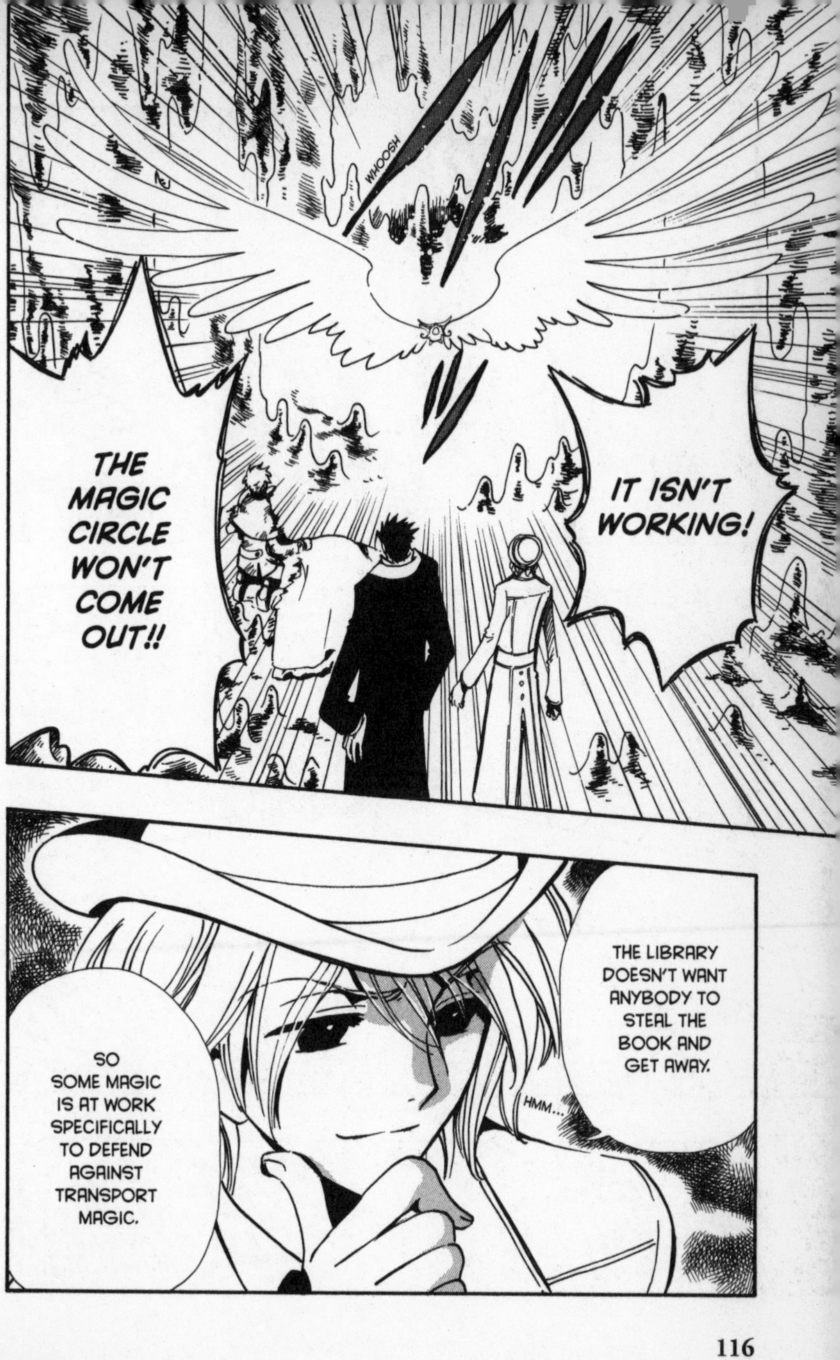
WHOOSH
IT ISN'T WORKING!
THE MAGIC CIRCLE WON'T COME OUT!!
THE LIBRARY DOESN'T WANT ANYBODY TO STEAL THE BOOK AND GET AWAY.
HMM...
SO SOME MAGIC IS AT WORK SPECIFICALLY TO DEFEND AGAINST TRANSPORT MAGIC.

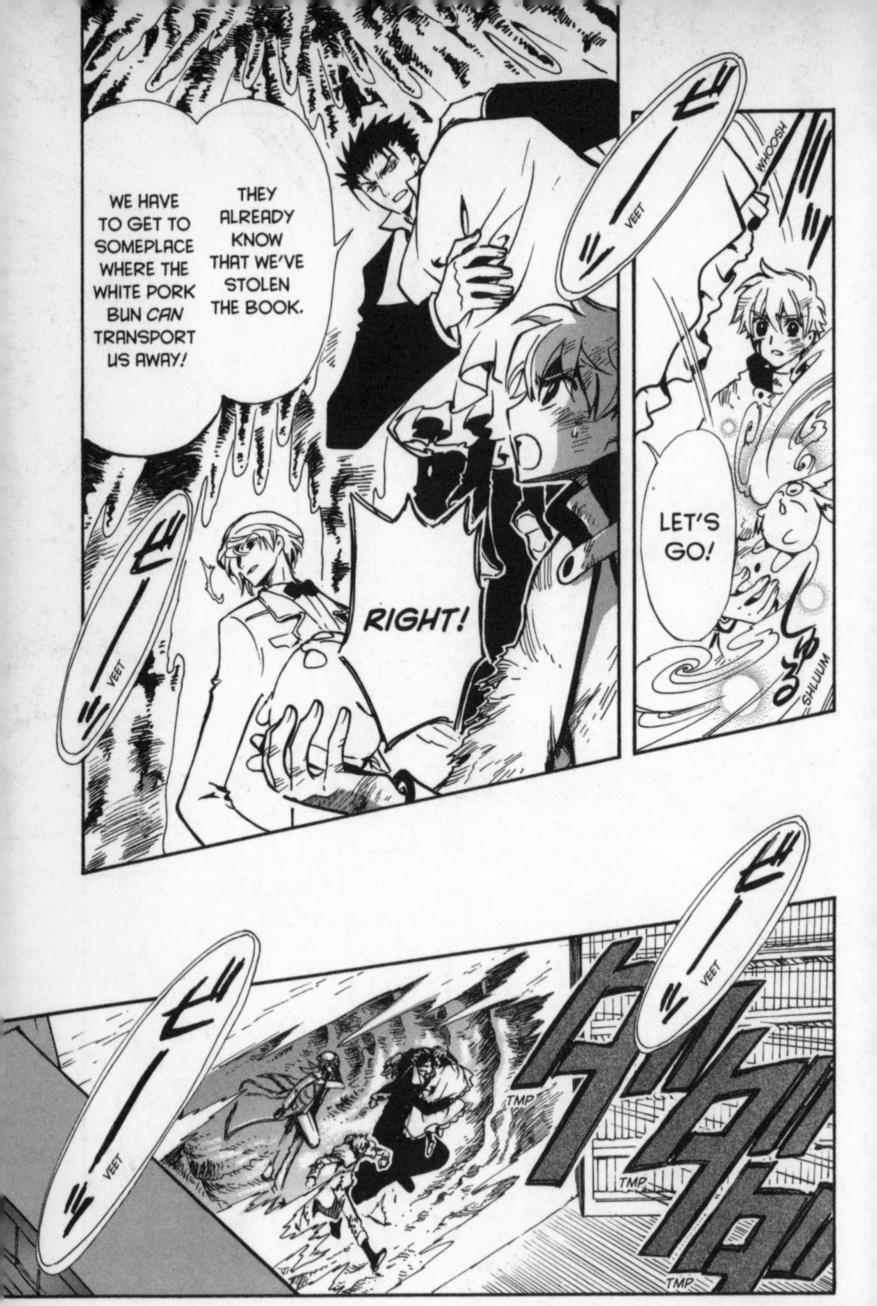
WHOOSH
VEET
LET'S GO!
SHLUUM
THEY ALREADY KNOW THAT WE'VE STOLEN THE BOOK.
WE HAVE TO GET TO SOMEPLACE WHERE THE WHITE PORK BUN *CAN* TRANSPORT US AWAY!
RIGHT!
VEET
VEET
TMP
TMP
TMP
VEET

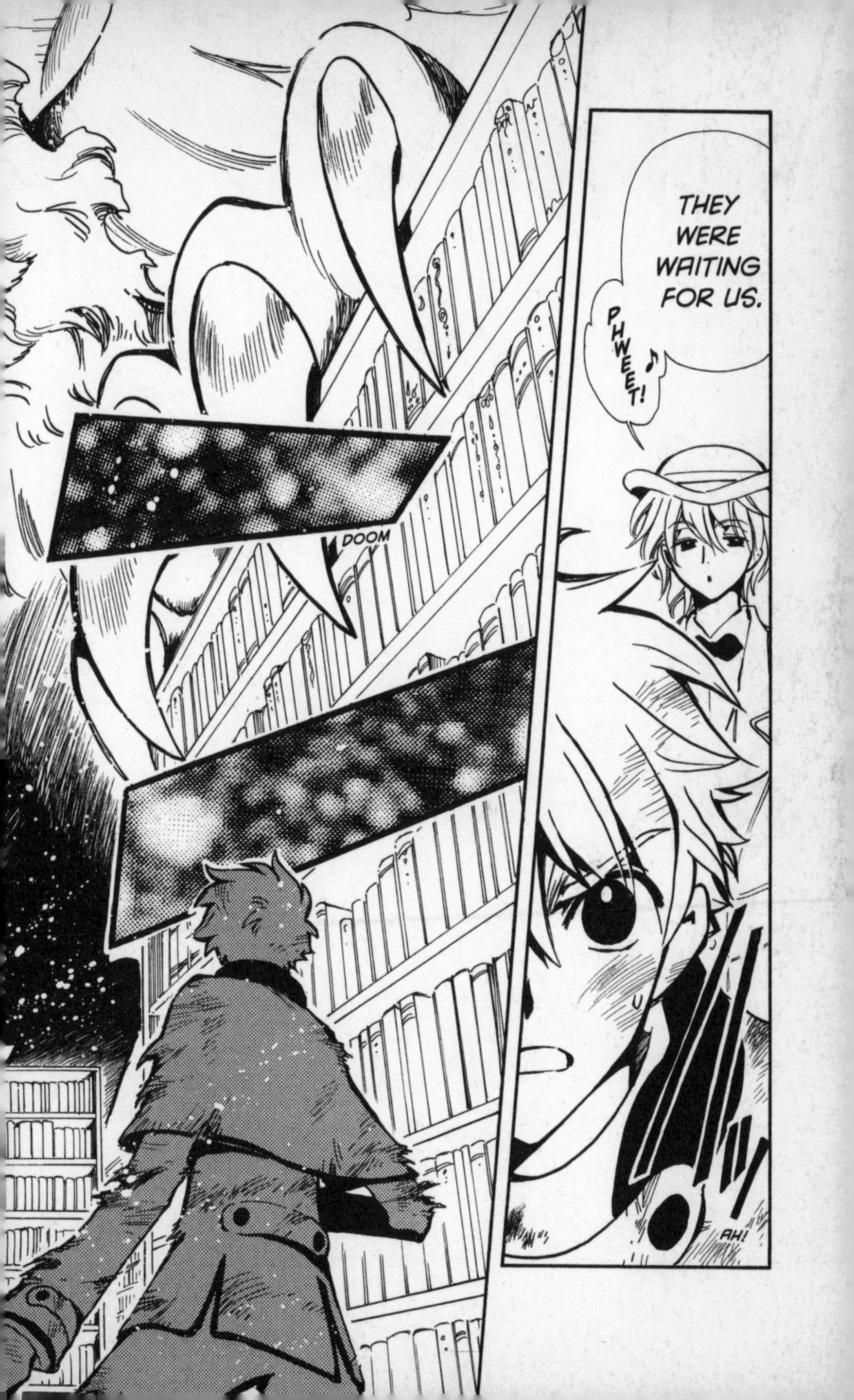
THEY WERE WAITING FOR US.
PHWEET! ♪
AH!
DOOM

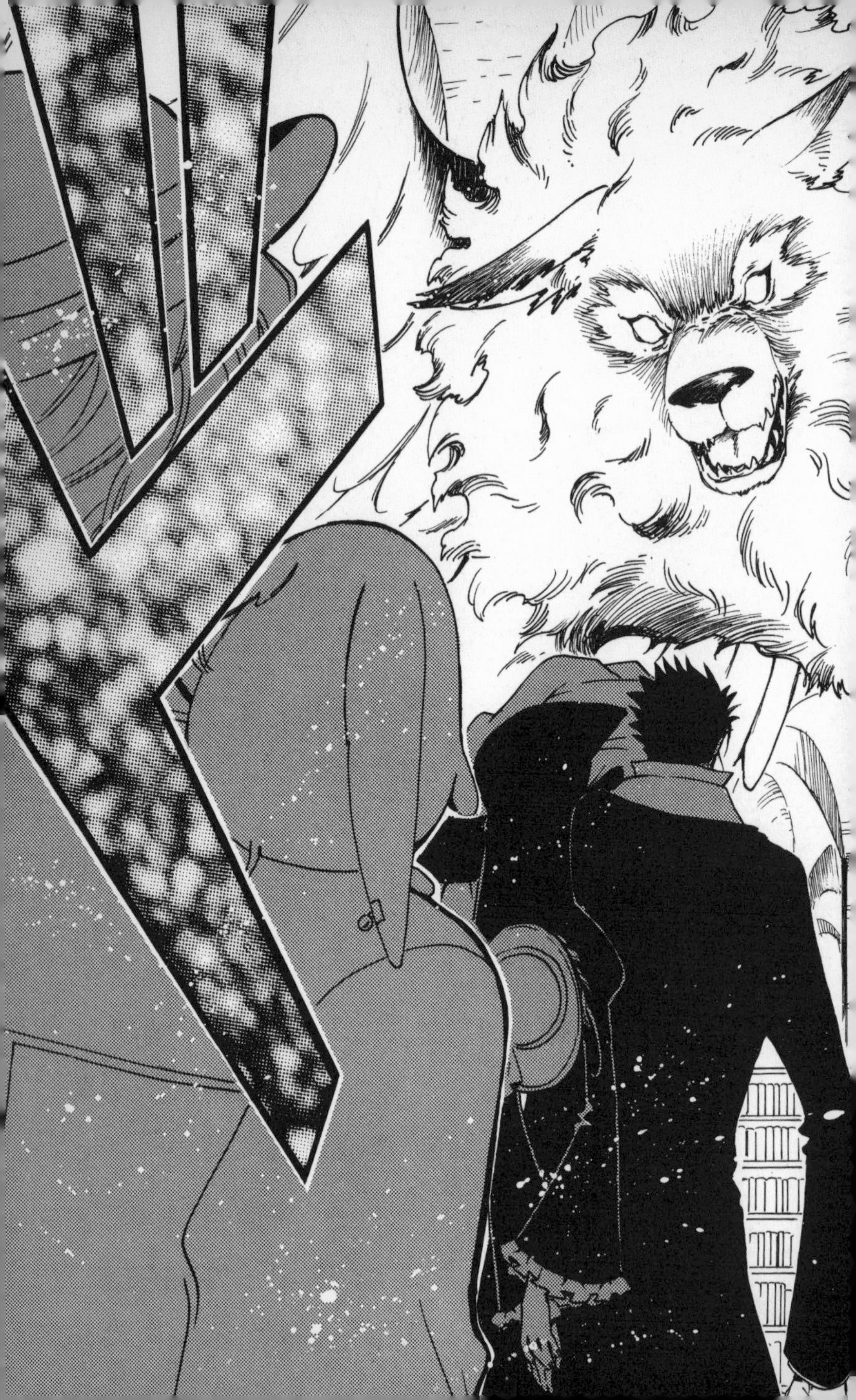

ツバサ

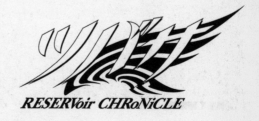

RESERVoir CHRoNiCLE

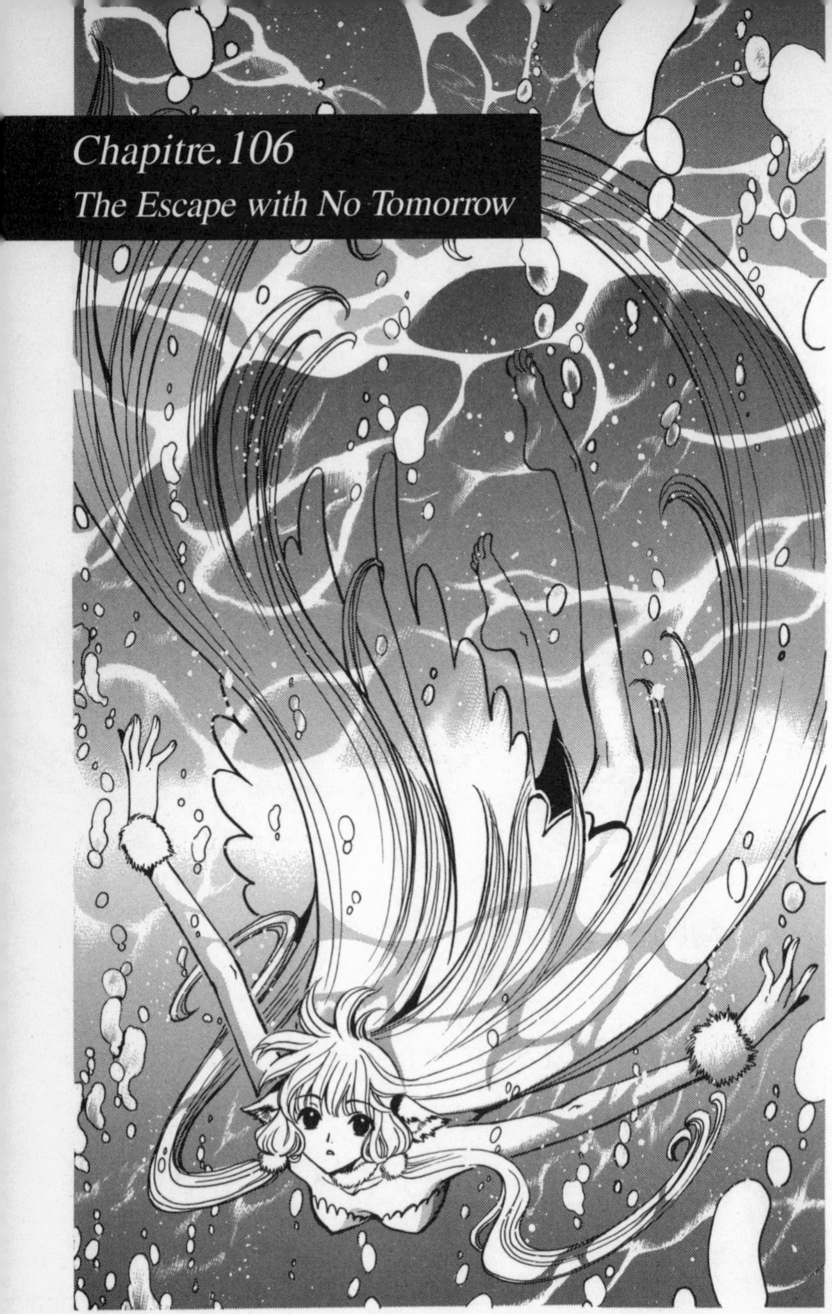
Chapitre. 106
The Escape with No Tomorrow

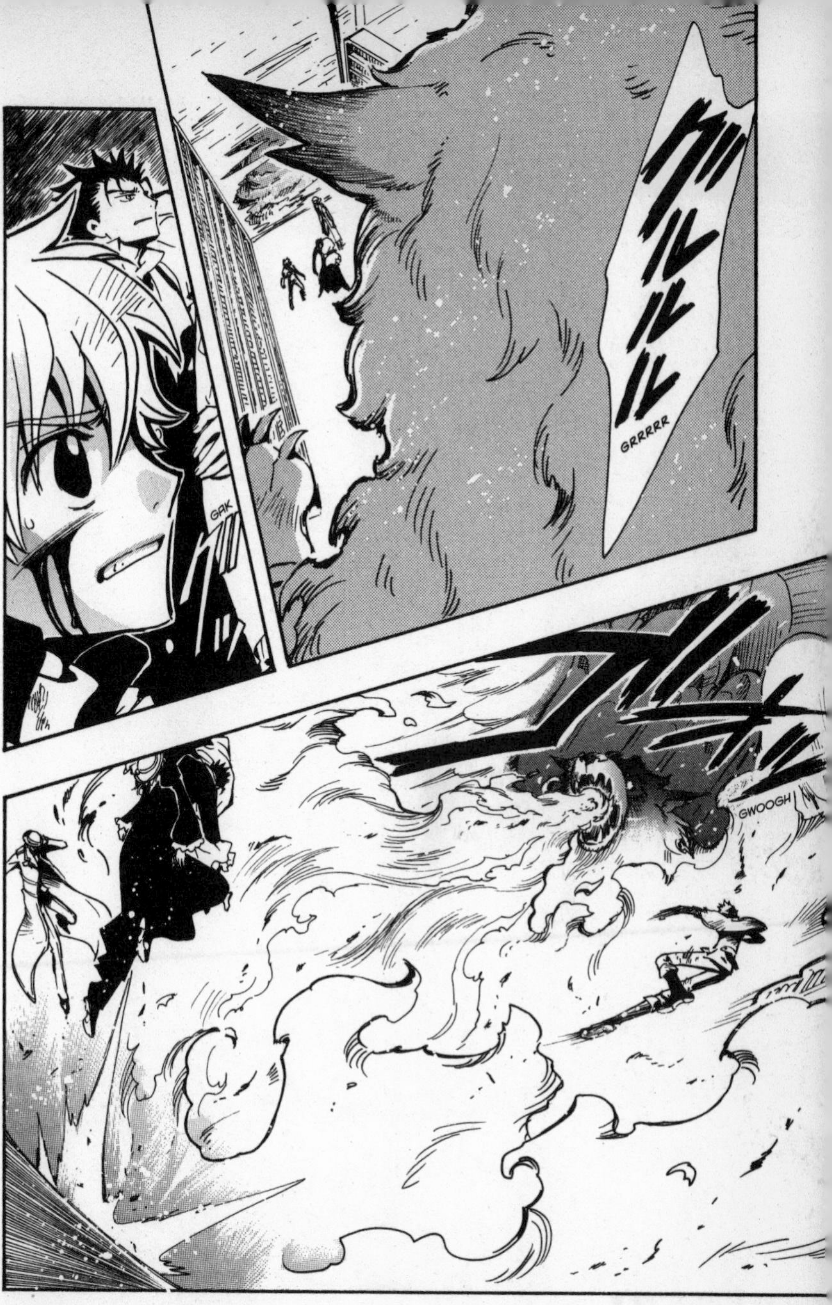
GRRRRR
GAK
GWOOGH

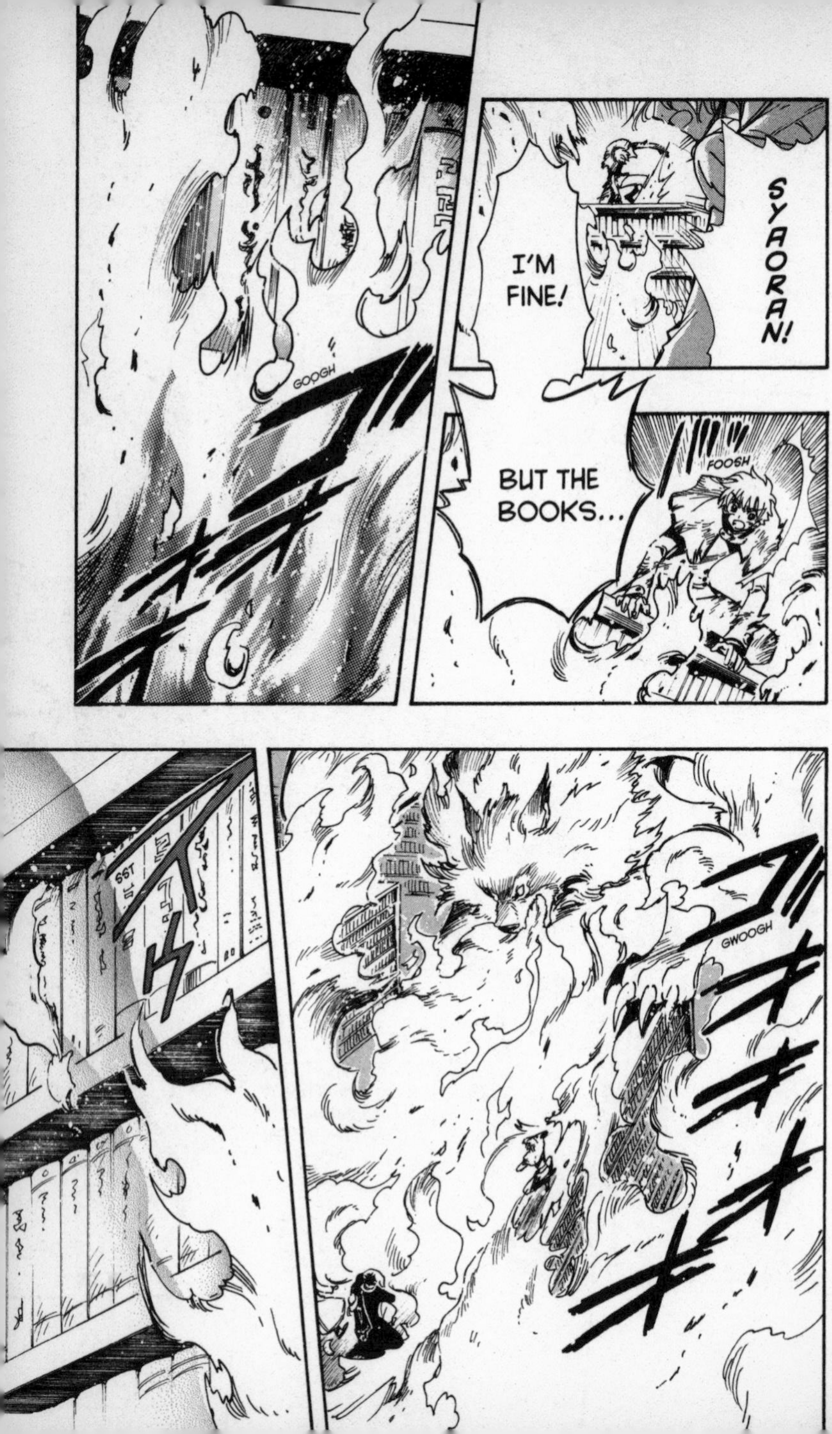
SYAORAN!
I'M FINE!
FOOSH
BUT THE BOOKS...
GOOGH
GWOOGH

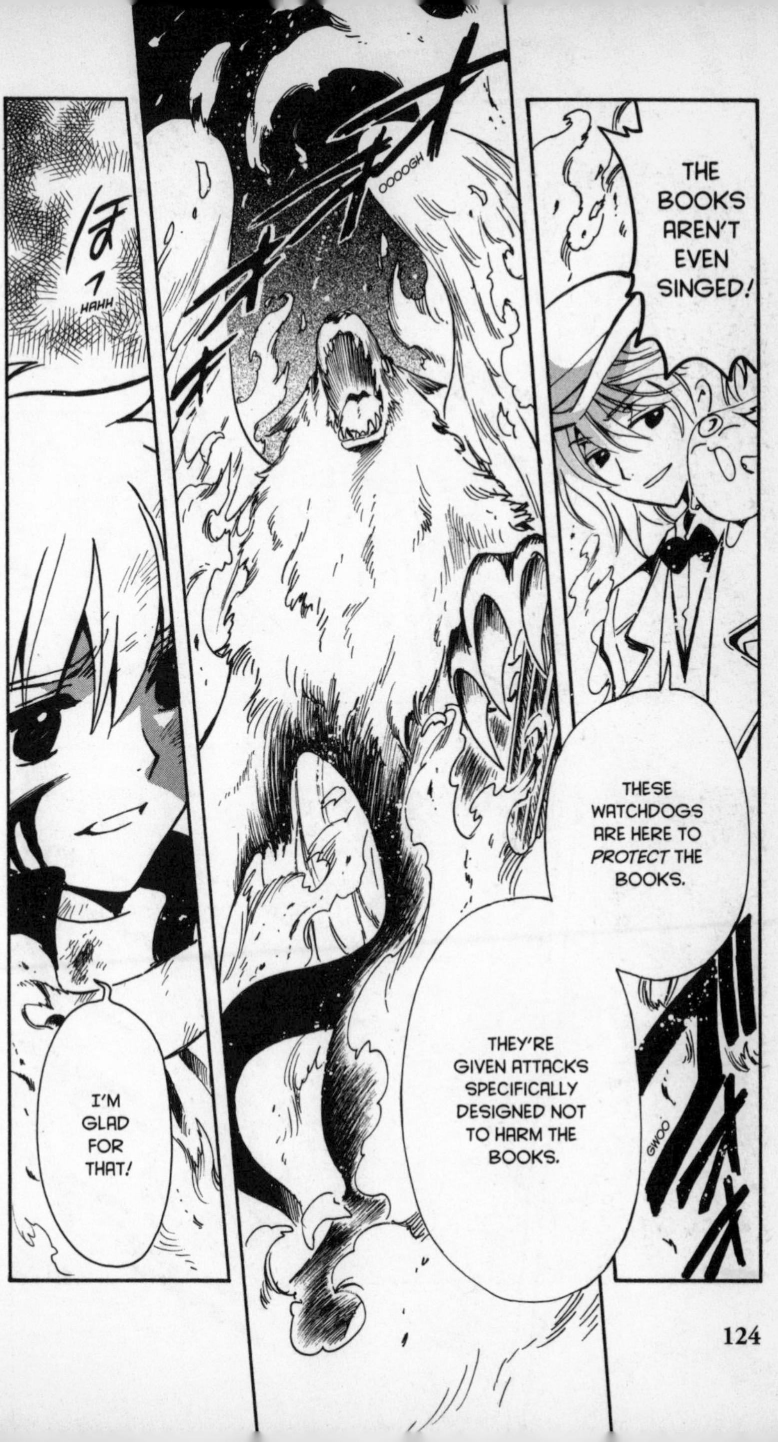
THE BOOKS AREN'T EVEN SINGED!
THESE WATCHDOGS ARE HERE TO *PROTECT* THE BOOKS.
THEY'RE GIVEN ATTACKS SPECIFICALLY DESIGNED NOT TO HARM THE BOOKS.
GWOO
OOOOGH
HAHH
I'M GLAD FOR THAT!

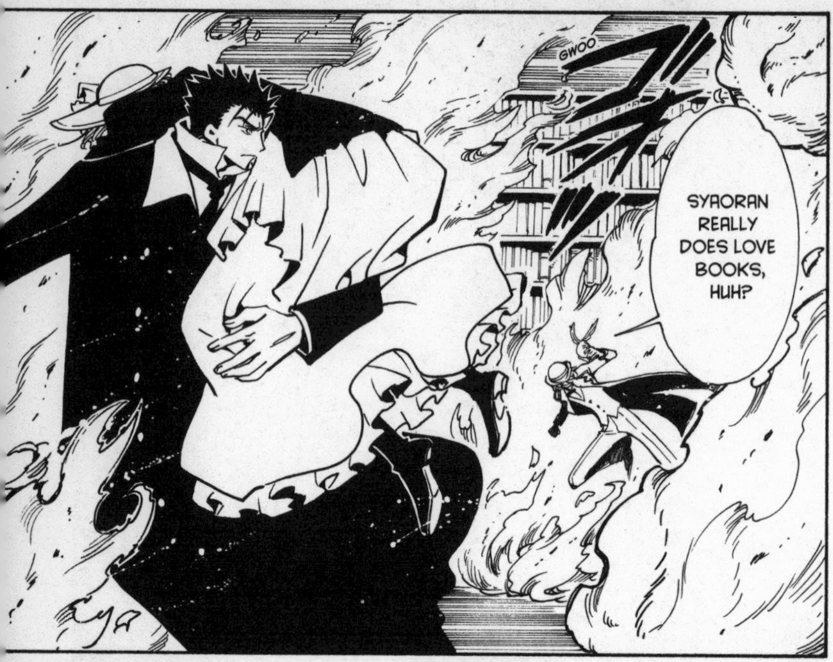
GWOO
SYAORAN REALLY DOES LOVE BOOKS, HUH?

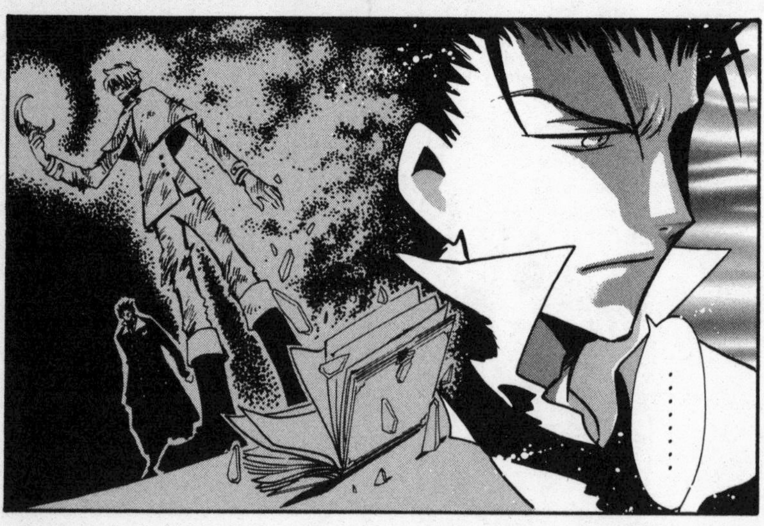
......

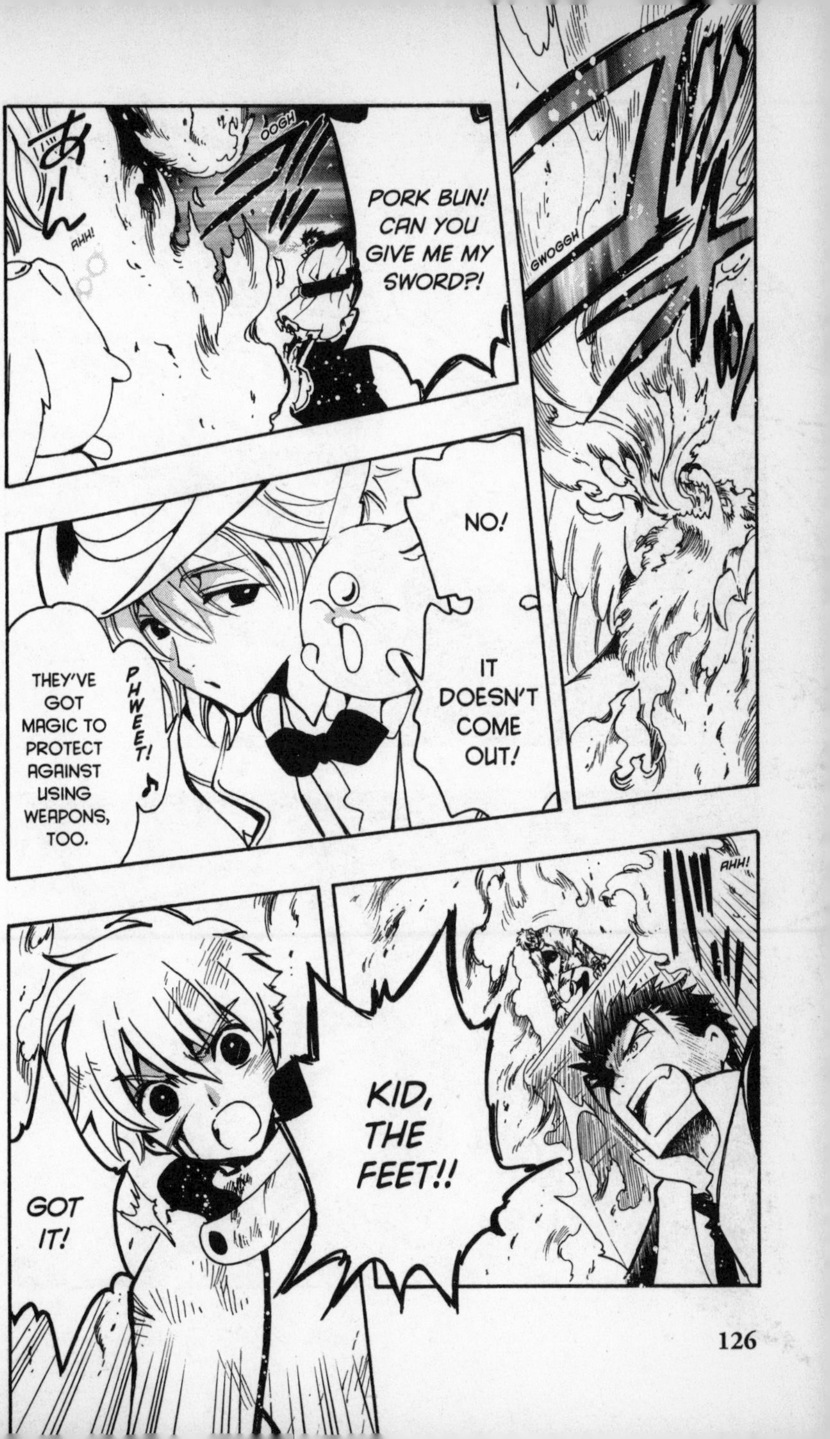
GWOGGH
OOGH
PORK BUN! CAN YOU GIVE ME MY SWORD?!
AHH!
NO!
IT DOESN'T COME OUT!
PHWEET!
THEY'VE GOT MAGIC TO PROTECT AGAINST USING WEAPONS, TOO.
AHH!
KID, THE FEET!!
GOT IT!

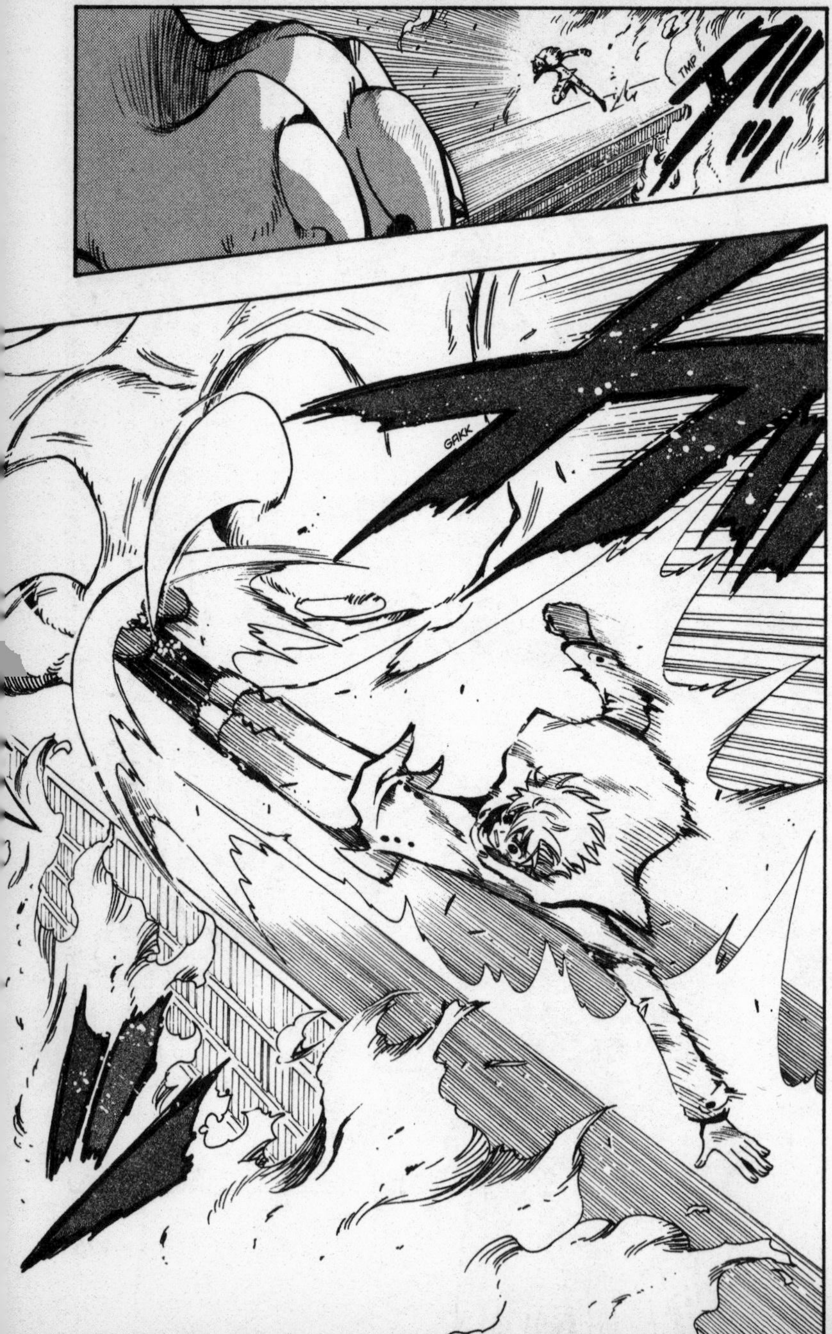
TMP
GAKK

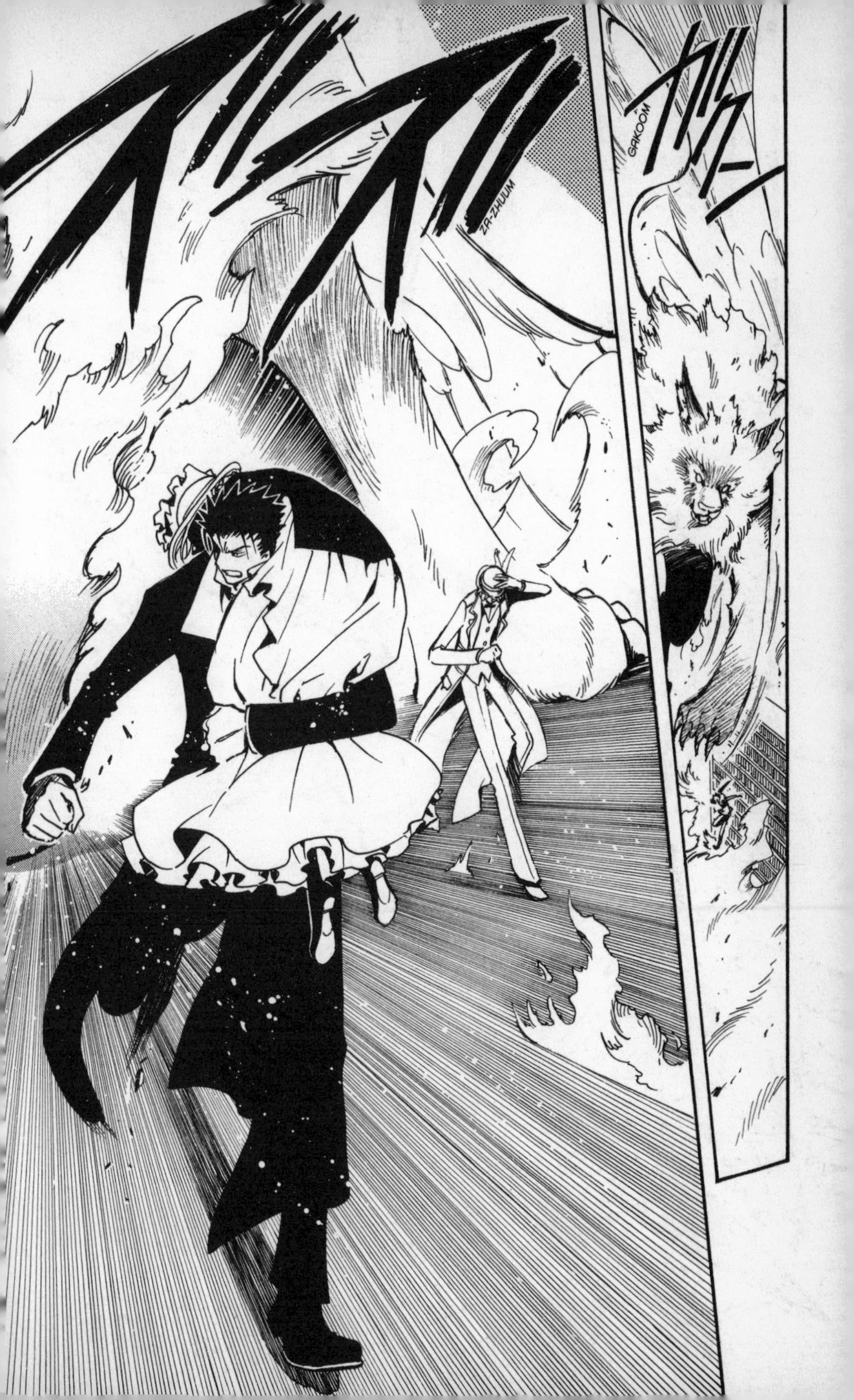
GAKOOM
ZA-ZHUUM

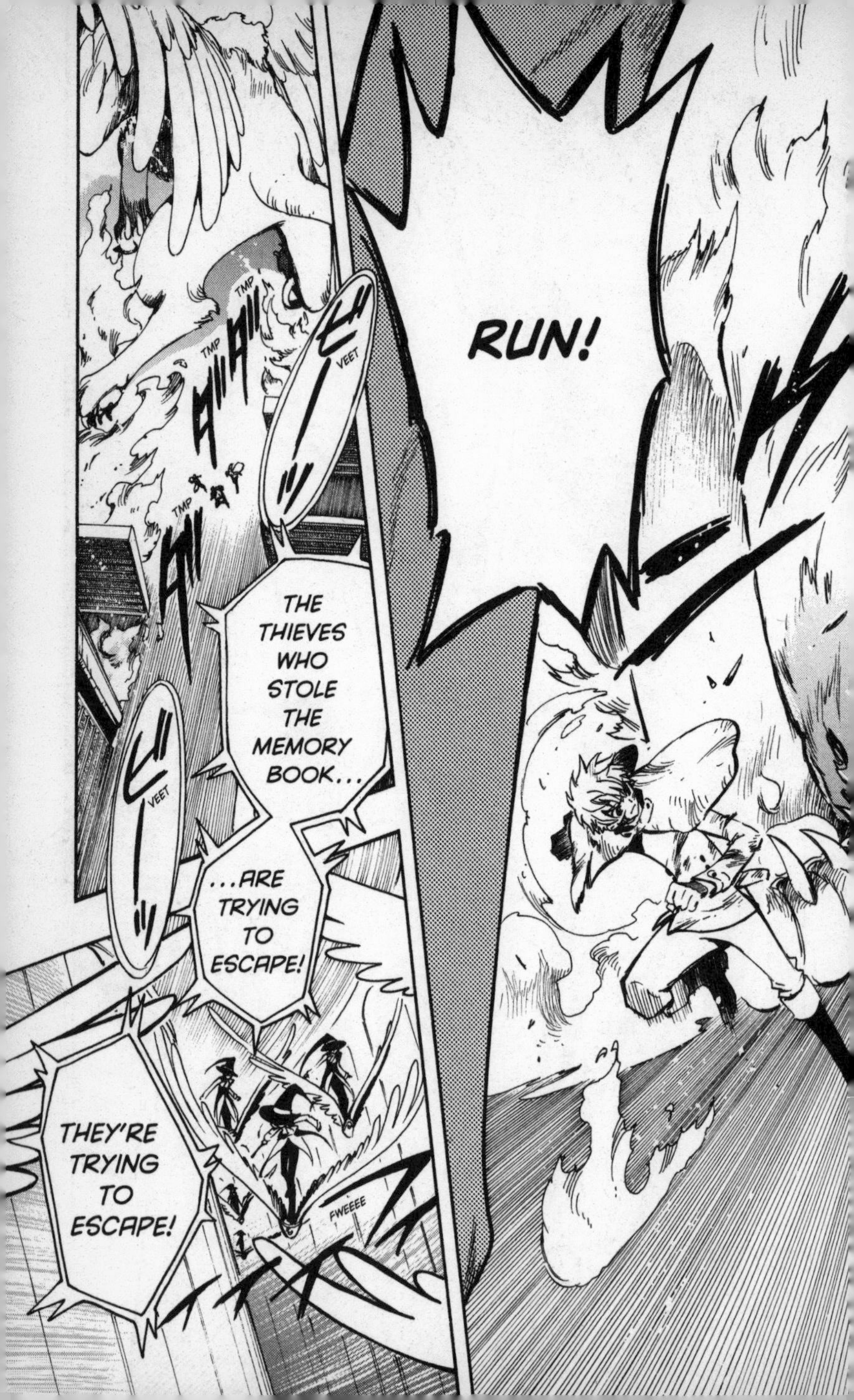
RUN!
VEET
TMP
TMP
TMP
THE THIEVES WHO STOLE THE MEMORY BOOK...
VEET
...ARE TRYING TO ESCAPE!
THEY'RE TRYING TO ESCAPE!
FWEEEE

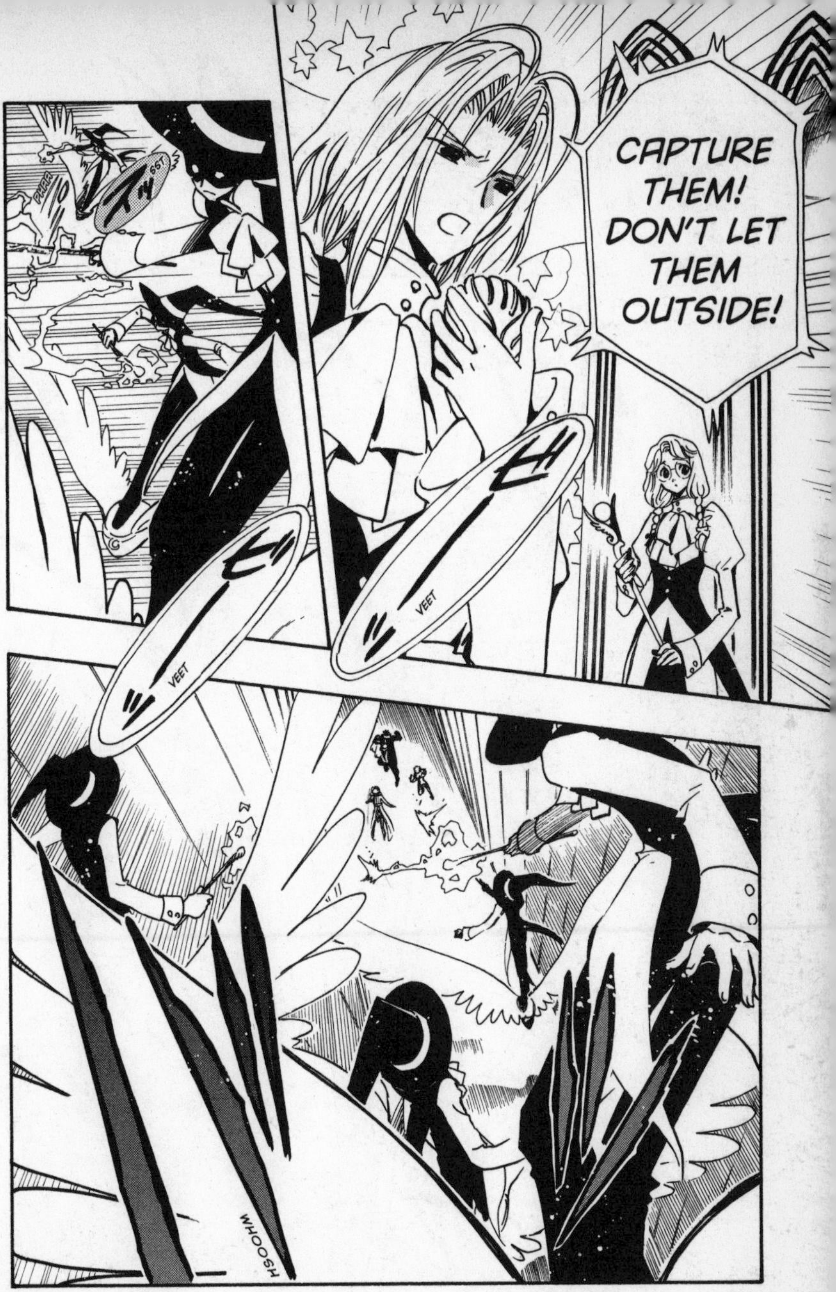
CAPTURE THEM! DON'T LET THEM OUTSIDE!
VEET
PWAA
SST
VEET
WHOOSH

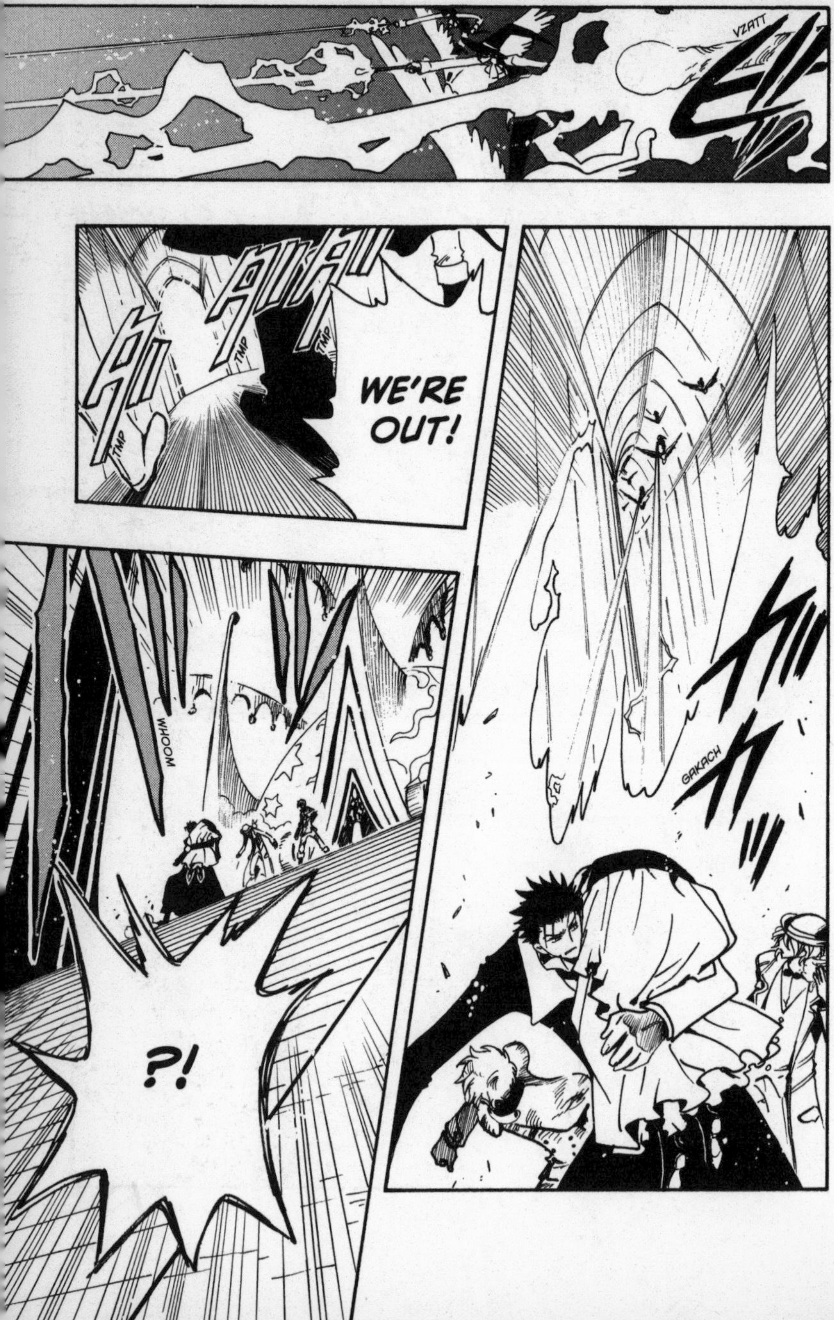
VZATT
TMP
TMP
TMP
WE'RE OUT!
GAKACH
WHOOM
?!

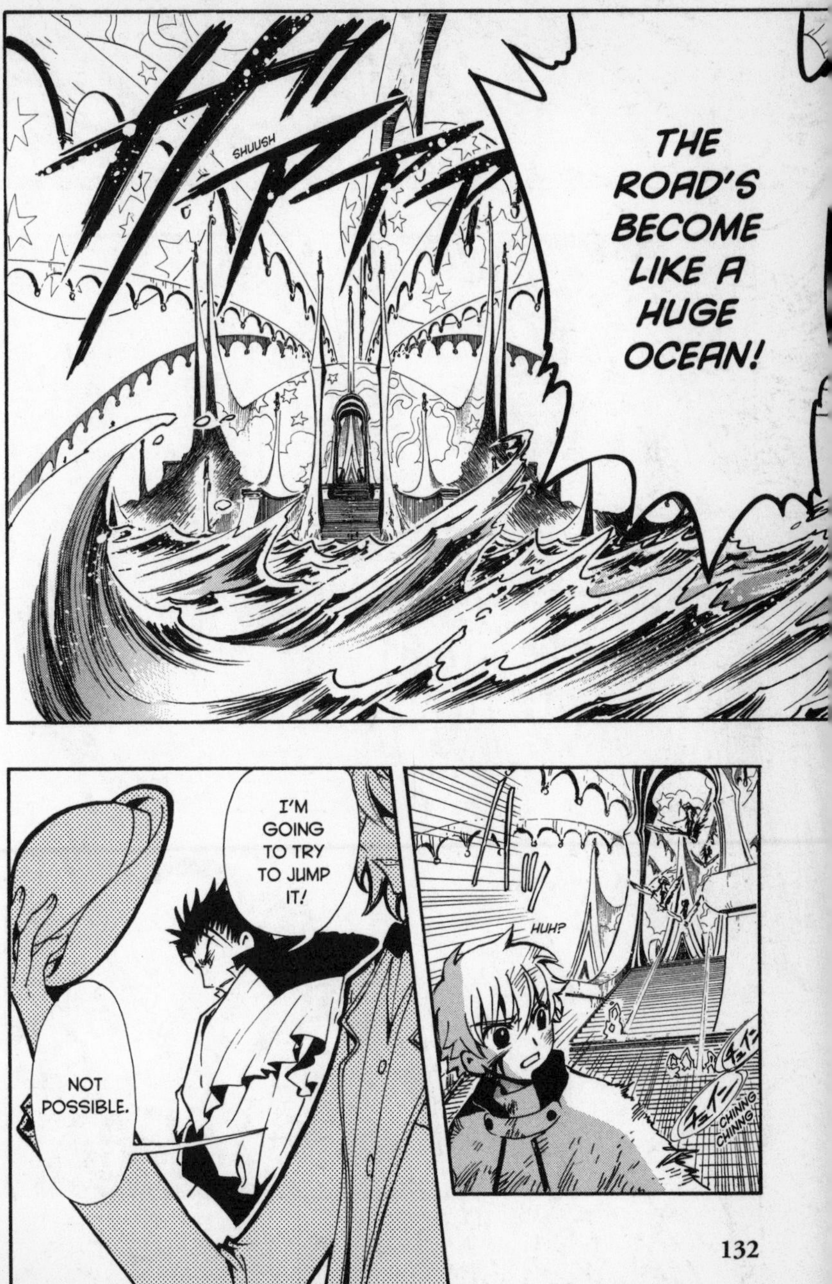
SHUUSH
THE ROAD'S BECOME LIKE A HUGE OCEAN!
HUH?
CHINNG CHINNG
I'M GOING TO TRY TO JUMP IT!
NOT POSSIBLE.

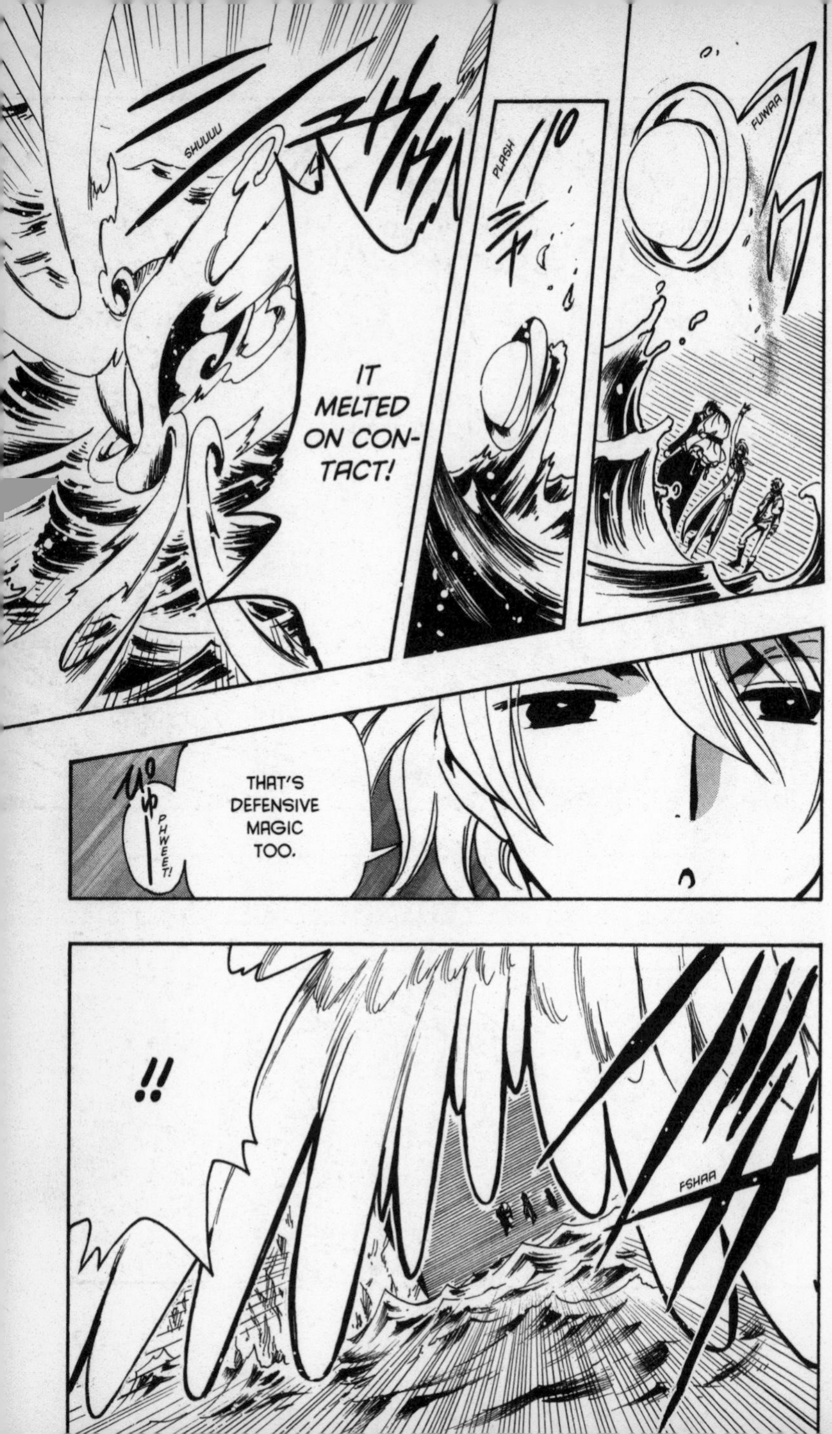
FUWAA
PLASH
SHUUUU
IT MELTED ON CON-TACT!
THAT'S DEFENSIVE MAGIC TOO.
PHWEET!
FSHAA
!!

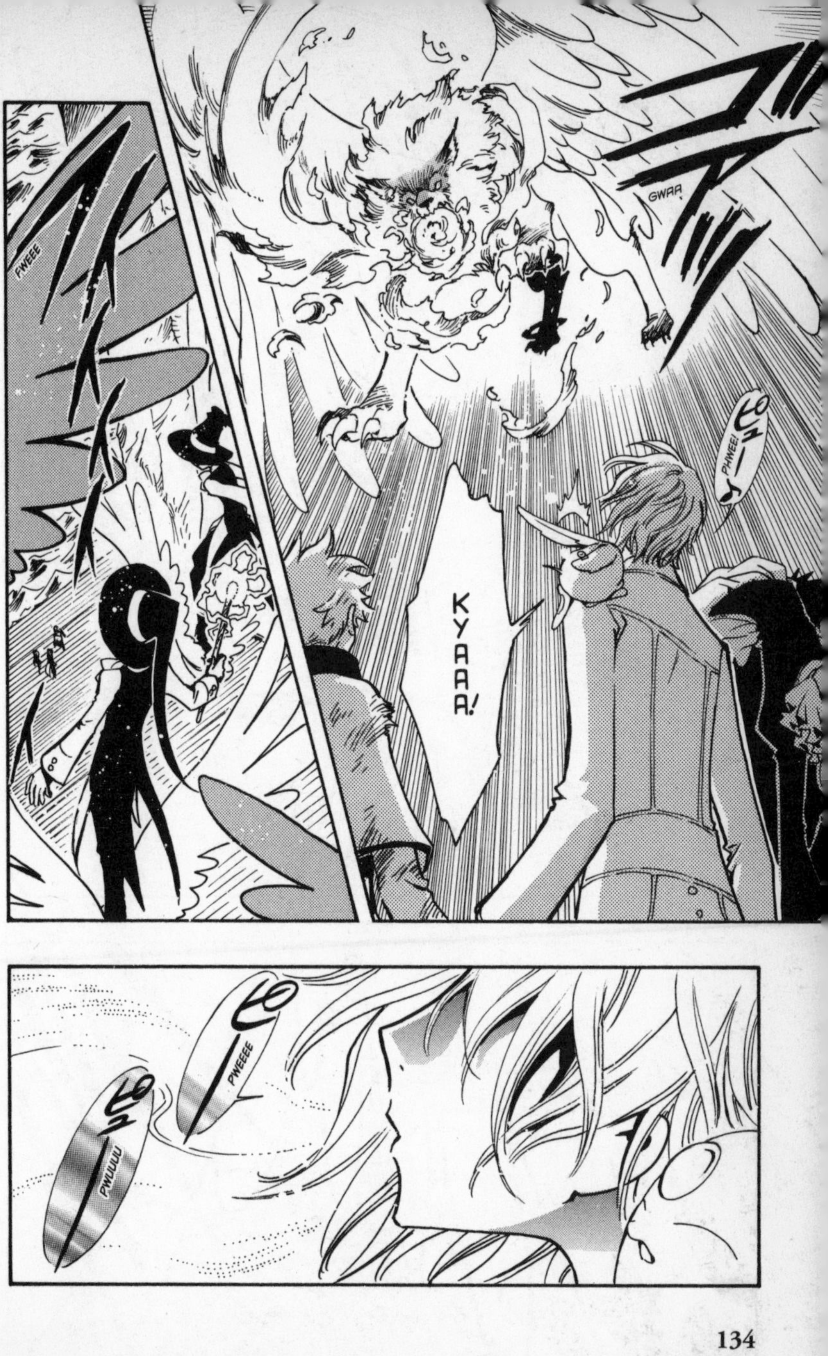
GWAA
PHWEE!
KYAAA!
FWEEE
PWEEEE
PWUUUU

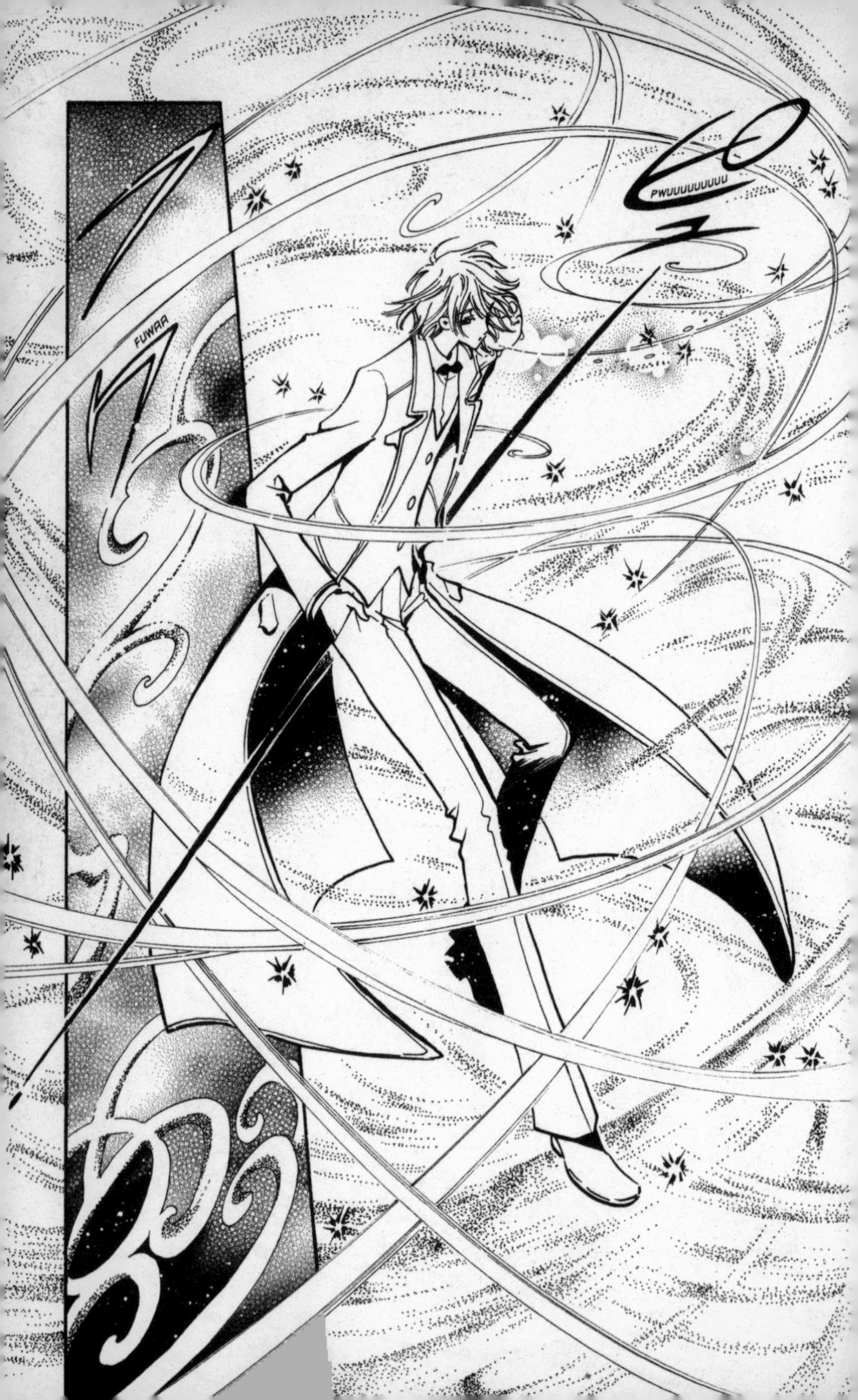
PWUUUUUUUUU
FUWAA

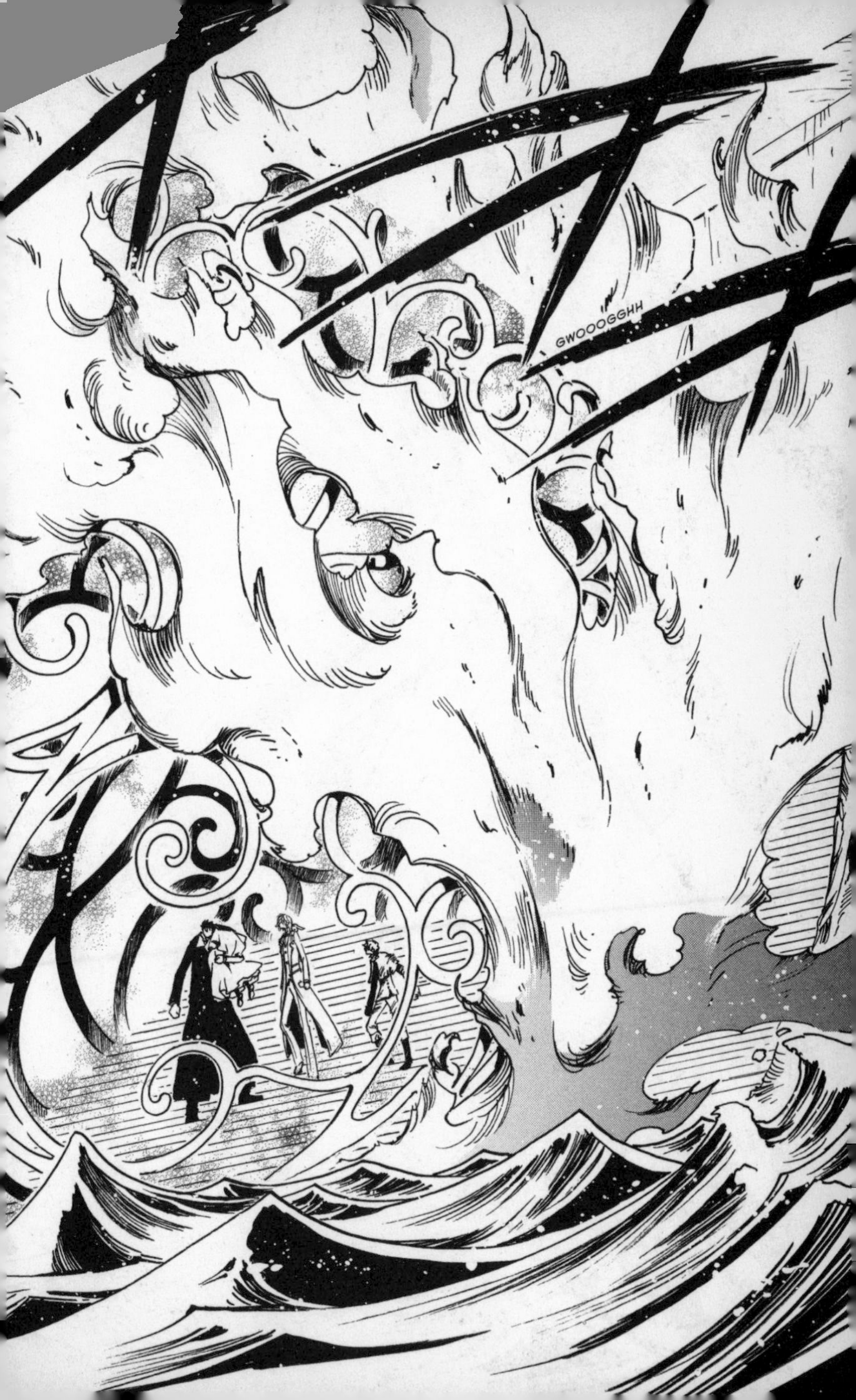
GWOOOGGHH

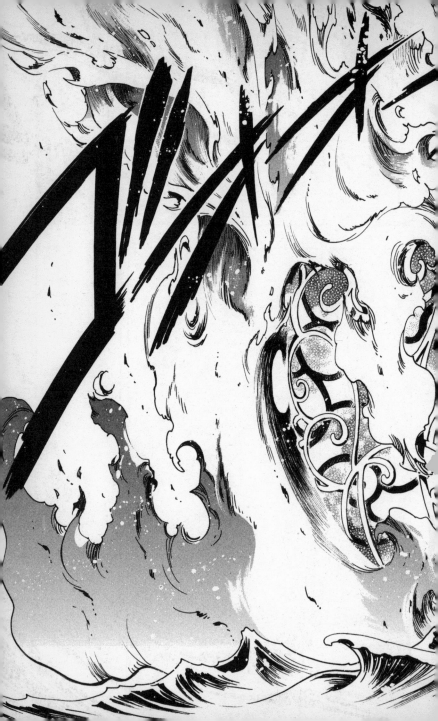

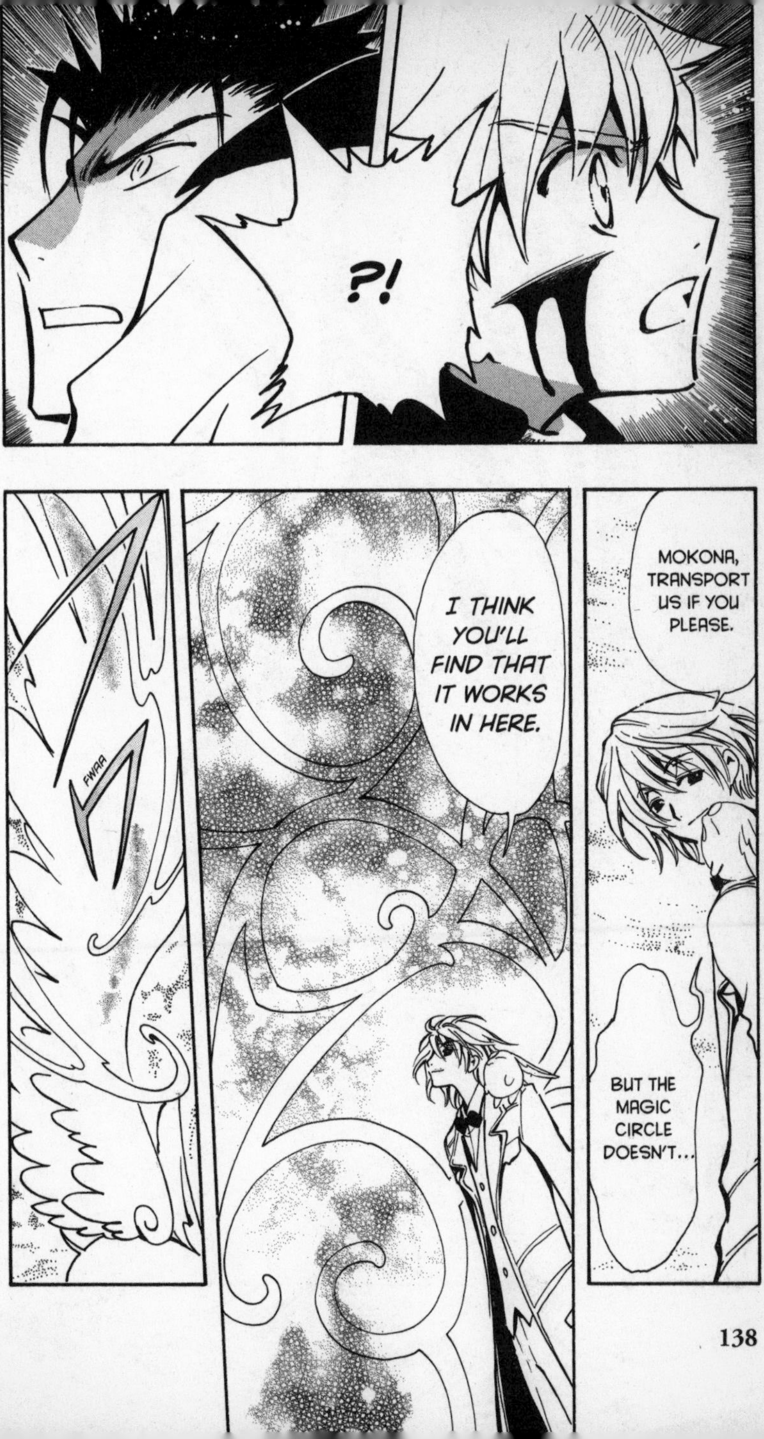
?!
MOKONA, TRANSPORT US IF YOU PLEASE.
BUT THE MAGIC CIRCLE DOESN'T...
I THINK YOU'LL FIND THAT IT WORKS IN HERE.
FWAA

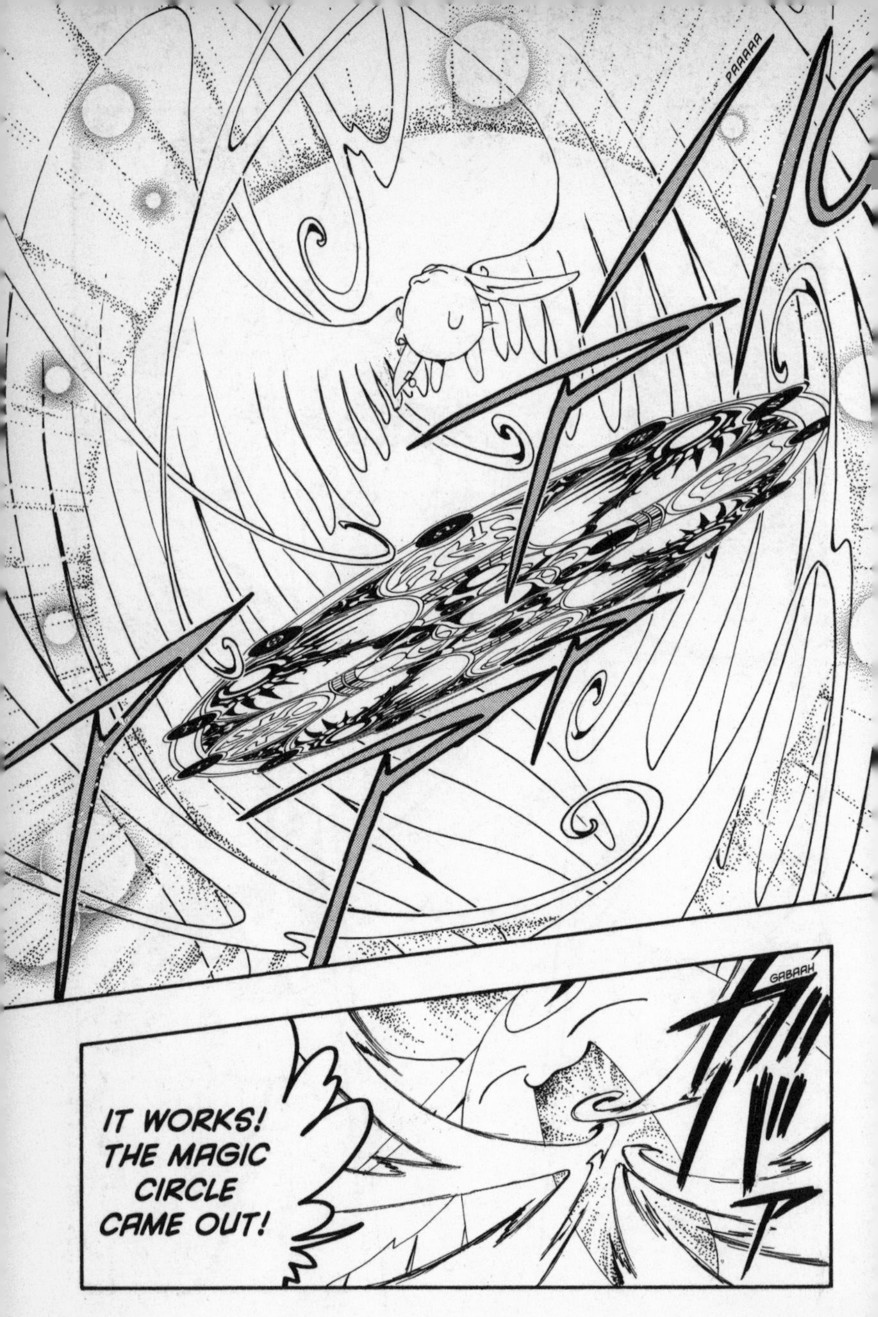
PAAAAA
GABAAH
IT WORKS! THE MAGIC CIRCLE CAME OUT!

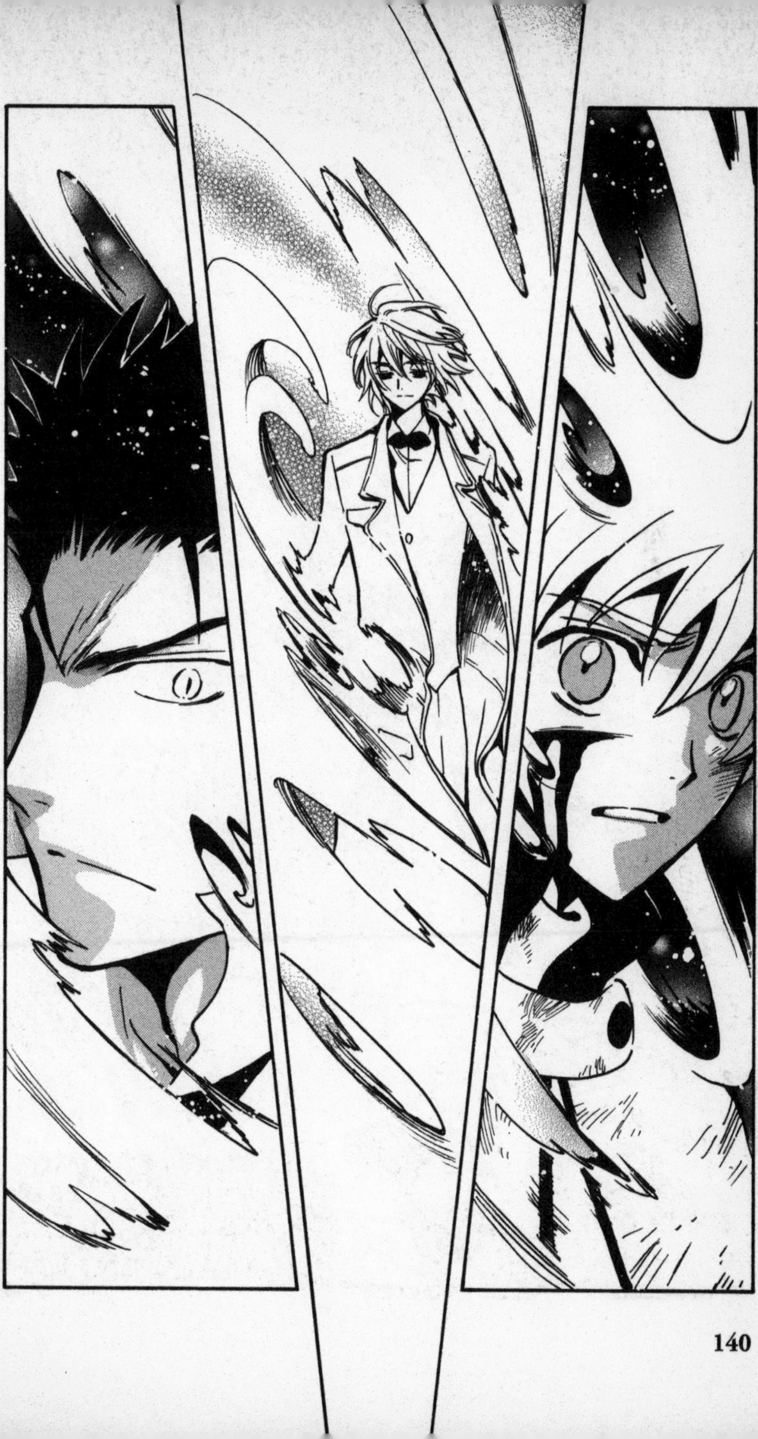

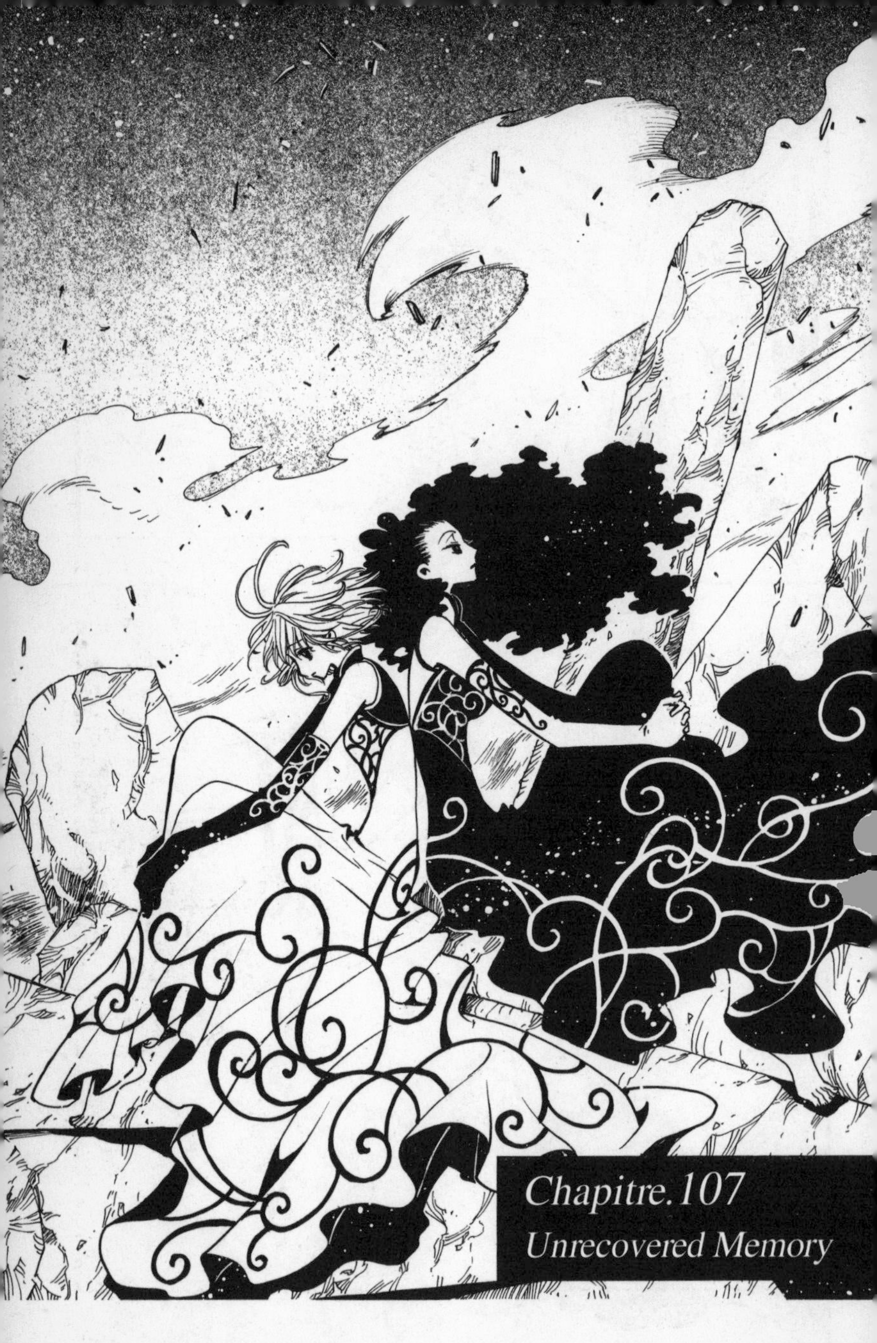

Chapitre.107

Unrecovered Memory

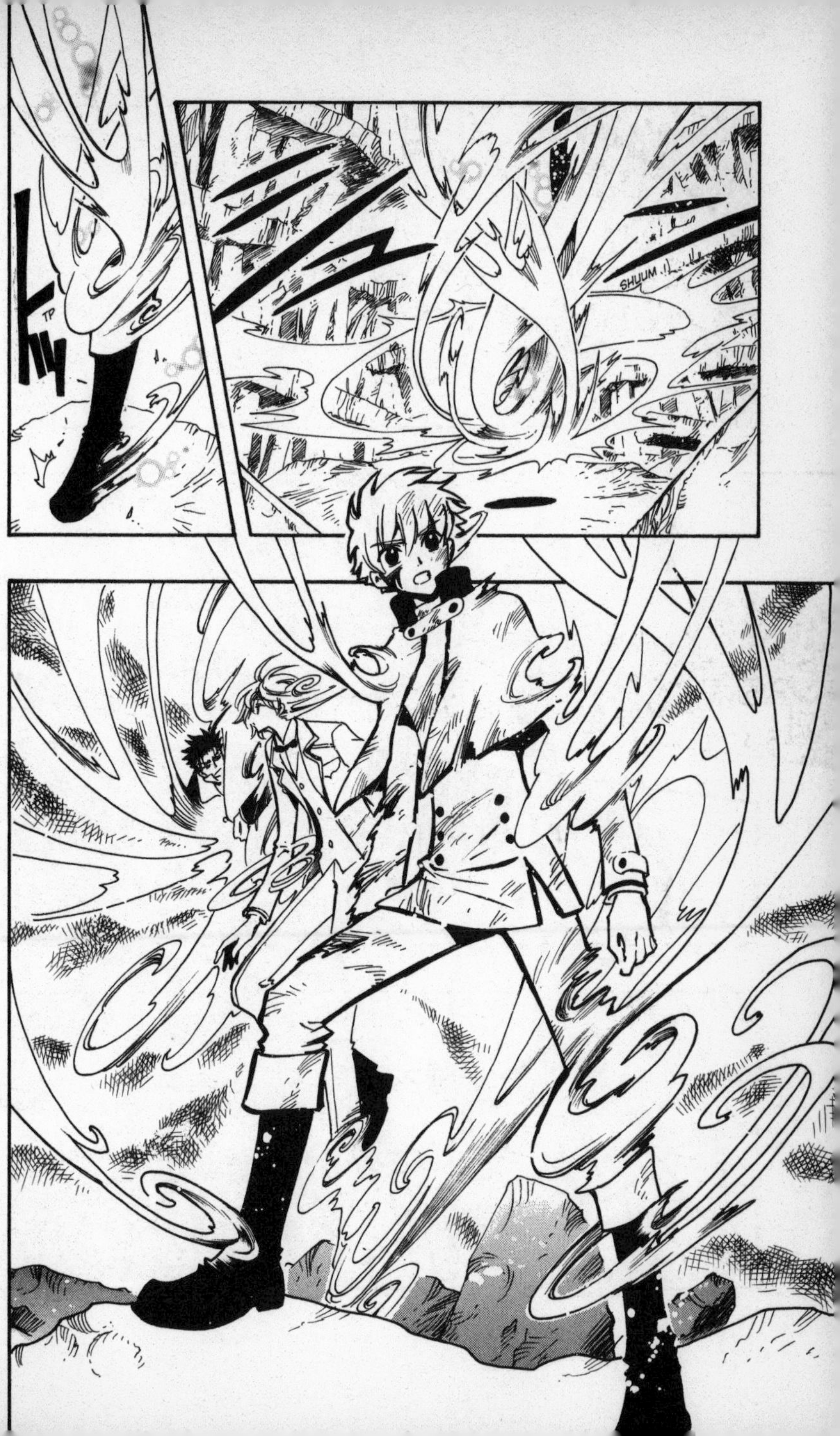
SHUUM
TP

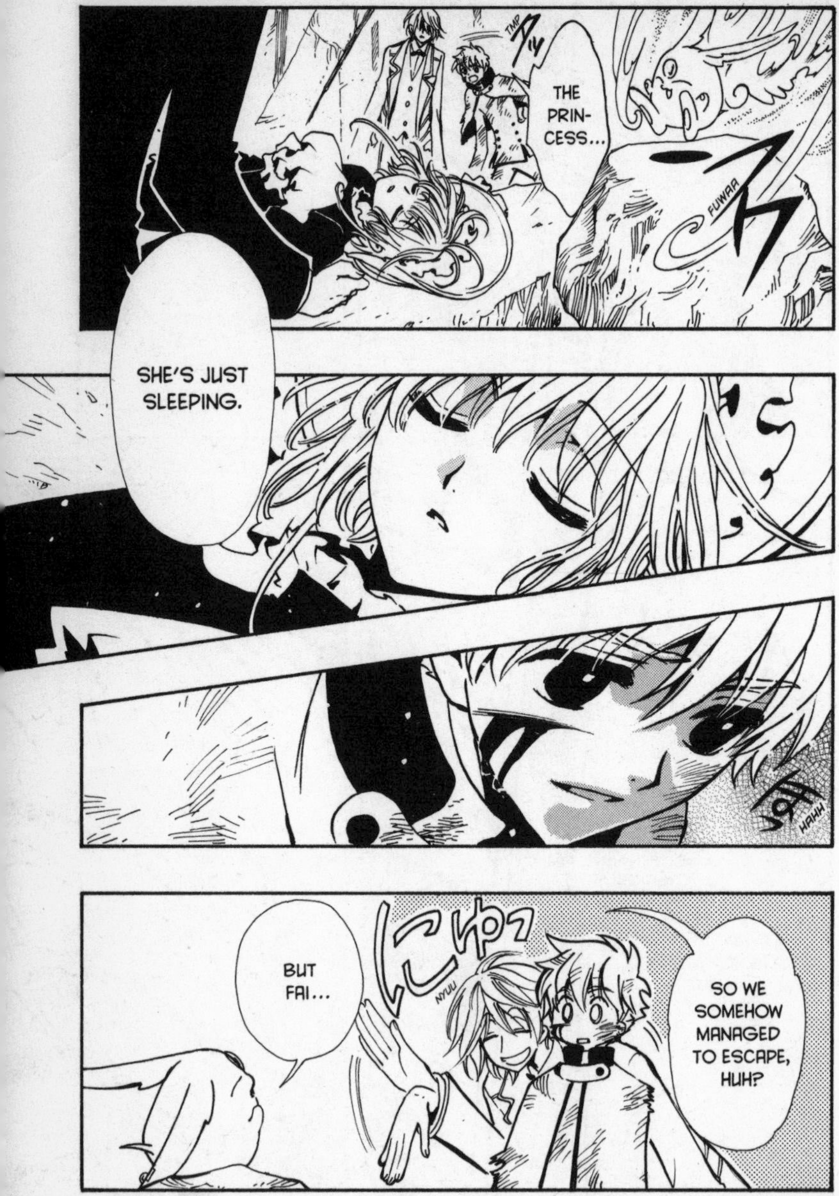
TMP
THE PRIN-CESS...
FUWAA
SHE'S JUST SLEEPING.
HAHH
SO WE SOMEHOW MANAGED TO ESCAPE, HUH?
NYUU
BUT FAI...

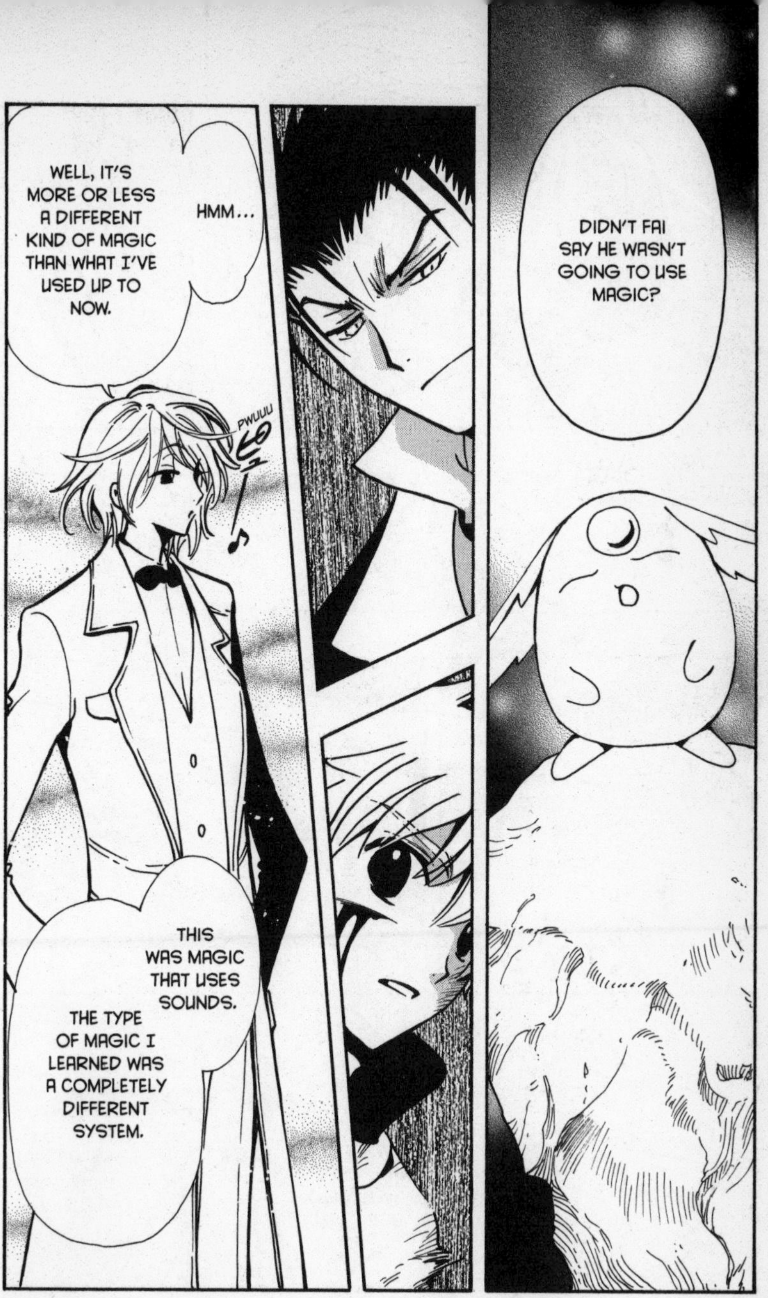
DIDN'T FAI SAY HE WASN'T GOING TO USE MAGIC?
HMM...
WELL, IT'S MORE OR LESS A DIFFERENT KIND OF MAGIC THAN WHAT I'VE USED UP TO NOW.
PWUUU
THIS WAS MAGIC THAT USES SOUNDS.
THE TYPE OF MAGIC I LEARNED WAS A COMPLETELY DIFFERENT SYSTEM.

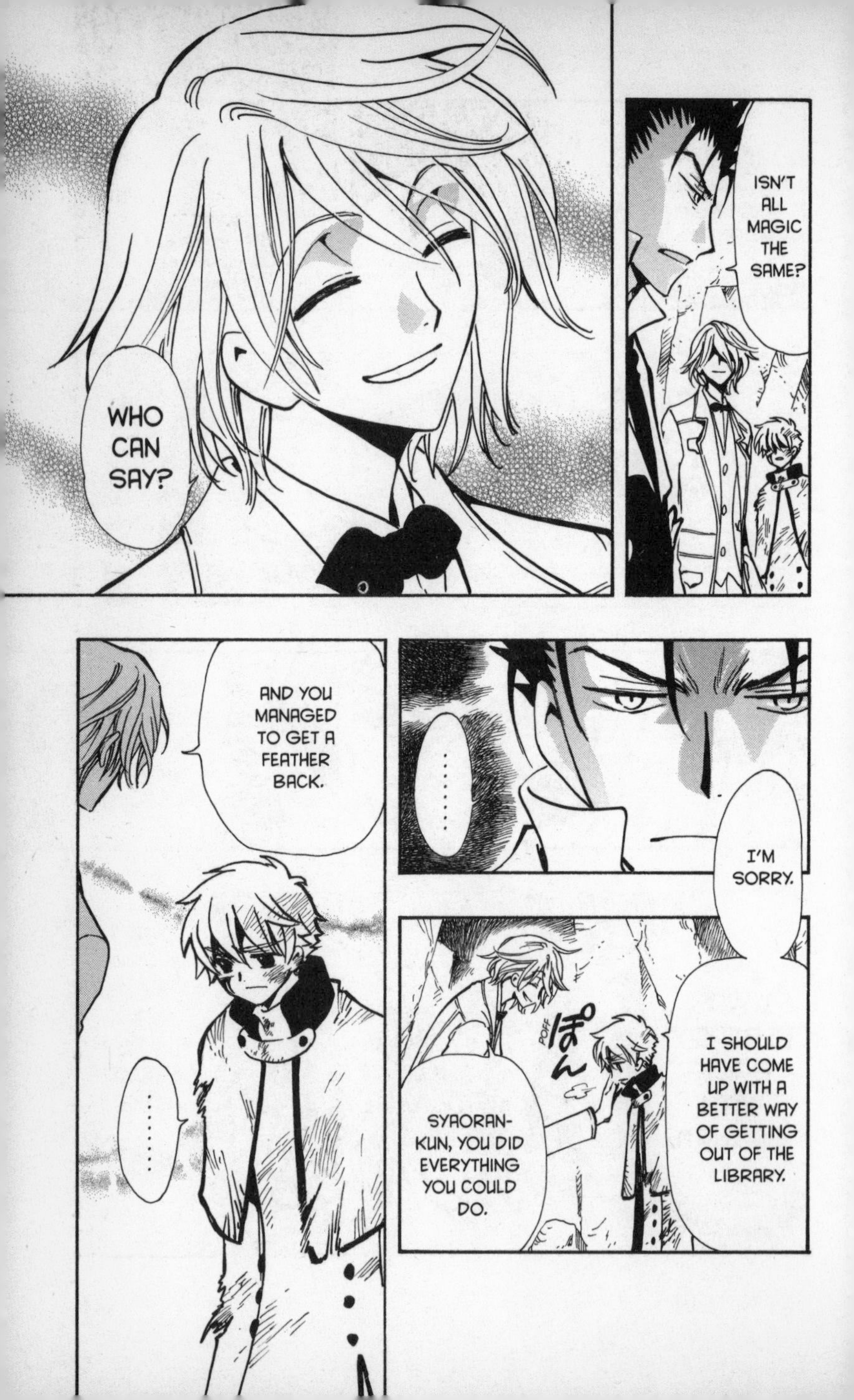
ISN'T ALL MAGIC THE SAME?
WHO CAN SAY?
……
I'M SORRY.
I SHOULD HAVE COME UP WITH A BETTER WAY OF GETTING OUT OF THE LIBRARY.
POFF ぽん
SYAORAN-KUN, YOU DID EVERYTHING YOU COULD DO.
AND YOU MANAGED TO GET A FEATHER BACK.
……

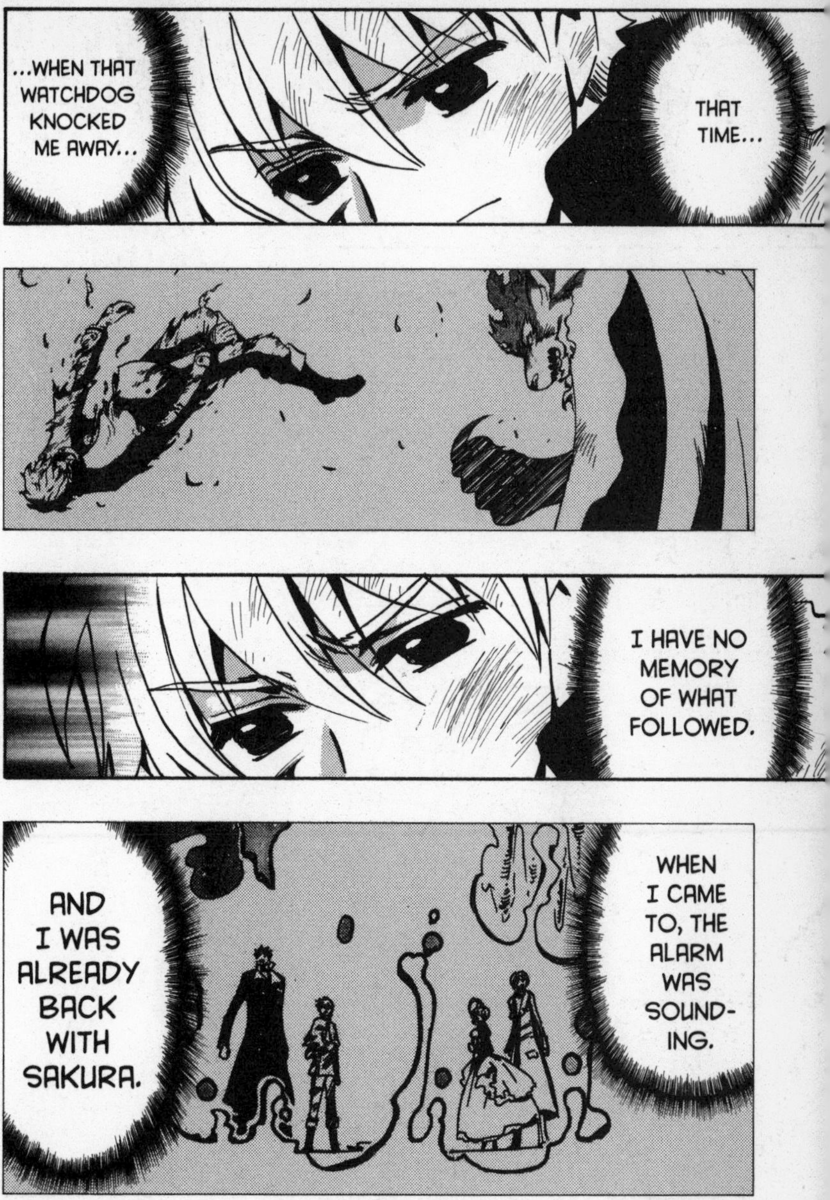
THAT TIME...
...WHEN THAT WATCHDOG KNOCKED ME AWAY...
I HAVE NO MEMORY OF WHAT FOLLOWED.
WHEN I CAME TO, THE ALARM WAS SOUND-ING.
AND I WAS ALREADY BACK WITH SAKURA.

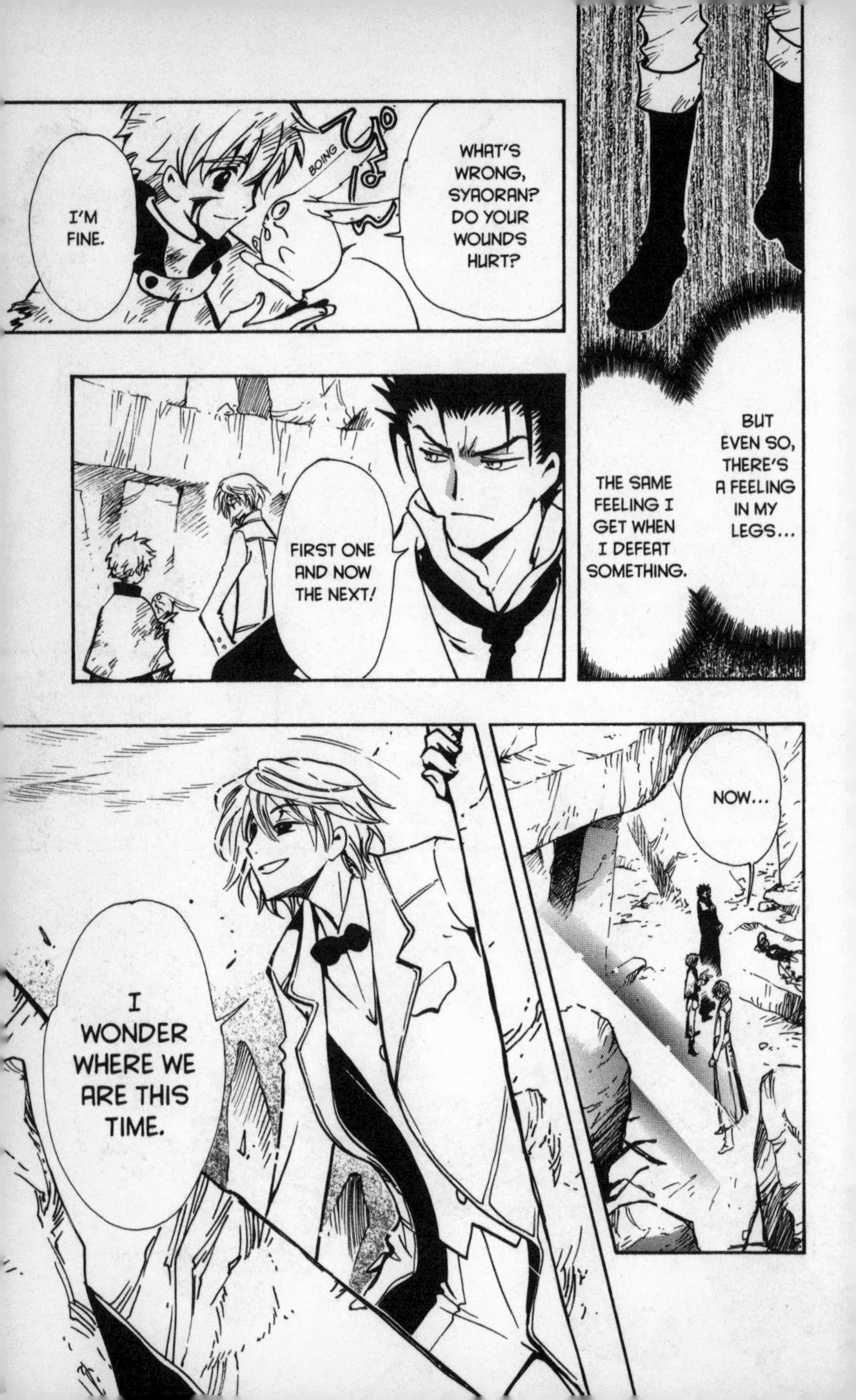
BUT EVEN SO, THERE'S A FEELING IN MY LEGS...
THE SAME FEELING I GET WHEN I DEFEAT SOMETHING.
WHAT'S WRONG, SYAORAN? DO YOUR WOUNDS HURT?
BOING
I'M FINE.
FIRST ONE AND NOW THE NEXT!
NOW...
I WONDER WHERE WE ARE THIS TIME.

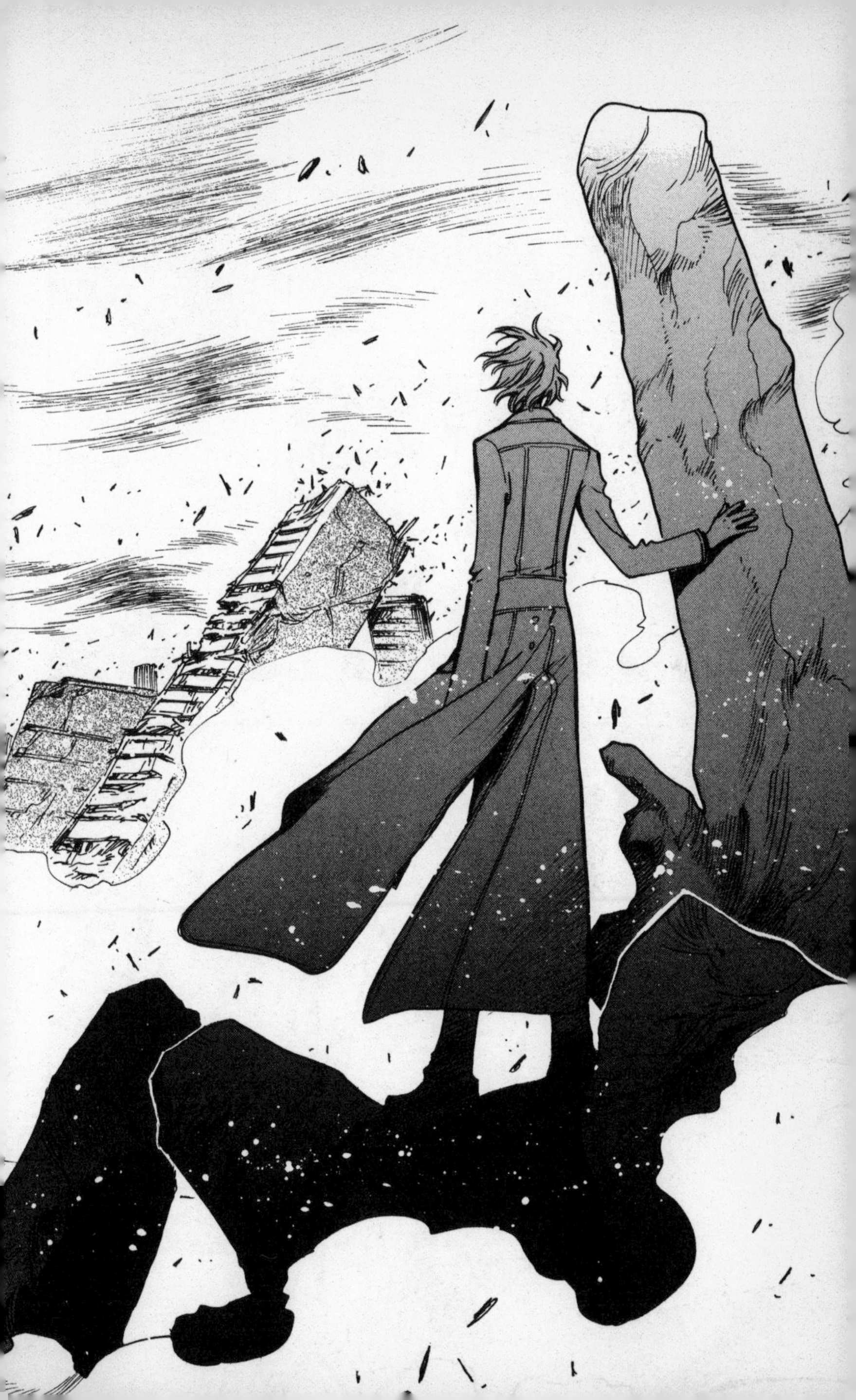

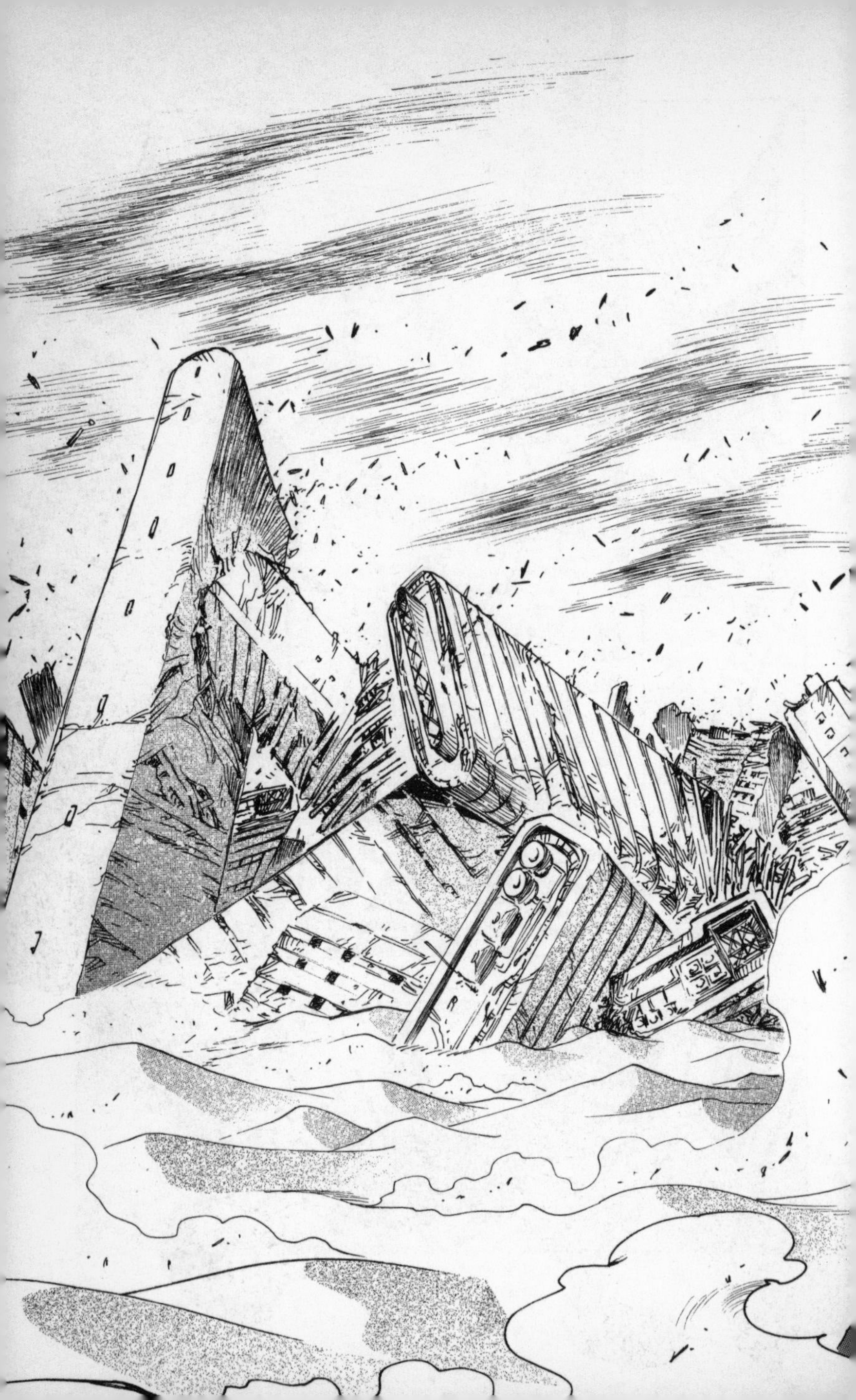

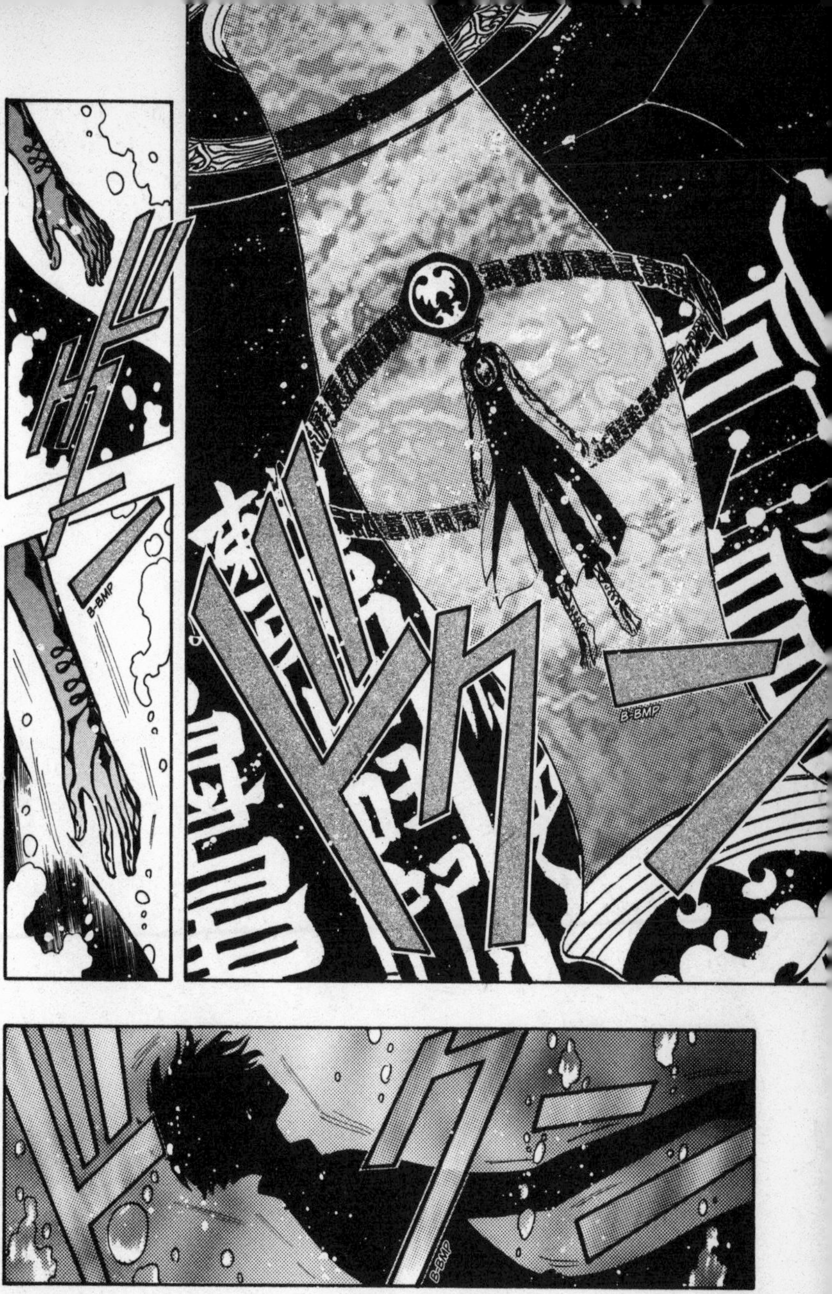
B-BMP
B-BMP
B-BMP

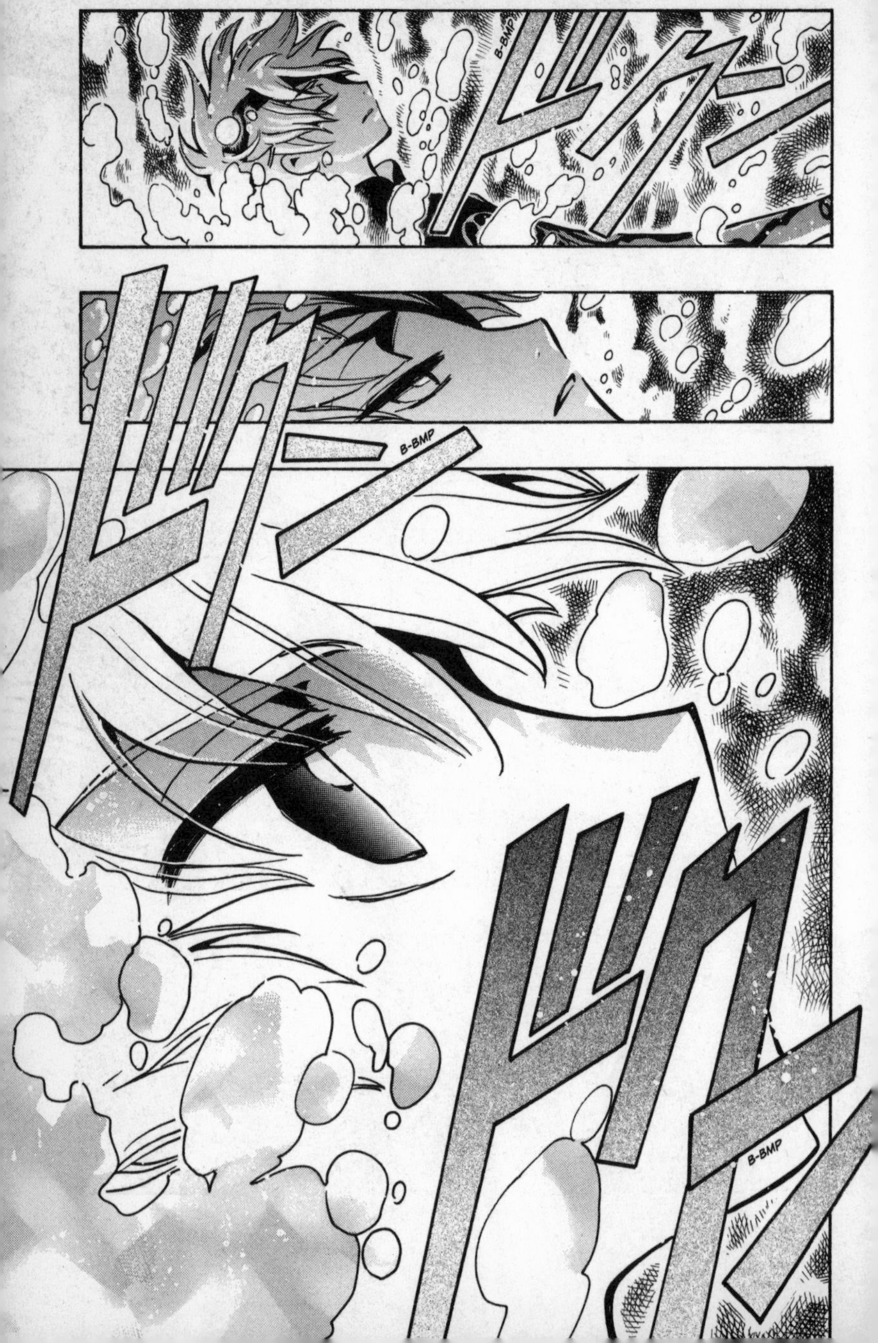
B-BMP
B-BMP
B-BMP

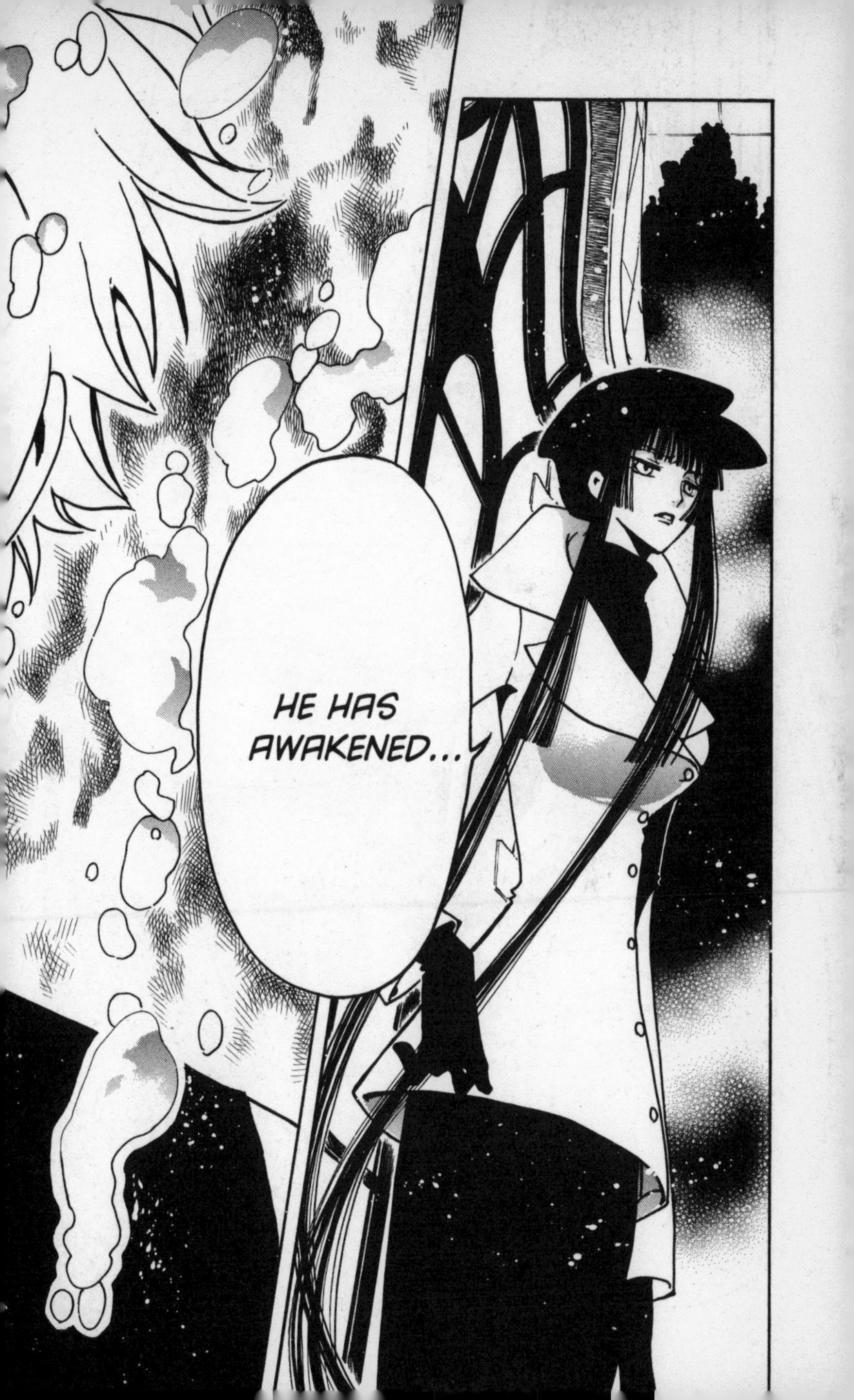
HE HAS AWAKENED...

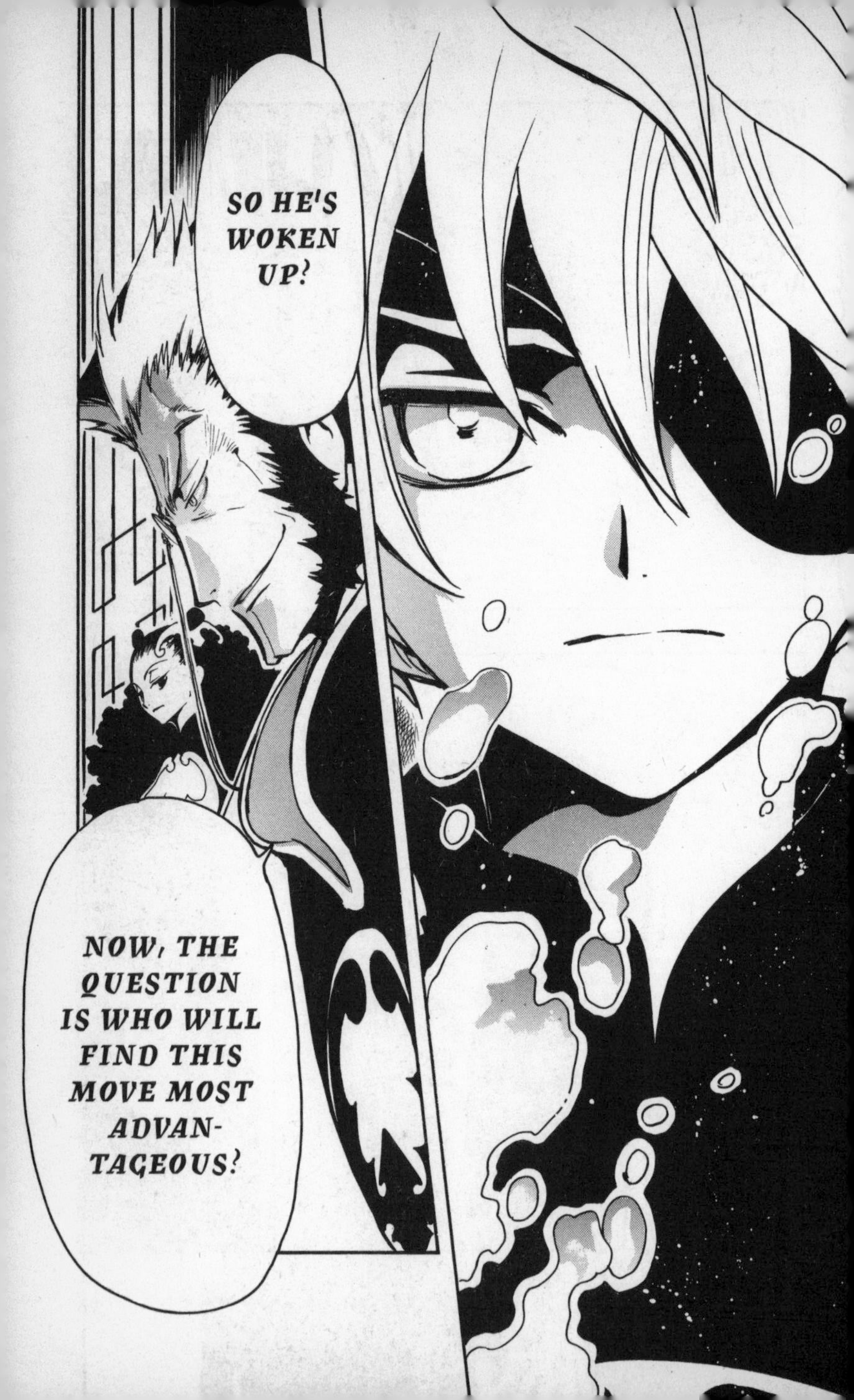
SO HE'S WOKEN UP?
NOW, THE QUESTION IS WHO WILL FIND THIS MOVE MOST ADVAN-TAGEOUS?

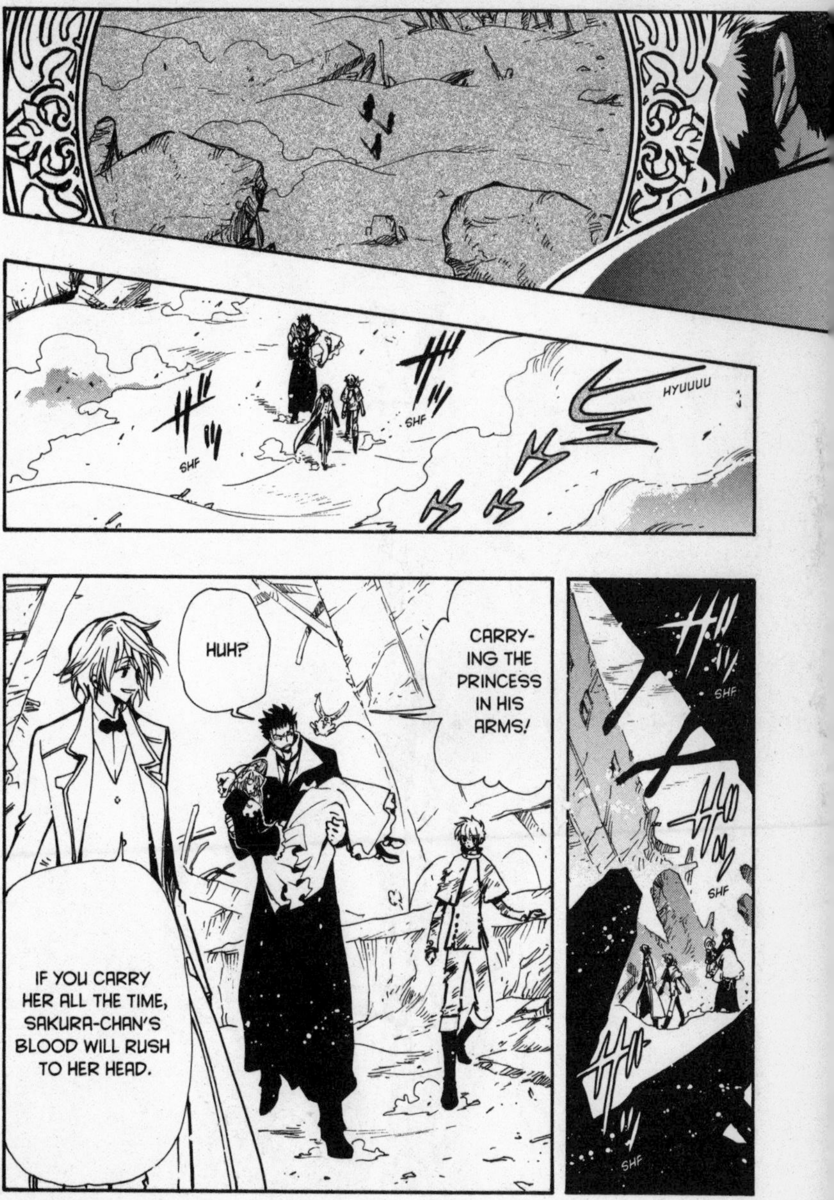
HYUUUU
SHF
SHF
SHF
SHF
SHF
CARRY-
ING THE
PRINCESS
IN HIS
ARMS!
HUH?
IF YOU CARRY
HER ALL THE TIME,
SAKURA-CHAN'S
BLOOD WILL RUSH
TO HER HEAD.

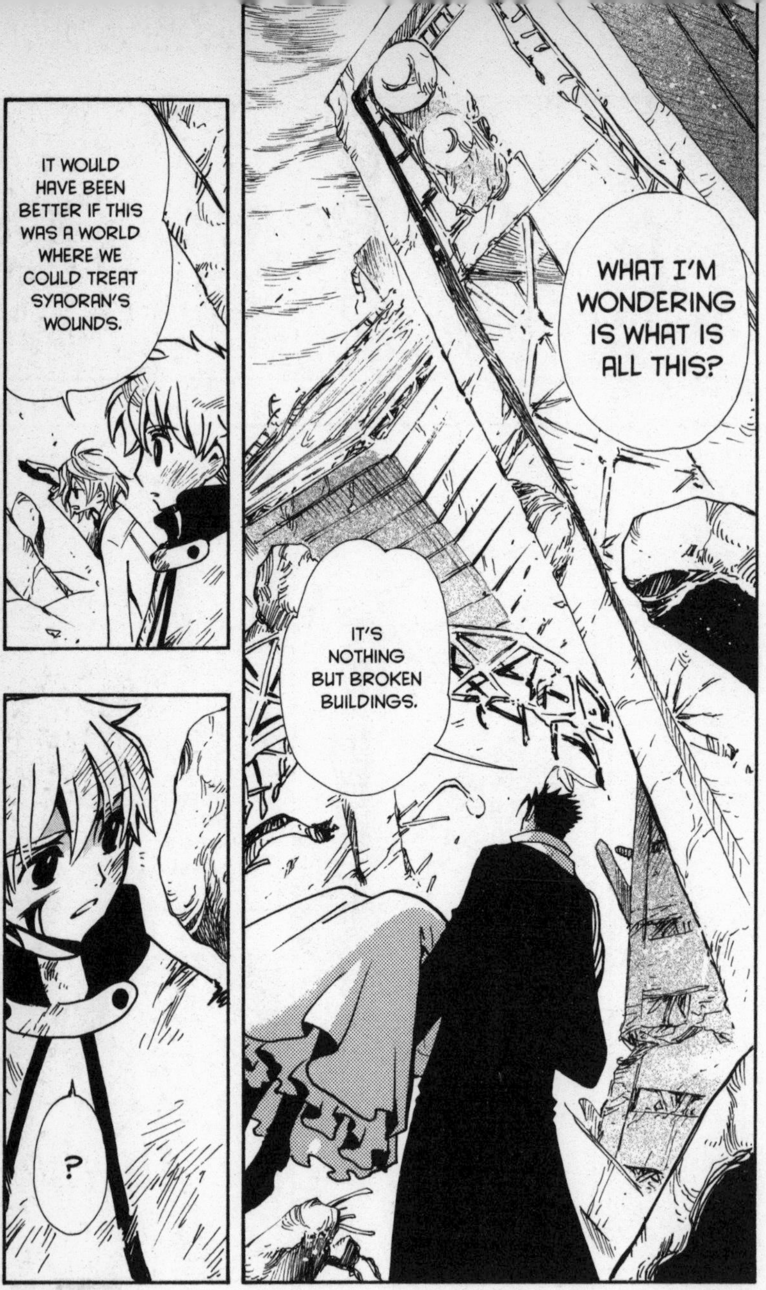
WHAT I'M WONDERING IS WHAT IS ALL THIS?
IT'S NOTHING BUT BROKEN BUILDINGS.
IT WOULD HAVE BEEN BETTER IF THIS WAS A WORLD WHERE WE COULD TREAT SYAORAN'S WOUNDS.
?

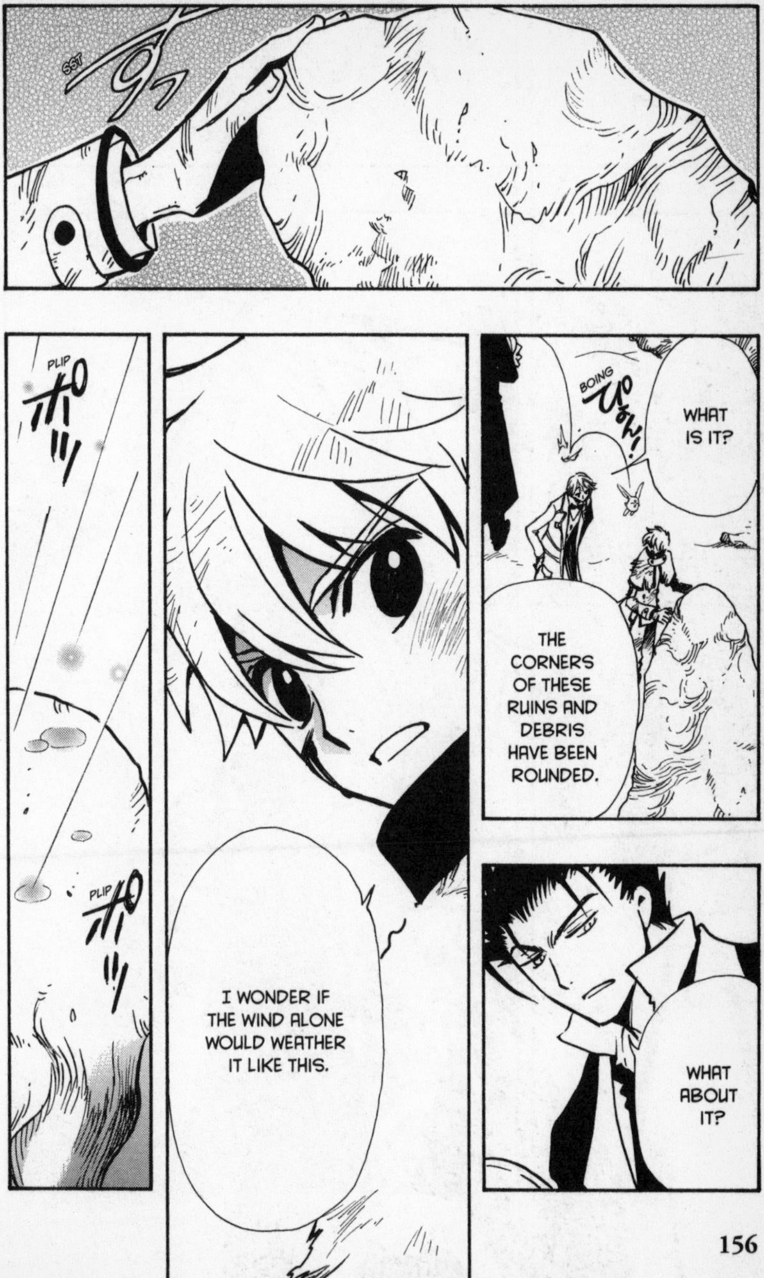
SST
WHAT IS IT?
BOING
THE CORNERS OF THESE RUINS AND DEBRIS HAVE BEEN ROUNDED.
WHAT ABOUT IT?
I WONDER IF THE WIND ALONE WOULD WEATHER IT LIKE THIS.
PLIP
PLIP

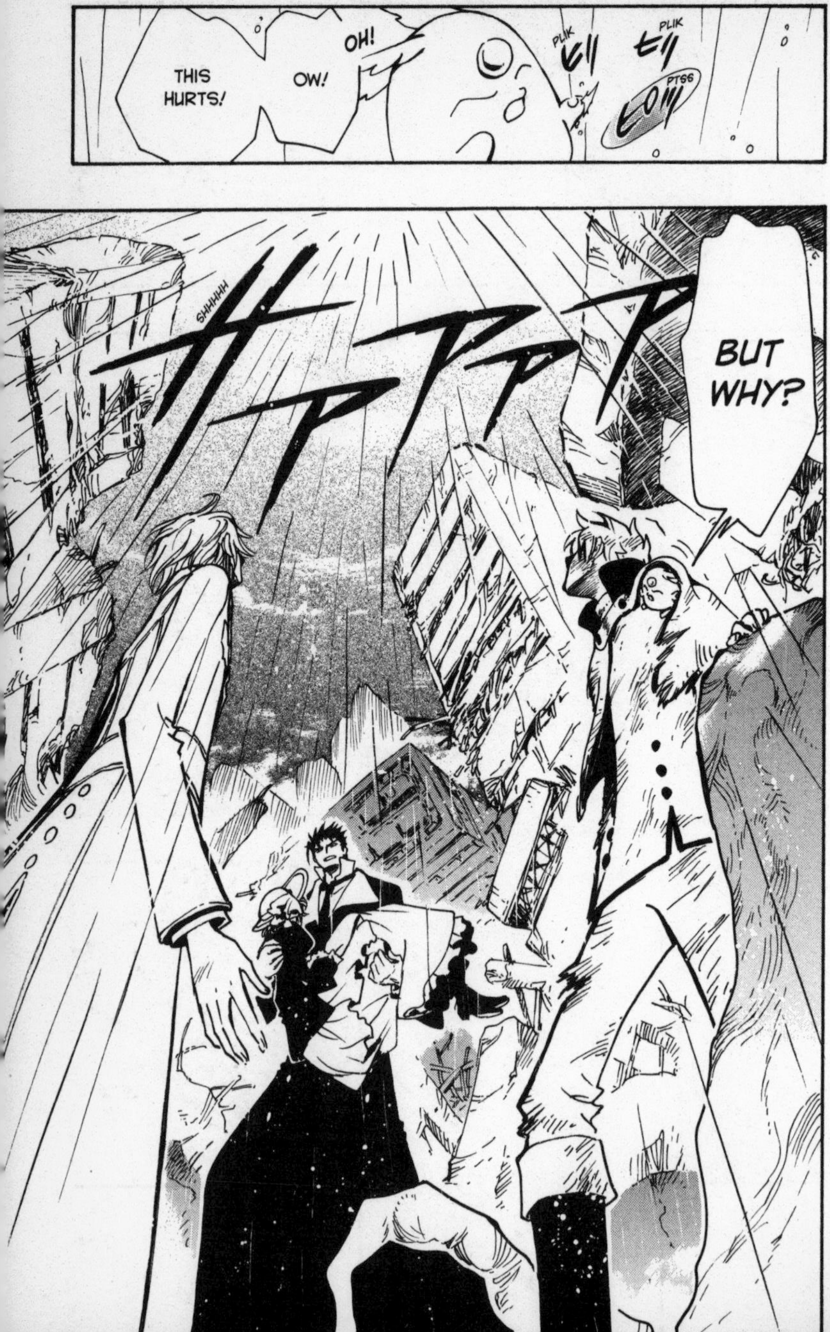
PLIK
PTSS
PLIK
OH!
OW!
THIS HURTS!
BUT WHY?
SHHHHH

ツバサ

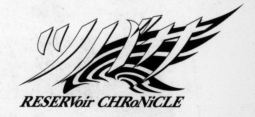

RESERVoir CHRoNiCLE

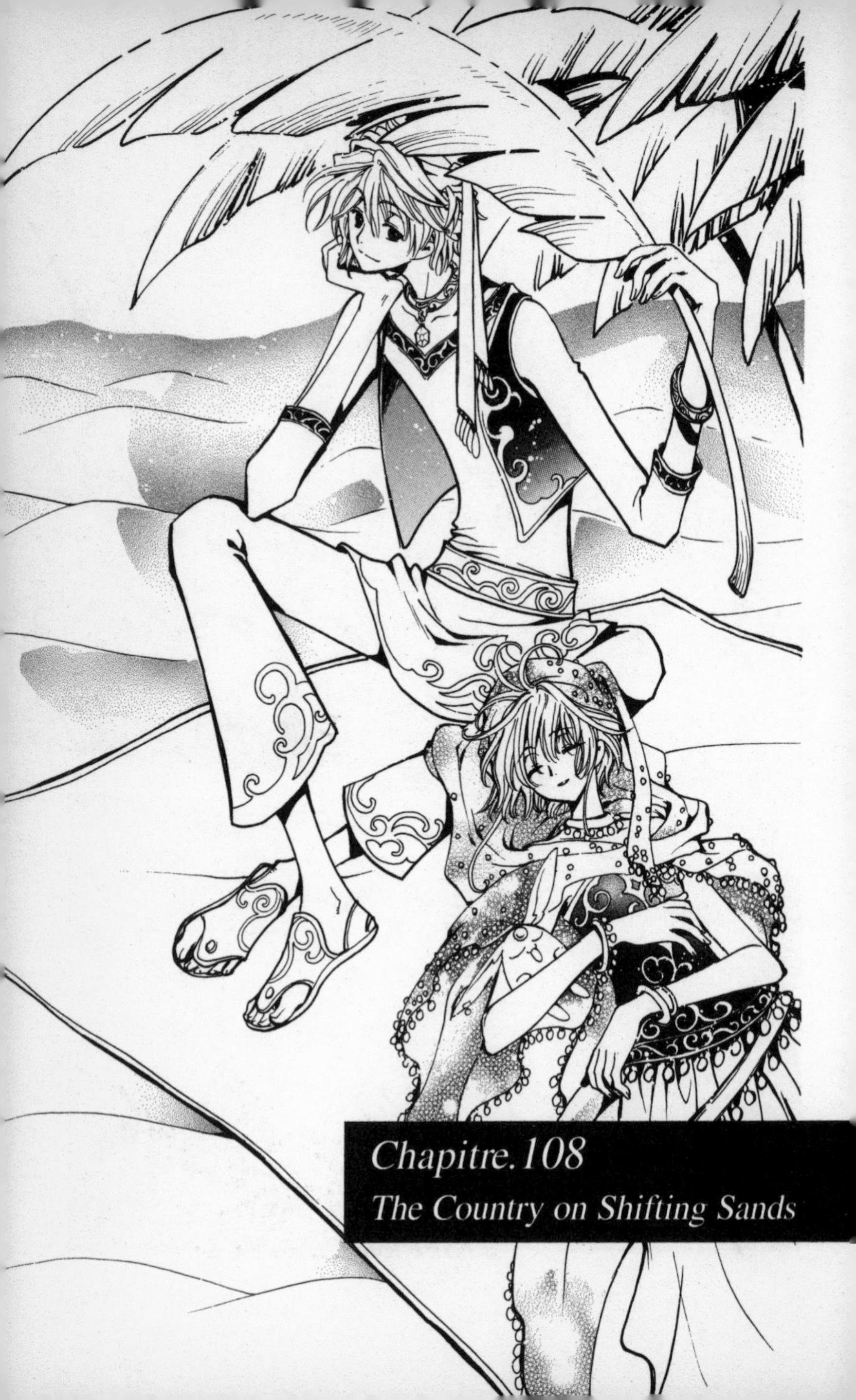

Chapitre. 108

The Country on Shifting Sands

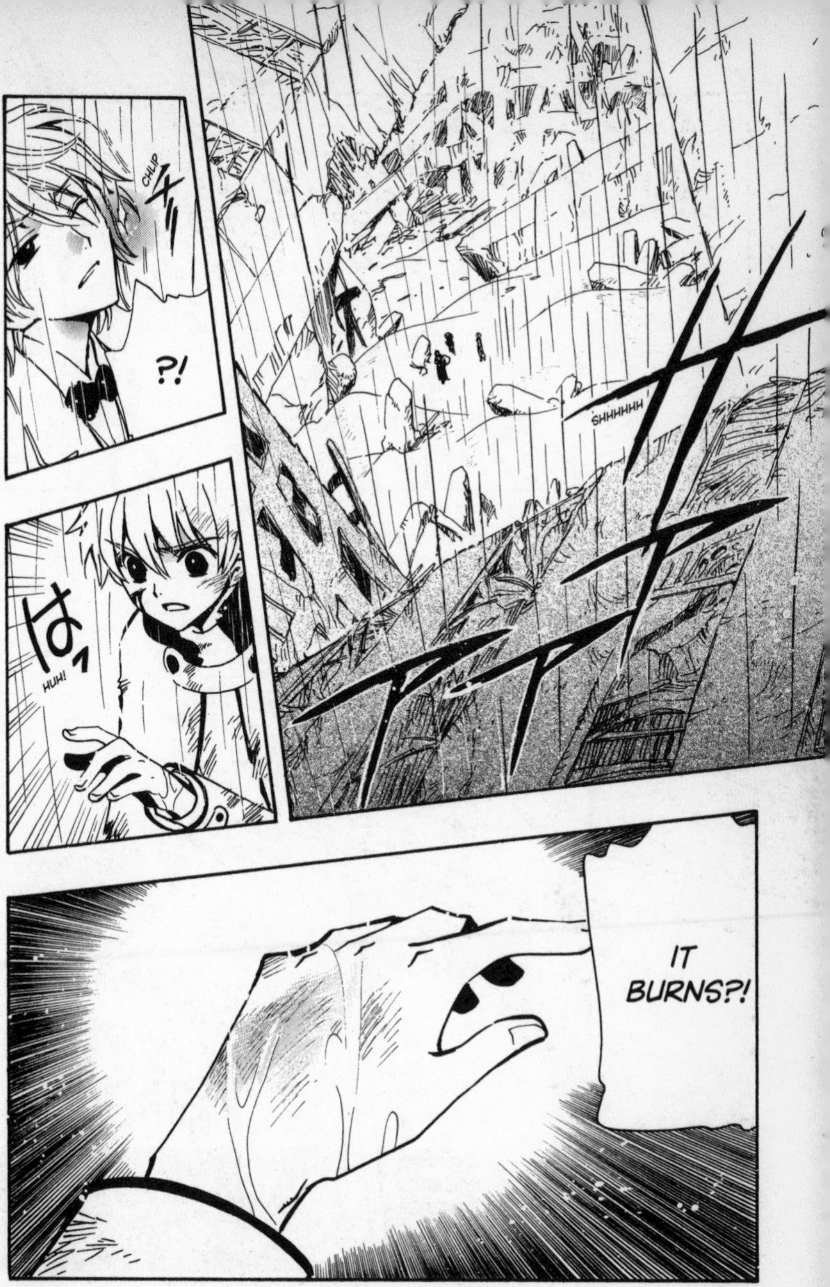
SHHHHHH
CHLIP
?!
は
HUH!
IT BURNS?!

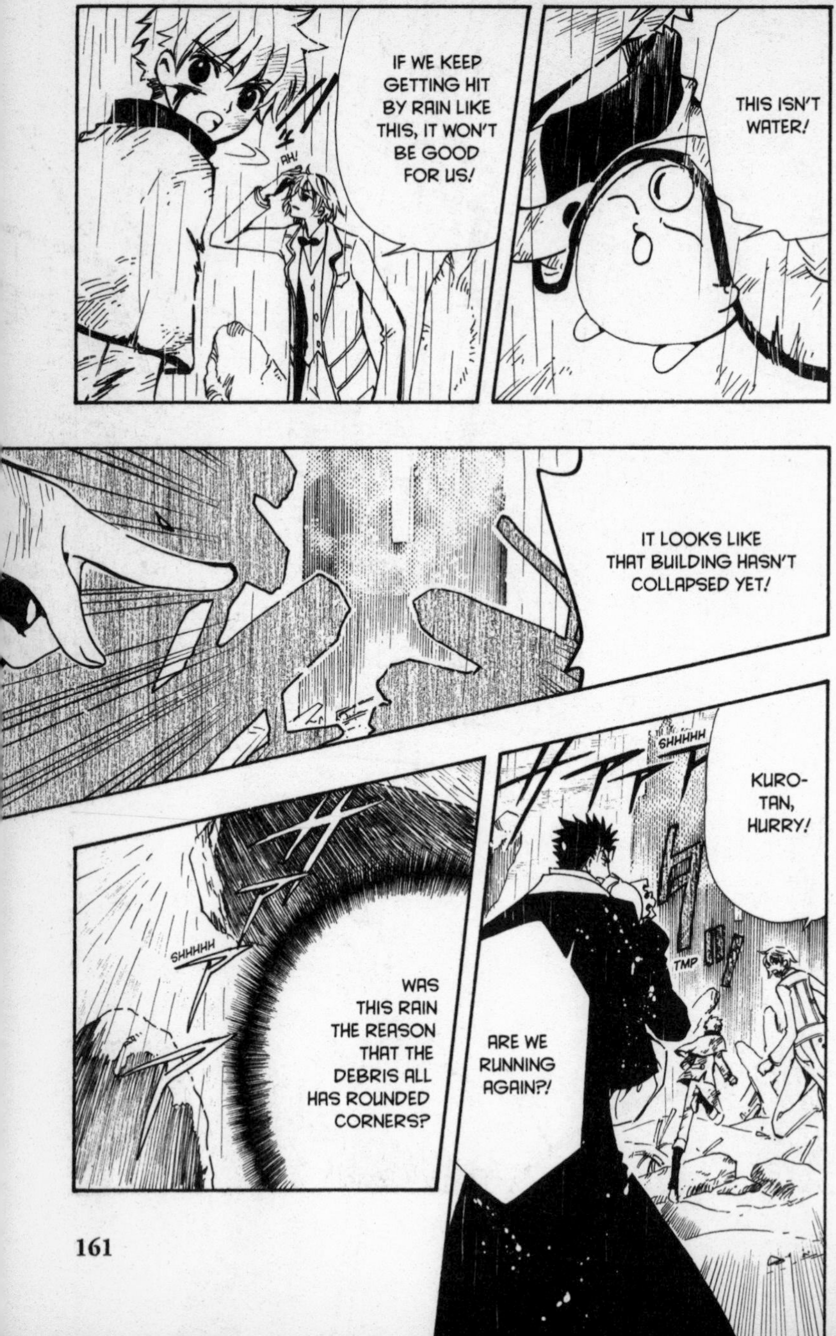
THIS ISN'T WATER!
IF WE KEEP GETTING HIT BY RAIN LIKE THIS, IT WON'T BE GOOD FOR US!
AH!
IT LOOKS LIKE THAT BUILDING HASN'T COLLAPSED YET!
SHHHHH
KURO-TAN, HURRY!
TMP
ARE WE RUNNING AGAIN?!
SHHHHH
WAS THIS RAIN THE REASON THAT THE DEBRIS ALL HAS ROUNDED CORNERS?

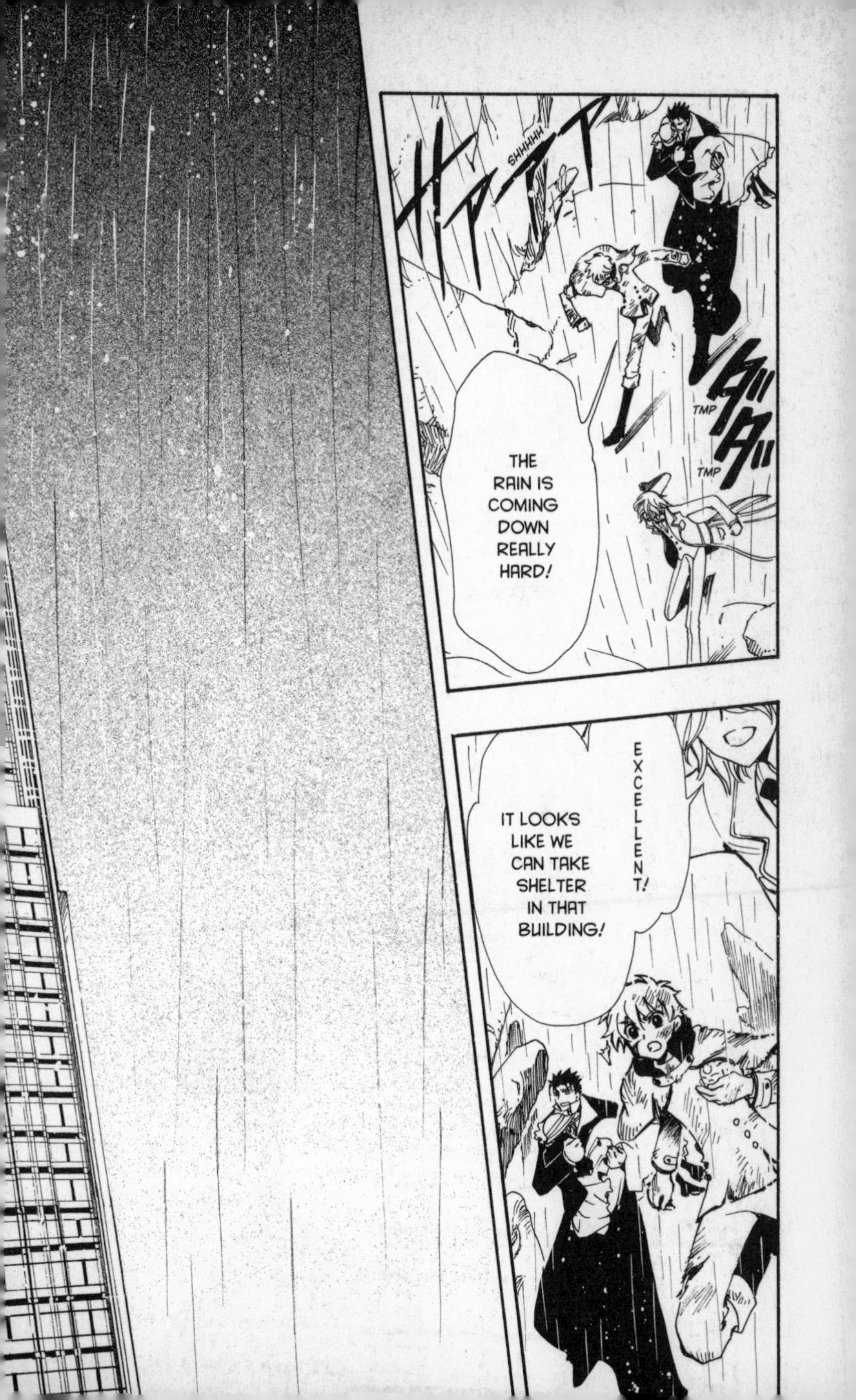
SHHHHH
TMP
TMP
THE RAIN IS COMING DOWN REALLY HARD!
EXCELLENT!
IT LOOKS LIKE WE CAN TAKE SHELTER IN THAT BUILDING!

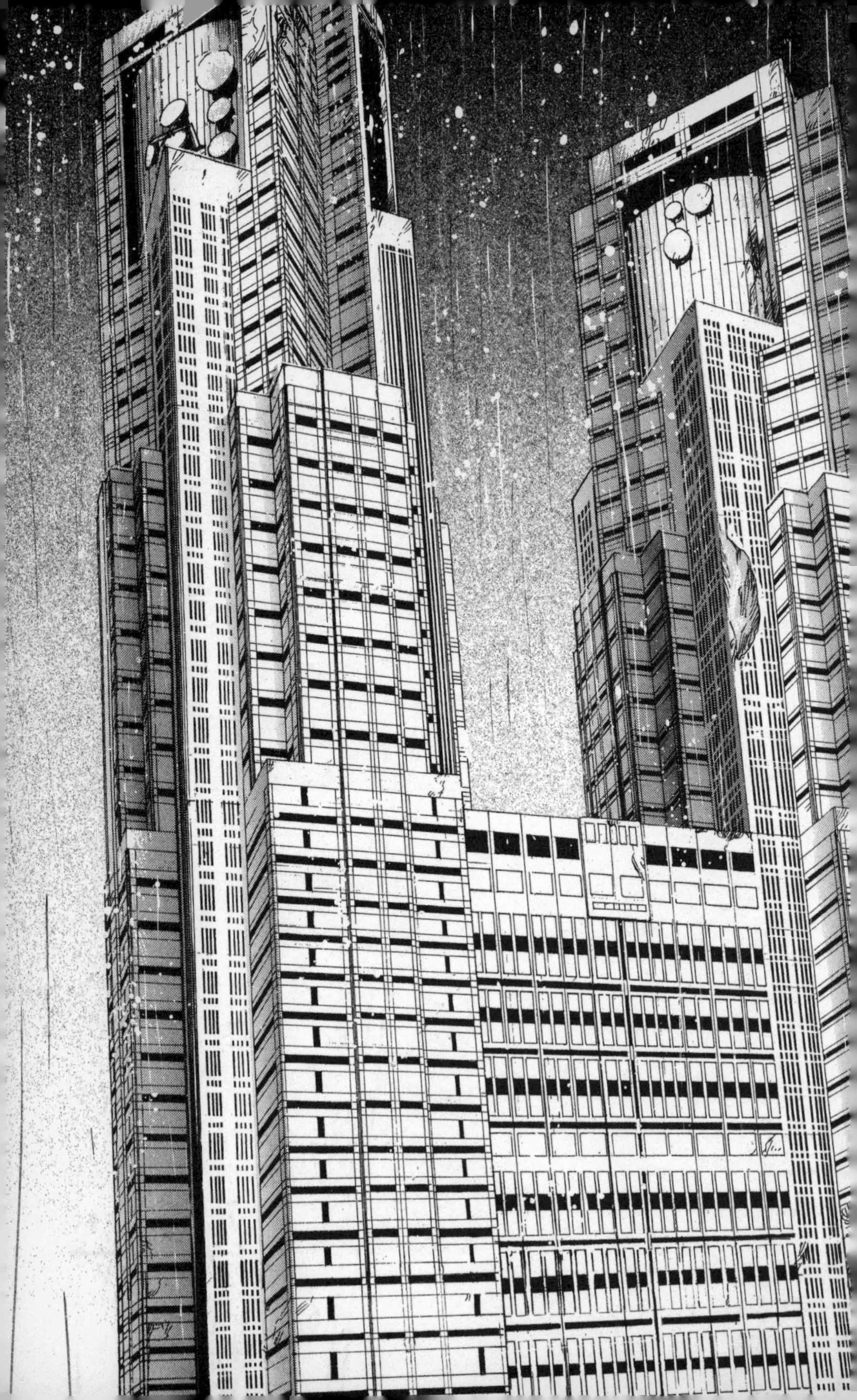

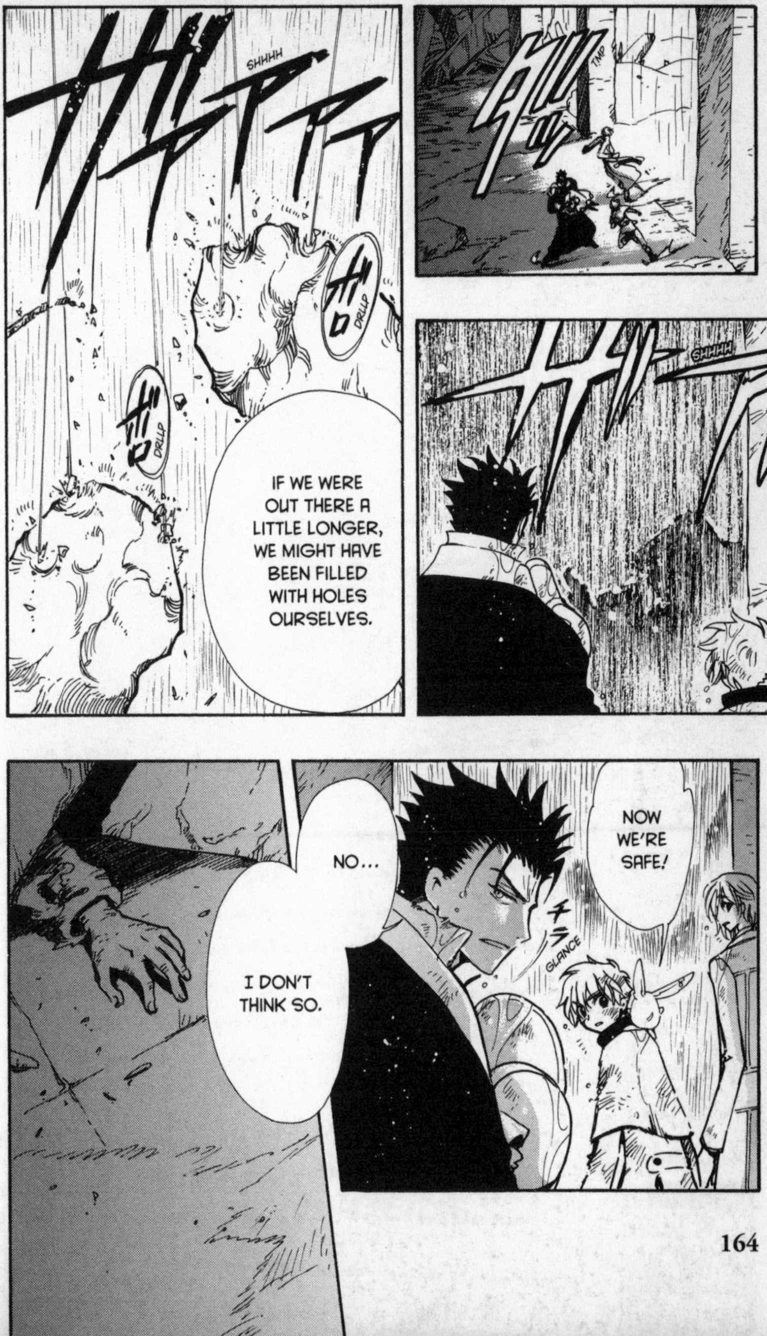
TMP
SHHHH
SHHHH
DRLLP
DRLLP
IF WE WERE OUT THERE A LITTLE LONGER, WE MIGHT HAVE BEEN FILLED WITH HOLES OURSELVES.
NOW WE'RE SAFE!
GLANCE
NO...
I DON'T THINK SO.

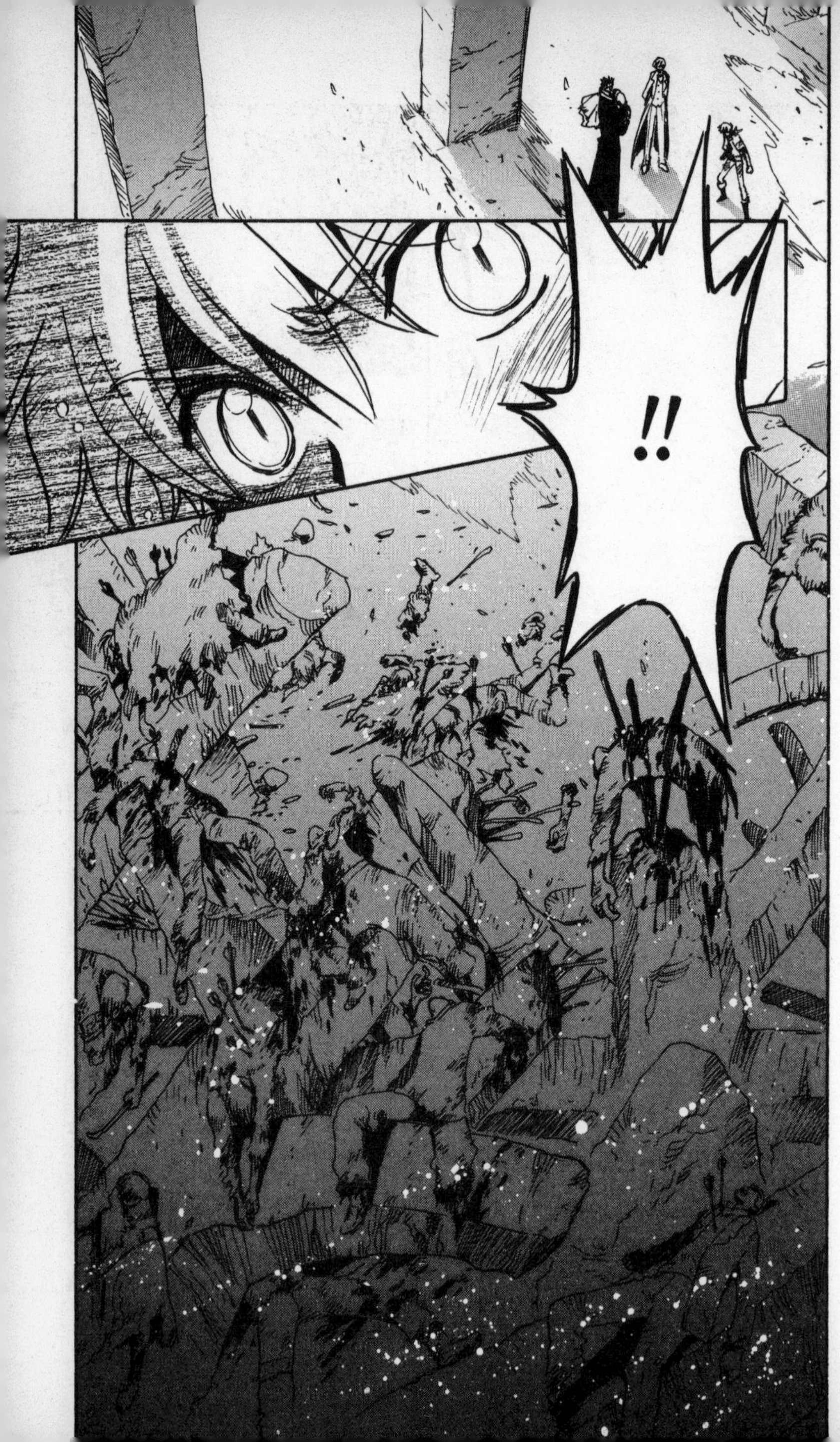
!!

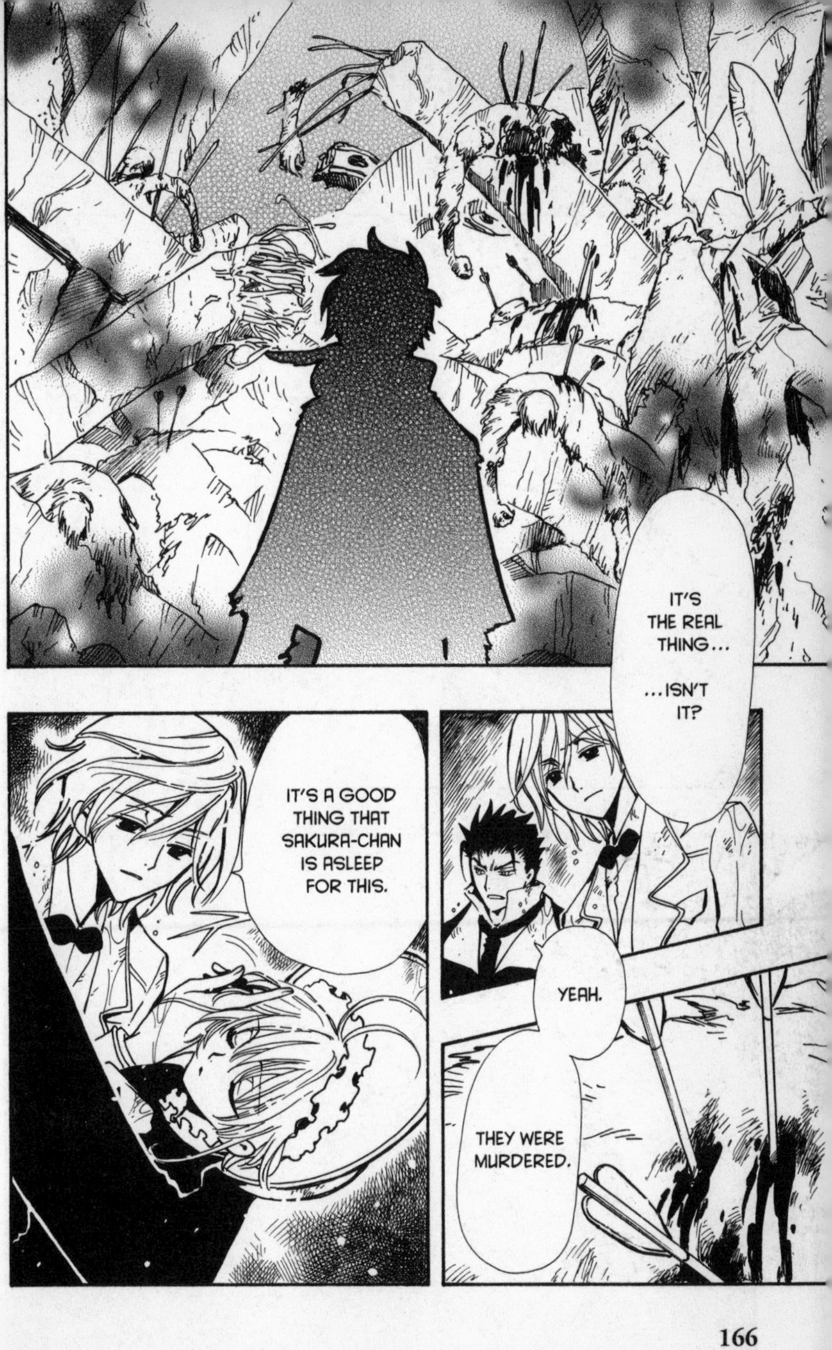
IT'S THE REAL THING...
...ISN'T IT?
YEAH.
THEY WERE MURDERED.
IT'S A GOOD THING THAT SAKURA-CHAN IS ASLEEP FOR THIS.

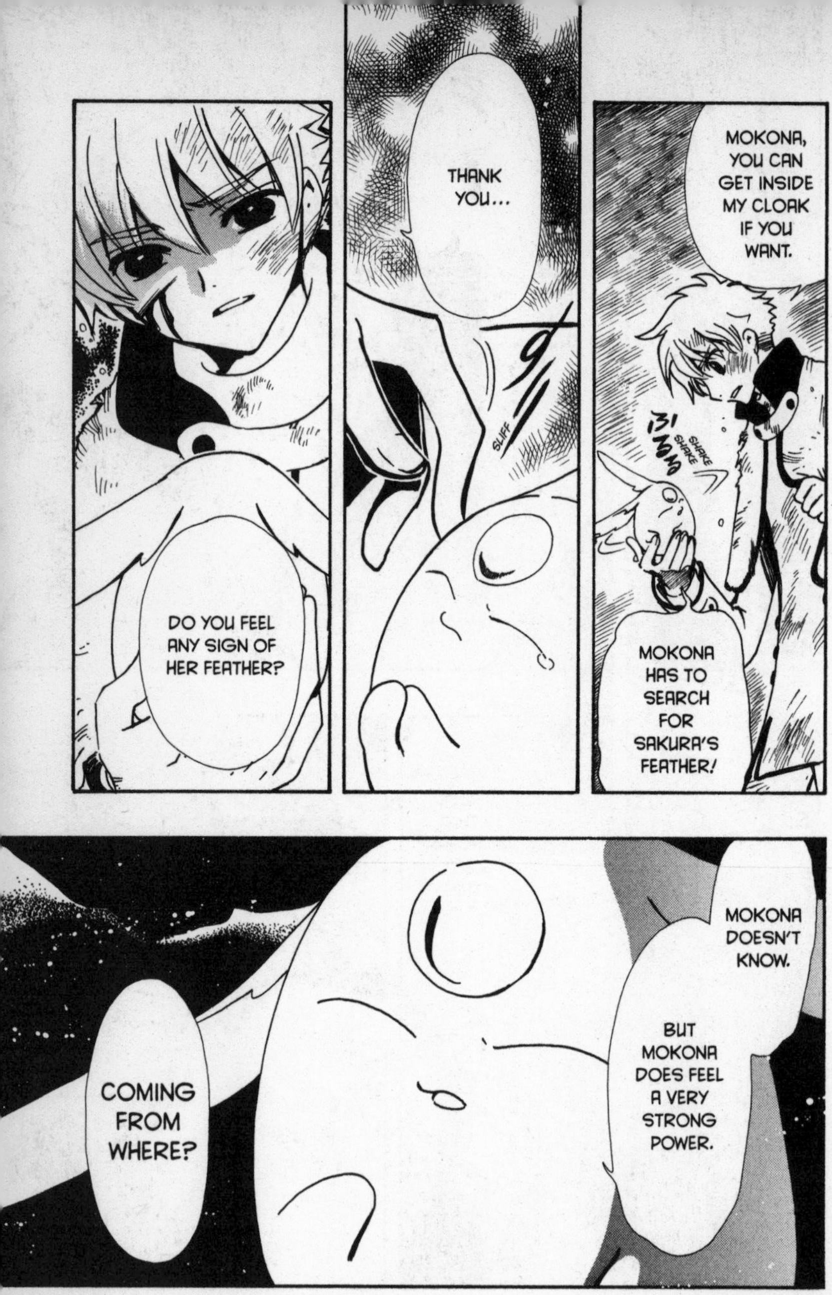
MOKONA, YOU CAN GET INSIDE MY CLOAK IF YOU WANT.
SHAKE SHAKE
MOKONA HAS TO SEARCH FOR SAKURA'S FEATHER!
THANK YOU...
SNIFF
DO YOU FEEL ANY SIGN OF HER FEATHER?
MOKONA DOESN'T KNOW.
BUT MOKONA DOES FEEL A VERY STRONG POWER.
COMING FROM WHERE?

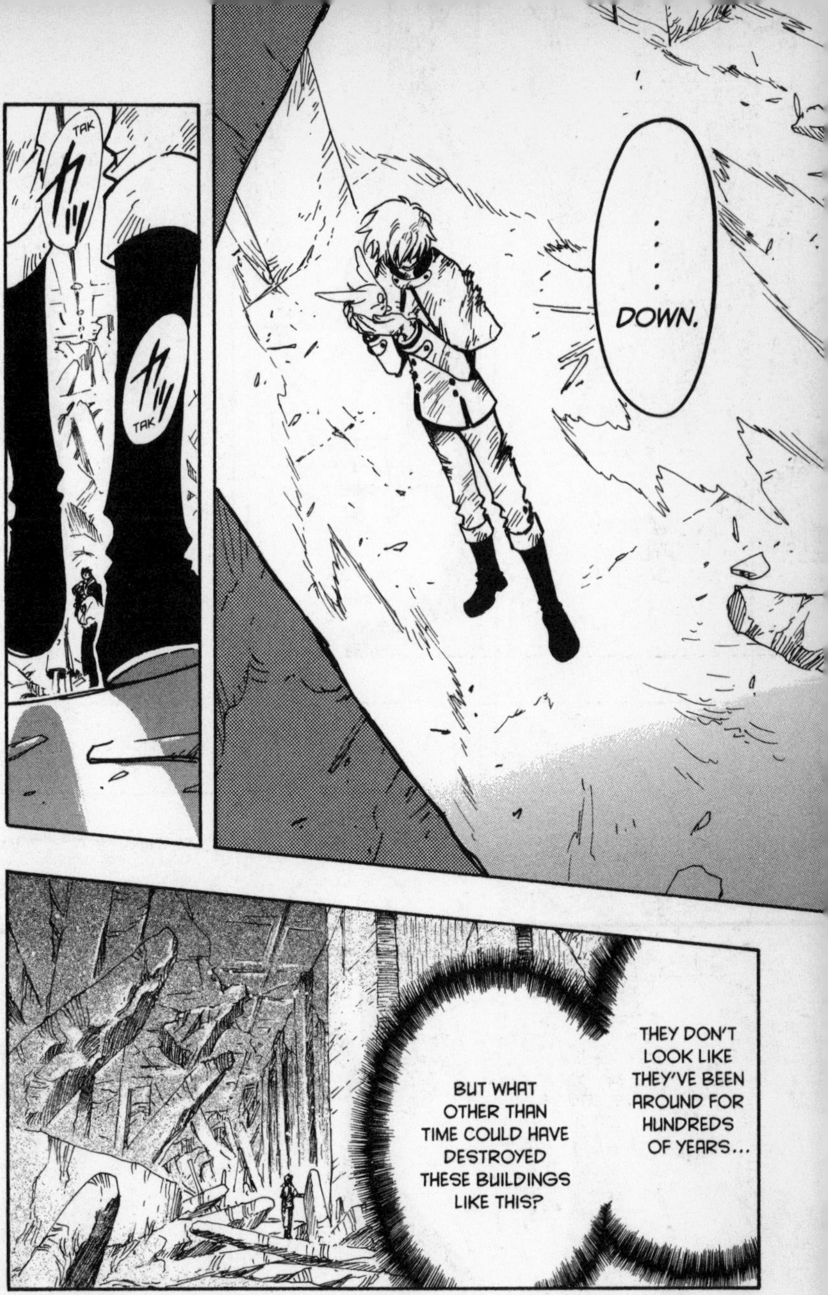

...DOWN.
カッ TAK
カッ TAK
THEY DON'T LOOK LIKE THEY'VE BEEN AROUND FOR HUNDREDS OF YEARS...
BUT WHAT OTHER THAN TIME COULD HAVE DESTROYED THESE BUILDINGS LIKE THIS?

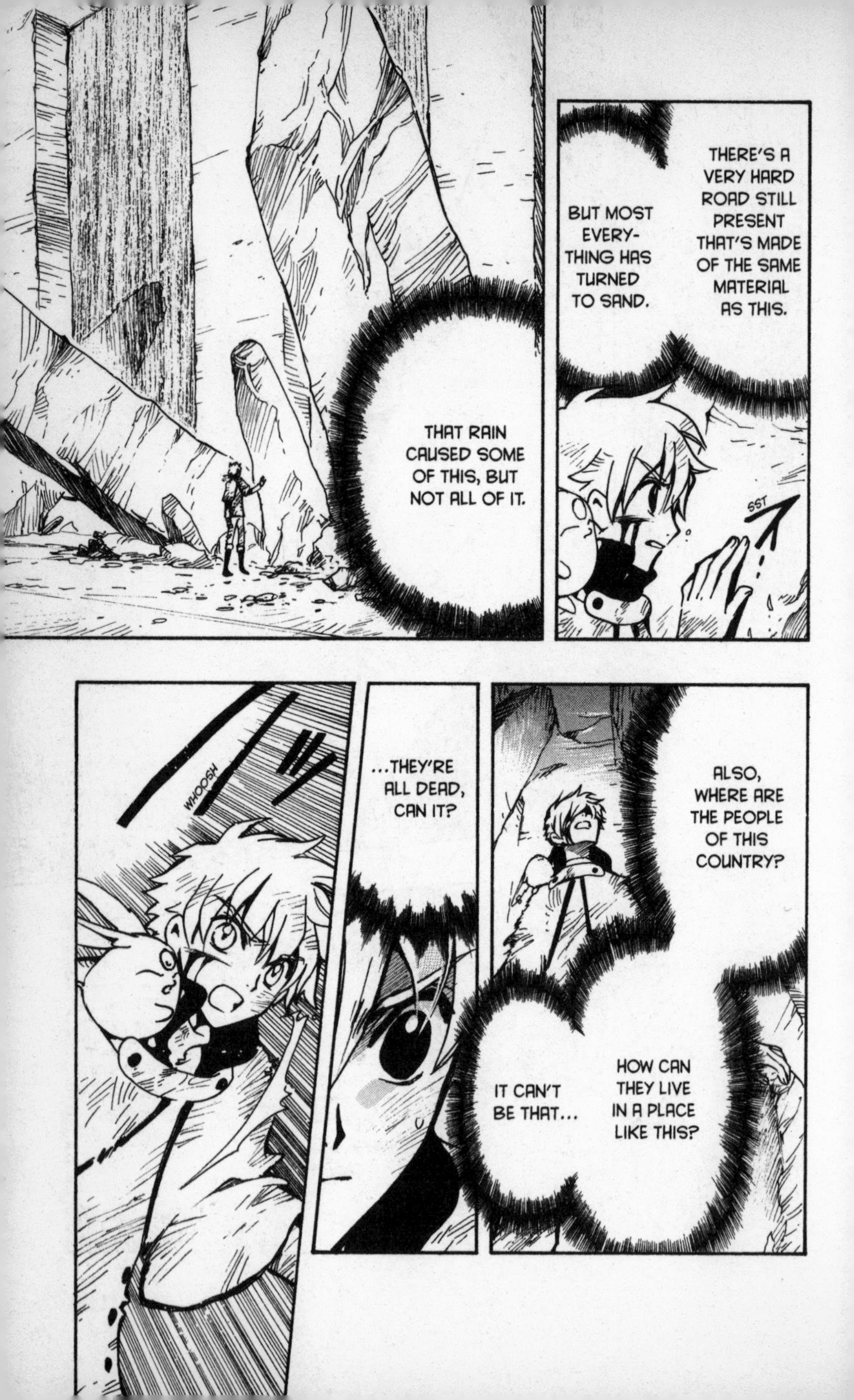
THERE'S A VERY HARD ROAD STILL PRESENT THAT'S MADE OF THE SAME MATERIAL AS THIS.
BUT MOST EVERY-THING HAS TURNED TO SAND.
SST
THAT RAIN CAUSED SOME OF THIS, BUT NOT ALL OF IT.
ALSO, WHERE ARE THE PEOPLE OF THIS COUNTRY?
HOW CAN THEY LIVE IN A PLACE LIKE THIS?
IT CAN'T BE THAT...
...THEY'RE ALL DEAD, CAN IT?
WHOOSH

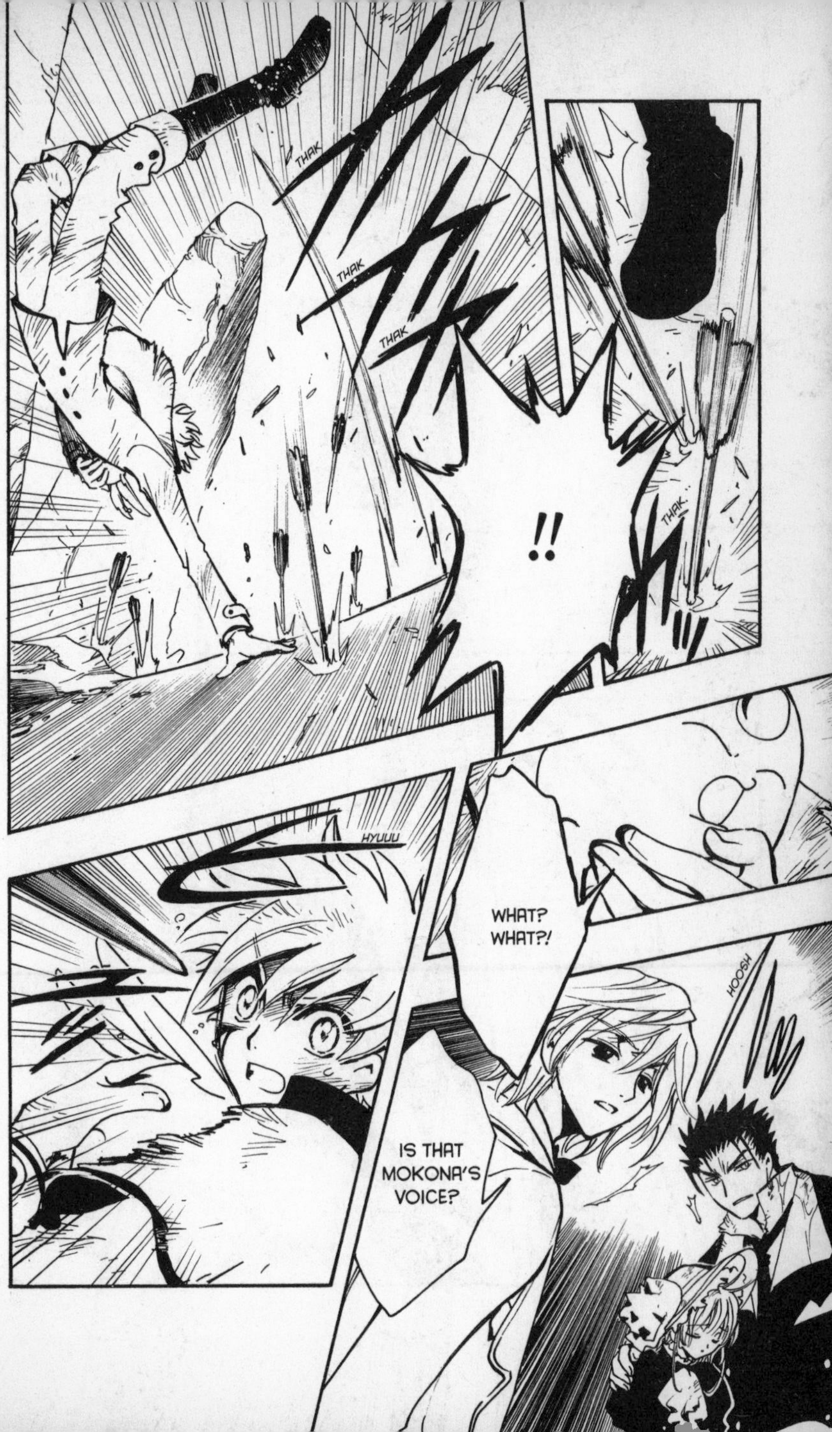
THAK
!!
THAK
THAK
THAK
WHAT? WHAT?!
HOOSH
IS THAT MOKONA'S VOICE?
HYUUU

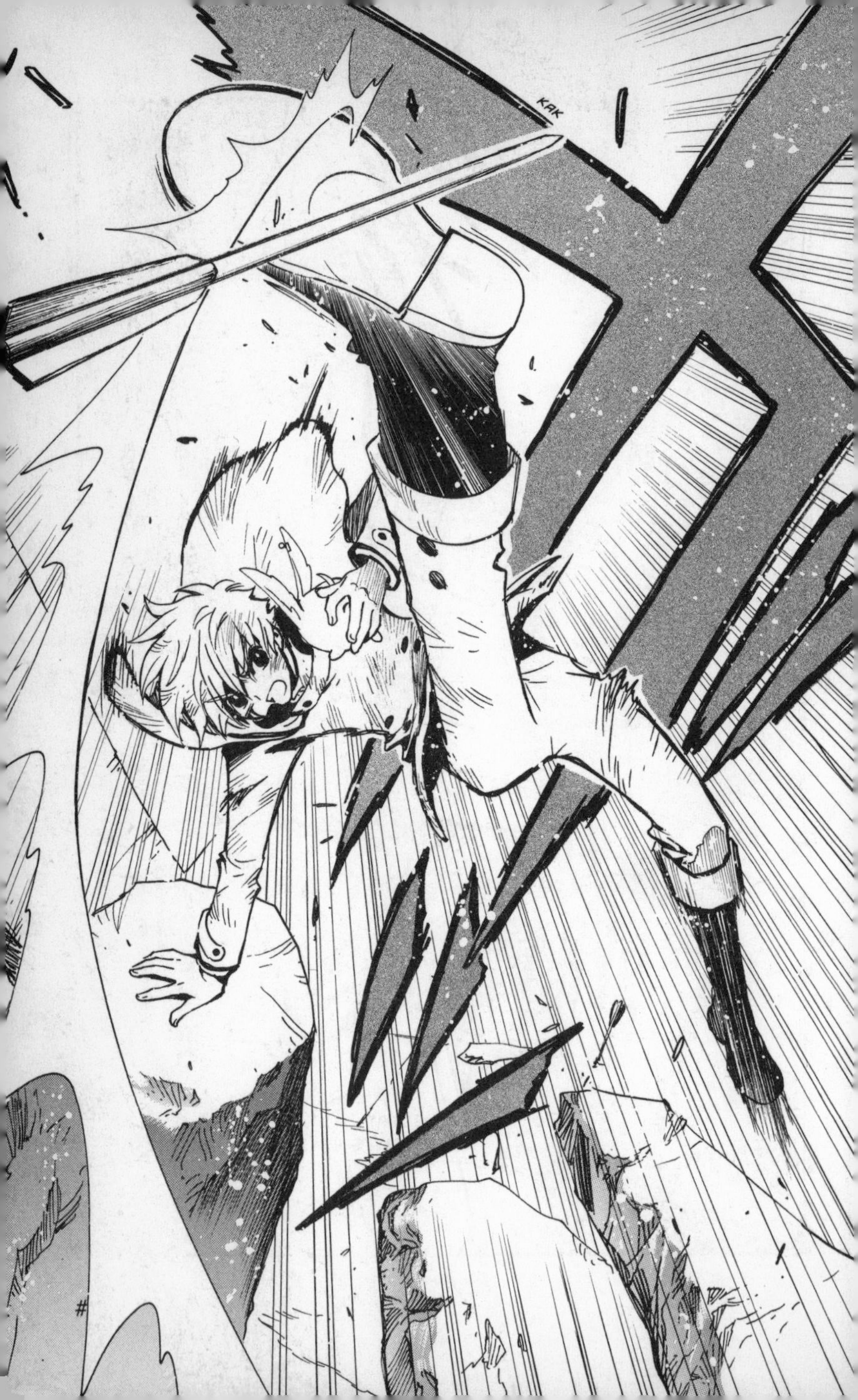
KAK

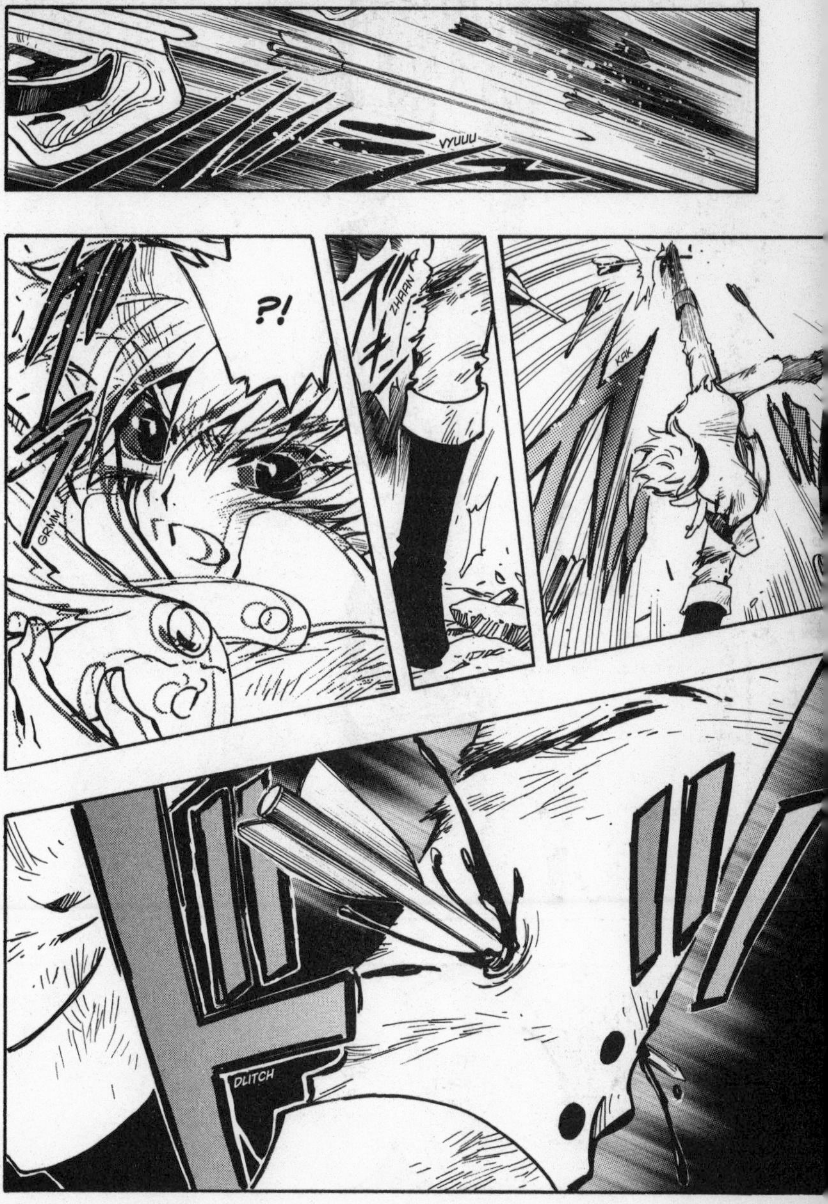
VYUUU
KAK
ZHAAN
?!
GRMM
DLITCH

SYAORAN!!

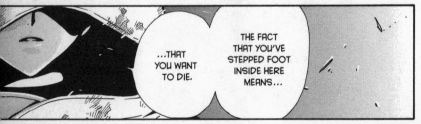

THE FACT THAT YOU'VE STEPPED FOOT INSIDE HERE MEANS...

...THAT YOU WANT TO DIE.

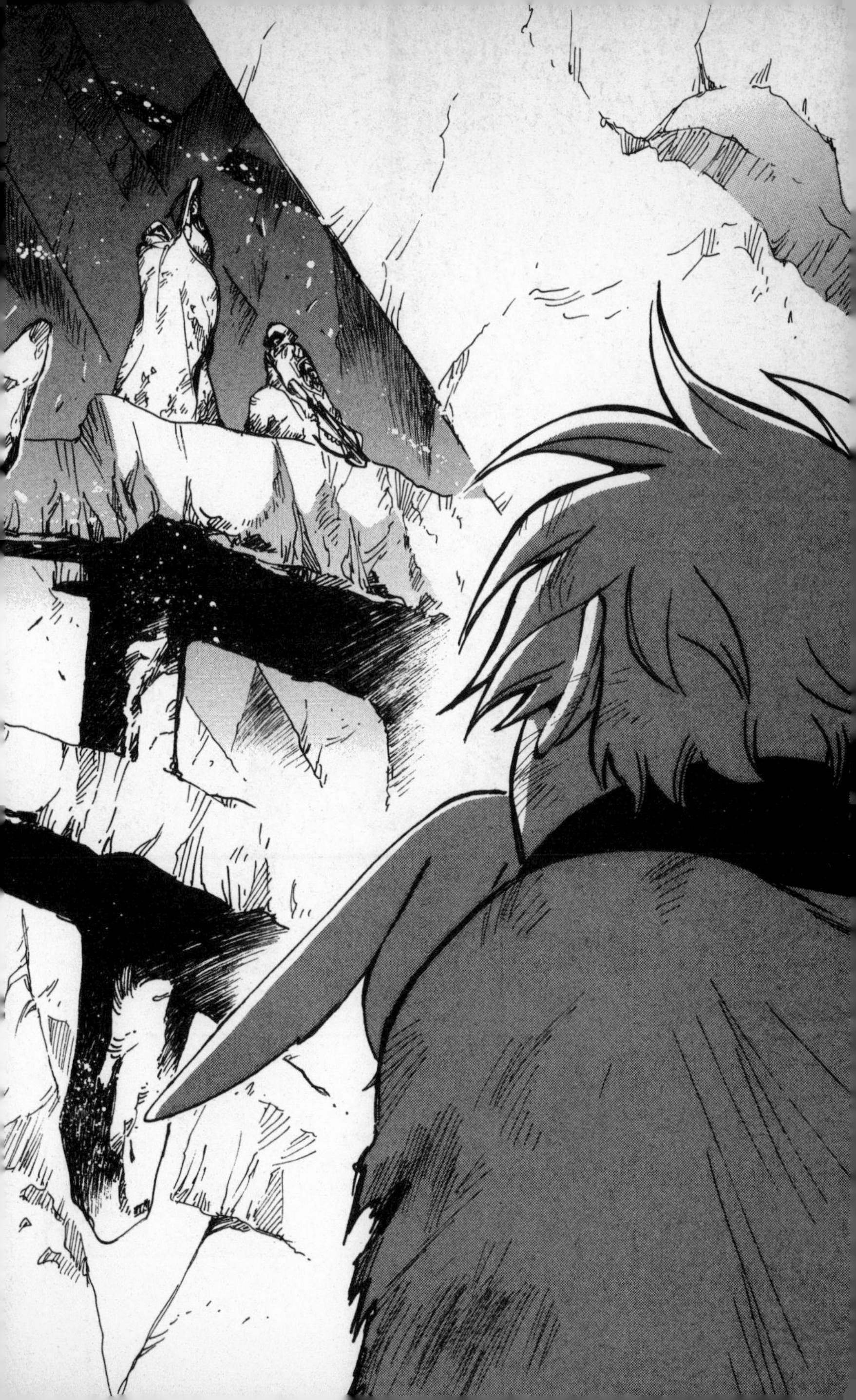

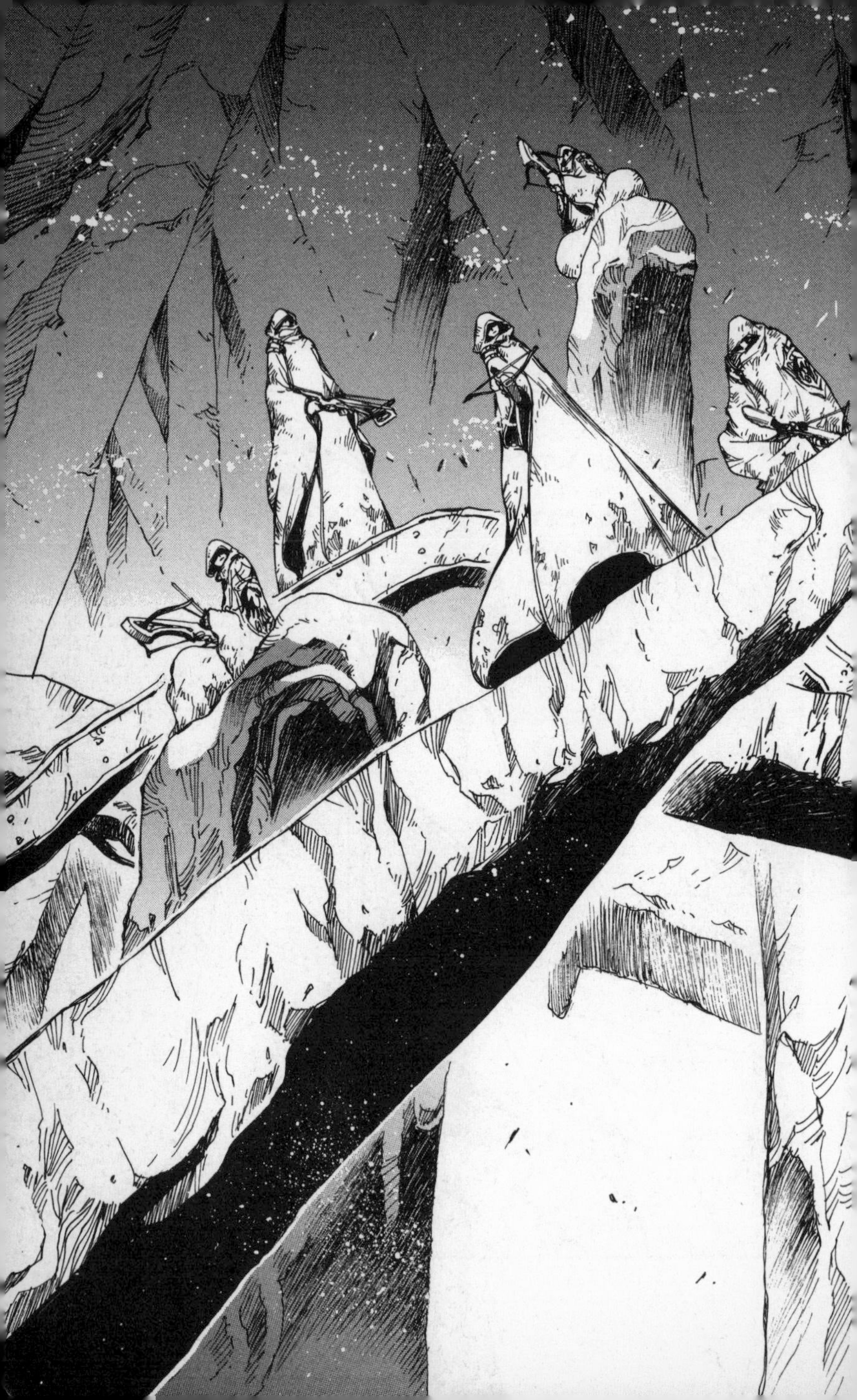

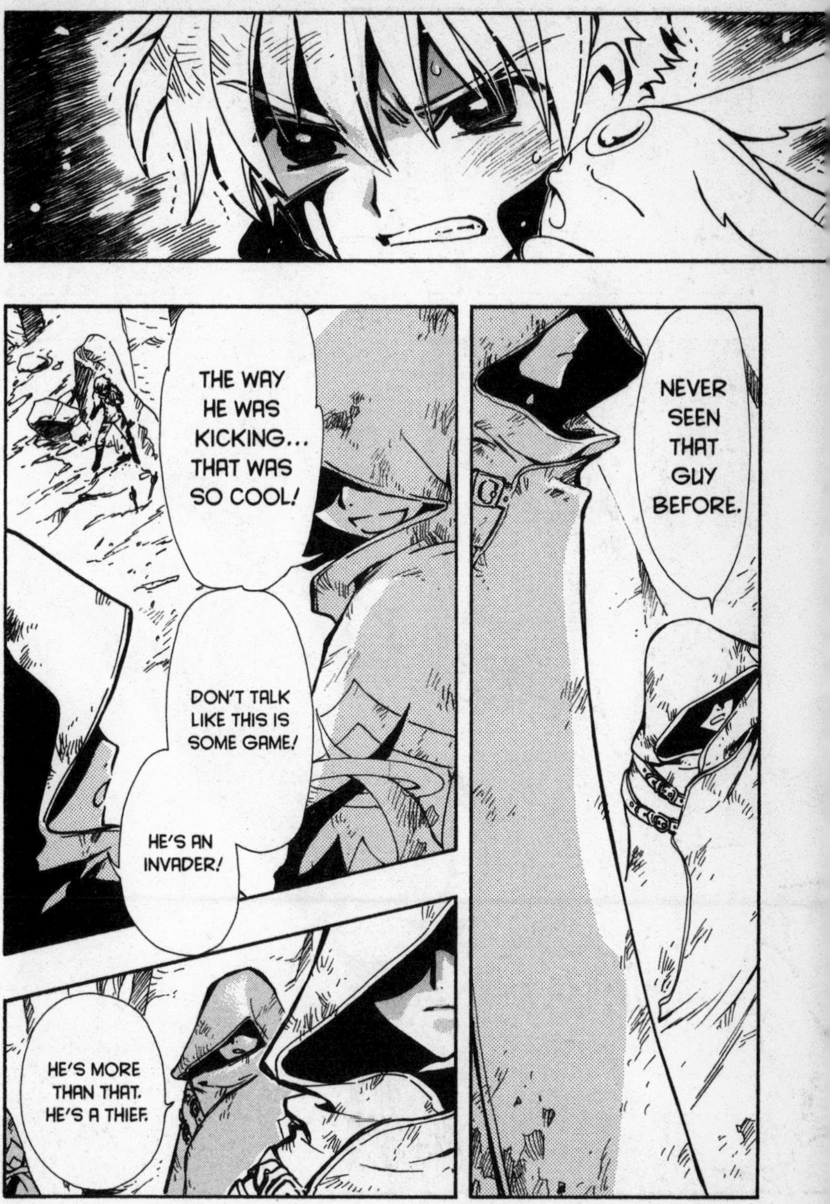
NEVER SEEN THAT GUY BEFORE.
THE WAY HE WAS KICKING... THAT WAS SO COOL!
DON'T TALK LIKE THIS IS SOME GAME!
HE'S AN INVADER!
HE'S MORE THAN THAT. HE'S A THIEF.

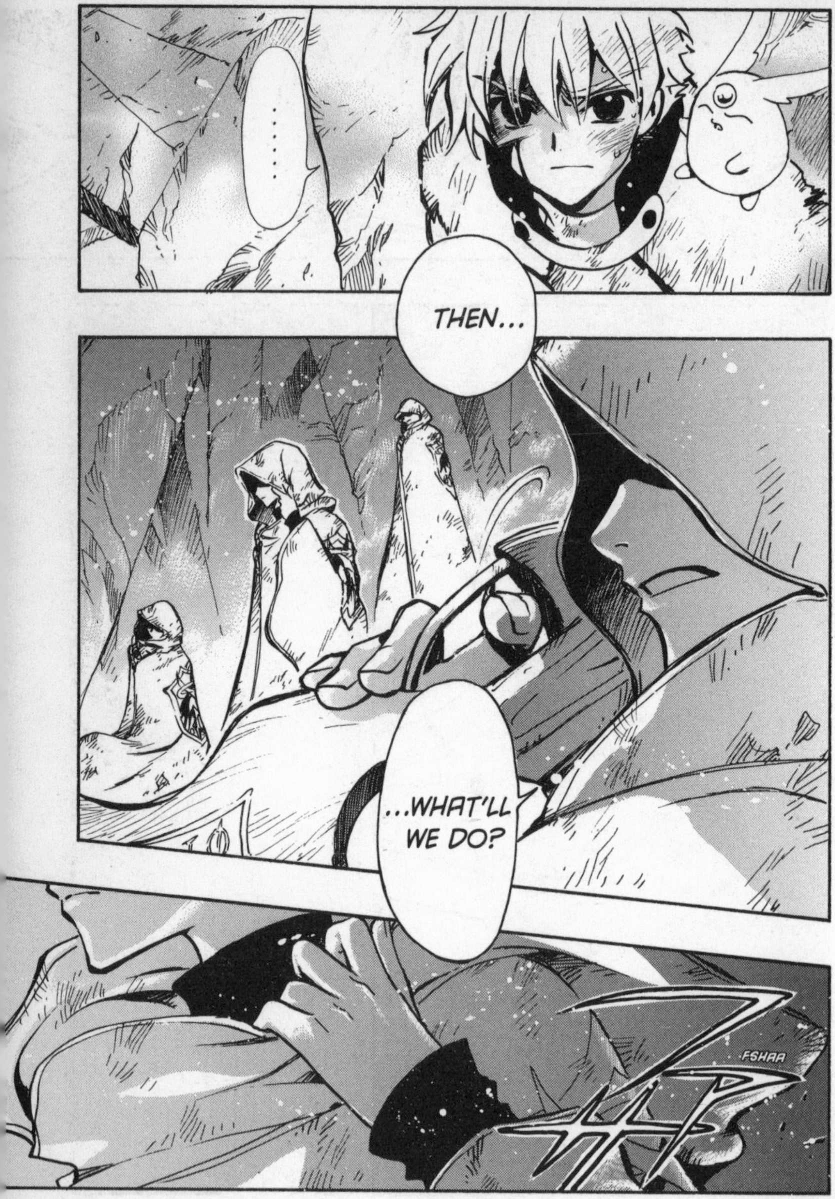
......
THEN...
...WHAT'LL WE DO?
FSHAA

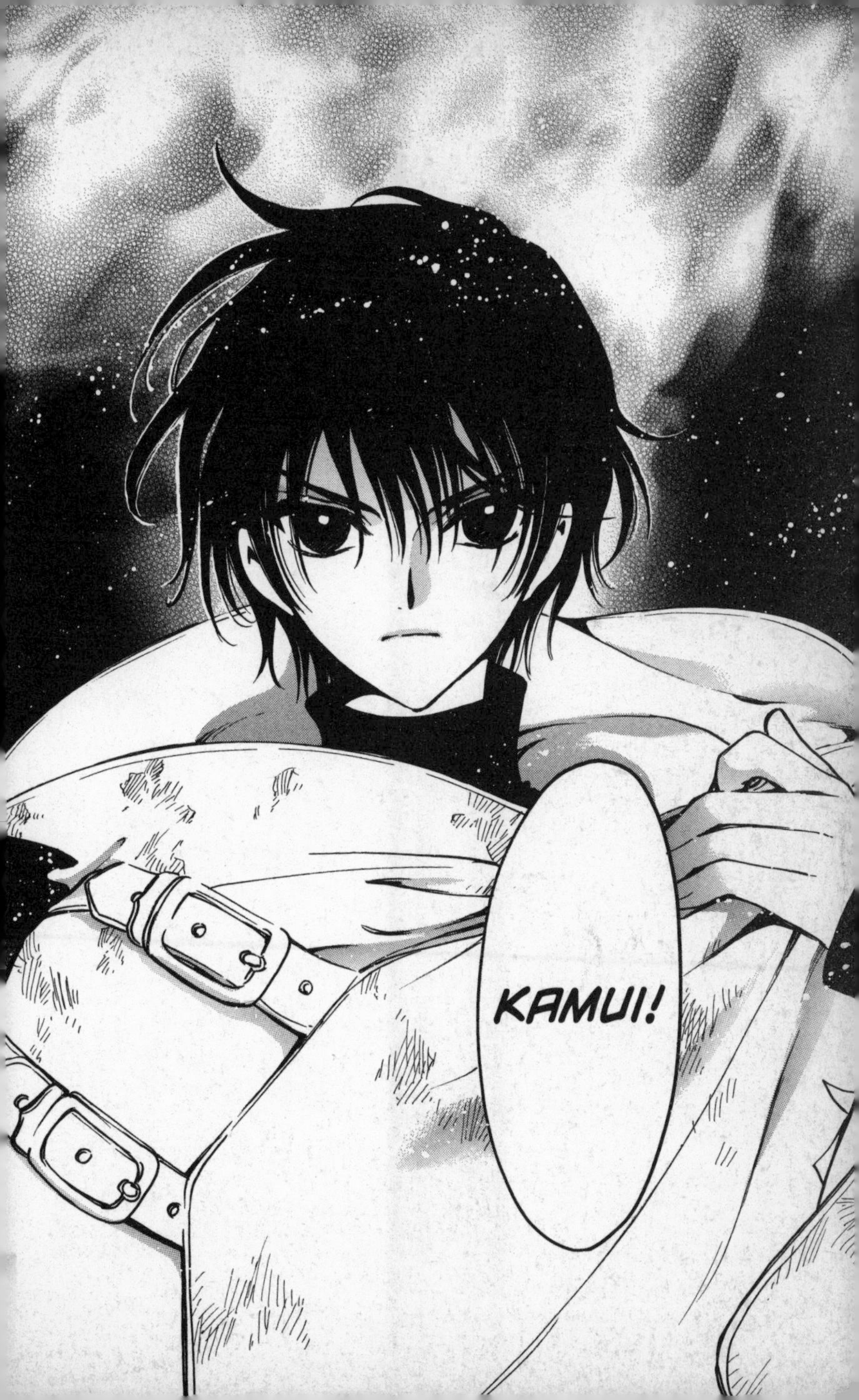
KAMUI!

To Be Continued

About the Creators

CLAMP is a group of four women who have become the most popular manga artists in America—Ageha Ohkawa, Mokona, Satsuki Igarashi, and Tsubaki Nekoi. They started out as *doujinshi* (fan comics) creators, but their skill and craft brought them to the attention of publishers very quickly. Their first work from a major publisher was *RG Veda*, but their first mass success was with *Magic Knight Rayearth*. From there, they went on to write many series, including Cardcaptor Sakura and Chobits, two of the most popular manga in the United States. Like many Japanese manga artists, they prefer to avoid the spotlight, and little is known about them personally.

CLAMP is currently publishing three series in Japan: Tsubasa and xxxHOLiC with Kodansha and Gohou Drug with Kadokawa.

Translation Notes

Japanese is a tricky language for most Westerners, and translation is often more art than science. For your edification and reading pleasure, here are notes on some of the places where we could have gone in a different direction in our translation of the work, or where a Japanese cultural reference is used.

Sandwiches, page 16

Although they haven't reached the popularity of *onigiri* (rice balls) as a lunchtime meal, sandwiches can be ordered in most every cafe or found in any supermarket or convenience store. However it is very unusual for a sliced-bread sandwich to be served with a crust. The depiction of sandwiches at the magic cafe is typical of the look of sandwiches in Japan.

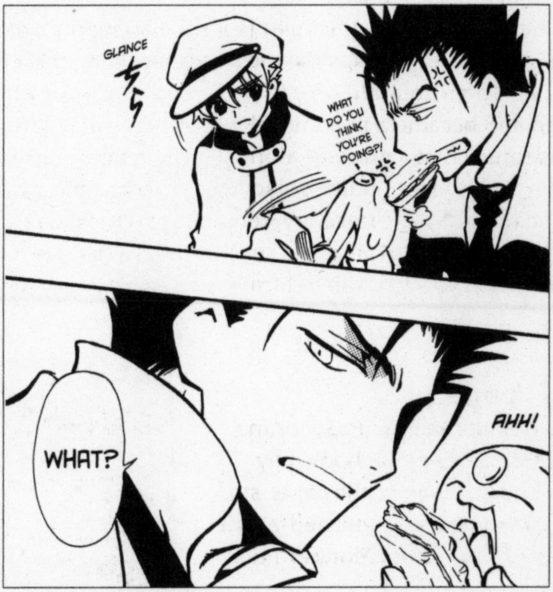
WHAT DO YOU THINK YOU'RE DOING?!
GLANCE
AHH!
WHAT?

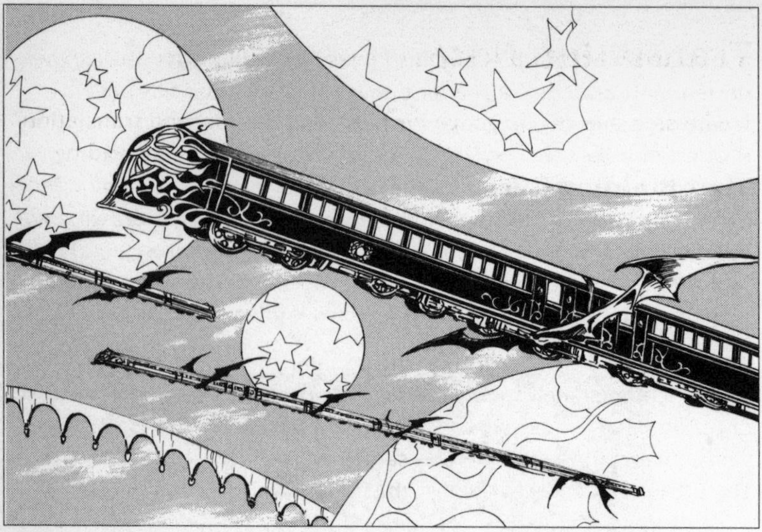

Flying Trains, page 26

Flying trains are a popular theme in Japanese animation, manga, and fantastical literature. Perhaps the most famous flying train is Leiji Matsumoto's *Ginga Tetsudô 999* (*Galaxy Express 999*) which began as a manga and became a popular television show and several animated feature films. Another along the same line is *Ginga Tetsudô no Yoru* (Night on the Galactic Railroad), a thoughtful and whimsical coming-of-age novel by Kenji Miyazawa which was turned into a beautiful animated film and several different stage productions. CLAMP's bat-winged trains are following in that same tradition.

Stealing, page 44

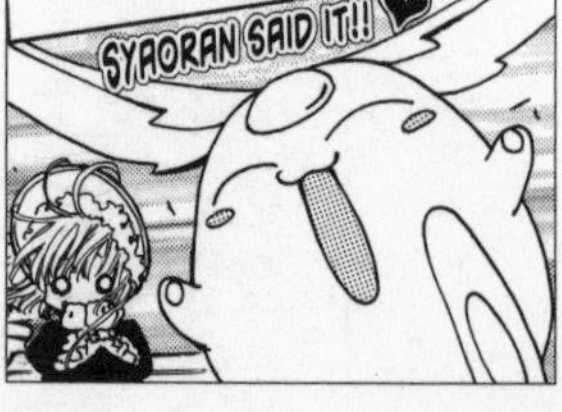
SYAORAN SAID IT!!

Mokona's gleeful reaction to Syaoran's determination to steal the book may stem from Japan's love of the caper story. Exemplified by the manga-turned-anime *Lupin III* by manga artist Monkey Punch about a world-class thief and his James Bond—like adventures, the daring theft and the subsequent police investigation has been a staple of Japanese entertainment for many decades.

That Building, page 163
CLAMP had a bigger purpose for including this intricate drawing of a building than just proving they can draw cool structures. Nearly all Japanese people would recognize the twin-tower design of the Tokyo Metropolitan Government Building (also known as Tokyo City Hall)

that stands in the high-rise district of the downtown center of Shinjuku. It was built in the early 90s and has been, not only a center for Tokyo's city government, but also a tourist attraction with the top floor open to the public. Followers of CLAMP's famous series X might also recognize it as the setting for many of the manga's scenes. It's also been featured in other movies, television shows, anime, and manga.

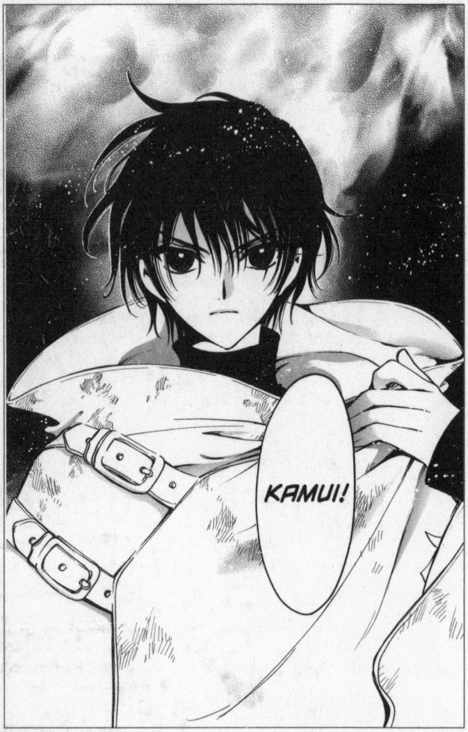
KAMUI!

Kamui, page 178
Followers of CLAMP's series X will also recognize the series' troubled and moody main character, Kamui.

TOMARE!

[STOP!]

You're going the wrong way!

Manga is a completely different type of reading experience.

To start at the *beginning*, go to the *end*!

That's right! Authentic manga is read the traditional Japanese way—from right to left. Exactly the *opposite* of how American books are read. It's easy to follow: Just go to the other end of the book, and read each page—and each panel—from right side to left side, starting at the top right. Now you're experiencing manga as it was meant to be.